CORPORATE GOVERNANCE AND FIRM ORGANIZATION

Corporate Governance and Firm Organization:

Microfoundations
and
Structural Forms

Edited by

ANNA GRANDORI

OXFORD
UNIVERSITY PRESS

OXFORD
UNIVERSITY PRESS

Great Clarendon Street, Oxford OX2 6DP

Oxford University Press is a department of the University of Oxford.
It furthers the University's objective of excellence in research, scholarship,
and education by publishing worldwide in

Oxford New York

Auckland Bangkok Buenos Aires Cape Town Chennai
Dar es Salaam Delhi Hong Kong Istanbul Karachi Kolkata
Kuala Lumpur Madrid Melbourne Mexico City Mumbai Nairobi
São Paulo Shanghai Taipei Tokyo Toronto

Oxford is a registered trade mark of Oxford University Press
in the UK and in certain other countries

Published in the United States
by Oxford University Press Inc., New York

A catalogue record for this title is available from the British Library

Library of Congress Cataloging in Publication Data
Data available
ISBN 0–19–926976–9

10 9 8 7 6 5 4 3 2 1

Typeset by Newgen Imaging Systems (P) Ltd., Chennai, India
Printed in Great Britain
on acid-free paper by
Biddles Ltd., King's Lynn, Norfolk

Acknowledgements

This book is based on the international conference Corporate Governance and Firm Organization: Nexuses and Frontiers, organized for the Centennial of Bocconi University in Milan, 5–6 December 2002, by Anna Grandori, Bocconi University, with the collaboration of Nicolai Foss, Copenhagen Business School, and Mark Ebers, EGOS Standing Group on Business Network Research. The collaborating institutions and colleagues are warmly thanked for their contributions. The precious contribution of Jacqueline Fuchs in the organization of the Conference is also gratefully acknowledged. I am grateful to Paul Windolf, Siegwart Lindenberg, Mark Roe, and Margaret Blair for valuable feedback and comments on the Introduction, and to Jacqueline Fuchs for language editing. I wish to thank warmly all authors for the challenging, thoughtful, and accurate cross-reviewing of their chapters in this book.

Anna Grandori
Bocconi University of Milan
February 2004

Contents

Part III Explaining Difference and Change in Corporate Governance Systems: Beyond the Convergence/Divergence Dilemma

List of Figures

List of Tables

Notes on Contributors

ANNA GRANDORI holds a chair of Organization, is Director of the Research Center of Business Organization, and Director of the Ph.D. Program in Business Administration at Bocconi University, Milan, where she is also professor of methodology of research in the Ph.D. program. She received her Laures degree in economics from Bocconi University and conducted graduate studies in business administration at Harvard Business School. Her core underlying research interest—building bridges between the economic and social and the behavioral sciences—is manifest in many of her publications in both economic and organizational journals (for example, *ASQ, JEBO, Organization Science, Organization Studies, Human Relations*) on decision making, knowledge, networks, and the theory of the firm, and in her last book (*Organization and Economic Behavior*, Routledge, 2000). She has been co-editor of *Organization Studies* (1992–9), a member of the Coordinating Committee of EGOS (1989–96), Scientific Director of the European Science Foundation Program 'European Management and Organization in Transition' (1993–7), and Editor-in-Chief of the *Journal of Management and Governance* (2000–). Some of her books published in English have been translated into Chinese and Japanese.

RUTH V. AGUILERA is an Assistant Professor at the College of Business and the Institute of Labor and Industrial Relations at the University of Illinois at Urbana-Champaign. She received her Ph.D. in Sociology from Harvard University. Her current research interests lie at the intersection of economic sociology and international business and include comparative corporate governance, global mergers and acquisitions, and employment relations. She has published several book chapters on different issues surrounding corporate governance, co-edited a book that compares Eastern and Western European corporate governance, and has had several articles published in academic journals such as *Academy of Management Review, International Journal of Human Resources*, and *Organization Studies*.

MASAHIKO AOKI, who obtained his doctorate from the University of Minnesota, is Takahashi Professor at the Department of Economics at Stanford University and President of the Research Institute of Economy, Trade and Industry (RIETI) in Japan. Current research interests include corporate governance, political economy of public finance, and comparative institutional analysis. Recent publications include *Toward a Comparative Institutional Analysis* (MIT Press, 2001).

MARGARET MENDENHALL BLAIR is a Professor of Law at Vanderbilt University Law School, teaching corporate law, corporate finance, and corporate governance. She recently completed an appointment as the Sloan Visiting

Professor Georgetown University Law Center and Research Director for Georgetown's Sloan Project on Business Institutions. From 1988 through 1999, she was a scholar in residence at the Brookings Institution, and she continues as a non-resident Senior Fellow at Brookings. she also serves as a director of Sonic Corp. Professor Blair holds a Ph.D. in Economics from Yale University, and is a renowned scholar in the field of corporate governance. The author of numerous books and articles, she has influenced scholars and policy-makers working on enterprise reform and corporate governance in Europe and Asia. She has also collaborated with Professor Lynn Stout on Team Production theory and the behavioral foundations of corporate law. Professor Blair recently published articles on the economic reasons for the emergence of corporate law and on historical insights affecting current debates about corporate governance reforms. Her work has appeared in publications such as the *Virginia Law Review*, the *Journal of Corporation Law*, and the *UCLA Law Review*. Her other areas of expertise include business ethics, human capital issues, the role of intangible assets, and financial market institutions.

JOHN CHILD holds the Chair of Commerce in the Birmingham Business School, University of Birmingham, UK. His M.A. and Ph.D. are from the University of Cambridge, which also awarded him a higher doctorate (Sc.D.) for his outstanding scholarly work. In 2002 he was elected a Fellow of the Academy of Management, and in 2003 received the first Distinguished Contribution Award of the International Academy for Chinese Management Research. He was Editor-in-Chief of *Organization Studies* from 1992 to 1996. Professor Child is author or co-author of seventeen books and over 120 articles in learned journals. His new book on *Organization: Contemporary Principles and Practices* will be published by Blackwell in 2004.

ALVARO CUERVO-CAZURRA, Ph.D. in management from the Massachusetts Institute of Technology and Ph.D. in business economics from the University of Salamanca, is an assistant professor at the University of Minnesota's Carlson School of Management. His current research lies at the intersection of strategic and international management, studying how firms change and develop resources to become competitive and then become international. Another line of research deals with corporate governance issues, studying the role and behavior of boards of directors.

BRUNO S. FREY, Professor of Economics at the University of Zurich, received an honorary doctorate in economics from the Universities of St Gallen and Göteborg. Current research interests include behavioral economics, public choice, and law and economics. He has numerous articles published in professional journals, and sixteen books including *Not Just for the Money, Economics as a Science of Human Behaviour, Arts & Economics, Inspiring Economics, Successful Management by Motivation* and *Happiness and Economics*.

JOSEPH LAMPEL is Professor of Strategy at Cass Business School, City University London. He previously worked at Stern School of Business, New York University, University of St Andrews, Scotland, and University of Nottingham Business School. Joseph Lampel is the author with Henry Mintzberg and Bruce Ahlstrand of the *Strategy Safari* (Free Press/Prentice-Hall, 1998). He is also the editor with Henry Mintzberg, James Brian Quinn, and Sumantra Ghoshal of the fourth edition of *The Strategy Process* (Prentice-Hall, 2003), and editor with Jamal Shamsie and Theresa Lant of *The Business of Culture: Emerging Perspectives in Media and Entertainment*, Lawrence Erlbaum (forthcoming). His work has also appeared in *Strategic Management Journal, Organization Science, Journal of Management Studies, Sloan Management Review, R&D Management, International Journal of Project Management, International Journal of Technology Management, Advances in Strategic Management, and Journal of New Product Innovation*.

RYON LANCASTER is a doctoral student of sociology and management at Northwestern University. His research interests include organizational change and economic sociology. He has published articles on organizational learning and the role networks play in price-setting behavior, and is completing his dissertation on the bureaucratization of the Catholic Church in the twelfth century.

WILLIAM LAZONICK is University Professor at the University of Massachusetts Lowell and Distinguished Research Professor at INSEAD. He holds a Ph.D. in Economics from Harvard University, and was previously an economics professor at Harvard and Columbia. He specializes in industrial development and international competition, and is the author or editor of nine books and some eighty academic articles (see http://faculty.insead.edu/Lazonick).

SIEGWART M. LINDENBERG (Ph.D. Harvard, 1971) is Professor of Theoretical Sociology at the University of Groningen, the Netherlands. He is one of the directors of the Interuniversity Center for Social science theory and methodology (ICS) and a member of the Royal Netherlands Academy of Arts and Sciences. His main interests lie in the areas of groups, organizations, and corporate governance, and micro-foundations of theories of cooperation and collective phenomena. He is also coordinator of the *Groningen Project on Assessing Sustainable Corporate Performance*. His list of publications and other research interests can be accessed via his homepage www.ppsw.rug.nl/~lindenb.

PATRICK MORETON, M.B.A. (Harvard, 1991), Ph.D. (University of California, 2002), is an Assistant Professor of Organization and Strategy at the Olin School of Business at Washington University in St Louis. His current research and teaching interests include business creativity, the value basis of business strategies, and the interaction between business strategy and corporate governance.

MARGIT OSTERLOH, Ph.D. from the Max-Planck Institute for Human Development, Free University Berlin, is full Professor of Business Administration at the Institute for Organization and Administrative Science, University of Zurich. Her current research interests are on organization science, management of innovation and technology, and women in organizations. She is author or co-author of eight books, 104 articles published in scientific journals and edited books. Main topics: process organization, knowledge and motivation management, participation, behavioral decision theory, corporate virtue, women in organizations, methodology of social sciences.

MICHAEL PIORE is David W. Skinner Professor of Political Economy at the Massachusetts Institute of Technology. His current research focuses on three areas: the organization of product design and development; changes in the structure and organization of the labor market, and the enforcement of labor standards in the process of globalization. His most recent book, *Innovation–The Missing Dimension*, co-authored with Richard Lester, will be published by Harvard University Press in the Fall of 2004. He has written numerous articles and papers on a wide range of subjects in labor economics. His books include *Beyond Individualism*, *The Second Industrial Divide*, *Birds of Passage*, and *Internal Labor Markets and Manpower Analysis*.

ANDREA PRENCIPE, Ph.D. from SPRU, University of Sussex, is Associate Professor of Business Administration at the Faculty of Economics of University G. d'Annunzio (Italy) and Fellow at SPRU. His research interests include the coordination and division of innovative labor in multitechnology industries and organizational learning and memory in project-based organizations. Main publications include articles in *Administrative Science Quarterly*, *Industrial and Corporate Change, Research Policy*, and *Journal of Management and Governance* and a book on systems integration with Oxford University Press.

SUZANA B. RODRIGUES received her Ph.D. from the University of Bradford in the UK. She is Professor of International Business at UFMG, Brazil, and is also a Senior Research Fellow and Director of the M.Sc. in International Business at the University of Birmingham, UK. Her current research interests concern the interface of corporate governance with organization studies and international management. Professor Rodrigues has published in the *Journal of Management Studies*, *Organization Studies*, and the *Journal of Management and Governance*. She is co-author with John Child of *Corporate Evolution*, to be published by Blackwell in 2005.

MARK J. ROE is a Professor of Law at Harvard Law School, where he teaches both corporations law and corporate bankruptcy, as well as advanced seminars on the two topics. Roe's writings include *Strong Managers, Weak Owners: The Political Roots of American Corporate Finance* (Princeton, 1994), *Political Determinants of Corporate Governance* (Oxford, 2003), 'Delaware's Competition', 117 *Harvard Law Review* 1568 (2003); 'Rents and their Corporate Consequences', 53 *Stanford Law Review* 1463 (2001); 'Political Preconditions to Separating Ownership from Corporate Control', 53 *Stanford Law Review* 539 (2000); and 'Backlash', 98 *Columbia Law Review* 217 (1998). He received his J.D. from Harvard Law School and his B.A. from Columbia College.

GIUSEPPE SODA, Ph.D., Associate Professor of Organization Theory, Director of the Department of Organization and Human Resources at Bocconi University School of Management. Research interests include networks and the impact of human capital on performance. Main publications include articles and books on inter-firm networks and organizational design.

STEEN THOMSEN, Ph.D., is Professor at the Department of International Economics and Management at Copenhagen Business School, and chairman of the Danish Corporate Governance Network. Current research interests include the corporate governance of firms with concentrated ownership. Main publications include sixteen journal articles, mainly on ownership and corporate governance structures in Europe, and three books on the Danish corporate governance system.

BRIAN UZZI, Ph.D. in sociology from the State University of New York at Stony Brook, is Associate Professor of Management and Sociology at the Kellogg School of Management at Northwestern University. Current research interests focus on the role of networks and complexity theory in imagination and change in creative industries, including law, finance, and the Broadway musical industry. His main publications include numerous articles on embeddedness and network theory in the *American Sociological Review, Administrative Science Quarterly*, and *Science* as well as a book, *Athena Unbound* (Cambridge University Press, 2000), on the networks and careers of men and women scientists in the hard sciences.

PAUL WINDOLF, Ph.D. from the University of Münster, habilitation at the University of Marburg, is a full Professor of Economic Sociology at the University of Trier (Germany). Current research interests include corporate networks, corporate governance, and economic institutions from a comparative perspective. Recent publications: *Corporate networks in Europe and the United States* (Oxford University Press, 2002); *Expansion and Structural Chang: Higher Education in Germany, the United States, and Japan, 1870–1990* (Westview, 1998); L'évolution du capitalisme moderne: La France dans une perspective comparative'. *Revue française de sociologie* 40 (1999).

TODD ZENGER, Ph.D. from UCLA, is a chaired Professor of Organization and Strategy at Washington University in St Louis. His research focuses on the economics of organization, including work on the theory of the firm, boundary choice, and compensation. This research has appeared in several top journals including *Strategic Management Journal, Administrative Science Quarterly, Academy of Management Journal, Academy of Management Review, Organization Science, Management Science, and the Journal of Law, Economics, and Organization*.

Introduction

Reframing Corporate Governance: Behavioral Assumptions, Governance Mechanisms, and Institutional Dynamics

ANNA GRANDORI

'Corporate governance' (CG) is a core concern across a variety of fields in the social sciences and ranks high on the agenda of policy-makers. The recent scandals involving giant US firms testify to the importance of corporate governance issues in the organization of modern economies. These scandals have contributed to doubts about any presumed superiority of prevailing corporate governance models over other models, and about the adequacy of available theories for analyzing and designing forms of governance. These doubts had already been voiced in research for some time, and this book is based on an international conference organized well before the acute pathological events that occurred in the US.

This book challenges the two major approaches in the field—the so-called shareholder and stakeholder perspectives—as well as the theories behind them and the governance solutions that are usually derived from them. In particular, agency theory and the associated property rights approach have provided some useful core ideas for conceptualizing corporate governance issues. However, it has been criticized on various grounds, especially its use as a normative theory of shareholder value maximization. This book posits some new, specific, and differentiated challenges to agency theory on the one hand and to the 'shareholder value' application of it on the other.

Alternative perspectives, such as the stakeholder approach and historical and institutionalist studies on the varieties of capitalism, have suffered from various limitations: they are descriptive rather than explanatory, lack substantial underlying theories, and do not lead to any conclusive empirical results on superior governance structures. Between these traditions, despite the urgency of the issue, there have been few attempts to define a theory-driven but empirically-based approach to corporate governance. This book responds to the need for realistic and pluralistic, yet precise and design-oriented models for corporate governance.

'Organization', as both an object and a science of design, is expected to make a special contribution to the emergence of such models. In fact, organization and administrative sciences draw from the various basic social sciences—in particular, law and economics, sociology and history that have inspired most research into corporate governance, but have a particular interest in, and specific conceptual equipment for, social engineering and for the design of adequate and even new organizational architectures. In addition, surprisingly little attention has been paid so far in the corporate governance debate to the organization of the firm. Legal regulation and property rights allocation have received most attention, but the internal (or otherwise private) systems of formal rules and social norms, as well as intra-firm and inter-firm organizational structures and processes, clearly affect and can contribute to proper governance—as many contributions to this book demonstrate. Furthermore, extending the analysis to organizational mechanisms enlarges the portfolio of governance mechanisms, thereby reducing the difficulties in finding better governance solutions. As a result, the book contributes both *new approaches* and *new solutions* to the corporate governance problem.

The contributing authors represent a unique collection, made up of scholars with different roots in basic social sciences, sharing a common interest in governance and organization, and adopting a critical innovative stance towards the orthodoxies in the field. Some of them are world leaders in research and thought on corporate governance, some are established scholars in organization and management theory and approach the problem of corporate governance from that perspective, some are leading or emerging researchers in new perspectives that can be of particular value if brought to bear on the corporate governance debate, and some are contributors of particularly original empirical elements in the evolution of corporate governance. In this introduction, I shall refer to some previous key works and the background of the contributors, highlighting the new ideas that the contributions to this book bring to the CG debate.

This introduction is organized around what I take to be the key messages of the book:

- a criticism of existing approaches to the 'principals' of corporations and the development of elements of a more general contingency theory of principals and governance arrangements;
- a criticism and an extension of the cognitive and motivational foundations of governance problems and possible solutions;
- an enlarged conception and portfolio of governance mechanisms;
- a broader conceptualization of the notion of governance form, including important elements of the organizational form of the enterprise and a range of new governance and organizational forms, emerging as superior solutions in the complex, innovative activities that characterize the modern economy;
- a criticism and reframing of the 'divergence' versus 'convergence' issue, suggesting a suspension of the debate around the descriptive 'dilemma'—namely, are corporate governance forms around the world converging

or diverging?—as unanswerable and relatively uninteresting, in favor of more predictive and prescriptive approaches to the 'variety of governance forms' problem.

Neither Shareholder nor Stakeholder Approaches: The Contingent and Combinative Choice of Right-Holders

A distinctive contribution of this book is to challenge the very foundations of the conventional wisdom of agency theory and property rights theory without 'rejecting' them. To appreciate this contribution, it is necessary to understand what these theories have successfully explained and the criticisms that have been made against them.

Agency theory (AT) and its property rights theory (PRT) development, like other strands of organizational economics, most notably transaction-cost economics, address the governance problem in its most difficult formulation. An agency *relation* is said to exist when one party (called the principal) transfers to another party decision rights to act 'in the interest of the principal' in a defined domain. Agency *theory* has modeled a subset of agency relationship in which both parties hold clear, measurable and adversarial objectives (maximize profit from effort or the utility of incentives; minimize the cost of effort or of incentives and monitoring, and so forth); alternative courses of action are known and can be ordered according to 'payoffs' by both parties (even if the principal might not know which action has been actually taken by the agent, or cannot observe the agent's behavior). An underlying 'behavioral assumption of opportunism' leads to the conclusion that the agency contract is not viable unless either incentive or control mechanisms are set up in the interests of the principal.

Even in this 'worst of all possible worlds', AT and PRT, as applied to the investor-manager relationship and to the assessment of governance structures, predict that a variety of governance structures are efficient under different circumstances. In particular, they explain widely observed regularities such as the prevalence of 'investor-owned' 'classical' firms in situations where agents' behavior is observable and financial capital investments are critical; while 'employee-owned' 'cooperative' firms are predicted in situations where behavior is very costly to monitor and human capital investments are critical (Alchian and Demsetz 1972; Hart and Moore 1990; Milgrom and Roberts 1992; Fama and Jensen 1983a, 1983b); as well as other ownership structures are contemplated according to how the costs of ownership, of contracting, and of decision-making are configured (Hansman 1996).

One of the most widespread objections raised so far to AT and PRT has not really challenged the theories themselves but mainly the particular applications or misapplications of them. I refer to the claim that those theories are not value-neutral because they 'assume' that financial investors are principals—that is, they advocate a 'shareholder value maximization' approach. The objection is unsatisfactory because who the principals are is not an 'assumption' in AT and related property right theories, but rather a 'dependent variable'. It depends—among other things—on who the investors of firm-specific critical assets are. The most common application of this principle to the corporate governance problem has been to view financial investors as the category of actors who are 'typically' in that position (Shleifer and Vishny 1997) and who 'typically' see their interest as 'shareholder value maximization'. But the arguments that other actors may well be in that position and, even more so, that stock value maximization may not be in the best interest of shareholders themselves has already been made (Blair 1995; Hansman 1996), and anyway is not inconsistent with agency theory.

Another idiosyncratic application of AT and PRT has been to cast the problem of ownership structure as the selection of one owner among many candidates rather than contemplating the possibility of a plurality of principals. The reasons for this option have been set out above all by Hansman (1996), and justified in terms of costs of decision-making in the case of heterogeneous preferences over firm policies.

This trait of AT has been the distinctive target of criticism from the 'stakeholder' perspective in management. Plainly, the advocates of the stakeholder perspective propose to move to the other end of the continuum of interest representation: all actors having 'a stake' in the firm should 'participate' in its governance. Consequently, the 'stakeholder' view is an alternative to the 'shareholder' view, but not to agency theory. The main problem with the stakeholder view, however, is that, as such, it should be an application of an alternative theory capable of specifying who the stakeholders should be and why, and what types and degrees of participation are effective. This theory has never been worked out, however. Clearly, a simple claim that anyone whose interests are affected by the existence and behavior of firms is too broad, and makes any design task unmanageable (Aoki, this volume). In fact, the definition of stakeholder has often been restricted to those interested actors who have 'legitimate power' in the firm (Donaldson and Preston 1995). Unfortunately, this is a tautology, since the problem is precisely to understand which actors should have 'legitimate power'. Even worse, this definition can work as a conservative mechanism reinforcing whatever the existing power system happens to be—something which was certainly not the intention of the proponents of the approach.

Another peculiar trait of the current versions of AT and PRT is to treat property rights as a 'bundle'. In other words, 'ownership' is considered as a 'package' of residual rights of 'control' (which include decision rights, in these authors' formulations) and residual reward rights which can hardly be separated. There are arguments for this view, but this book contributes to dismantling them.

The original argument was made by Alchian and Demsetz (1972) who, considering a team production situation with observable inputs, justified the emergence of hierarchy (a supervising central agent) as a solution to the free-rider problem, and explained the assignment of residual reward rights to the controller as a response to the question 'who will control the controller?' In later PRT contributions, the focus on the hold-up problem and the idea that an actor has more incentives to invest in an asset the more he or she can determine the use of an asset, has led to the near-identification of ownership with control (Hart 1995; Hansman 1996). This argument suffers from serious empirical anomalies. One of the most important features of modern capitalism—the separation of 'ownership' and 'control'—becomes almost indefinable and inexplicable in that frame. In addition, the variety of 'hybrid' or otherwise mixed forms governing inter-firm relationships cannot even be defined, let alone explained, if we do not admit that property rights of different types are actually separated and allocated to different actors. Research on inter-firm networks is clear-cut on that and has gone some way already in specifying which configurations of property rights allocation are efficient and fair under what circumstances (for example, Daems 1983; Grandori and Neri 1999; Child 2002).

This book takes further steps in this direction, fully considering the advantages of the separation between 'ownership' and 'control' and, even more, between residual rights of reward, decision, control, use, and sale of rights. An important reason why AT and PRT underestimate, or even overlook, these advantages is their unilateral focus on the hold-up and conflict of interests dimension of governance, and a neglect of the knowledge and competence dimension of governance. Organization theory helps to overcome this limitation, offering some relevant propositions on the matter: namely, that decision rights should be assigned to actors possessing relevant knowledge, that decision rights cannot be separated from action rights in complex activities, and that control rights cannot easily be separated from action and decision rights in knowledge-intensive activity. The contributions to this book are sensitive to these organizational insights, and address governance issues in full awareness of the interactions and trade-offs between the knowledge and interest dimensions of governance, and are thus able to predict and explain more varied and hybrid configurations.

The contributions in the first part of the book offer approaches that could be seen as covering the middle ground between the traditional agency-based shareholder view and the stakeholder view. They use concepts from AT and PRT, but apply them in very novel ways, and typically integrate them with other economic and organizational models such as game theory, negotiation analysis, and certain neglected important principles of law. As a whole, they offer substantial elements for what can be called a 'contingency theory of principals', in a much wider sense than AT and PRT can provide.

Aoki starts out precisely by observing that an unrestricted and unqualified stakeholder approach makes the governance problem analytically intractable. He then restricts the 'players' to those actors who can be considered as claimant 'principals', that is, investors in firm-specific assets. The cases in which only one category of investors is 'essential', whereby property rights over firm assets are efficiently assigned to it, are, in that frame, special cases. Unlike the main property rights theory treatments, Aoki does not dismiss the possibility of multiple principals due to assumed 'high decision-making costs' between actors with different preferences. He acknowledges that the problem exists, and is actually exacerbated by the internal horizontal organization structure which—according to organization theory—is effective in multiple critical resource situations. In fact, the canvassed solution is not an undifferentiated, stable and costly group decision-making regime over firm policies and the division of surplus. Instead, Aoki applies some core ideas to the CG problem from his *Cooperative Game Theory of the Firm* (1984), as well as echoing some recent and traditional insights in organizational economics, such as Aghion and Bolton's analysis (1992) of shifting property rights between entrepreneurs and investors contingent on the firm's outcomes, and Williamson's early analysis (1970) of optimal levels of organizational slack contingent on the state of the environment (munificent/resource-rich versus competitive/resource-poor). Aoki proposes a game in which different categories of property rights (residual reward and control rights) shift between the different actors, contingently to the level of surplus (arguably, a higher level of surplus makes the negotiation easier and reduces decision-making costs). For high surplus levels, residual output value is shared among insiders (managers and workers), while external financial investors and their delegated controllers get fixed rewards. For low levels of surplus, the opposite occurs. In other words, the framework specifies the conditions under which multiple principal governance is superior (multiple critical resources), and also specifies which coalition of actors should become the principals contingent on the level of surplus.

Grandori and Soda resort to a negotiation analysis framework for identifying superior governance structures in pressure of multiple principals, and define a governance regime as a combination of an allocation of property rights and an array of other organizational mechanisms. Two categories of principals are considered: investors of human capital (highly qualified or 'high potential' managers) and investors of financial capital or their delegates in boards of directors. In this research framework, drawing on earlier work on organization structures as efficient and fairly negotiated agreements (Grandori 1991), Grandori and Soda conceive of superior governance structures as combinations of mechanisms that minimize the distance between principals' preferences. As expected, more than one solution is found. All actors prefer democratic, horizontal organizational structures over hierarchical ones (a diffused allocation of decision rights)—and this solution is aligned to the organizational arrangements expected to be effective in complex, competence-intensive task. But one coalition would go for a longer-lasting association between resources and long-term human capital investments and more fixed rewards to human capital providers, while another—to which many managers and few investors belong—would accept more risk transfers (residual rewards to managers) but would also demand more control rights (more management representatives on boards) and more resaleability of their assets (more mobility, short-term association with any firm).

Margaret Blair draws on her distinctive integrated law, economic and organizational approach (Blair 1996) to bring into the picture one of the fundamental contributions of commercial law to the definition of the firm— specifically in its incorporated form—although an almost neglected point in the law-and-finance-dominant approach to CG analysis. Far from being just a 'nexus of contracts' among parties with an identity, the corporation is a juridical person whose assets and interests are distinct from those of any of its constituencies, whether shareholders or stakeholders. The very separation between any input provider and the firm itself is the core juridical invention which made it possible to build long-lasting institutions and to 'lock-in' technical firm-specific assets in spite of the mobility of investors and suppliers. Strictly speaking, corporations are firms with no owners. The firm—as a juridical person—is the principal. Any analysis of CG should therefore consider the interests of the firm itself, based on its social function, above and beyond the interests of any party who 'has a stake' in it, or even who has made specific investments in it.

Child and Rodrigues further enlarge the perspective by pointing out that some external business partners can qualify as principals as well. Other firms can make, and increasingly do make, firm-specific investments in other firms. In those types of inter-firm alliances, in fact, property rights are shared in various forms and degrees among firms (Daems 1983; Child 2002). Analyses of the relationships between inter-firm alliances and CG are almost absent, however, and this essay contributes to filling up the deficit. There could be at least two broad types of relationships to analyze on these grounds: first, how the participation of a firm in partnerships and alliances is likely to modify the governance structure of the firm; and second, what governance structures are set up to conduct inter-firm collaborative activities. Child and Rodrigues's chapter addresses the second issue, by analyzing the governance structures of joint ventures—in particular of international joint ventures—as a case of firms with multiple other firms as principals with differentiated interests and competencies. Four basic solutions to this problem—or joint-venture governance structures—are canvassed, ranked according to principal firms' preferences which are expected to vary contingently with the degree of risk and with the distribution of competences among partner firms. The 'unbundling' of different categories of rights and their selective assignment to the parent as opposed to the joint-venture firm emerge as a fundamental way of achieving viable governance arrangements.

Moreton and Zenger's essay, in a way, addresses the other side of the network-governance nexus, that is, the effect that the structuring of external networks in which firms are embedded has on firm governance. The study adds new insights and aspects to the existing literature on how 'shareholder value maximization', intended as stock price maximization, can discourage innovation (O'Sullivan 2000). The authors, who have contributed to the understanding of how and to what extent 'high powered incentives' can be used in the governance of large enterprises (Zenger and Hesterley 1997), uncover the indirect but strong effects of a new set of incentives on managers to influence the judgement of financial analysts who assess the value of equity shares of traded firms. They find evidence that—aside from the influence costs that this relationship may entail—a major effect is the narrowing down of firm strategies to courses of action that are conventional, recognizable, easy to explain and communicate, and easy to evaluate by analysts. This phenomenon may erect a significant barrier to the evolution of firms in novel directions, to resource complementarity-based diversification across industry boundaries definitions, ultimately to the growth of the most important basis for value creation, namely, the capacity of firms to be unique collections of resources (Penrose 1959). In addition, the chapter contributes—thanks to its solid grounding in the theory of the firm—to overcoming the difficulties of assessing governance solutions directly in term of the quality of business strategies generated rather than in terms of the structures that are supposed to generate good choices (criticizing and avoiding common and faulty stereotypes on that ground, such as considering diversification per se as an index of managerial drift).

In sum, a first key contribution of the book is to set out the elements for an approach to CG that is able to prescribe governance solutions in conditions of multiple principals and multiple objectives, to define governance solutions not only in terms of ownership and governance bodies structures but also in terms of complementary organizational mechanisms and structures, and to explain the variety of efficient and equitable CG solutions according to relevant contingencies.

Beyond the Logic of Incentives and 'Alignment': From 'Behavioral Assumptions' to Empirically-based Theories of Preferences and Motivation

Another main objection usually made against AT and other economic theories of governance has been more theoretical, although it is derived from the usual criticism of economic models from outside economics: the model of rationality implied by AT is a standard expected value-maximizing model, with all the restrictive 'assumptions' that go with it in terms of actors' knowledge and calculative capabilities. In general, however, this type of objection mainly specifies the domain of application of those models rather than demonstrating that they are wrong. And it may well be that some (though surely not all) governance games are well-structured problems, with clear payoffs in which value-maximizing calculations are possible. Hence, a more pertinent response to the 'narrowness' of the value-maximizing model would be to develop an array of alternative or complementary models of decision-making applicable beyond those narrow conditions or able to better predict effective decision behavior (Grandori 1984, 2001c; Lindenberg 1990). In fact, none of the chapters that proposes to rethink the cognitive and motiv-ational foundations of governance does so by way of 'rejecting' utility theory and the possibility of value-maximizing altogether in favor of resorting to a mere (albeit more 'realistic') description of actual behavior. Rather, and more ambitiously, the chapters concerned with this issue argue that proper attention to cognitive processes allows one to specify the conditions for desirable outcomes better than the standard economic models.

A related criticism, also drawn from the typical repertoire of organizational and behavioral criticisms of economics, has been a reaction to the content of assumptions on preferences. Whereas agency theory and its more common applications 'assume' self-interest and opportunism, identification, loyalty, and trust (most notably in so-called stewardship theory) has been counter-assumed (Davis, Schoorman, and Donaldson 1997). Of course, in this 'best of all possible worlds' governance problems would be simply assumed away: managers identify with the firm and their duties, are good 'stewards' of own-ers or of the firm, and wish to maintain the trust that has been invested in them. The chapters in this book do not follow this easy path. Rather, and more ambitiously, the chapters concerned with this issue try to specify *motiv-ation content* in an empirically testable way rather than by assumption (Simon 1997) and to figure out what cognitive processes should be sustained that are *better* than those prescribed by standard economic models for achieving high-performance outcomes.

I will illustrate these general achievements in more detail, highlighting how three major assumptions of economic models applied to corporate governance, which usually go unquestioned, are actually challenged in this book:

- that economic behavior is primarily governed by economic means, that is, by proper incentives which 'align objectives';
- that 'objectives alignment' is a good thing; and
- that the content and shape of utility functions (what the objectives are) is a matter of 'assumption making'.

A conceptual itinerary on the first issue can be traced in the book, start-ing with the wide-ranging chapter by Michael Piore that revisits some core contributions by social scientists such as Weber and Polanyi on the nexus between economy and society and applies his own current thoughts on that nexus (Piore 2002) to the issue of corporate governance. Piore attributes current difficulties in finding effective governance solutions to a lack of understanding of what a new equilibrium between economy and society can be, after the crisis of the 'old industrial model'. In that model, there has been a sharp division of labor and of codes of behavior between the firm as the core economic institution and the family as the core social institution, but both were stable and clear institutions, thereby satisfying the requirements of identity, language and embeddedness imposed by human nature itself. Piore characterizes the current situation, especially after the 1990s, as simultaneously highly unstable, both in economy and society, and marked by loose, transversal identities. These changes, involving much more blurred boundaries between economy and society, have stimulated a dominant approach to governance that proposes an even sharper divide between an economy guided by a logic of market and gain, competition and mobility, and a society which, in addition of being 'marginalized' by the dominance of the economic realm, has lost any understanding of its own codes, hence its capacity to temper, integrate or otherwise complement the other realm.

Many other chapters in the second part of the book share the diagnosis that many of the currently critical problems in corporate governance have roots in the paradoxes and dysfunctions that 'the pursuit of gain', even in the format of 'shareholder value' and 'aligning objectives' to that goal, is likely to generate.

Paul Windolf's argument proceeds a conceptual basis rooted in classic sociology, akin to that of Piore. He also sees a core governance dilemma lying at the intersection of economic, social and political codes of behavior. Differentiation and autonomy in the systems are needed, otherwise they do not perform efficiently the function they are constituted for; furthermore, the very use by one system of the code of another system is what we call corruption (for example, the use of money for securing laws, or the use of friendship for securing business); and systems cannot complement and 'temper' one another if they are not different. Therefore, 'over-embeddedness' of any system into another is undesirable (Wrong 1961). On the other hand, systems need to be 'embedded' into one another (Granovetter 1985). In particular, economic relations should be embedded in social (and political) institutions to function effectively (North 1990).

Windolf's chapter also contributes to linking these macro considerations to a more micro analysis of how 'embeddedness' may work at the decision-making level (which is the central concern of the subsequent essays in Part II). Windolf instructively goes back to Max Weber's insights and brings them to bear on the CG problem. A core concern, if not *the* core concern, in *Economy and Society* was to 'free' the capitalistic enterprise from the personalistic interests and the uses of its patrimony by capitalists themselves. Windolf sharply observes that a core ingredient of capitalism, according to Weber—and a core difference from previous economic systems—was the organization of economic activities under an institution—the capitalist enterprise—capable of 'tempering' plain greed and unregulated self-interest-seeking (let alone self-interest-seeking-with-guile).

This useful connection to Weber (which parallels and complements Blair's argument on the advantages of institutionalizing the firm as a separate legal entity) leads to the second criticism of AT assumptions implied by this book. Among the many critiques of AT, it is rare to find any objection to the core assumption that 'objective alignment' is a desirable state of affairs. Although this is a matter on which, methodologically, it is legitimate to make assumptions, I will argue that the assumption is wrong and that the contributions to the second part of the book sustain this proposition.

In fact, in Weber's analysis, one important rationale for 'bureaucracy' as 'the best way of organizing' the capitalistic enterprise was its property of achieving a separation between personal and organizational goals, and a specialization in organizational sub-goals. Far from being a variant of 'sub-goal pursuit' as personal agendas, the specialization and differentiation of objectives was intended to generate sense of duty, task identification, and the pursuit of standards of technical excellence. In the organizational literature, despite the various criticisms of the bureaucratic model, this message has been retained and elaborated in founding concepts such as Simon's (1969) 'near-decomposability' of organization, and Lawrence and Lorsch's (1967) 'differentiation of cognitive and emotional orientations' of managers in the specialized organizational sub-units. To put it more explicitly: *the differentiation of objectives has cognitive and motivational advantages.*

Osterloh and Frey reinforce this argument, pointing out the dysfunctional consequences of aligning managerial objectives to profit-making. In particular, drawing on Frey's theory (1997; Frey and Jegen 2001) of 'crowding out', they predict that the intensive use of incentives and extrinsic rewards tends to 'crowd out' intrinsic motivation, thereby making shirking, free riding and even unlawful money-seeking maneuverings all the more likely. On descriptive grounds, they also show that the sensitivity of managerial behaviors to incentives may already be high at very low levels of contingent-pay incidence, making significant investments in it unwarranted.

Lindenberg also roots his analysis in cognitive research for offering insights into the functioning of opportunism as a likely consequence of the dominance of a 'gain frame'. Using recent insights from cognitive and motivational psychology and his own work on 'relational signaling' (Lindenberg 2000), Lindenberg convincingly argues that, paradoxically, the creation of wealth and collectively generated value, instead of coming about as a result of the pursuit of self-interest at the individual level, can be produced only by the partial suspension of calculative behavior itself. The reason is that the unconstrained pursuit of self-interest, and the related possibility of opportunism, is likely to destroy the very relationships from which value is generated. Hence, rational actors would choose to signal that they would refrain from opportunism in order to increase the probability that others would also behave trustworthily, rather than treating everyone else as a potential opportunist, thereby increasing the probability that all players involved in fact behaved opportunistically. This strategy is particularly compelling where the complexity of activities bars the possibility of control and where there is potentially 'joint production' in a long-lasting relationship, that is, where repeated transactions among given partners potentially generate surplus value. A corollary of this relational perspective is that, when a principal is aware that he is engaged in a 'joint production' game and that no 'value' can be generated, let alone maximized, without the cooperation of other players, it is rational for him to have an interest in the satisfaction of other actors' objectives (after all the term 'inter-est' means 'to be' 'inter', and it is not at all contradictory to say that the best way of serving one's interest is to be not entirely self-interested).

Lindenberg then turns to the issue of how the players of the governance game—especially principals—can give credible signals of relational commitment. On this basis, the author usefully brings organizational justice theory and research (Greenberg 1995) into the governance debate, highlighting how 'procedural justice' in particular (practice of open communication, record of kept promises, adherence to voice-giving procedures, and so on) can and should inform the working of corporate governance (in fact any form of governance) if it is to be sustainable.

Grandori and Soda's study includes the most explicit quest for an empirical assessment of what the content and shape of preferences of key actors actually are.[1] In other words, the third departure from the 'assumptions' of economic models of CG included in this book is that assumptions—in their strict sense of non-testable postulates—should not be made at all on preferences. Rather, following the methodological prescription that assumptions should be made only on matters where testing is not possible (Simon 1997), and that this is not the case with preferences, the research advances *testable hypotheses* on how actors' preferences on governance mechanisms should be configured and tests them (Grandori 2001*b*). As could be expected, some interesting surprises emerge with respect to usual expectations and to dominant economic theory 'assumptions' on preferences. For example, it emerges that a critical matter of exchange in agency relationships is the extent of the delegation of power on which the relation is based in the first place, and that both 'principals' and 'agents' assign positive preferences to high managerial discretion. This result was theoretically predicted by the researchers, for the knowledge (rather than interest) reason—quite neglected in agency and property right theory—that decision rights should be allocated where the relevant knowledge resides. Similarly, the 'cost of effort' does not appear to

---

[1] Although they do not emphasize this feature methodologically, other chapters in Part I of the book—notably, those by Child and Rodrigues, and Moreton and Zenger—also rely critically on the prediction and empirical test of preferences.

be such a major problem: according to classic motivation theory, work has intrinsic benefits and managers are not concerned with avoiding effort. In sum, another key message of the book is that some of the supposed 'evils' of governance, of the supposedly troublesome traits of modern corporations, like the 'separation between ownership and control' and the 'misalignment of objectives', have roots in healthy and valuable properties of firm organization, and that of the modern corporation in particular, like the separation between private and organizational goals and patrimony, and organizational differentiation. Hence, the proper way to address 'differentiation' (between ownership and control and between units' objectives) is by no means to reduce it but to integrate what has been (properly) separated and differentiated (a core principle in organization theory). This leads to the question of what the portfolio of integration mechanisms is.

Beyond the Logic of Control: Enlarging the Portfolio of Governance Mechanisms

The CG debate has been focused on a surprisingly limited set of governance mechanisms—surprising at least from the point of view of organizational scholars approaching the field and the problem of CG, as I and other contributors to this book are. In fact, in a recent effort at systematizing and comparing the variety of basic coordination and control mechanisms envisaged and assessed in organization theory (Grandori 2001a), at least the following had to be considered:

- price-like mechanisms (including incentives, market prices, transfer prices, queues and rationing, fees), often coupled with the complementary mechanism of exit; and voting mechanisms (the parallel of pricing for regulating collective actions rather than transactions);
- negotiation, with its repertoire of signals, hostages and pledges, brokers, and mediators as complements;
- teams and communities, based on all-to-all communication and involving various degrees of knowledge-sharing and reciprocal monitoring;
- hierarchy (more or less inclusive of decision and control rights);
- formal rules and social norms (internal or external to the system to be governed, and differing in their levels of generality); and
- property rights allocations (ownership of assets, rights to residual rewards, residual control rights).

In the CG debate—both in the academy and in policy-making—only four types of governance mechanism are typically considered:

- pricing and exit—that is, 'market-like'—mechanisms (including incentive structures, markets for corporate control and the like) and voting mechanisms (voting rights attached to shares, composition of boards of directors, and so forth);

- hierarchical control (monitoring by 'principals' or by their delegates on agents);
- formal regulation, either of the court-enforceable or of the self-regulation variety; and
- property right allocation (separation of ownership and control, insider-outsider ownership, and so on).

Various chapters in this book contribute to enlarging the portfolio of governance mechanisms that can be employed to integrate the differentiated interests and inputs of the key actors in the governance game, but have so far been conspicuously absent from the CG repertoire: *negotiation, social norms, and community governance.*

All the contributions in Part I, as already discussed, highlight the importance of *negotiation* as a regulative mechanism. Both the Roe and Piore essays also point out that a major distinction between governance systems across time and space is the extent to which the distribution of economic surplus is regulated by negotiation between the actors contributing to it or by price-based competition and legal restraints.

The importance of rules is obvious in CG. What is less obvious in CG—although classic in organization theory and organizational sociology—is that regulatory systems are always also composed of informal, socially defined *norms* (ranging from general values and codes of conducts, heuristics, rules of thumbs, to conventions and routines). The importance of norms emerges also in other essays included in Part II of this volume; Lampel's essay is explicitly and analytically devoted to understanding the functioning of norms and the structure of effective normative systems of control. In fact, the obvious problem with norms is that social and informal regulation requires a high level of confidence in compliance, and the definition and acceptance of heuristics for evaluating non-compliance. Lampel's definition and clarification of the function of these second-level or 'shadow' norms, which manage deviations from primary norms of good conduct, contributes to the literature both on norms and on corporate governance. Using a cognitive perspective, Lampel stresses that the notion of 'non-compliance', as central as it is in economic literature as well, is far from obvious: when is a 'defection' a defection? How large should the deviation be? How many deviations are no longer interpretable as 'random'? Is non-compliance due to under-competence or to opportunism? (Shapira 2000; Lampel and Shapira 2001). Higher-level procedural norms are needed—as, by the way, higher-order procedural rules are needed in formal rule systems. As long as 'bystanders' have incentives and competence to enforce social norms, arguably the shift from a logic of trust and informal norms to a 'logic of suspicion' (Sabel 1993) and formal deterrence—surely more costly—is not necessary.

However, high levels of instability and uncertainty, and high levels of differentiation of knowledge and interests, are potential causes of failure of norm governance (Grandori 2001*a*). Lampel's essay indicates a remedy for this weakness of norms: the presence of 'metanorms' makes the application of primary norms sensible, circumstantiated, and not automatic, thereby increasing the flexibility of normative governance—hence its robustness in the face of uncertainty. A corollary of this statement could be that normative systems with a high density of 'shadow' procedural norms and a low density of low-level action-prescribing norms—in Lampel's terms, 'missionary regimes'—should be more effective under uncertainty. This proposition would be consistent with the prescription of organization theory to focus on mission statements rather than on norms of behavior in complex uncertain activities. And it would help in not reacting to the distortions generated by extreme monetary incentives by resorting to a generic rhetoric of 'shared culture' and 'social responsibility'. In particular, norm-based governance, and especially 'flexible' normative systems, leave social contracts very implicit and very incomplete. Hence they are likely to work only if combined with other governance mechanisms. Among them, some have been analyzed—as the formalized but socially defined and voluntary 'codes of conduct' (see Aguilera and Cuervo-Cazurra, this volume)—while others have been rather neglected in the CG field, such as that of 'communities'.

Community governance has received increasing attention in organizational literature, especially as a mechanism for the governance of knowledge. It can be conceived as a variant of 'team-like' governance, if, drawing on the elegant and underused Marschak's definition (1955), we conceive teams as groups of actors with homogeneous preferences and distributed information and knowledge; and communities as teams characterized by knowledge-sharing. A variety of communities have therefore been conceived, ranging from 'communities of practices' (Brown and Duguid 1991)—sharing common knowledge of the tacit and routine-based variety—to 'epistemic communities'—sharing basic knowledge and methods but exchanging and integrating differentiated knowledge in an explicit, articulated, and creative way (Cowan, David, and Foray 2000).

Lazonick and Prencipe's chapter reveals the extreme stability and robustness of community governance under varying property regimes. Lazonick and Prencipe draw on the literature on the governance of innovation—and on their earlier contributions to it—to understand how innovation in a large industrial corporation has been sustainable through a history of changes in formal top-governance structure. Community governance at the level of scientific and technical work, the consistent and persistent decentralization of decision rights (if not of property rights) has created the cognitive and motivational conditions for a pursuit of technical excellence and product innovation, in spite of the variety of proprietary regimes at the corporate level.

It could be argued that, in the governance of complex, distributed knowledge, communities can hardly be substituted by any other mechanism, and that the allocation of decision and control rights characterizing organization structure is more uniquely determined and perhaps more important than the allocation of property rights at the level of the general ownership structure of the firm.

In fact, community governance has been shown to be effective even if combined with different ownership structures, in the same firm or sector over time in different conditions, and across firms and sectors. This empirical proposition could be derived comfortably from the contingency view of principals and governance structures emerging in this book. In fact, the relevant contingencies which call for community governance at the work level—distributed and critical knowledge assets—are not changing in the described situations, while some other contingencies affecting the identity of owners have. First, the criticality of financial investments changed, and the difficulty of attracting them, as well as the general economic situation and the level of firm surplus. Hence—and this seems to me a corroborating case for Aoki's model—while organization structure remains stable and horizontal (that is, decision and control rights remain decentralized), property rights *strictu sensu* (residual control and reward rights, and ownership of technical and financial assets) shift towards financial investors. Second, the heuristics used by investors and their analysts changed, possibly sustaining isomorphism in the adoption of 'conventional' ownership structures, for legitimization purposes—as various studies in Part III of this volume highlight.

Neither Convergence nor Divergence: Non-proximate Endogenous and Exogenous Determinants of Corporate Governance Evolution

A good part of the CG debate has revolved around the question of whether governance systems around the world are 'converging' or 'diverging', and to what. As in the case of governance mechanisms, this question sounds somehow unsophisticated from a modern perspective informed by organization theory. In fact, there have been important and similar debates in the past about whether organization and management practices could be transferred across national boundaries, obeying an efficiency and task contingent logic, or, rather, whether organization and management are 'culture-bound' and 'institutionally constrained', hence necessarily 'different' (Hofstede 1980; Whitley 1992). The stereotypical 'parties' in these quarrels have been: the economics-oriented scholars supporting convergence toward most efficient solutions—at least within homogeneous industry or task segments of the economy; and the sociological and political science-oriented scholars supporting the thesis of the intrinsic 'variety of capitalisms'—very much in the same way as is now occurring in the CG field. In spite of the survival of these positions also in the organizational debate, some relevant objections to the use of a 'convergence versus divergence' frame have already been developed (Grandori 1991*b*, 2000).[2]

- The mere description of 'differences' is a somewhat touristic exercise unless we are able to specify which aspects of the differences are arbitrary and conventional, and/or functionally equivalent arrangements; which aspects are rankable in terms of efficiency and fairness; and which aspects are path-dependent and institutionally constrained.
- Differences in solutions may stem from the use (in theories as well as in different economic systems) of different efficiency parameters (transaction and production-cost efficiency, Pareto-efficiency, static or dynamic efficiency) and of different justice criteria.
- Realized solutions may be dominated by possible but not yet tried solutions.
- Economic organization models themselves can not predict any generalized convergence, as the notion of efficient organization is always contingent on the characteristic of tasks and transactions—which cannot be imagined to be homogeneous even at the micro level of a single firm, let alone of an entire industry or an entire nation.

In the light of the contributions to this book that we have discussed thus far, and of the specific contributions gathered in Part III, the 'convergence versus divergence' frame looks inadequate for all these reasons—and for some additional ones.

First, all 'realized' current corporate governance systems, especially if considered as 'nationally' or even 'continentally' homogeneous, far from having any claim of optimality or of being the 'best practices' among those which have been tried, have been demonstrated to have serious weaknesses; hence, reform of all of them is more interesting than convergence toward any of them.

Second, even if we were to consider convergence toward new solutions (Van den Berghe 2002) rather than toward any existing solution, the variety of contingencies should produce a variety of effective arrangements rather than convergence toward a 'hybrid' or *in medio stat virtus* point. In fact, differences and variety in organization and governance solutions need not be due to the variety of institutional and cultural 'contexts', to organizational inertia, or to path dependencies—and therefore to all possible 'inefficiencies of history' (North 1990). Many of the observed differences can be predicted as efficient responses to variations in the type of resources and activities to be governed and to the configuration of actors and of their preferences. This

---

[2] I was directly involved in this debate—and took the position that the question was wrongly asked and empirically undecidable—in my capacity as scientific director of the European Science Foundation Research Programme EMOT (European Management and Organization in Transition), 1993–7 (co-director Richard Whitley).

type of 'contingency view' of structure is quite consolidated in the organization theory tradition, but it could be innovative in the CG field,[3] where it has often been plainly maintained that 'economic criteria' would predict convergence while political, legal, and sociological views would imply divergence (Thomsen, this volume). This is not so. Economic and efficiency criteria themselves predict a lot of variation (and even divergence) in governance structures.

Thomsen's chapter in Part III of the book also contributes to revealing some additional limits of the convergence or divergence frame. First, the convergence or divergence question further increases the difficulty of comparative analysis of different systems by adding a dynamic dimension, being the divergence and convergence referred to *change* in differences rather than simply on differences. In order to handle such a question properly in empirical research, any observed change in a short time span should be cast within the long-term dynamics of those systems, so as to make it possible to distinguish chance variations, short-term oscillations, extreme and unlikely variations destined to regress to the mean, from systematic convergence or divergence (Campbell 1969).

Third, it is obviously possible that some traits of a complex system change in one direction while other traits change in another: that is, some traits converge while variations are generated on other traits (Aguilera and Cuervo-Cazurra 2001), so that no general trend can be meaningfully identified.

Fourth, the models behind both the convergence and the divergence hypotheses are all based on rather traditional 'contextual' explanations; that is, they consider independent variables which pertain either to the proximate economic context (for example, the globalization of markets) or to the proximate institutional context (for example, CG regulative laws). Both perspectives neglect the endogenous forces that are likely to generate change in many systems and in governance systems in particular. And both perspectives neglect the background, structural, exogenous forces (like demography) that are likely to affect the configuration and dynamic of systems, often more strongly than more proximate and 'intended' causes (like law and regulation).

---

[3] The so-called contingency research on corporate governance in the management field (Daily and Cannella 2003) is not contingency theory in the organization theory sense. In fact, the typical design of contingency studies in CG has been a model in which performance is the dependent variable and an array of structural variables are the independent variables (incentive schemes, board composition, and so on). The question is whether and how different governance structures affect performance. A proper contingency theory needs three classes of variables rather than two: the dependent variable should be the governance structure (rather than performance); the independent variable should be contingency on which the efficiency of each structural arrangement depends; the 'fit' between those two variables should affect performance. The improper design of much 'contingency' research on CG in management may be one explanation of why this research has not produced any 'conclusive results', as the leaders of this approach themselves admit (Daily and Cannella 2003).

Let me summarize and condense some original and unconventional elements that the chapters in this book—especially the empirical studies gathered in Part III—contribute to renewing the comparative study of governance systems, in consideration of endogenous change and background structural factors of change.

Michael Piore, in the historical notes included in his chapter, casts the change of the 'US model' in a different light, suggesting that it has changed much as political regimes change: because of internal laws of alternation in the distribution of power and because of background demographic and social structure changes. The stylized market- and regulation-based external control system was not always there. Actually, Piore dates its 'birth' to quite recently, when, in the 1980s, employers exerted 'militant pressures' for freeing management to govern the enterprise at their full discretion. This led to the collapse of the previously long-lasting (since the 1930s) bargaining-based, more insider-dominated system. Changes in the composition of society, double-career families, the emergence of professional or social group identities, and the decline of firm-centered identities contributed to the crisis of the old regime—although, as Piore observes, they do not necessarily find proper responses in the new regime.

A political interpretation of the evolution of CG systems and the importance of the work question in particular is quite consistent with Roe's theses (2003) on the political determinants of corporate governance. Among those determinants, Roe's chapter in this volume highlights the critical role of labor relations and trade unions as determinants of governance structures. He sets out the original thesis that the present differences in ownership concentration between Europe and the United States may in fact be largely due to the different ways of governing labor relations. Where the division of economic surplus is chiefly regulated by the mechanism of collective negotiation, the presence of powerful actors on one side creates incentives to set up a 'countervailing power' on the other side; hence, powerful unions and concentrated ownership reinforce each other. Even more, Roe's analysis suggests prospects that the reinforcement of ownership concentration is an 'unintended consequence' of polities that favor labor!

The 'concentrated ownership' and 'concentrated union power' governance arrangement may certainly raise concerns and surely entails costs, especially for minority investors and firms' capacity to attract investments and to grow. There are trade-offs, however. Organized labor voice can be an important additional tool for controlling managerial behavior, whereas organized workers, especially at the firm level (Van den Berg forthcoming), may have better incentives and information for controlling managers (Kochan 2003). In addition, direct negotiation over firm surplus may also have equity and efficiency advantages—as pointed out by Roe, Piore, Aoki, and Blair in this volume and elsewhere. It could be added that these advantages should have more weight where surplus is created by firm-specific and long-lasting association of participants. Actually, it would be possible to argue that some of the observed variations across time and space in the importance of bargaining-based systems are due to the extent to which those 'long-lasting, specific associations' between participants are or are not at the basis of firm existence.

The difficulties of interpreting these changes in terms of convergence or divergence emerge even more clearly from the interesting empirical evidence presented by Thomsen (although somehow paradoxically, given that the framing of that chapter is to a large extent informed by the convergence/divergence debate).

Thomsen's study indicates that the governance solutions prevailing in the US and UK are undergoing another change, especially after the scandals that recently occurred in the US. After the US drift toward a 'market competition and external law constraint' of the 1980s, Thomsen shows that in the 1990s quite a few traits of the US–UK system actually seem to have converged to European standards: higher concentration of ownership, increasing levels of internal ownership, increasing separation of management and control through independent board members, ethical investments by pension funds, more negotiated governance between different stakeholders. This dynamic, however, can also be seen as a 'convergence' to standards and practices which were also present in the US system in earlier historical phases.

In other words, the observed changes may be consistent with an *alternation model of change* rather than with a convergence or divergence model. In fact, in governance matters there may be forces that after some time push any system out of its configuration, whichever it was. The reason lies in the costs that any governance system entails, and in the difficulty of achieving a fair distribution of resources in a static way. As in political governance, 'alternation' between systems may represent a dynamic solution to that problem (Lindblom 1959; Grandori 2001a; Nickerson and Zenger 2003). The different advantages and disadvantages of the various arrangements on different performance parameters and for different actors can compensate each other over time.

In fact, according to Thomsen's chapter, CG practices in European countries seem to have evolved in the 1990s in the opposite direction (de-concentration of ownership, more market and external law regulation). However, this trend need not be a case of convergence toward the US/UK model or to any other salient focal point. The oscillation may well continue beyond the point of maximal similarity among the systems and start another divergence drift.

In response to this 'alternation' or 'oscillation' hypothesis on my part, and to my question whether he had elements on former variations before the 1990s, Thomsen inserted in his chapter the data on the long-run stock market index, which does confirm that the 1990s were indeed a period of unusual, extreme stock exchange activity. Therefore, it is not surprising that more market-oriented practices diffused in those years (as, it seems, occurred in other stock-euphoric periods in the past). In sum, the elements provided by Thomsen are consistent with the idea that the 1990s have been outliers: more a case of an extreme variation which is likely to regress to the mean, an 'oscillation', than a case in convergence toward the US/UK model as a superior governance system—which was in fact changing, during the same years, the other way around. As Thomsen notices, another result supporting the diagnosis that the observed changes have been quite period-specific is the absence of any common industry effect on changes.

Both Cuervo-Cazurra and Aguilera's chapter and Lancaster and Uzzi's chapter provide complementary empirical elements on the specificities of the 1990s, and a valuable call for attention to the possibility that sociological forces may drive the homogenization of management practices at least as much as economic ones. Contrary to how the phenomenon is seen in the CG debate, convergence can be a case in 'social isomorphism' and 'legitimation-seeking' rather than in economic efficiency (Powell and Di Maggio 1991; Aguilera and Cuervo-Cazurra 2004). In fact, both the phenomena analyzed in the two studies, respectively the adoption of voluntary 'codes' of good governance in various countries and the adoption of 'corporate-like' governance structures (rather than partnership-like) in US law firms, escalated in the 1990s. And in both papers, the authors argue that those homogenizing trends responded in part to economic reasons and in part to symbolic and social conformist reasons. Beyond this common trait, the two studies make a number of further distinctive contributions.

Aguilera and Cuervo analyze the adoption of codes in the frame of a wider organizational perspective on cross-national differences in organizational solutions (Aguilera and Jackson 2003) and as a diffusion process (Alvarez and Engwall 1999). A relevant result of their study is to empirically support the thesis that the dynamics of change is different on different governance traits. The adoption of codes, by itself, was a generalized tendency in the 1990s, thereby reducing differences at that level. However, the speed of adoption was not equal, and actually reinforced the pre-existing differences, whereas common-law countries, with stronger initial legal regulation, were more likely to adopt voluntary regulation as well. In other words, on those grounds, legal and voluntary regulation is more complementary than fungible. The contrary is found, instead, for specific 'anti-director' provisions. Other aspects generating variety between governance systems, within the overall homogenizing trend to adopt codes, are that the content and issuers of codes have been different.

Another interesting organizational insight offered by Aguilera and Cuervo's chapter into the evolution of CG around the world comes from casting the problem of diffusion of management recipes as a case in knowledge transfer. The frame proves to have heuristic power, as the study actually detects that some of the patterns which are known for knowledge transfers (such as that transfer is difficult beyond certain levels of differentiation between the knowledge nodes) hold for governance practice transfers as well;

and that the mere establishment of connection channels does not imply that any transfer occurs (Grandori 2001*c*).

Lancaster and Uzzi's chapter crisply shows the powerful effects of 'background' social factors, rather than transaction-specific and proximate context factors, on CG. In particular, it highlights the role of demographic changes in labor market structure and labor force composition and preferences, in the comparatively interesting setting of law firms. In fact, professional firms are the typical case in which employee ownership—of the partnership variety—is traditionally supposed to be effective. Empirically, Lancaster and Uzzi describe the recent trend away from the 'sacred' model of professional partnership in the US, whereby law firms concentrate, assume incorporated structures, and institute new employee-like roles which structure careers in a more conventional and hierarchical way. They explain the observed trend as a response to the increased incidence in the relevant labor force of women and minorities who do not perceive equal opportunities of becoming partners (thereby finding the partnership structure less attractive); and to the growth rates of firms, which may decrease the expectation of becoming partners for everybody. Although not formalized in the tested propositions, another interesting finding in this chapter is that large prestigious law firms are much less likely to conform to the incorporation trend. Again, the extent to which firms are long-lasting, specific associations of essential resources, or short-term associations with shifting participants emerges as an important determinant of what the superior governance arrangements are.

Finally, this chapter on law firms concurs with the study on the changing proprietary arrangements at Rolls-Royce by Lazonick and Prencipe in indicating that those changes are viable to the extent they do not disrupt the epistemic and deontological communities guiding and controlling professional work. Hence, it seems essential that the shift of some of the formal and institutional traits of governance toward more hierarchical internal structures and more market-driven external control is complemented by a persistently decentralized and team-like operative organization structure.

In conclusion, important determinants of CG arrangements and of their change lie outside and beyond the traditional proximate contingencies of investors' legal protection (and more generally of the 'institutional context') and of markets' efficiency and the 'economic context'. They include background social factors, in particular demographic and political factors, and social legitimization factors. As well, endogenous dynamics of 'alternation' and oscillations are likely to drive CG system change (as any organizational change). A paradoxical, somehow extreme way of expressing the challenge of this book toward the entire convergence-divergence debate (beyond the proposal to abandon the dilemma altogether) is to advance an opposite interpretation of the 'facts': (1) the 1990s may have represented an extreme oscillation, as such destined to regress to the mean; (2) the 1990s' convergence may have been driven more by social and ideological factors, while economic efficiency would require, and will restore, differentiation and contingency design.

Concluding Remarks: Implications for Design

In governance, as in organization, there is one solid law: there is no one best way of organizing. This does not mean that all ways of organizing are good; nor that 'institutional contexts' can justify any differences in solutions (what could we ever contribute to the design of institutions in this way?); nor that everything should be contingent (some abstract and procedural governance and organization principles may well be universally superior) (Grandori 2001*b*).

This book distinctively contributes both to identifying which traits of governance solutions are more universally superior and which are not, and to devising new forms and new 'contingencies' for their design. A new set of propositions, regarding the 'degree of contingency' of different mechanisms as well as on new governance forms, starts with the statement that the allocation of residual reward rights is more contingent than the allocation of decision and control rights. In fact, a decentralized, participatory, team-like, even democratic, relationally and procedurally just organization structure is consistently found to be superior in the governance of complex activities, which the direction of modern firms can generally be maintained to be (Aoki, Lampel, Lindenberg, Osterloh and Frey, Windolf, and Grandori and Soda). However, this allocation of decision and control rights can be compatible and even complementary, with varying allocations of other property rights. In particular, it is viable in combinations of collective, partnership-like and hierarchical ownership and reward structures. In fact, ownership structures in a stricter sense—how ownership of assets and residual reward rights are allocated—is found to vary in a more pronounced way, across time and space, according to relevant contingencies. The resulting configurations open up the variety of structural alternatives to new governance forms. In addition, these propositions constitute a challenge to and a possible extension of current property rights theory (Hart and Moore 1990), which do not consider the possibility of separating 'residual control rights' from other property rights (actually it defines ownership as residual control).

The book also offers new propositions on the nature of these contingencies. They are distinctively not nation-specific. They are much more fine-grained. They predict efficient variety within nations and even sectors. One major contingency is the state of the variables defining the key actor, namely, the firm. In one of the most innovative essays by an economist, on 'the theory of the firm revisited', one of the few surviving attributes that can define a 'firm-like organization' (if not a firm) is indicated in the 'long lasting association of input owners' (Demsetz 1991). But it turns out that there are fundamental differences among firms in this respect—which indicate a need and a line for revision of even the 'revisited' theory of the firm. More than one essay in this book suggests the hypothesis that the extent to which the firm is a long-lasting association of inputs is a variable. And some of the observed differences in governance systems across time and space could find an explanation in that variable. Firms constructed as long-lasting associations between unique, specific, non-substitutable resources demand different governance structures from firms constructed as unstable associations between mobile and shifting participants. Arguably, the 'resource-based firm' calls for more insider-dominated systems and for more concentrated ownership (Blair, Roe, Piore). Rather, the 'project-based firm' allows, and it is even based on, sustained mobility and change in the identity of both financial and human capital providers; hence, it arguably calls for a larger poll of potential contributors, a wider range of investors, and a more 'externally-dominated' governance. Another contribution of the studies included in this book has been to show that, contrary to conventional expectations, these two basic types of mechanism configurations can be both further combined with reward, career, and control mechanisms of a different nature, namely, more market-like mechanisms, or more hierarchical mechanisms, or more representative and democratic mechanisms—thereby giving raise to further efficient variations in governance structures (Lancaster and Uzzi, Grandori and Soda, Child and Rodrigues).

A second major contingency is the state of the environment, surprisingly even less considered as a variable in most common treatments of governance structures. Aoki's chapter sets out a core hypothesis in this respect, as powerful as it is simple: the basic 'economic contingency'—namely, expansion or recession—should matter, more precisely favoring insider coalitions under expansion and resourcefulness. Other essays on the variation of corporate governance mechanisms over time indirectly support this hypothesis, and contribute in indicating other background, base-rate, structural, environmentally relevant factors, such as demographic trends (Thomsen, Lazonick and Prencipe, Lancaster and Uzzi, Piore, Roe).

In conclusion, this book, bringing organizational insights into the CG debate, has direct implications for the design of corporate governance mechanisms, whose profile is different from that usually prescribed on the basis of economics and law only. And although this book is not directly concerned with devising the proper institutional 'rules of the game' in which these organizational choices should be embedded (North 1990), it does have indirect implications for it, claiming that the design of law and regulatory mechanisms should take into account the requirements imposed by the internal functioning of firm organization: in particular, if the so-called 'knowledge economy' means anything precise, the need for democracy and the need for change.

References

Aghion, P. and Bolton, P. (1992). 'An Incomplete Contracts' Approach to Financial Contracting', *Review of Economic Studies*, 59: 473–94.

Aguilera, R. and Cuervo-Cazurra, A. (2004). 'Codes of Good Governance Worldwide: What is the Trigger?', *Organization Studies*, 25: 417–46.

—— and Jackson, G. (2003). 'The Cross-National Diversity of Corporate Governance: Dimensions and Determinants', *Academy of Management Review*, 28: 447–65.

Alchian, A. and Demsetz, H. (1972). 'Production, Information Costs and Economic Organization', *American Economic Review*, 62: 777–95.

Alvarez, J. and Engwall, L. (1999). *The Production and Diffusion of Managerial Knowledge*. London: Routledge.

Aoki, M. (1984). *The Cooperative Game Theory of the Firm*. Oxford: Oxford University Press.

Blair, M. (1995). *Ownership and Control: Rethinking corporate governance for the 21st Century*. Washington, DC: Brookings Institution.

—— (1996). *Wealth Creation and Wealth Sharing: A Colloquium on Corporate Governance and Investments in Human Capital*. Washington, DC: Brookings Institution.

Brown, J. and Duguid, P. (1991). 'Organizational Learning and Communities-of-Practice: Toward A Unified View of Working, Learning, and Innovation', *Organization Science*, 2/1: 40–57.

Campbell, D. (1969). 'Reforms as Experiments', *American Psychologist*, 24: 409–29.

Child, J. (2002). 'A Configurational Analysis of International Joint Ventures', *Organization Studies*, 23: 781–815.

Cowan, R., David, P., and Foray, D. (2000). 'The Explicit Economics of Knowledge Codification and Tacitness', *Industrial and Corporate Change*, 9/2: 211–53.

Daems, H. (1983). 'The Determinant of Hierarchical Organization of Industry', in A. Francis, J. Turk, and P. Willman (eds.), *Power Efficiency and Institutions*. London: Heinemann.

Daily, C. and Cannella, A. (2003). 'Corporate Governance: Decades of Dialogue and Data', *Academy of Management Review*, 28: 371–82.

Davis, J., Schoorman, F., and Donaldson, L. (1997). 'Toward a Stewardship Theory of Management', *Academy of Management Review*, 22: 20–47.

Demsetz, H. (1991) 'The Theory of the Firm Revisited', in O. Williamson and S. Winter (eds.), *The Nature of the Firm: Origins, Evolution and Development*. Oxford: Oxford University Press.

Donaldson, T. and Preston, L. (1995). 'The Stakeholder Theory of the Corporation: Concepts, Evidence and Implications', *Academy of Management Review*, 20: 65–91.

Frey, B. (1997). *Not Just for the Money: An Economic Theory of Personal Motivation*. Cheltenham, UK and Brookfield, US: Edward Elgar.

—— and Jegen, R. (2001). 'Motivation Crowding Theory: A Survey of Empirical Evidence', *Journal of Economic Surveys*, 15: 589–611.

Fama, E. and Jensen, M. (1983*a*). 'Agency Problems and Residual Claims', *Journal of Law and Economics*, 26: 327–49.

———— (1983*b*). 'Separation of Ownership and Control', *Journal of Law and Economics*, 26: 301–25.

Grandori, A. (1984). 'A Prescriptive Contingency View of Organizational Decision Making', *Administrative Science Quarterly*, 29: 192–208.

—— (1991). 'Negotiating Efficient Organization Forms', *Journal of Economic Behavior and Organization*, 16: 319–40.

—— (1993). 'Notes on the Use of Power and Efficiency Constructs in the Economics and Sociology of Organization', in S. Lindenberg and H. Schreuder (eds.), *Interdisciplinary Perspectives on Organization Studies*. Oxford: Pergamon Press.

—— (2000). 'Conjectures for a New Research Agenda on Governance', *Journal of Management and Governance*, 4/1: 1–9.

—— (2001a). *Organization and Economic Behavior*. London: Routledge.

—— (2001b). 'Methodological Options for an Integrated Perspective on Organization', *Human Relations. Millennium Special Issue*, 54/1: 37–47.

—— (ed.) (2001c). 'Rationality, Cognition and Governance: A Roundtable in Memory of Herbert Simon', *Journal of Management and Governance*, 5/3–4.

—— and Neri, M. (1999). 'The Fairness Properties of Interfirm Networks', in A. Grandori (ed.), *Inter-firm Networks: Negotiated Order and Industrial Competitiveness*. London: Routledge.

Granovetter, M. (1985). 'Economic Action and Social Structure: The Problem of Embeddedness', *American Journal of Sociology*, 89: 481–510.

Greenberg, J. (1995). *The Quest for Justice on the Job*. Thousand Oaks, CA: Sage.

Hansman, H. (1996). *The Ownership of Enterprise*. Cambridge, MA: Harvard University Press.

Hart, O. (1995). *Firms, Contracts and Financial Structure*. Oxford: Oxford University Press.

—— and Moore, J. (1990). 'Property Rights and the Nature of the Firm', *Journal of Political Economy*, 98: 1119–58.

Hofstede, G. (1980). *Culture's Consequences: International Differences in Work-Related Values*. London: Sage.

Kochan, T. (2003). 'Restoring Trust in American Corporations: Addressing the Root Cause', in M. Huse (ed.), 'Roundtable on Renewing Paradigms of Corporate Governance', *Journal of Management and Governance*, 7/3: 223–31.

Lampel, J. and Shapira, Z. (2001). 'Judgmental Errors, Interactive Norms and the Difficulty of Detecting Strategic Surprises', *Organization Science*, 12: 599–611.

Lawrence, P. and Lorsch, J. (1967). *Organization and Environment*. Cambridge, MA: Harvard Business School Press.

Lindblom, C. (1959). 'The Science of "Muddling Through"', *Public Administration Review*, 19: 78–88.

Lindenberg, S. (1990). 'Homo Socio-oeconomicus: The Emergence of a general Model of Man in the Social Sciences', *Journal of Institutional and Theoretical Economics*, 146: 727–48.

—— (2000). 'It Takes both Trust and Lack of Mistrust: The Working of Cooperation and Relational Signaling in Contractual Relationships', *Journal of Management and Governance*, 4: 11–33.

March, J. and Simon, H. (1958). *Organizations*. New York: Wiley.

Marschak, J. (1955). 'Elements for a Theory of Teams', *Management Science*, 1: 127–37.

Meyerson, D., Weick, K., and Kramer, R. (1996). 'Swift Trust and Temporary Groups', in R. Kramer and T. Tyler (eds.), *Trust in Organizations: Frontiers of Theory and Research*. Thousand Oaks, CA: Sage.

Milgrom, P. and Roberts, J. (1992). *Economics Organization and Management*. Englewood Cliffs: Prentice-Hall.

Nickerson, J. and Zenger, T. (2003). 'Being Efficiently Fickle: A Dynamic Theory of Organizational Choice', *Organization Science*, 13: 547–66.

North, D. (1990). *Institutions, Institutional Change, and Economic Performance*. Cambridge: Cambridge University Press.

O' Sullivan, M. (2000). *Contests for Corporate Control*. Oxford: Oxford University Press.

Penrose, E. (1959). *The Theory of the Growth of the Firm*. New York: Wiley.

Pettigrew, A. (1992). 'On Studying Managerial Elites', *Strategic Management Journal*, 13: 162–82.

Piore, M. (2002). 'Economics and Sociology', *Revue Economique*, 53: 291–300.

Powell, W. and Di Maggio, P. (eds.) (1991). *The New Institutionalism in Organizational Analysis*. Chicago: University of Chicago Press.

Pugh, D., Hickson, D., Hinigs, C., and Turner, C. (1969). 'An Empirical Taxonomy of Structures of Work Organizations', *Administrative Science Quarterly*, 14: 115–26.

Roe, M. (2003). *Political Determinants of Corporate Governance*. Oxford: Oxford University Press.

Sabel, C. (1993). 'Constitutional Ordering in Historical Context', in F. Scharpf (ed.), *Games in Hierarchies and Networks*. Boulder, CO: Westview Press.

Shapira, Z. (2000). 'Governance in Organizations: A Cognitive Perspective', *Journal of Management and Governance*, 4: 53–67.

Shleifer, A. and Vishny, R. (1997). 'A Survey of Corporate Governance', *Journal of Finance*, 52: 737–83.

Simon, H. (1969). *The Sciences of the Artificial*. Cambridge, MA: MIT Press.

—— (1997). *An Empirically-based Microeconomics*. Oxford: Oxford University Press.

Tversky, A. and Kahneman, D. (1981). 'The Framing of Decisions and the Psychology of Choice', *Science*, 211: 453–8.

Uzzi, B. (1996). 'Social Structure and Competition in Interfirm Networks: The Paradox of Embeddedness', *Administrative Science Quarterly*, 42: 35–67.

—— and Lancaster, R. (2002). 'Social Embeddedness and Price Formation in the Large Law Firm Market', paper delivered at the international conference 'Perspectives on competition and cooperation', University of Umea, 5–7 May.

Van den Berg, A. (forthcoming). 'The Contribution of Worker Representation to Solving the Governance Structure Problem', *Journal of Management and Governance*.

Van den Berghe, L. (2002). *Corporate Governance in a Globalizing World: Convergence or Divergence?* Dordrecht: Kluwer.

Whitley, R. (ed.) (1992). *European Business Systems: Firms and Markets in their National Contexts*. London: Sage.

Williamson, O. (1970). *Corporate Control and Business Behavior*. Englewood Cliffs: Prentice Hall.

Wrong, D. (1961). 'The Oversocialized Conception of Man in Modern Sociology', *American Sociological Review*, 26: 182–93.

Zenger, T. and Hesterley, W. (1997). 'The Disaggregation of Corporations: Selective Intervention, High Powered Incentives and Molecular Units', *Organization Science*, 8: 209–22.

PART I

Contingent Structures and Multiple Rightholders:
Co-Designing Governance and Organization

1

Comparative Institutional Analysis of Corporate Governance

MASAHIKO AOKI

A Modicum of Historical Background

I myself started to get interested in the subject of corporate governance (CG) more than 20 years ago. I became interested in it as a natural outcome of having worked on the theory of the firm as an organization of managers, workers, and investors. When I had an occasion to visit Harvard in 1979–1980, however, very few people in the Department of Economics, except for the late Professor Harvey Leibenstein, had an interest in CG. Most of them had not even heard the terminology. CG was then strictly a subject matter of lawyers and my first systemic exposure to it was through auditing a small seminar at Harvard Law School. My first book in English, *The Cooperative Game Theory of the Firm*, published in 1984, was an attempt to integrate an economist's approach to the theory of the firm with the corporate governance theory in law that evolved from that personal experience. The references in the book contained a number of writings by legal scholars and legal documents on CG, but the text itself did not have any reference to CG. While writing the book, I debated whether or not I should use the term or not. Regrettably in retrospect, I did not because I felt the term might alienate my potential audience, economists. Instead I used the term 'legal models of decision-making structure of the firm' in a primitive attempt to capture the nexus between management and governance. Ironically, the book was then received more warmly by legal scholars than economists.

The term 'corporate governance' all of a sudden began to capture the attention of economists in the late 1980s and early 1990s. It happened in a particular atmosphere in the US at that time, when the competitive threat of German and Japanese companies alarmed the American business community. It was said then (for example, at a conference on CG organized by the American Academy of Sciences in 1991) that the erosion of competitiveness of American industries was due to the 'short-termism' of the top corporate executives subjected to the constant pressure of stock market signals, whereas their German and Japanese counterparts were insulated from such pressure through the bank-oriented corporate finance and governance. With the perceived reversal of competitiveness in the mid-1990s, however, references to the 'short-termism' were replaced by references to 'flexibility' without much change in the substance of the argument, whereas the bank-oriented system became perceived as out of date because of a series of banking crises all over the world throughout the 1990s. As the force of global capitalism emanating from Wall Street exerted such a stormy influence in the second half of the 1990s, market-oriented corporate financing and governance was declared victorious. All of us know well, however, that CG may mean more than just stockholders' sovereignty, that other stakeholders also matter in the mechanisms of CG. Indeed, some of us have been earnestly doing research on this premise. However, an influential survey article on CG by Shleifer and Vishny (1997: 737) bluntly limited their scope thus: 'CG deals with the ways in which suppliers of finance to corporations assure themselves of getting a return on their investment.'

Then, all of a sudden, another shock hit the scene: the Enron and World-Com debacles. These events themselves do not necessarily invalidate the Shleifer-Vishny concept of CG. I suppose they would say that the ways securities and auditing regulations were formulated and practiced were wrong and could be remedied by a more rational design. For reforming the American CG system, they may be right. But in my view what the events teach us is, among other things, that any CG arrangement cannot be absolutely superior to others over time and over space. By saying this, I do not intend to advocate the return to a romantic era of bank-oriented CG system. Given changing environments, it will never be a viable universal solution. However, I would argue that it is a good time to reconsider such issues in broader perspectives like the following: Why is there a variety of CG arrangements? What are the nexuses between the past and possible subsequent trajectories of a CG system? Besides financial markets, do the polity and social and labor relations matter in the formation of a CG arrangement? How can each CG arrangement be improved by legal design? Can and should diverse arrangements eventually be harmonized?

What is CG? The CIA Approach

The issues just mentioned are comparative by nature. But for comparative studies to be productive, it is desirable to go beyond being just descriptive and to work within a unified conceptual and analytical framework for an understanding of diverse CG arrangements. It is also desirable for such a framework to be useful for accommodating insights from different disciplines. In *The Cooperative Game theory of the Firm* (Aoki 1984), I made a primitive attempt to present such a framework. I tried to view the firm as a coalition of the stockholders (financial resource suppliers) and the workers (firm-specific human resource suppliers) and specify conditions under which a cooperative Nash solution may, or may not, become a self-binding agreement. Law, institutional set-ups for labor and financial markets, social norms, and so forth constitute such conditions for evolving in diverse forms (US, UK, Japanese and German). One thing remained unsatisfactory, however. The manager was considered to be performing a mediating role to achieve such a stable solution under surrounding institutional constraints, but he was not explicitly treated as a strategic player. This was certainly a point to be remedied.

In a recent book of mine, *Toward a Comparative Institutional Analysis* (Aoki 2001), I was able to present a more satisfactory—at least for me—framework for comparative and trans-disciplinary CG. It is based on a generic conceptualization of institutions based on a game-theoretic framework. A game may be described by a tripartite arrangement composed of a set of players, sets of their activated action choices, and the consequence function, which maps each profile of chosen actions by all the players to some consequences. I argue that statutory law constitutes an element determining a form of the consequence function, together with technology, historical legacies, and so on. I then conceptualized an institution in one particular domain of repeated social game (economic, political, or social) as a salient characteristic of its equilibrium reflected in 'shared beliefs among players regarding the ways how the game is being played'. An institution as such is a summary representation of a stable equilibrium outcome of strategic plays among the players.

Based on this generic conceptualization, I formulated the concept of CG as follows. Let us consider the domain of CG composed of three types of strategic players: the manager, the investors, and the workers. CG is *a set of self-enforcing rules (formal or informal) that regulates action choices of those players contingent on evolving states*. In particular, managers' beliefs (expectations) regarding possible actions of other players in critical contingencies—such as in the state of corporate financial difficulties—that may constrain his or her action *ex ante* are essential elements of a CG arrangement.

There are some merits in considering an institution in general, and a CG arrangement in particular, as an equilibrium phenomenon (Aoki 2001: 14–20). Among other things, it provides a rigorous framework for understanding a particular CG arrangement as 'nexuses (linkages)' of various elements (such as rights to property, control, rewards, and information, as well as a mode of social relationships). It also provides a rigorous framework for understanding various modes of nexuses (complementarities) between a CG arrangement on the one hand and an organizational architecture and political-economy arrangement on the other. Under the game-theoretic framework, the nexuses of the first type may be often analyzed in terms of *linked games*. The idea is that a particular profile of strategies in one particular domain of a game may not be sustained as an equilibrium (or there may be many other equilibria) when that game is played separately, but it may become a (unique or distinct) equilibrium when the game is simultaneously played with another game and players belonging to both domains coordinate their own strategies in both games to achieve higher payoffs. That is, linking games may create externalities to some or all players. For example, Granovetter's celebrated notion of social-embeddedness may be related to this idea (Granovetter 1985). A certain mode of transaction (for example, relational contracting) may not be feasible among strangers in the bazaar but, if buyers and sellers are continuously in social contracts, it may become a viable alternative because they may be afraid of being ostracized from the domain of social exchange if they default on such contracting. Social embeddedness may be relevant to an understanding of certain types of corporate governance arrangements (for example, corporate grouping found in India, Chile, and elsewhere) (see Granovetter 1992, 1994; Khanna and Palepu 1999, 2000). I will shortly provide another example of linked games for understanding a CG arrangement based on property rights.

Nexuses of one particular arrangement in the corporate governance domain with particular institutional arrangements in other domains (such as the polity and financial and labor markets) may be conceptualized as *institutional complementarities* and their viability and implications can be analyzed in terms of strategic complementarities within the game-theoretic framework: that is, in terms of how an equilibrium profile of strategic choices of agents in one domain can become strategically complementary to, or conditional on, the equilibrium choices of other agents in other domains. In this way, we can understand the conditional robustness of an overall institutional arrangement of the economy in general, and that of a CG arrangement in particular, as well as the multiplicity of such arrangements. It is often difficult to change a CG arrangement by a mere modification of corporate law unless it is accompanied with complementary changes in other institutions such as in labor and financial markets. I will shortly provide a few examples of institutional complementarities surrounding CG arrangements.

There is another type of nexus surrounding CG, namely, the nexuses between the arrangements of a system and the possible subsequent trajectories feasible for that system. Although I will not elaborate on this here, there is one thing I would like to note. In a game-theoretic analysis, there is usually a multiplicity of equilibria. Usually, game theorists regard a multiplicity of equilibria as troublesome, and they have spent a great deal of research effort, without decisive success, on the so-called refinement of the equilibrium to enable them to identify only one equilibrium out of many possible Nash equilibria. However, I consider that the multiplicity of equilibria of games should not be regarded as bothersome in comparative institutional analysis. On the one hand, by making institutions susceptible to equilibrium analysis, it can be made clear that institutions are humanly devised, yet can be neither arbitrarily designed nor implemented in a discretionary manner. On the other hand, once an institutional bifurcation occurs, even if two economies are exposed to the same technological and market environments afterwards, the subsequent overall institutional arrangements of the two economies may well differ, depending on their respective interim institutional trajectories—the phenomenon known as path dependence. Thus, equilibrium and historical analyses are mutually complementary and are both indispensable to comparative institutional analysis.

Having laid out the basics of the game-theoretic framework for comparative institutional analysis, let me move on to examine some interesting examples of linked games and institutional complementarities regarding generic CG arrangements. My purpose here is to illustrate the potential explanatory power of the game-theoretic approach so that arguments remain abstract and generic.

The Hartian Property Rights Approach as a Special Case

The first example is drawn from the celebrated contributions of Oliver Hart and his associates (Grossman and Hart 1985; Hart 1995; Hart and Moore 1990). We reinterpret their major insights in the context of our framework. First, consider the simplest domain of organization constituted of one employer and one worker who invest respectively in relation-specific (firm-specific) human investments. Suppose that the organizational architecture is designed in such a way that the skill of the employer is 'essential' in the Hart sense while the worker's is not. This corresponds to a situation in which the manager's task is indispensable to the productive use of physical assets used by herself as well as by the worker so that the worker cannot enhance his productivity without her direction (information processing), even if he owns the entire set of physical assets. On the other hand, the manager can (at least partially) realize her value even without the trained worker if she owns the physical assets. In this case, the second-best solution is for the manager to acquire the ownership of the entire set of physical assets. Only in this way is the manager motivated to accumulate her own essential human assets. The indispensability of the manager's skill may be thought of as consisting of her ability to dictate the use of physical assets to the workers in a productive manner in unforeseeable events, when contract is incomplete. Thus, the ownership of physical assets and the hierarchical coordination of production by the manager and the physical labor of the propertyless worker are 'linked'. In other words, proprietary firms can win out in competition with other ownership arrangements, in which the hierarchical mode is conventional in the organizational architecture in the economy. However, as we will see later, there can be other modes of organizational architecture (production coordination), so that *the nexus of this type is to be regarded as a rather specific case, albeit an important one*, even if we limit our attention to generic CG arrangements.

When the manager-cum-owner becomes cash-constrained, she must then raise funds from outside investors through debt contracts (when the cash constraint is moderate) or from stockholders through equity contracts (when it is severe). This situation can be analyzed as a three-person repeated game between the investor, the manager, and the worker. In this game, the investor controls the supply of funds, the manager invests/shirks in relation-specific human capital and is engaged in hierarchical coordination, and the worker invests/shirks in relation-specific human capital and is engaged in production using physical assets. One kind of such model can be obtained simply by augmenting the Tirole's model (2001) with the explicit addition of the worker. One can derive the following implication from such model: *a value-enhancing takeover by a new stockholder may not necessarily be efficiency-enhancing when the worker retaliates against the 'breach of trust' by a new manager with non-cooperation* (Shleifer and Summers 1988; Aoki 2001: ch. 11:1).

Institutional Complementarities between Co-determination and Corporatism

In the previous model, it is assumed that the worker may be subjected to the efficiency wage discipline: that is, the worker invests in relation-specific human capital and uses it in the second-best manner in the anticipation of the employer's sharing the surplus with him, as far as the manager has kept her promise to do so. Imagine, however, that a wage rate is fixed by a corporatist agreement between the trade union and the employers' association at the national level and each management is obliged to comply with it. Suppose that, in order to elicit a worker's cooperation under this institutional environment, the employer (suppose too for a while she is a manager-cum-owner just like the Hartian proprietor) allows the worker to participate in the 'residual rights of control' (Grossman and Hart 1986)—the rights to decide on the use of human and physical assets in contractually unspecified events—provided that the worker has always cooperated (made an effort) in past periods, and otherwise keeps the residual rights of control to herself and does not make any payment beyond what is determined in the corporatist agreement. In a symmetric way, the worker makes a reciprocating effort provided that the employer has always partially relinquished residual rights of control to the worker in the past, and otherwise shirks. Let us assume that the worker can reduce the cost of his effort by participating in the residual rights of control, possibly because of improvements in working conditions, participation in workplace design, pleasure derived from more autonomous control of his work, and so on. This implies that the participation of the worker in the residual rights of control transforms the organizational architecture from a functional hierarchy to a participatory hierarchy. On the other hand, there may be some reduction in the employer's utility in the event of partial relinquishment of residual rights of control, for she may not implement the work plan that she likes best. Still, it can be one equilibrium over periods in which the reciprocating cooperative strategies are sustained by both parties. We cannot make a definite Pareto-ranking between this equilibrium and the Hartian equilibrium.

When the equity of the original owner of the firm is still too small relative to the required capital, she inevitably needs to abandon her ownership rights. However, in this case the governance structure cannot be the same as the shareholder governance discussed in the previous section because the worker participates in the residual rights of control. Suppose that both the worker and investors (shareholders and creditors) are able to veto a management action respectively that they prefer less than the status quo, or the reappointment of the manager for the next round of the game, depriving her of an opportunity to obtain employment continuation value. Thus, the worker and investors can exercise separate control rights over the management. Let us call this governance arrangement 'co-determination'. Then, any unilateral new action that would hurt the worker can be blocked by a worker's veto and by the manager's career concerns. On the other hand, assume that, although the investors supply full financing, they have little useful inside information for facilitating the smooth operation of the participatory hierarchy within the firm, and thus are passive in formulating a business plan. The possibility of restructuring after initial financing can be perceived only by the manager, who has invested in firm-specific human assets. However, the investors can threaten to withdraw finance and the workers can be uncooperative if they so choose. In this setting, it can be proved that *participatory hierarchy and co-determination are institutionally complementary to corporatist wage-setting*. There may be a stock value-enhancing management plan that can be chosen under stockholder governance but not under co-determination if it is expected to have a welfare-reducing impact on the worker and incite a retaliatory uncooperative choice of efforts by the workers. *Co-determination and stockholder sovereignty governance are thus not necessarily Pareto-rankable.* Also, it is interesting to note that under co-determination more external financing takes the form of long-term debt contracts, as the interests of debt-holders and those of the worker are more congruent than under functional hierarchy (Aoki 2001: ch. 11:2).

Knowledge Sharing and Relational Contingent Governance: Benefits and Costs

As already mentioned, there has been a persistent stream of thought in the CG literature that the corporation actually is, or at least ought to be, run in the interests of various stakeholders, including the workers, but not in the sole interests of the stockholders. Even Adolph Berle, who was engaged in a harsh debate against such view in the early 1930s, was converted to it in his later career. Recently Jean Tirole, an analytical economist, made this comment in his Presidential Address to the Econometric Society: 'I will, perhaps unconventionally for an economist, define corporate governance as the design of institutions that induce or force management to internalize the welfare of stakeholders .... There is unfortunately little formal analysis of the economics of the stakeholder society' (2001: 4). Relying on recent developments in contract and control theory, he pointed out that it is difficult to theoretically design multi-task incentives for the manager to satisfy diverse interests of the stakeholders or an effective arrangement for the division of control rights among stakeholders. Even if that is so, it is possible to design a CG arrangement in which control rights *shift* (as opposed to being divided) between stakeholders contingent on events in the corporate organizational domain: more specifically, between the insiders (the managers and workers) on one hand and a designated agent of the investors on the other, contingent on the (corporate financial) outcome of the stage game in a repeated game context. Thus, I call this governance arrangement 'relational-contingent governance'. I first derive this mechanism theoretically as a second-best solution to a free-riding problem inherent in the organizational architecture of the knowledge-sharing type.

Suppose that both the manager's skill and the worker's skill become essential in the Hartian sense. This corresponds to the situation in which both the manager and the worker cannot generate surplus value without mutual cooperation, even if they own the entire (or relevant) set of physical assets. In this situation, an ownership arrangement cannot resolve the governance problem. I interpret this situation as one in which the information-processing activities of both manager and worker are crucial inputs for each to be productive. Catching its essential aspect in the simplest form, let us assume that they are symmetrical in their contribution to the organizational output but that each of them cannot precisely observe the other's level of effort. This type of production organization is referred to as 'team' (Alchian-Demsetz-Holmstrom) or as horizontal hierarchy in contrast to the functional hierarchy in which the indispensability of agents' skills is asymmetric. In this type of organization, free-riding on other members' efforts becomes an inherent moral-hazard problem that cannot be resolved by sharing the outcome among the members alone. There must be an external discipline.

Suppose that this organization (let us refer to it as the 'H-firm' and its manager and worker as 'insiders') needs some outside financing for productive activity. It is provided by numerous investors who expect a certain level of financial returns. They cannot, however, observe even the aggregate output value of the H-firm ex post, but can observe only the court-verifiable event of its termination. They entrust the enforcement of financial contracts to a particular *relational monitor* ('R-monitor') who can observe the aggregate output value of the H-firm at the end of each period and then exercise control rights contingent on it according to a contract agreed with the H-firm at the beginning of the period. The R-monitor requires a certain expected level of income per period for this service payable from the current output of the H-firm.

In this setting, it can be proved that the following nexus of contingent contracts is the second-best CG arrangement for the free-riding problem

(Aoki 2001: ch. 11:3). It divides the entire range of the H-firm's possible output value at the end of each period into the following four regions in the order of highest to lowest, and specifies control rights to be exercised by either the insiders or the R-monitor on each of them. In the highest region, *insider-control region*, both investors and R-monitor get a fixed amount of returns and the residual output value is equally shared exclusively among the insiders. In the next highest *R-monitor-control region*, control rights to output shift to the R-monitor. The R-monitor pays the same rate of return to the investors as in the insider-control region, pays the agreed minimum income to the insiders, and acquires the non-negative residual. The H-firm continues to the next period. In the next lower *bailing-out region*, the payment schedules are the same as the previous region except that the output value level is so low that the residual borne by the R-monitor becomes negative. However, the H-firm is still sustained to the next period. This corresponds to the case in which the R-monitor bails out the H-firm comprised of the wealth-constrained insiders. In the lowest *termination region*, the R-monitor terminates the H-firm after making contractual payments of the minimum income to the insiders and a fixed rate of return to the investors lower than the expected investors' rate. Deficits after the termination are to be borne by the R-monitor.

The nexus of contracts just described defines a basic mechanism of governance regarding both the disposition of the H-firm's output and its continuation at the end of each period. Since control rights shift between the insiders and the R-monitor in a punctuated manner contingent on the value of the H-firm's output, we may call this arrangement 'relational-contingent governance'. In the insider-control region, the insiders become the residual claimants, as in the case of an insider-controlled firm. However, if such a status were to extend over the entire range of output value, the moral hazard inherent in H-firms would become unavoidable. Further, if the value of output is very low, it may not be sufficient to guarantee the minimum required income of the insiders. For these two reasons, if the value of output falls below a certain level, the residual claimant status shifts to the R-monitor. If the value of output falls even further to below the termination point, the H-firm is terminated and its members have to accept inferior outside options. This efficiency-wage-like discipline can provide incentives for the insiders not to shirk. The outside option value may be taken as a parameter by the insiders of an individual H-firm, but its lowering can be regarded as a (general equilibrium) outcome of the convention of horizontal hierarchies prevailing in organizational architecture: that is, if all firms are structured as H-firms relying on the context-oriented skills of their members, and individuals' skills are geared toward a particular firm, they cannot freely move between the firms without suffering a loss in their employment continuation value. Thus, the effectiveness of relational-contingent governance is enhanced when horizontal hierarchies are established as a convention in the organizational field. Conversely, as we have discussed, horizontal hierarchies are run more efficiently when relational contingent governance are institutionalized. Thus, *the convention of horizontal hierarchies and contingent relational governance are mutually reinforcing and institutionally complementary.*

Since some costs of termination may be born by investors, in practice there may be incentives for the R-monitor to terminate a financially troubled H-firm even when the H-firm should be bailed out. To counteract these incentives, some positive values—rents—needs to be expected for the R-monitor over time and across H-firms for credibly committing to a bailing-out operation whenever it is appropriate to do so. We can then discern one important dilemma inherent in the mechanism of relational-contingent governance. On the one hand, if rents are not sufficiently high, the R-monitor may be motivated to terminate firms that should be bailed out: that is, valuable organization-specific assets may be destroyed even when mildly poor performance occurs due to uncontrollable stochastic events but not to the actions of insiders. On the other hand, if the rents made possible by bailing-out are too high, the monitoring agent may be motivated to bail out a firm that should not be. If such expectation prevails, the mechanism of relational-contingent governance fails to provide proper incentives *ex ante* for the insiders of horizontal hierarchies to make sufficient effort. The tendency is known to economists as the 'soft-budget constraint' syndrome (Kornai 1980). Which syndrome prevails in a particular economy depends on the relative magnitudes of those costs and rents facing relational monitors. Explicit contracts of relational-contingent governance are hard to write in practice because of the complexity of the contractual environments. Further, it may not be possible to determine the rents for each firm, but they may be specified and generated only in a broader institutional context in which they are embedded. In actuality, one cannot assume that costs and rents are arranged in such a way that the second-best solution can be implemented with precision in each organization domain.

It is reasonable to expect that one or another of the syndromes may prevail. Yet, in environments in which rents and costs remain fairly stable, if not balanced exactly in a second-best way, expectations regarding the possible behavior of R-monitors, whoever they may be, may become predictable, and firms of the horizontal hierarchy type may accordingly be disciplined while being able to accumulate and preserve organization-specific assets in a more or less steady fashion. However, when there is an environmental change that drastically transforms the parameter values defining the costs and rents of bailing-out, so that expectations regarding the monitoring agent's possible actions become uncertain, the provision of effective relational-contingent governance will become problematical.

The above discussion has been conducted at a highly abstract level. In particular, I have been silent about who relational monitors can be and what their incentives to bail out financially depressed firms are. There are several institutional possibilities of contingent governance relationships: (*a*) between firms and their main bank; (*b*) between subsidiary corporations and their holding/management company; (*c*) between an entrepreneurial start-up firm and a venture capital company; (*d*) between state-owned enterprises and the government; or (*e*) between banks and the government regulatory agency. These possibilities and their inherent syndromes are discussed in Aoki (2001: 300–5).

The Silicon Valley Model as a New Mode of CG

We discussed in the previous section CG issues for the production system in which information is symmetrically shared among its members. In contrast, we may conceive of a system whose members jointly, but competitively, pursue some systemic objectives with information differentiation among them as its inherent characteristic. For example, consider a cluster of entrepreneurial firms as observed in Silicon Valley. Each firm is engaged in the development of a module product that is expected to constitute a part of a complex innovative product system. In each modular design multiple entrepreneurial firms compete so that their information processing is hidden, or *encapsulated*, from one another. This information encapsulation allows another important systemic characteristic: each module can be developed independently of the design of other modules, as far as the interfaces and performance requirements among modules are standardized *ex ante* or *ad interim* and known to each entrepreneur. Then, an innovative system may be developed in an evolutionary manner by combining the best-developed product of each module *ex post*. When system development is extremely complex, this process may have a superior innovative capacity to cases in which system design is done in a hierarchical manner once for all, or design improvements may be done through intense information exchanges and sharing among a fixed set of design subunits. This is so because the process can create *option values* (Baldwin and Clark 2000) by allowing each module to experiment on diverse designs in the presence of high uncertainty. However, the option value cannot be obtained without costs. The costs are the duplication of development costs within each module. Further, if the cost of development by an entrepreneur has to be financed by outside investors so that possible returns are to be shared with them, entrepreneurial incentives may be compromised without a proper governance arrangement. How can these costs of development be controlled?

Let us consider a game played by the venture capitalist (VC) and two groups of entrepreneurs, each competing for the development of a modular product that may constitute an innovation system. These two modular products may be combined through standardized interfaces. The VC finances the initial development funds to multiple entrepreneurs in each module design and then monitors their design development without necessarily observing their effort levels directly. It mediates a modicum of information sharing among entrepreneurs if necessary for the *ad interim* modification of interface. Eventually the VC selects only one entrepreneur for each module for the completion of its project and realizes its values by bringing it to public offering or arranging an acquisition by an existing company. The realized values can be shared between the VC and the selected entrepreneurs according to *ex ante* share contracts, but other entrepreneurs do not get anything. It is essentially a tournament game played among entrepreneurs refereed by the VC; and we may call this arrangement 'VC governance by tournament'. The VC is linked to other financial markets for raising funds, but I do not consider this aspect here.

We can now take stock. The arrangement can create option value at the cost of duplicated development efforts and financing (Baldwin and Clark 2000). The tournament provides additional incentives for the entrepreneur, in contrast to the stand-alone development effort, because marginal benefits of additional effort are composed of marginal expected benefit obtained in the event of winning plus marginal gains obtained from the enhanced probability of winning (Aoki 2001: ch. 14). However, as the number of entrepreneurs competing in each modular design increases, these incentive effects are diluted so that there is an optimal number of entrepreneurs to compete in each module development, depending on the degree of uncertainty involved in development and the expected value of final products (Aoki and Takizawa 2002). Particularly interesting is the following proposition. *If the total value of an innovative system is expected to be high, and if the VC's selection of winning entrepreneurs is believed by entrepreneurs to be precise, then it is possible that, even for the same share allocation between entrepreneurs and financiers, VC governance by tournament can elicit higher development efforts from entrepreneurs than arm's-length financing, and that its effect, together with the creation of option value, can compensate the social costs of duplicated development efforts.*

Concluding Remarks on the Role of Law

Using a simple generic model, I have shown that there may exist diverse CG arrangements associated with different organizational architectures. Also, I have argued that those arrangements are supported by complementary institutional arrangements in other domains (see Aoki 2001 for a more comprehensive treatment on this subject). This may indicate that a CG arrangement may have a robust property that may be hard to change unless complementary changes occur in other domains. Also, a mode of organizational architecture tends to evolve as a convention, although conscious design elements are also involved. Thus, a particular CG arrangement and a corresponding organizational architecture may co-evolve. Does all this indicate that an attempt to improve on a CG arrangement through the design of statutory law is bound to be futile? Obviously, this is not the case.

As I indicated before, statutory laws constitute an element of the consequence function of the game structure. In other words, they may provide information to the players about the possible outcomes of their actions if laws are enforced, although whether or not they are actually enforced is a matter determined through the strategic interplays between the enforcer and other players. Thus, laws affect the outcome of the game through the expectations of the players as well as their incentives. So statutory laws are not institutions per se in my conceptualization, but can induce the evolution of an institution. In particular, codified rules of corporate governance—that is, the legal rights afforded to various agents (particularly shareholders and employees) and the associated legal procedures—define the exogenous rules of the game in the corporate organization domain, and as such they may affect the beliefs and incentives of the agents and thereby corporate performance (La Porta *et al.* 1998). However, legal rules that are inconsistent with equilibria in complementary domains, particularly with a prevailing convention of organizational architecture, may not yield the outcome intended by the legislature in the corporate organization domain. For example, the Japanese Commercial Code provides minority shareholders with one of the strongest rights at stockholders' meeting. However, its governance arrangement is normally not considered to be stockholder-controlled.

On the other hand, sustainable legal rules for corporate governance may be understood as the codification of an equilibrium arrangement that evolved through a long history of complementary institutions (for example, co-determination in Germany; see Aoki 2001: ch. 6). A careful and systematic study is called for regarding the questions of how the initial institutional conditions, such as the legacies of old institutions and the prevailing informal rules (norms, social ethics, and so on), the kinds and level of the existing stock of human competence, can affect policy impact on subsequent legal evolution and, conversely, how formal rule-setting in the polity interacts with the evolution of the endogenous rules of the games (that is, institutions) in CG and other domains.

References

Alchian, A. and Demsetz, H. (1972). 'Production, Information Costs, and Economic Organization', *American Economic Review*, 62: 777–95.

Aoki, M. (1984). *The Cooperative Game Theory of the Firm*. Oxford: Oxford University Press.

—— (2001). *Towards a Comparative Institutional Analysis*. Cambridge, MA: MIT Press.

—— and Takizawa, H. (2002). 'Information, Incentives and Option Value: The Silicon-Valley Model', *The Journal of Comparative Economics*, 30: 759–86.

Baldwin, C. and Clark, K. (2000). *Design Rules: The Power of Modularity, vol.1*. Cambridge, MA: MIT Press.

Granovetter, M. (1985). 'Economic Action and Social Structure: The Problem of Embeddedness', *American Journal of Sociology*, 91: 480–510.

——(1992). 'Economic Institutions as Social Constructions: A Framework for Analysis', *Acta Sociologica*, 35: 3–11.

——(1994). 'Business Groups', in N.J. Smelser and R. Swedberg (eds.), *Handbook of Economic Sociology*. Princeton: Princeton University Press.

Grossman, S. and Hart, O. (1986). 'The Costs and Benefits of Ownership: A Theory of Vertical and Lateral Integration', *Journal of Political Economy*, 94: 691–719.

Hart, O. (1995). *Firms, Contracts, and Financial Structure*. Oxford: Clarendon Press.

——and Moore, J. (1990). 'Property Rights and the Nature of the Firm', *Journal of Political Economy*, 98: 1119–58.

Khanna, T. and Palepu, K. (1999). 'Policy Shocks, Market Intermediaries, and Corporate Strategy: The Evolution of Business Groups in Chile and India', *Journal of Economics and Management Strategy*, 8: 271–310.

————(2000). 'Is Group Affiliation Profitable in Emerging Markets?: An Analysis of Diversified Indian Business Groups', *Journal of Finance*, 55: 867–91.

Kornai, J. (1980). *Economics of Shortage*. Amsterdam: North-Holland.

La Porta, R., Lopez-de-Silanes, F., Shleifer, A., and Vishny, R. (1998). 'Law and Finance', *Journal of Political Economy*, 106: 1113–55.

Shleifer, A. and Summers, L. (1988). 'Breach of Trust in Hostile Takeovers', in A. J. Auerbach (ed.), *Corporate Takeovers: Causes and Consequence*. Chicago: University of Chicago Press.

Shleifer, A. and Vishny, R. (1997). 'A Survey of Corporate Governance', *Journal of Finance*, 52: 737–87.

Tirole, J. (2001). 'Corporate Governance', *Econometrica*, 69: 1–35.

2

The Neglected Benefits of the Corporate Form: Entity Status and the Separation of Asset Ownership from Control

MARGARET M. BLAIR

For most of the last two decades corporate law scholarship has been dominated by the view that a corporation is a legal fiction, a mere nexus through which individual investors, entrepreneurs, and suppliers of various factors of production contract with each other (Fama and Jensen 1983; Easterbrook and Fischel 1991).[1] This approach to understanding corporate law has provided insights into some important problems. But it has obscured other problems and has contributed to neglect and misunderstanding of one of the most important functions of corporate law: the creation of a legal and institutional basis for accumulating enterprise-specific physical capital, as well as specialized organizational and other intangible capital, and for 'locking in' that capital by discouraging premature asset withdrawal by managers, investors, or their heirs (Blair 2003). Corporate law helps accomplish these things because a corporate charter creates a separate legal entity—a fact that contractarian legal scholars tend to dismiss as unimportant in understanding how corporate law affects the relationships among participants in a corporation.

Research on this article has been supported by the Georgetown-Sloan Project on Business Institutions. I would like to thank Jeff Bauman, Dan Ernst, Bill Klein, Mitu Gulati, Bill Bratton, Michael Diamond, Jill Fisch, Henry Hansmann, Roger Conner, and participants at workshops at Vanderbilt Law School, Fordham Law School, and Georgetown University Law Center, for advice and feedback on an earlier version of this chapter. Colleen Dunlavy provided me with copies of a few early nineteenth-century corporate charters and advice about how to track down more. Aaron McCants, Erin Peters, and Katherine Goyer provided helpful research assistance. I also want especially to thank Christopher Baer of the Hagley Library in Wilmington, DE, Laura Bedard of Georgetown University Law Center Library, and Amy Forster Rothbart, of University of Wisconsin, for helping me track down historical documents.

[1] The most important strand of the 'nexus of contracts' approach to understanding corporate law focuses on the 'agency costs' associated with the problem of making certain that individuals who are authorized to make decisions for the corporation act in the interests of the corporation, and do not steal or expropriate the corporation's property for their own use (Fama 1980; Fama and Jensen 1983; Jensen and Meckling 1976; Easterbrook and Fischel 1991). But much of that literature assumes that the investors (especially shareholders) are the 'owners' of the corporation and its property, and therefore this strand of literature pays little attention to the problem, addressed in this chapter, of assets being inappropriately or prematurely taken from the firm by shareholders, acting individually or as a group.

This chapter argues that the separate entity status of corporations transforms the relationships among corporate participants in ways that cannot be replicated through a collection of contracts. Corporations can buy and sell assets and enter into contracts that are independent of the specific individuals who have contributed resources to the enterprise, or who make decisions for the corporation, or who hold claims against the corporation. Since neither the investors, nor the managers, nor any other participant in the corporate enterprise owns the corporation's property, none of them can use ownership of critical assets to 'hold up' or control the others.

In previous work with Lynn Stout, we have argued that shareholders in widely traded corporations should not be regarded as the 'owners' of corporations since they yield nearly all of the important control rights and other indicia of ownership to boards of directors (Blair and Stout 2001) at the time the corporation is formed. We have further argued that shareholders as a class are better-off because they have, in the corporate form, a mechanism for committing capital to an enterprise and yielding control rights to directors almost irrevocably (Blair and Stout 1999). In this chapter, I further explain why entity status for corporations is so transformative, and I offer empirical evidence that helps explain the paradoxical notion that shareholders as a class are better-off if they cannot dictate corporate policy to directors.

The evidence I offer comes from a review of the emergence of corporate law in the early nineteenth-century United States. I show that business organizers began seeking out corporate status to organize their businesses because the separate entity status of corporations, and the resulting separation of the roles of managing the enterprise from that of contributing capital to the enterprise, helped solve certain contracting problems that arise in enterprises that are especially complex, long-lived, or large in scale.[2] In the first section, I describe how the Industrial Revolution and rapid expansion of transportation and communications capabilities in the late eighteenth and early nineteenth centuries opened up opportunities for business people to begin operating large-scale enterprises, with activities spread over wide geographical areas and over long periods of time. In response, business people began experimenting with new organizational forms, other than general partnerships, that would help them solve the unique contracting problems that arise in such businesses. Two legal forms were used with growing frequency during this period: the unincorporated joint-stock company and the corporation. In the second section, I explain why, over time, business organizers with increasing consistency chose the corporate form—even though it was originally much more costly to use—while the use of unincorporated joint-stock companies died out. I argue that the unincorporated joint-stock company evolved out of partnership law and, because

---

[2] The historical details and the structure of the argument in this article are drawn from Blair (2003).

courts treated these firms as partnerships, their organizers could not prevent them from being broken up by individual members or their heirs. Corporate law in the US, however, appears to have evolved out of the body of law that applied to religious, eleemosynary, and civic institutions with recognized public purposes.[3] Hence, the courts were willing to recognize business corporations as separate legal entities with potentially unlimited life, giving them the potential ability to protect the assets of the enterprise from being broken up to satisfy the demands of individual resource contributors or their heirs.

In the third section, I tell the story of how I. M. Singer & Co., a highly successful and innovative business partnership, was reorganized as the Singer Manufacturing Company in 1863. The purpose for the reorganization was not to raise new capital or provide investors with limited liability (the usual explanations given for the attraction of incorporation), but to prevent the heirs of the partners from forcing a premature liquidation of assets used in the business and to provide a mechanism for settling future disputes between the former partners or among subsequent investors. Finally, in the fourth section, I suggest how the lessons of this insight into the role of corporate law might be applied to the problem of building effective institutions of capitalism in developing and transition economies.

The Industrial Revolution and the Need for Long-Lived Business Entities

Although the United States was not a world leader in industrial production or in finance in the late eighteenth and early nineteenth centuries, it did lead the world in developing the corporate form of organization for business purposes. In 1800, there were only 335 chartered business corporations in the US (Davis 1917), and most of them had been chartered after 1790. By 1890, there were nearly 500,000 chartered business corporations in the US (Votaw 1965: 24), far more than in any other country (Wright 2002: 159–61). By then the US had also become a world leader in industrial production. How did this happen? This section argues that, as business people began undertaking larger, more complex, and more long-lived business ventures, innovating to take advantage of expanding markets and new mass production technologies, they began experimenting with new organizational forms that had what we can now see as corporate-like features. They also began seeking corporate charters from state legislatures. Over the first half of the nineteenth century, states responded to this demand reluctantly, granting such charters at first only occasionally. But then, by mid-century, states

---

[3] In England, by contrast, it appears that corporate law might have evolved out of partnership law, but that process was stopped by the Bubble Act of 1720, which made it illegal to trade in the membership shares of unincorporated joint-stock companies. See discussion below.

were granting corporate charters more and more freely, until by 1860 most states had adopted some sort of generalized incorporation law.

In 1800, most commercial activity consisted of small transactions between individuals who produced goods in their homes and other individuals who wanted to buy and use them, or between the individual producers and merchants who bought products in large quantities from many households and transported them to other markets where they were then sold to households that wanted to buy and use them. Only a few types of commercial activity—trading expeditions, banking, and insurance, for example—required a significant amount of capital investment that would be tied up over an extended period of time. And even for these activities, the capital commitments were usually for only a few years at a time. From 1800 to 1860, however, the US underwent a massive transformation in technology, transportation, and communications that greatly increased productive capabilities in agriculture, mining, and manufacturing, and massively expanded access to markets. With the exception of the US postal system, most of the transportation, communications, and manufacturing infrastructure put in place during the first six decades of the nineteenth century was not financed or managed by federal or state government, but rather was accomplished by private business people (Ratner, Soltow, and Sylla 1979: chs. 5 and 7).

This industrial revolution brought new opportunities to business people to undertake productive ventures, such as building and operating roads, bridges, railroads, or factories, that had the potential to continue in operation for decades. In the early 1800s, a group of business people who wanted to undertake a long-term joint business venture, such as building a canal or a factory for manufacturing textiles, had three choices about how they could organize their enterprise.[4] They could form a general partnership in which the participants would jointly own and manage the assets of the business and share responsibility for the liabilities of the business; they could form an unincorporated joint stock company, which was a special type of partnership that used trust law to separate the assets of the enterprise from the personal assets of the partners (or 'members' as they were sometimes called), which made it easier to raise capital from passive partners; or they could attempt to form a chartered corporation. A partnership could be formed by a handshake or a relatively simple contract binding the partners together for purposes of engaging in the business activity. The formation of a joint stock company required a more complex contract in which a trust was created, the resources contributed by investors were put into the trust, and trustees were assigned to manage the trust for the benefit of the investors. Investors were then given tradable claims to any distributions from the trust. Still, these contracts could be drawn up among private individuals and no

---

[4] A single individual could operate a business as an individual proprietorship, but for purposes of this chapter I will consider only organizational forms that involve more than one person.

involvement of the government was required. To form a corporation, however, business people had to go to their state legislatures and ask them to pass a special act granting the business organizers a charter to create a separate legal entity to hold the assets to be used in the enterprise.

Why were business people willing to go to the trouble and expense of seeking a special act of the legislature if they could easily use the other two organizational forms? Why were organizers of corporations willing to yield property rights over the assets used in production to a separate legal entity, rather than to hang on to a direct pro-rata claim on the assets as they would in a partnership? To understand the answers it is helpful to think about the contracting problems facing organizers of large complex businesses such as those that entrepreneurs first began assembling and operating in the early to mid-nineteenth century and that continue today to dominate commercial activity.

In previous work of my own and with Lynn Stout, I have described the problem of assembling and coordinating the use of complex inputs for long-term or continuous production as a 'team production' problem (Blair 2003; Blair and Stout 1999). 'Team production', as the phrase is used by economists, refers to production that requires various inputs of differing types from two or more individuals and for which the output is not easily separable into pieces or portions that are attributable to the various inputs individually (Alchian and Demsetz 1972). When inputs are complex and difficult to specify in advance, and when outputs are 'nonseparable' and risky, it is virtually impossible to draft complete contracts that can help govern the relationships among the participants in the joint production process over an extended period of time. Any contract that specified the division of the output in advance would introduce perverse incentives into the relationship (Alchian and Demsetz 1972; Holmstrom 1982; Blair and Stout 1999). But any contract that failed to specify the division of the output would likely lead to costly 'rent-seeking' behavior among the participants over time as the joint surplus was realized.

The three types of organizational structures mentioned above are all based, not on detailed contracts among participants, but on agreements among participants about process rules for governing how decisions will be made among the participants over the course of the venture. Under the rules of partnership that would have applied in the early 1800s, business people could form a partnership simply by agreeing to act as partners in undertaking a certain business activity, and to share the profits and liabilities associated with the business (Hillman 1987; 1971: iii). Partnership assets were considered to be the joint property of the partners; contracts entered into by any partner with outside parties in connection with the business were legally binding on all partners. Unless the partnership agreement specified otherwise, the agreement would be assumed to be at will. This meant that any partner could terminate the relationship at any time and for any reason, thereby forcing the other partners to either liquidate the assets of the business or buy out the share of the departing partner. An exception to this default rule would be made if the partners had specifically agreed to continue in the relationship for a certain period of time or until certain conditions were met (such as the completion of a particular discrete project or venture). In such a case, any partner could still exit the partnership at will and force dissolution, but the exiting partner might be required to pay damages. A partnership would automatically be dissolved if a partner died, became insane, or became bankrupt (Hillman 1987; Kent 1971: iii).

Each partner in a business venture organized as a partnership hence had tremendous power over the other partners. Individual partners could enter into contracts that bound the other partners, could incur debts that the other partners could be held liable for, and could threaten to pull out, forcing dissolution of the business, if they did not get what they wanted out of the partnership. And each time a partner pulled out, or died, or had to exit the partnership for some other reason, the partnership had to be reorganized to keep the business going.

While partners had considerable power to protect themselves against unfair expropriation of the benefits of team production by other partners, the set of relationships embodied in the partnership was vulnerable to disruption by disputes among partners, as well as the death or even bad luck of one or more partners. This complicated the relationships not only among the partners but between the partnership and suppliers and customers who surely knew and understood that the partnership was highly vulnerable to being broken up. Thus, while partnerships provided a potential solution to the 'team production' problem, they could be difficult to manage over an extended period of time.[5] Participants in a large network of business relationships in which mutual success depends on numerous individuals making team-specific investments over a sustained period of time require more assurance of continuity and financial stability.

Understanding the vulnerability of the partnership form, business people began using a variation on the partnership form called a 'joint stock company'. As early as the seventeenth century, joint stock companies were used in Europe to undertake trade missions (Hansmann, Kraakman, and Squire 2002). In the earliest joint stock companies[6] a group of merchants would pool their 'stocks' (the goods they had for trade) and collectively hire

---

[5] Business historian Alfred Chandler tells us that traditional business partnerships in the early nineteenth century were generally 'short-lived' (Chandler 1977: 8). Nonetheless, a few major corporations, such as DuPont, Carnegie Steel, and Baldwin Locomotive Works, managed to operate as partnerships over several decades in the nineteenth century, not converting to corporate form until early in the twentieth century. See Blair (2003: 449–54) for a discussion of why these ventures were able to function effectively as partnerships for so long.

[6] The British East India Company was chartered in 1600; the Dutch East India Company was chartered in 1602.

a ship to undertake a trade mission. The charters that these groups had been granted by their respective kings gave them monopolies over rights to trade as well as the rights to establish colonies in certain parts of the world.[7] The companies' ships would go out on their trade missions, and when they returned the stock of goods acquired in trade would be divided among the merchants and the 'company' essentially dissolved, to be reformed under the same charter for the next trade mission. Eventually, some chartered companies decided to quit dividing up the proceeds at the end of each trade mission, and instead commit their initial capital for an extended period. In 1623, the Dutch East India Co. was granted the right of perpetual existence. Under this new arrangement, the company members would no longer be able to demand repayment at the end of each voyage, since some funds or stocks would always be retained for the next trade mission. But member merchants could instead, with the approval of other members, sell their 'shares' in the company, much the way members of the New York Stock Exchange can today sell their 'seats' or membership in the exchange. In 1654, the British East India Company also adopted a rule of perpetual existence, accompanied by full transferability of shares (Hansmann, Kraakman, and Squire 2002).

During the late seventeenth and eighteenth centuries in the US, entrepreneurs pursuing other kinds of businesses, especially banking and insurance, formed similar organizations. Many of these organizations sought charters from the states to give them special privileges (such as the right to issue currency). But by the late eighteenth century, entrepreneurs pursuing business ventures that did not require any special monopoly or franchise from the state were increasingly using unchartered joint stock companies for such businesses as land speculation and settlement (Livermore 1968), harvesting and selling natural resources such as coal,[8] small manufacturing, especially of textiles (Seavoy 1982; Bagnall 1893), and building canals and roads.[9]

Legally, unchartered joint stock companies were partnerships in which partners agreed to place the assets used in the business into a trust controlled by a group of trustees, in exchange for transferable claims on distributions

---

[7] The charters also gave them extended life. But they did not legally partition the assets by creating a separate legal entity to own the property. At any point in time, the assets of these companies consisted of the 'joint stocks' of the merchants who were members of the company at that time.

[8] Blair (2003) traces the history of the Lehigh Coal Mine Company and the Lehigh Navigation Company in the early nineteenth century. Both were unincorporated joint stock companies. In the 1820s, the two companies merged and were granted a charter by the Pennsylvania legislature as the Lehigh Coal and Navigation Company.

[9] Sowards and Mofsky (1969) note that there is no record of how many unchartered joint stock companies may have been formed in the late eighteenth and early nineteenth centuries, precisely because such organizations were not granted charters, nor were they otherwise registered.

from that trust.[10] In this way, the promoters were able to achieve some degree of commitment of resources to the business venture (assets in the trust could stay in the trust, even as individual investors sold their 'shares' to other investors). This form also made it possible for some investors to be passive since control rights over the assets were vested in the trustees of the trust. This, to some extent, separated the role of control from the role of investment in the business and made it possible to raise capital from a larger number of investors.

But the commitment of resources was only partial. Because the courts regarded unchartered joint stock companies as a species of partnership, members were regarded as holding pro rata direct interests in the property of the partnership. Although the organizers of a joint stock company could agree among themselves to commit funds to the partnership trust indefinitely, these agreements apparently were not binding on the heirs of the members.[11] So if a joint stock company member were to die, the heirs could compel dissolution just as partners in an ordinary general partnership could compel dissolution.

Moreover, a joint stock company did not completely separate the role of investing from the role of controlling the company. Because courts at the time regarded joint stock companies as a species of partnership, they took the position that the members selected the trustees and could therefore withdraw authority from the trustees at any time. Hence, members were regarded as still legally in control of the enterprise, and could for this reason be held personally liable for debts of the business, just as individual partners could be held personally liable for debts of an ordinary general partnership.

Apparently, these problems were not considered trivial. In a pamphlet published in 1823 by seven business people attempting to organize The Schuylkill Coal Company and seeking a charter from the state legislature in

---

[10] In England, the Bubble Act of 1720, passed in the wake of a financial collapse and associated market scandals, made it illegal to trade in shares of unchartered joint stock companies in England. This greatly slowed the development of this organizational form in England for more than a century, until the Bubble Act was repealed in 1825 (Harris 1994). During that period, the British Parliament granted charters for joint stock companies only very reluctantly, which also slowed the development of the chartered corporate form. England did not clean up the confusion and pass a general incorporation act that clearly permitted business people to organize themselves into companies and receive a charter simply by registering until the passage of the Companies Act of 1844 made incorporation more widely available (Mahoney 2000; Hunt 1935).

[11] Ireland (1996) traces the history of court cases in England, noting that before about 1837 English courts consistently found that shareholders in joint stock companies, whether incorporated or not, had a direct property interest in the assets of the firm. In the US, it appears that courts followed this line of reasoning for unincorporated joint stock companies but not for chartered corporations, which, as I explain in the next section, were always understood under American law to be separate legal entities.

Pennsylvania, the organizers listed the following reasons why they needed a charter (Schuylkill Coal Company 1823):

1. To have the real estate of the Company, consisting of the coal lands which they hold, and such limited additional quantity as they may be allowed to acquire, with the necessary and appropriate improvements for the working of the mines, exempted from the laws of succession or inheritance, which govern the cases of natural persons or individuals. 2d. That the Company should be exempted from the ordinary laws of partnership, so far as they subject the estates of the several individuals who compose the Company to all the liabilities of the Association. 3d. To be recognized in law by a corporate name, and to be perpetuated, notwithstanding the demise or change of the members who may at any given time compose the Company.

The pamphlet goes on to stress the particular problem that would arise if a member of an unincorporated joint stock company were to die:

If one of the partners die, his undivided interest will descend by inheritance, or pass by devise to his heirs, who may consist of numerous children, in infancy, or numerous collateral relations, widely spread, and difficult of recognition. The operations of the Company must, on this event, immediately cease, and the joint estate be sold for division, or be otherwise divided between the survivors and the heirs of the deceased member, according to the decree of a proper legal tribunal, perhaps after a tedious suit, involving intricate questions of partnership claims, accounts, and settlements.

The promoters of the Schuylkill Coal Company were clearly aware of the possibility of using trust law to try to protect the assets of the enterprise. But they were not confident that organization as an unincorporated joint stock company, and the use of the business trust, would provide adequate protection:

Some of these difficulties may indeed be avoided by complicated trusts, covenants, and stipulations; but these, plain men of business cannot themselves frame, nor without difficulty understand; and when framed under the advice of the best legal abilities, they are subject nevertheless, to various constructions, and end but too frequently in vexatious and injurious controversies, which prudent men will anxiously avoid.

The organizers of the Schuylkill Coal Company obviously believed, and the legal record we have supports the idea, that, if the enterprise were organized under a corporate charter granted by the legislature, these problems could be solved.

How Corporations Succeeded in Locking in the Capital, and Separating Investment from Control

The earliest incorporated entities in the US were either chartered trading companies that had received their charter from the English king before the

Revolution or they were eleemosynary institutions, municipalities, towns, settlements, or chartered banks or insurance companies. Occasionally corporations were chartered to carry out some public works project, such as building a road or bridge or canal or providing a supply of water to some municipality (Livermore 1968).[12] As late as 1826, James Kent (1971: ii. 221–2) noted that, under English law, corporations were either 'ecclesiastical' or 'lay', the former being religious societies that incorporated in order to provide a mechanism for holding property over time as individual members came and went. Lay corporations, Kent further noted, 'are again subdivided into eleemosynary and civil'. In the former category were hospitals, colleges, and universities, or other institutions organized to provide charitable services to the indigent. Civil corporations, he further parsed the category, 'are either public or private'. By public corporations Kent meant entities that exist for 'public political purposes such as counties, cities, towns, and villages'.

Only the final subdivision of 'private' corporations included business corporations. Clearly, in all these categories the primary reason why the state would provide a charter incorporating the entity was to provide a mechanism for holding property for some public, charitable, educational, or religious use, so that such property would not be owned by the individuals who at any point in time might be managing the organization or charged with making decisions about the use of the property. Since the property held by an incorporated entity was not owned by individual human persons, it could not be passed to the heirs of such persons but would continue to be the property of the institution, even as its 'managers' (mayors or bishops or presidents, for example) might come and go. It is with respect to this type of corporation that the law developed the concept of a separate legal 'person' or 'entity'. And it is out of this body of law that business corporations in the US appear to have evolved.

Of Kent's categories, private corporations were the only ones that might engage in strictly commercial activity, although in the late eighteenth century even corporations in this category were expected to provide some needed service.[13]

After the American Revolution, the new American states began, tentatively at first, granting corporate charters to business promoters to establish banks or to build turnpikes or provide other needed services. Because of

---

[12] Votaw (1965: 19) notes that 'the concept of *persona ficta* did not begin with commercial associations but with religious, educational, and municipal associations'.

[13] State courts apparently regarded it as an inappropriate use of legislative power for a legislature to grant corporate status for purposes that were not regarded as in the public interest. See, for example, *Curries Admin.* v. *Mutual Assurance Soc'y*, 14 Va. (4 Hen. & M.) 315347–348 (1809) arguing that 'it may often be convenient for a set of associated individuals to have the privileges of a corporation bestowed upon them; but if their object is merely private or selfish; if it is detrimental to, or not promotive of, the public good, they have no adequate claim upon the legislature for privilege.'

the special public purpose nature of the businesses that were granted corporate status, it was important that the business property be held separately from the personal property of the individual business promoters, and that it not be subject to being subdivided or otherwise broken up. Ronald Seavoy (1982: 4), for example, notes that 'the new classes of incorporated businesses were usually fairly large-scale and they often had a high risk factor'. Incorporating a business, he added 'helped protect the collective ownership of real property [and] facilitated the mobilization of capital'.

Although state courts would later struggle with the implications of entity status for business corporations in certain situations, and wavered about the extent to which business corporations should be understood as being like partnerships or different from partnerships, the separateness of the incorporated entity from its members or participants was rarely at issue. The whole point of the charter was separateness. In fact, courts eventually took the position that they might 'pierce the veil' of the separate entity in order to reach through to the individual persons associated together in the entity only if 'the notion of legal entity is used to defeat public convenience, justify wrong, protect fraud, or defend crime'.[14]

It is legal separateness that I regard as the singular accomplishment of corporate law, the characteristic that provided the benefit business organizers so eagerly sought. In prior work with Stout (Blair and Stout 1999) I have argued that an important feature of the corporate form that helps to solve the 'team production' problem is that control rights are delegated to a board of directors. Delegation of control rights helps ensure that none of the participants in the enterprise can exercise too much control over factors that affect the outcome for the other participants. This makes it easier for all of the participants in the enterprise to make credible commitments to cooperate with each other. In Blair (2003) I argue that another critical feature of the corporate form that made it the preferred way of organizing large, complex businesses was that a corporation is a separate legal entity with potentially perpetual life, and is the legal owner of the assets used in the business. Holding the property in corporate form rather than in a partnership or joint stock company made it easier to commit resources to long-lived, specialized business enterprises.

In connection with the separate legal status of corporations, early corporate charters and general incorporation statutes made several provisions that tended to facilitate the locking in of capital committed to the corporate enterprise. First, as already noted, neither shareholders nor their heirs could compel dissolution of the enterprise. Second, early corporate charters provided that organizers designate a 'par value' for each share of stock issued. The initial shares in the company might often be issued to subscribers for

---

[14] See *United States* v. *Milwaukee Refrigerator Transit Co.*, 142 F 247, 255 (C.C.E.D. Wis. 1905), as cited in Presser (1991: 1–7).

a fraction of par value, and the corporation would begin its business with the money raised from these initial installments. But when this approach was used, charters always provided that the corporation could go back to the subscribers at any time in the future and require them to pay the rest of the promised commitment (Dodd 1954).[15] Thus, from the time of the earliest corporations, financial investors who wanted to participate in a business organized as a corporation had to make substantial financial commitments, and these commitments were considered part of the corporation's permanent capital.

Once committed, the capital paid into a corporation by its initial investors could be very difficult to recover. Early charters and statutes typically specified that shareholders or 'members' could not withdraw their capital unless the enterprise were to be formally dissolved. Charters did provide that investors could receive dividends out of operating profits but not out of the permanent capital of the corporation (O'Kelley and Thompson 1999). But shareholders did not have a legal right to receive any dividend at all unless it was declared by directors. Also, early case law emphasized that the resources that had been invested in corporations no longer belonged to the shareholders but, rather, remained the property of the corporation unless and until paid out in the form of dividends.[16]

The final feature of corporate law in the nineteenth century that supports the idea that the corporate form facilitated the lock-in of capital investments is the 'trust fund' doctrine. The modern trust fund doctrine holds that, in an insolvent corporation, the directors have fiduciary duties running to creditors because corporate assets are held in trust to satisfy creditors first. This doctrine was articulated clearly in an 1824 case[17] in which Justice Story wrote:

It appears to me very clear upon general principles, as well as the legislative intention that the capital stock . . . is to be deemed a pledge or trust fund for the payment of the debts contracted by [the corporation]. The public, as well as the legislature, have always supposed this to be a fund appropriated for such a purpose. The individual stockholders are not liable for the debts of the [corporation] in their private

---

[15] In fact, prior to the nineteenth century, corporate charters commonly did not specify a par value for their shares, and in such cases there was no legal limit to the assessments that could be made against shareholders (Handlin and Handlin 1945). Thus the idea of corporations as separate legal persons for purposes of holding property preceded the idea of limited liability. Limited liability began to be a characteristic of some corporate charters in the 1810s, but the state of California did not provide for limited liability for business corporations until well into the twentieth century (Friedman 1973; Weinstein 2002).

[16] See for example *Brightwell* v. *Mallory*, 18 Tenn. (1 Yer.) 196, 197–198 (1836), noting that 'the money in the [corporation] is the property of the institution, and to the ownership of which the stockholder has no more claim than a person has who is not at all connected with the [corporation]'.

[17] *Wood* v. *Dummer*, 30 F. Cas. 435, (C.C.D. Me. 1824)(No. 17,944). This case concerns a bank, but its reasoning has been widely applied to business corporations of all types.

capacities. The charter relieves them from personal responsibility, and substitutes the capital stock in its stead. Credit is universally given to this found [*sic*] by the public, and as the only means of repayment. During the existence of the corporation it is the sole property of the corporation, and can be applied only according to its charter, that is, as a fund for the payment of its debts.... If the stock may, the next day after it is paid in, be withdrawn by the stockholders without payment of the debts of the corporation, why is its amount so studiously provided for, and its payment by the stockholders so diligently required?

Thus, the corporate form made it possible for investors in shares as well as creditors, employees, and suppliers to enter into long-term relationships with a firm with a greater assurance that the pool of assets would remain in the business to keep the business going forward.

In the next section, I illustrate this function of corporate law by telling the story of the I. M. Singer & Co. partnership, which developed and patented a functional sewing machine and began building a substantial marketing organization in the 1850s. But by the 1860s the partnership ran into problems that could be solved only by forming a corporation.

Why I. M. Singer & Co. Had to Incorporate

The story of the rise of the Singer Manufacturing Co. provides an example in which the corporate form was used not to raise financial capital or to achieve the benefits of limited liability, but to lock in existing capital, provide a mechanism for settling any subsequent disputes among the leading participants in the firm, and ultimately support the development of a massive marketing organization.

The Singer Manufacturing Co. had its start in 1851, when Isaac Merritt Singer was granted a patent on a machine that would make a continuous series of stitches. Singer had formed partnerships with a number of people who provided workshop space, equipment, and financial capital while he worked on his machine design. But, once he had his patent, he got out of those various partnerships and formed a new partnership with Edward Clark, a lawyer who had pushed through the patent application for Singer (Brandon 1977).

During the next ten years, the market for sewing machines grew, slowly at first, as Singer and several other sewing machine manufacturing firms tried to convince the male breadwinners of households that it was worth spending what amounted to a very substantial amount of money relative to typical household net worth on a device that, from their point of view, had no purpose other than to make women's work easier and faster. Moreover, the various sewing machine manufacturers were continually suing each other over patent infringement claims. Indeed, Singer's design, while containing novel components, was based partly on a prior machine patented by Elias Howe in 1846. The patent wars among Howe, Singer, and the other manufacturers absorbed most of the partnership profits, and virtually all of Clark's time and energy during the years from 1851 to 1856.[18] In the fall of that year, the three leading manufacturers, together with Elias Howe, who among them held dozens of patents on sewing machines and their various improvements—including all of the most important patents—agreed to form the first 'patent pool'. The parties contributed all of their relevant patents to a single pool, and agreed that, for a fee of $20 per sewing machine sold, they could all use each others' patents.[19]

With the patent wars settled, I. M. Singer & Co. manufactured and sold 2,564 machines in 1856, and by 1860 production and sales had reached 13,000 machines. Singer and Clark were rapidly becoming very wealthy people and, though still organized as a conventional general partnership, were beginning to build a substantial manufacturing, distribution, and sales organization. They had established sales offices in many major US cities, as well as in Paris, Glasgow, and Rio de Janeiro, and were even thinking about establishing manufacturing operations abroad. Singer and Clark, though they didn't particularly like or trust each other, had managed to establish a reasonably successful working relationship, and had begun building substantial intangible assets in their brand and unique marketing organization.

Meanwhile, however, Singer was thoroughly enjoying his new wealth and was living an unusually flamboyant life. In 1860, a series of incidents had brought public attention to the fact that Singer had domestic relationships with, and numerous children by, at least four women, only one of whom he was legally married to. To escape the wrath of the woman with whom he had been living the longest and most openly, who called herself Mrs Isaac Singer, and with whom he had fathered eight children, Singer fled to England.[20]

Apart from the unseemliness and notoriety of this lifestyle (which might have had a negative impact on the ability of the firm to market Singer machines to 'respectable' households), why did this matter to Clark? The problem, Clark could easily foresee, was that, if the firm were still organized as a partnership at the point when Singer died, the valuable business which the two of them had built over the previous years would be destroyed in the legal battles over claims to Singer's estate. Singer's heirs, however many of them there might be, would all have some legal claim to some share of the

---

[18] Brandon (1977: 99) describes reports that newspapers of the era carried about the latest developments in the 'Sewing Machine Wars'.

[19] The first five dollars of this fee was to go to Howe, who held that key early patent and had won a series of court battles defending his claim. Another part of this fee was set aside for fighting future patent infringement battles against any other manufacturers who might attempt to use the devices covered by patents in the pool, and the rest would be divided among the three manufacturing firms in the pool (Brandon, 1977: 98).

[20] This woman was Mary Ann Sponsler, who had been Singer's most frequent and public companion for nearly twenty years, even though Singer had never been legally divorced from Catherine Haley Singer, with whom he had fathered two children (Brandon 1977: 162–3).

business, and it would probably require years of court battles to establish who was to get what. Clark feared that, without liquidating much of the firm, he would not be able to come up with enough cash to prevent catastrophe by buying out Singer's share from the heirs.

The solution to this problem, Clark also realized, was to incorporate the business, and Clark hoped as part of the bargain to ease Singer out of active management. By 1860, most states had passed generalized incorporation statutes, and the corporate form was being used widely enough to make Clark aware of its advantages. Once incorporated, the business assets would no longer be the joint property of Clark and Singer but would belong to the corporation. Equity shares would be issued to Clark and Singer, each of whom would provide a pro-rata claim on any distributions from the business. But any such distribution would be at the discretion of the board of directors of the company, and could not be compelled by either former partner or by the executor of the estate, nor would it likely be compelled by any court of law handling the proceedings. Heirs could be given equity shares in the business out of Singer's estate, and they could thereby become passive investors in the business. All this could happen without disturbing or breaking up the assets and governance structure of the business.

The company by this time had no need to raise additional capital (it was generating cash faster than it could reinvest it), nor were there any particular concerns about limiting the liability of shareholders: the firm had little or no debt (except perhaps small amounts of trade credit from materials suppliers), and class action lawsuits for fingers injured by sewing machine thread guides and pressure feet had not yet been invented. The only function that incorporation served was to make sure that the substantial organizational capital that had been accumulated by the firm could not be torn apart, or its reputation easily destroyed, as a result of the messy personal affairs of one of the partners.

According to Singer's biographer, it took more than three years for Clark to get Singer to agree to incorporation of the business. But in August of 1863, I. M. Singer & Co. was dissolved, and the business was reorganized as the Singer Manufacturing Company. The firm by then had 22 patents and capital assets of $550,000. Within four years after incorporation, it had established manufacturing and sales operations overseas, becoming the first American firm to produce and market extensively in Europe (Davies 1969). According to Chandler (1977), Singer was also the first manufacturing company to establish a sales force of its own salaried employees rather than rely on sales agents. The Singer organization that developed in the 1860s and 1870s included retail branches in virtually every community in the US of at least 5,000 population (as well as in many communities in Europe and South America). Each branch office included, at a minimum, a general salesman, an instructor (often a female employee hired to teach other women how to use the machines), a mechanic (to assure customers that machines could be promptly repaired if they broke down), and a bookkeeper (Chandler 1977: 403).

One other detail of the transition of I. M. Singer & Co. to the Singer Manufacturing Company, provided by Singer's biographer Ruth Brandon, suggests that the governance structure established in the newly organized corporation was designed to serve a mediating function, as the team production theory suggests, rather than to establish agents to act on behalf of shareholders, as the standard principal-agent theory of the corporation argues. Brandon (1977: 179) says that

Singer had only agreed to the end of the partnership [in which he knew he would lose his ability to make extraordinary demands on the other participants] under certain conditions, the principal one being that neither of the partners would be president of the new company while the other was alive, and that both would "retire from active participation in the management of the business." In other words . . . if Singer was to become a non-executive director, then so must Clark. If he [Clark] was so determined to dissociate Singer from the business, this was the price he had to pay.

The agreement they ultimately reached was that Singer and Clark would each take 40 per cent of the shares of the new company in exchange for their interests in the partnership, with the rest to be subscribed to by four senior officers of the firm (who were each required to buy 175 shares at $200 per share), and twelve other employees of the company who were offered the opportunity to buy shares. A young manager, Mr Inslee Hopper, was named president. The initial board of trustees would include Singer, Clark, Hopper, George Ross McKenzie who had been a trusted agent of the firm for a number of years, William F. Proctor, and Alexander F. Sterling.

While Singer did retire from active involvement in the company after that, Clark did not, and after Singer died in 1875 (Brandon 1977: 193), Clark became president in 1876 (Chandler 1977: 403). Chandler credits Clark and McKenzie with building an integrated organizational structure that became a model for many other large manufacturing and distribution companies in the late nineteenth and early twentieth centuries.

Under-appreciated Lessons (and a Proposed Application)

The stories of the Schuylkill Coal Company's reasons for wanting a corporate charter and of Edward Clark's reasons for wanting to incorporate the Singer Manufacturing Co.[21] suggest an important lesson that I believe

---

[21] See Blair (2003) for other historical facts and anecdotes about the development of US corporate law in the nineteenth century that also support the arguments made in this chapter.

has been greatly under-appreciated by contemporary corporate scholars: the corporate form of organization was a brilliant mechanism for raising capital because it permits passive investment by *separating the role of contributing capital from the role of managing or controlling the business.* Contemporary scholarship on corporations places a huge emphasis on the so-called agency costs that result from this separation, and an enormous amount of paper and ink have been used to discuss and analyze methods of controlling these agency costs.[22] But little regard is paid to the apparent fact that, however great and troubling these agency costs are, they must be relatively trivial compared with the benefits arising from this separation.[23] These benefits, I argue, have to do with the improved ability business people had to create long-term wealth-generating organizations once these roles were separated. That the benefits must be huge is clear from the fact that organizers of large complex businesses for at least the last century and a half have consistently chosen the corporate form over other possible business organizational forms where they have had the choice, even when doing so was initially more costly than using other legal forms.

A primary benefit of the corporate form, this chapter has argued, arises from the fact that passive investors yield ownership rights over the assets they contribute to the legal entity created by corporate law. In yielding ownership rights, they give up the right to withdraw the financial capital or other contribution they have made, and agree to accept in return only the distributions from the business that are ordered by the board of directors which has been given legal authority to make decisions for the corporate entity. This has the effect of reassuring and encouraging investment by all of the participants in the enterprise, including other financial investors as well as managers and specialized technicians, suppliers who make specialized investments to meet the needs of this particular corporation, and customers who buy the corporation's products on the promise that the products will live up to certain minimum performance or quality standards, or will be replaced or repaired by the corporation.[24] All of these participants depend

[22] Blair and Stout (1999: n. 1) lists more than a dozen leading articles that approach the analysis of corporate law and governance from the perspective of minimizing agency costs. These articles are just the tip of the iceberg. A quick search of the Social Science Research Network database, which generally includes only articles written since about 1997, turned up 315 articles with the phrase 'agency costs' in the title or abstract.

[23] Fama and Jensen (1983) were the first to point out that the so-called 'separation of ownership from control' provided benefits because it permitted specialization by corporate participants either in management or in risk-taking. In this chapter and in previous work (such as Blair 2003) I suggest that the benefits go far beyond mere specialization benefits, and include the capacity implicit in the use of the corporate form to create stable institutions that can support the accumulation of intangible assets such as brand or reputation value, intellectual capital, and organizational capital.

[24] The idea that customers as well as other corporate stakeholders will be more willing to do business with a company that appears to be stable and financially secure has been

on the continued existence and financial viability of the corporation, characteristics which would be very difficult to achieve if financial investors could for any reason, or no reason at all, withdraw their contribution at will. In other words, the ability to lock in the capital provided by investors until, in the judgement of *directors* (not of the investors themselves), it is no longer needed to enhance the development of the business, is critically important to the creation of complex, productive commercial enterprises.

One situation in which the failure to appreciate the full significance of this feature of the corporate form has probably been costly has been in the advice that US scholars and consultants have given to developing and transition economy countries in recent years. Many emerging market and transition economy countries in today's world face a lack of institutional, cultural, and legal supports for corporate organizations that is similar in many ways to the environment faced by entrepreneurs and business people who built and led the first large and complex industrial, transportation, communication, and marketing firms in the nineteenth century US. They lack competitive product markets, sophisticated courts that can adjudicate complex contracts, an independent accounting profession and accounting rules developed to provide accurate information for investors, good internal information systems, strong independent financial institutions, deep and liquid capital markets, and powerful social norms about the appropriate roles and behavior of corporate managers and investors (Black and Kraakman 1996). Scholars and consultants who advised Russia in the early 1990s to rapidly privatize Russian industries, and who helped them draft corporate codes to govern the new corporations created to own and run these industrial enterprises, have conceded that they failed to appreciate just how important these institutional, legal, and cultural supports to capitalism are in developed countries (Black, Kraakman, and Tarassova 2000).[25]

illustrated in recent months by a hostile takeover contest in the US involving PeopleSoft Corp. and Oracle Corp. Shortly after PeopleSoft announced in the spring of 2003 that it planned to merge with J. D. Edwards, another software company, Oracle Corp. announced a tender offer for PeopleSoft. Oracle CEO Larry Ellison initially announced that, once Oracle acquired PeopleSoft, he intended to stop selling PeopleSoft's products (which compete with Oracle's products) and move PeopleSoft's customers to Oracle's own products (see, for example, Sorkin and Flynn 2003). PeopleSoft responded with a full-page advertisement in several major newspapers claiming that the Oracle tender offer was primarily intended to put PeopleSoft out of business by creating an uncertain environment for purchasers of its products. 'Customers will not commit millions of dollars to enterprise software that is subject to such uncertainties', said the ad, which was signed by the seven members of PeopleSoft's board (see *Washington Post*, 2 July 2003: E12). Oracle then responded with a series of full page ads accusing PeopleSoft's board of 'forgetting its fiduciary responsibilities' by rejecting Oracle's all-cash offer (see *Washington Post*, 8 July 2003: A11).

[25] Black, Kraakman, and Tarassova (2000) have been frank in their assessment and self-criticism of 'what went wrong' in the effort to privatize industry in Russia and establish functioning mechanisms of corporate governance. They note that rapid privatization led to massive self-dealing and asset stripping by corporate insiders rather than an effort by the new private sector 'owners' and managers to do a better job of managing the assets to improve

The aggressive privatizers who were advising much of Russia, the former Soviet Union, and eastern Europe believed that the biggest economic problem in these countries was that, under centralized economic control, capital assets had been grossly misallocated. They also believed that, if claims to those capital assets were in the hands of private investors, those investors would then have the incentive to reallocate the assets to more efficient uses.[26] In fact, they believed specifically that 'large outside shareholders', if given an opportunity to invest in Russian corporations, would 'have incentives to make good investments' (Black and Kraakman 1996: 3).

This analysis failed to appreciate what business organizers in the early nineteenth century US understood: that, where there is no active financial market that makes it easy for an investor to sell his or her claim on an enterprise at anywhere near its full value, passive investors in a firm who are neither deeply rooted in the community where a business operates nor deeply committed to the long-term success of the business are likely to try to pull their capital out at the first sign of trouble. They may even pull their capital out simply because they prefer to spend or invest their money elsewhere and cannot readily convert their holdings to cash by selling them. Worse yet, such investors, if they are also in a position of sufficient control to permit them to do so, are likely not only to withdraw the share of the assets that they 'own' or have some kind of claim to, but may loot the assets of a troubled company rather than go to the effort to try to make the company work better.

Advocates of early and rapid privatization (steeped in the principal-agent view of corporate governance) saw the central corporate governance problem to be addressed by corporate law in the transition economies to be 'protecting minority investors against exploitation by managers or controlling shareholders' (Black and Kraakman 1996: 3). While doubtless this was and remains a major problem, another equally important problem is how to encourage investors and corporate managers not to yank capital out of the enterprises but to leave it in and redirect it to better more productive uses.

The dramatic bloodless revolution that took place in the former Soviet Union and Communist bloc countries in the early 1990s presented an unprecedented set of problems and opportunities. Perhaps there was nothing that Western advisers could have done to prevent the deep corruption and destructive asset-stripping that continues to occur in Russian and other former Soviet bloc corporations.[27] But an appreciation of US history and of

productivity and create wealth. They blame the failure largely on the deep corruption of powerful leaders who were in positions to simply take control of productive enterprises and loot them.

[26] As Black, Kraakman, and Tarassova (2000) state in the opening line of the abstract of their article: 'In Russia and elsewhere, proponents of rapid, mass privatization of state-owned enterprises (ourselves among them) hoped that the profit incentives unleashed by privatization would soon revive faltering, centrally planned economies.'

[27] My comments here are not intended as a criticism of the people who plunged into the intellectual challenge of advising Russia and former Soviet countries in the 1990s—a truly

the importance to economic development generally of the ability provided by the corporate form to lock in capital and separate financing from control might at least help explain why China's transition to capitalism has proceeded with continued rapid economic growth and much less asset-stripping and looting than has taken place in Russia. In China, product markets have been decontrolled gradually, while new corporate-like organizations led by entrepreneurial business people have been permitted to emerge to compete with state-owned enterprises. Meanwhile, subsidization of the state-owned enterprises has been gradually withdrawn, forcing the managers of those enterprises to make them more competitive or to shut them down and redeploy their assets. But Chinese managers have been far less likely than Russian managers have been to loot the firms for their own personal benefit. A lesson of this essay is that perhaps this is because the 'ownership' of the assets in the state-owned enterprises has remained separated from control of those assets.[28]

As efforts to advise developing and transition economies continue, scholars, consultants and advisers from such international institutions as the IMF, World Bank, and Asian Development Bank (Metzger 2003) are likely to provide more sound advice if they keep in mind the economic function that legal entity status, and the separation of financing from control that accompanies it, played historically and still play today.

More broadly, economic and legal scholars interested in corporate governance and public policy in any context need to keep these important functions of the corporate form in mind as they think about whether, and if so how, corporate law and governance rules should be reformed.

References

Alchian, A. and Demsetz, H. (1972). 'Production, Information Costs, and Economic Organization', *American Economic Review*, 62: 777–95.

Bagnall, W. (1893). *Textile Industries of the United States*. Cambridge, MA: Riverside Press.

Black, B. and Kraakman, R. (1996). 'A Self-Enforcing Model of Corporate Law', *Harvard Law Review*, 109: 1911–82.

daunting task. They are instead meant as a criticism of the state of social science knowledge these advisers were equipped with at the time.

[28] Black, Kraakman, and Tarassova (2000: 1752) note that managers of state-owned enterprises in Russia prior to privatization may not have been completely honest, but that the scale of dishonesty was limited by, among other things, 'bureaucratic controls [that] kept managers away from direct access to the payments that a company received for its goods, and provided oversight of those who had access to money'. This observation resonates with Weber's argument (1930) that bureaucracy is important to capitalistic enterprises because it helps to achieve a separation between personal and organizational goals.

——, ——, and Tarassova, A. (2000). 'Russian Privatization and Corporate Governance: What Went Wrong?', *Stanford Law Review*, 52: 1731–808.

Blair, M. (2003). 'Locking in Capital: What Corporate Law Achieved for Business Organizers of the 19th Century', *UCLA Law Review*, 51: 387–455.

—— and Stout, L. (1999). 'A Team Production Theory of Corporate Law', *Virginia Law Review*, 85: 247–328.

—— —— (2001). 'Director Accountability and the Mediating Role of the Corporate Board', *Washington University Law Quarterly*, 79: 403–47.

Brandon, R. (1977). *A Capitalist Romance: Singer and the Sewing Machine*. Philadelphia: J. B. Lippincott Co.

Chandler, A. (1977). *The Visible Hand: The Managerial Revolution in American Business*. Cambridge, MA: Belknap Press.

Davies, R. (1969). '"Peacefully Working to Conquer the World": The Singer Manufacturing Company in Foreign Markets, 1854–1889', *Business History Review*, 43: 299–325.

Davis, J. (1917). *Essays in the Earlier History of American Corporations*. Cambridge, MA: Harvard University Press.

Dodd, E. (1954). *American Business Corporations Until 1860: With Special Reference to Massachusetts*. Cambridge. MA: Harvard University Press.

Easterbrook, F. and Fischel, D. (1991). *The Economic Structure of Corporate Law*. Cambridge, MA: Harvard University Press.

Fama, E. (1980). 'Agency Problems and the Theory of the Firm', *Journal of Political Economy*, 88: 288–307.

—— and Jensen, M. (1983). 'Separation of Ownership and Control', *Journal of Law and Economics*, 26: 301–25.

Friedman, L. (1973). *A History of American Law*. New York: Simon & Schuster.

Handlin, O. and Handlin, M. (1945). 'Origins of the American Business Corporation', *Journal of Economic History*, 5: 1–23.

Hansmann, H., Kraakman, R., and Squire, R. (2002). 'Legal Entities, Asset Partitioning, and the Evolution of Organizations'. Working paper, Yale Law School, February.

Harris, R. (1994). 'The Bubble Act: Its Passage and Its Effects on Business Organizations', *Journal of Economic History*, 54: 610–27.

Hillman, R. (1987). 'Private Ordering Within Partnerships', *University of Miami Law Review*, 41: 425–71.

Holmstrom, B. (1982). 'Moral Hazard in Teams', *Bell Journal of Economics*, 13: 324–40.

Hunt, B. (1935). 'The Joint-Stock Company in England, 1830–1844', *Journal of Political Economy*, 43: 331–64.

Ireland, P. (1996). 'Capitalism without the Capitalist: The Joint Stock Company Share and the Emergence of the Modern Doctrine of Separate Corporate Personality', *Legal History*, 17: 41–73.

Jensen, M. and Meckling, W. (1976). 'Theory of the Firm: Managerial Behavior, Agency Costs and Ownership Structure', *Journal of Financial Economics*, 3: 305–60.

Kent, J. (1971). *Commentaries on American Law* (1st edn. 1826). New York: Da Capo Press.

Livermore, S. (1968). *Early American Land Companies: Their Influence on Corporate Development* (1st edn. 1939). New York: Octagon Books.

Mahoney, P. (2000). 'Contract or Concession? An Essay on the History of Corporate Law', *Georgia Law Review,* 34: 873–93.

Metzger, B. (2003). 'International Financial Institutions, Corporate Governance and the Asian Financial Crisis'. Draft chapter for Thomas Heller and Lawrence Liu (eds.), *The Ecology of Corporate Governance: The East Asian Experience* (forthcoming).

O'Kelley, C. and Thompson, R. (1999). *Corporations and Other Business Associations: Cases and Materials* (3rd edn.). Gaithersburg, MD: Aspen Law and Business.

Presser, S. (1991). *Piercing the Corporate Veil.* West Group. New York: Boardman.

Ratner, S., Soltow, J., and Richard Sylla, R. (1979). *The Evolution of the American Economy.* New York: Basic Books.

Schuylkill Coal Company (1823). *Remarks and Observations Showing the Justice and Policy of Incorporating 'The Schuylkill Coal Company', respectfully addressed to the publick, and particularly to the Members of the Legislature* (pamphlet in the collection of the Hagley Library).

Seavoy, R. (1982). *The Origins of the American Business Corporation, 1784–1855.* Westport, CT: Greenwood Press.

Sorkin, A. and Flynn, L. (2003). 'Oracle Takes $5 Billion Jab at PeopleSoft', *New York Times,* 7 June, C1.

Sowards, H. and Mofsky, J. (1969). 'Factors Affecting the Development of Corporation Law', *University of Miami Law Review*, 23: 476–94.

Votaw, D. (1965). *Modern Corporations.* Englewood Cliffs, NJ: Prentice Hall.

Weber, Max (1930). *The Protestant Ethic and the Spirit of Capitalism.* New York: Scribner.

Weinstein, M. (2002). 'Limited Liability in California: 1928–1931'. Working paper. Los Angeles: Marshall School of Business, University of Southern California Law School.

Wright, R. (2002). *The Wealth of Nations Rediscovered: Integration and Expansion in American Financial Markets, 1780–1850.* Cambridge: Cambridge University Press.

3

Governing with Multiple Principals: An Empirically-Based Analysis of Capital Providers' Preferences and Superior Governance Structures

ANNA GRANDORI AND GIUSEPPE SODA

Introduction

Labor, as one of the three fundamental factors of production and value generation—namely, capital, land, and labor—is increasingly contributing to economic activity in the form of 'investments' of human capital rather than just in the form of services sold. In fact, concepts like those of 'human capital' or 'human assets' have come to be commonly used (Becker 1964; Williamson 1979; Hart and Moore 1994) for representing the 'potential' for value generation, the stock of knowledge, and competence resources which are combined with other assets for generating valued services. The firms, sectors, and activities involving investments of critical human assets are of growing importance in economic life, such as, for example, the high-tech and new economy sectors.

By 'critical' investments we mean important or essential investments of human capital (Hart and Moore 1990), investments of high value or

This research has been conducted as a project of the Bocconi Center of Research on Business Organization (CRORA) and co-financed by Bocconi University and by four major firms—Unicredito, Pilkington, Egon Zehnder International, and Pirelli—whose support is gratefully acknowledged. We are also indebted to the leaders of the Italian business community who contributed in the launching of the CRORA project, providing insights on current organizational concerns of the key actors who actually govern corporations (Luciano Balbo; Giuseppe Crisci; Gianfilippo Cuneo; Alberto Meomartini; Giuseppe Morchio; Alessandro Profumo; Paolo Scaroni). The empirical analysis on masters alumni was made possible by the collaboration of the Master programs of the Politecnico di Milano, S. Anna di Pisa, CUOA Padova, and Bocconi; we heartily thank the Program Directors and Alumni Associations. The analysis of the control group of 'high potential managers' was made possible by the collaboration of three of the largest Italian firms; we are grateful to the human resource directors who supported and organized the enquiry. The organization of the board members' questionnaires was supported by Assogestioni and AIFI, which are warmly thanked.

poor substitutability (contributions that are necessary for other assets to be usable). They are typically made when knowledge and competence (capital) and tasks (the service or action) cannot be easily separated, when it is technically unfeasible for one actor, possessing the relevant knowledge, to 'direct' another in respect of what tasks to perform (Demsetz 1991)—something that in turn tends to occur when knowledge is sophisticated, difficult to codify, and diffused among different specialists, when tasks are complex, and when tight complementarities link human and technical resources (Alchian and Demsetz 1972; Grandori 2001*a*).

One of the possible responses, recommended by theory and partially adopted in practice, is to allocate a 'bundle of property rights', in a broad sense of the term, throughout the firm and to all capital providers, including human capital providers (and, at the extreme, allocated only to them). These rights include decision and control rights as well as rights to residual rewards and to partnership in ownership (Fama and Jensen 1983; Blair 1995, 1996; Hart and Moore 1990; Hansman 1996). The forms and degrees of this diffused right allocation are debatable; however, since they can have different incentive, risk-bearing, and information-processing properties, they might require different complementary organizational mechanisms in order to be viable.

This assessment is elaborated in the first section of this chapter by a consideration of the properties of a wide array of governance mechanisms. The second section envisages and assesses complementary and superior ways of combining these mechanisms so as to solve governance problems. The third section considers the possibility that the various possible ways of allocating rights may be ranked in different ways by the different categories of capital providers, in particular by financial capital providers and human capital providers. The fourth section advances and tests hypotheses on expected preferences.[1]

The chapter improves on standard approaches to corporate governance design in several ways. It makes it possible to model a wider variety of governance arrangements than is usually envisaged. It explores the structural consequences of fully considering the providers of human assets as 'principals' rather than agents, by framing the structural optimization problem as a negotiation game between the providers of different types of assets. It considers a wider spectrum of relevant governance mechanisms, bridging economic and organizational theories of governance.

---

[1] The methodological approaches applied here—the search for superior combinations of complementary coordination mechanisms (rather than the comparative assessment of given governance forms packaging them in historically pre-defined ways); the empirical test (rather than the untested 'assumption') of preferences; and a negotiation approach to governance and organization forms with respect to the preferences of the relevant players—have been developed in Grandori (2001*b*, 1997*b*, 1991).

Assessing Multiple Governance Mechanisms

To the extent that corporate governance is a problem of devising ways of allocating rights of action, decision, and rewards so as to generate Pareto-improvements (the generation of larger surpluses and an expected fair division of them), it is, to a large extent, also a problem of coordination and of human resource management. Organization theory and the human resource management literature have produced much that could and should be considered in corporate governance design. In particular, they can provide useful tools for *enlarging the portfolio of decision and control mechanisms*, since, in a way, this is one of their distinctive specialties as disciplines. In fact, seen from an organizational perspective, the range of governance mechanisms considered in the current corporate governance debate looks quite restricted. The considered mechanisms are based on three coordination logics: *price-like mechanisms* (incentives and compensation packages), *authority-like mechanisms* (board composition and the like), and external *rule-like mechanisms* (legal provisions on transparency and protecting minority shareholders). Theoretically, recent discussions and systematization of basic coordination and governance mechanisms and their properties include other possibilities (Miller 1992; Grandori 2001*a*):

- Negotiation and team-like decision and control can bring about credible commitments and effective controls between key actors as well as sustain effective and creative problem-solving and task-selection (Varian 1990; Bazerman 1986; Hatchuel 2001).
- 'Incentives' mechanisms can and should include intrinsic rewards from work since, under the usual strict 'extrinsic motivation' assumption, not only does incentive design become more difficult than it is in practice, but it is likely to produce biasing arrangements—'crowding out' the precious (although elusive) resource of intrinsic motivation (Osterloh and Frey, Chapter 9, this volume).
- Rule-like mechanisms can include the 'internal legal system' of the firm as well as the systems of social norms (whether firm-specific, industry-based, societal values and frames, or ethical codes and routines) which can reduce opportunism and ensure cooperation to a considerable extent (Lindenberg and Lampel, Chapters 10 and 11, this volume).

In the present framework and study, we will consider an array of governance mechanisms regulating the allocation of both extrinsic and intrinsic reward rights; the allocation of decision, control, communication and action rights; and the right to exit and to make or withdraw investments in human capital. Each right is considered here to be separable, in principle, from any other; and any coupling among them is to be justified in terms of complementarity (Milgrom and Roberts 1995) and tested empirically.

Reward Rights

Both theoretically and empirically, there has been a recent demand for and trend toward the variabilization of reward. It is a response to pressure by financial capital providers to make their agent-managers more accountable (Useem 1996). However, even if we consider managers just as agents of financial investors, and even if we use standard agency theory, it does not follow that the sensitivity of managers' rewards to variations in shareholder wealth should be maximized. The mechanism of encouraging performance with contingent pay entails growing marginal costs and decreasing marginal benefits, and yields an 'optimal incentive' intensity which varies as a function of a number of variables. In particular, it is lower the more uncertain the activities are (due to exogenous variance), the less measurable performance outcomes are, and the less performance is attributable to agents' actions (due to low discretion or interdependence with other actions) (Milgrom and Roberts 1992). Theoretically, the incidence of performance-related pay should therefore not be very high in the governance of the agency relationship in risky and complex activities—as some empirical research (Bloom and Milkovich 1998) confirms (though it may be high where activities remain in known causal relations with clear outcomes, but activities are poorly observable and relevant information and discretion remain with the agent).

Is the allocation of residual reward rights likely to be different if investments in human capital are involved? The answer should be 'yes': human capital providers would then be in the position of 'residual claimants', and should be interested in more decision rights over the firm conduct (rather than being just 'delegated' power to decide and act in the interest of the principals) and should hold more rights to the residual economic results of that conduct. Within some limits, however. In fact, since human capital investments are not easily diversified, human capital investors are likely to be more risk-averse than other investors. If they were to bear the entire risk of the activity, they would bear more risk than necessary and firm conduct would be distorted (Jensen and Meckling 1976). In addition, the presence of investors of other non-human resources, who are also in the position of residual claimants, limits the share of residual reward rights allocated to human capital investors.

The *form* of 'residual rewards' is also likely to be different. A relevant alternative here is between pay contingent on individual or group performance, and residual rewards contingent on firm performance (through partnerships, employee shareholding, stock options, and profit-sharing mechanisms). In fact, these solutions are widely used in human capital-intensive firms, such as in the cases of professional partnerships, or as incentive architectures for upper-echelon management.

In sum, we expect that the efficient allocation of residual reward rights to both agents and human capital investors should have upper bounds, and intermediate values of residual rewards should be superior to extreme ones (in particular to very high levels of contingent pay), especially in innovative and risky activities.

Decision and Control Rights

Organization science has consistently shown that the more complex the tasks are and the more diffuse the relevant knowledge and information is, the more decentralized are the effective and efficient allocations of decision rights. This is a very important complement to agency and property rights theories, which have somehow 'forgotten' the very reason for and benefits of separating 'ownership from control', for concentrating on the costs that this separation generates (agency costs and hold-up problems). Decision and control rights, even 'residual' ones, should be allocated, first and foremost, to those actors having the knowledge to take those decisions. And if tasks are complex (outputs are difficult to evaluate), and competence is highly specialized, or tacit, or 'team'-embedded (inputs are difficult to evaluate), residual control rights should be allocated together with residual decision rights (Alchian and Demsetz 1972; Ouchi 1979).

Therefore, we expect extensive decentralization to agents of decision rights in their own area of specialized action—this is what an agency relation is for—especially in complex activities; and we expect an even more extensive diffusion of decision and control rights where the investment of human assets is involved. In this last case, decision and control rights demanded by human capital providers should apply to firm conduct more extensively, not only and specifically a specialized area of decision and action.

The *forms* in which 'residual decision and control rights' are granted should therefore be different where managers are in a 'principal' rather than in an 'agent' position. The relevant alternative here is between rights of action and decision in individual and group work (autonomy) and rights of decision and control over firm conduct (representation on boards of directors, voting rights, and other forms of corporate democracy).

The decentralization of decision rights, on the other hand, is also expected to have upper bounds, generated not only by agency costs (as stressed in economic models) but also by the risks of uncoordinated behavior of the system as a whole (as highlighted by organization theory)—the costs of errors, misunderstanding, loss of information, and so on.

Organization theory suggests two powerful remedies that can mitigate these problems without reducing the effective degree of separation between 'ownership and control' and without reducing the effective degree of differentiation of knowledge and objectives within the firm. They are: the *intrinsic rewards* generated by high discretion and autonomy and by the richness and intrinsic interest of task content (as an alternative to extrinsic 'objective aligning incentives'); and decentralized *coordination by teaming* (as an alternative to centralized coordination by hierarchy and to decentralized coordination by prices). These two mechanisms can be expected to generate sufficient levels of self-control and peer control to mitigate 'shirking' problems and sufficient communication to solve many coordination problems.

In sum, we expect the effective mix of decision and control mechanisms to be characterized by generally high levels of autonomy and discretion in all conditions involving distributed knowledge (any professionalized and managerial work); and we expect intrinsic rewards from the job to be generally important. In addition, if investors of critical human capital are present, we expect that they are more interested in being represented at the institutional level and have more formal residual control rights.

Investments in Human Capital and Exit Rights

A way of reducing the risk of firm-specific human capital investments, and actually a way of diversifying, at least over time, those investments is to shorten the investment time horizon and to maximize the resalability of work experiences and positions in new ventures and new positions. This contributes to explaining the shortening of the length of stay of managers in single positions and firms.

Another reason why granting 'exit rights' in the short term to human capital investors may be effective is innovation. While we have been accustomed to a model of the innovative firm as 'resource based' (Penrose 1959), involving long-term specific investments of resource providers to sustain 'competitive advantage' (Barney 1991), this model is likely not to be the only effective one and to be rather outdated in the so-called knowledge economies. Mobility generates input variety and sustains innovation. Therefore, the popular question 'how to retain high-potential managers' may be misconceived. The issue is not to retain the 'same' human capital investors, any more than it is to retain the 'same' investors of technical and financial assets. The relevant issue is how to have at any point in time a good collection of investors—where 'good' is likely to imply that it is a shifting combination.

On the other hand, there are countervailing forces, encouraging the longevity of relations. The main force is represented by the development and/or transfer of specific or co-specialized competences to the firm, the tasks, the co-workers. This may be thought of as an interest of the firm and of the investors of other resources in it rather than of the human capital investor, but interests may be more congruent. In fact, the manager or professional should wish to increase the value of his or her human capital by enriching it with new knowledge and experience. The only way to gain it is to expose oneself to the acquisition of some knowledge and experience that may not be transferable in order to have access to other knowledge and learning which is transferable. In addition, in this way the 'human capital provider' is likely to obtain some co-investment by the firm in the development of the firm-specific components of his human capital.

Hence, we expect job tenure to find a lower bound in the technically minimum period required to construct and use profitably firm-specific competencies, and to find that the costs of the investments in the development of human capital relevant for the current work experience are shared between the firm and the human capital provider (as a private expense).

The countervailing needs posed by investments in firm-specific human asset and the realization of returns on human capital investments (through reselling of experience) is likely to affect also the *forms* of regulating mobility and not only its speed. The possibility that the divide between internal and external labor markets may be ill-suited for interpreting governance in human capital-intensive economies has been advanced by one of the experts on the concept of internal labor markets (Piore 2001). More specifically, on the problem to hand, in a study on governance mechanisms of human and social capital in the new economy (Grandori *et al.* 2002), we have hypothesized and found that *both* 'free' market-like human-capital mobility across firms *and* internal labor markets should be less efficient than competence-based social and professional networks, especially in innovative ventures for which evaluating human resource potential is quite difficult *ex ante*. In fact, personal networks among human capital providers function as certifiers of competence and reliability (Karpik 1989) and network governance may allow the formation of team-specific or network-specific but not strictly firm-specific competences. The participation by human capital investors in projects in teams can provide a guarantee that each individual member will not withdraw before due time, as they would damage their co-workers and their own reputation in subsequent ventures. Alternatively, managerial and professional embeddedness in networks of relationships can provide new participants in projects, so that projects and firms can survive individual mobility. Therefore, network governance of mobility may raise the 'upper bounds' that otherwise are likely to limit the incentive to invest by financial capital providers in projects where human and social capital provided by other actors is critical (see Hart and Moore 1994 for the argument that those upper bounds exist).

In sum, it is possible to specify an expected set of mechanisms effective for governing the continued association of critical human capital with other assets:

- High managerial discretion is a universal requirement in the governance of both agency relations and human capital co-investment relations (irrespectively of industry or other contingency). If human capital investments are involved, a wider set of property rights should be allocated to managers (residual decision and control rights on firm conduct).
- High incidence of team work and high levels of intrinsic reward from work are organizational mechanisms complementary to high discretion. Instead, as a corollary, work effort should not be a core concern, and should not be perceived as a relevant cost—as usually assumed in agency

theory applications to corporate governance—since effort is to a large extent a benefit (if it does not become over-stressful and over-strenuous).

- 'High-powered incentives' and performance-related pay can be expected to be less universally efficient. There are trade-offs. Hence, we expect that the relation between the relative incidence of performance-related pay and its net benefits is U-shaped, that is, the superior configurations should be found at intermediate levels. If managers are 'human capital investors', that is, principals rather than agents, we should find that relatively higher levels of 'residual reward rights' are acceptable to them as a complementary mechanism to wider residual decision and control rights.

- The degree of mobility and the length of job tenure of human capital investors is expected to assume intermediate values in order to 'optimize' the trade-off between resalability of experiences on one hand and the exploitation of investments in firm-specific competences on the other hand.

- Human capital mobility across firms is expected to be better governed by professional networks or brokered/certified markets rather than by either 'external labor markets' or 'quasi-internal labor markets' (networks of former co-workers).

The space of governance possibilities, defined by the above hypotheses, can be operationalized in a web of dimensions. A framework operationalizing eight dimensions is outlined in the next paragraph. That 'governance mechanisms web' is proposed as a useful analytical tool for measuring, comparing, and designing governance solutions on the basis of different inputs. The first input is the theoretical profile of effective mechanisms, discussed above. Actually observable effective solutions can be located or ranked with respect to those predictions. A further input is the (eventually different) preferred combinations of those mechanisms by the providers of different sorts of capital, namely, financial and human. Preference gaps on the 'governance-web' may be minimized to support the design of maximum joint utility structures. Those combinations of mechanisms which generate more value for all involved parties may be regarded as 'complementary', that is, it may be said that the use of each mechanism increases the value of the application of the others (Milgrom and Roberts 1995). It is to this task that we turn now.

Expected Preferences of Different Capital Providers

Most available analyses of 'complementarities' of governance mechanisms are *ex post*, that is, the existence of complementarities is detected by correlations between the combined use of mechanisms and some performance or generated value variable. However, the analysis would be stronger if we were able to predict which combinations should generate more value. In our case, this would imply a prediction of the configuration of key actor preferences over governance mechanisms and of those combinations which can generate more value. We expect more than one superior combination for various reasons:

- the capital provider groups may well be internally differentiated, allowing the formation of 'coalitions' or matches between complementary types of human and financial capital providers;
- even if the 'game' were between two actors, each with just one preference structure, if there is cooperative potential, then a set of non-dominated solutions rather than one optimal solution typically exists (Luce and Raiffa 1958); and
- there is substitutability between different types of governance mechanisms, especially between control and incentive mechanisms: that is, they can be equi-functional to achieve similar outcomes (Coles, McWilliam, and Sen 2001).

There are reasons to expect that financial and human capital providers will rank some of the listed attributes in different ways according to preference. In spite of the common interest in not applying technically inefficient mechanisms (for example, unable to convey complex information where needed, board too large to take any decisions, and so on), there might be distributive issues on rights and resource allocation grounds.

We have said that preferences should be empirically assessed rather than assumed. As for any empirical endeavor, however, hypotheses on expected configurations will strengthen the interpretation of results. Where do we expect convergence and where do we expect divergence, and in what direction, on the various dimensions?

On some dimensions, *complementary preferences* can be expected, thanks to the quasi-indifference of some parties or genuine convergence of interests. In particular, we expect that high levels of discretion and autonomy should be preferred by everybody, as managers get more intrinsic rewards and the firm more competent and timely decisions. It is unlikely, however, that managers are quasi-indifferent with regard to the content of their activities, as in classical employment contracts (Simon 1951). Rather, the reverse is more likely to be true—human capital providers are extremely concerned with the content of their work, while financial capital providers may be quasi-indifferent toward the nature of performed tasks as long as the results are positive, as they do not have the relevant knowledge for selecting tasks and actions (the classical configuration of an employment relation is reversed). Therefore, we also expect that rich jobs providing high levels of intrinsic motivation and extensive team decision-making are ranked high, as complementary mechanisms.

On other aspects we can expect *conflicting preferences*, although in the form of variable-sum games with both need and space for compromise (rather than zero-sum games). These should include:

- managerial representation in boards of directors (involves distributive elements with regard to the available 'places' but also an everyone's interest in obtaining reliable representation and information);
- interfirm mobility (more in the interest of human capital providers for maximizing career opportunities, while the providers of other assets may prefer a relatively longer stay of firm-specific human capital);
- incidence of contingent pay (should be relatively more praised by financial investors than by human capital investors, but preferences may converge if relevant decision rights at the firm strategy level are granted to managers);
- the distribution of the costs of development of human capital (involves a distributive negotiation between the manager, investing in himself or herself, and the firm having incentives to invest only in firm-specific competence development);
- the form of governance of human capital mobility (networked careers tend to restrict access and personnel search, creating opportunity costs—especially for firms—and allowing managers to collude and eventually drain larger shares of rent than their contributions justify; hence, network governance is more interesting for 'career owners' while other investors should prefer a higher dose of either external or internal labor-market discipline); and
- on work effort there might be conflict at the margin on 'over-stress' (working hours beyond contractual levels).

Operationalizing and Testing the Model: A Study of Italian Capital Providers

Methods, Samples, and Variables

This section presents a comparative analysis of governance structure preferences of two groups: human capital providers and financial capital providers.

The human capital providers are managers, which can be considered 'critical human resources' for the firms employing them. This sample of managers (MGR) has been drawn from the population of people who have completed one of the main Italian master's programs in the last ten years. The incidence of postgraduate degrees in the Italian management population is still quite limited; hence, a master's degree from one of the best universities can be considered a significant human asset that firms try to attract (a similar proxy has also been employed in other studies: for example, Uzzi and Lancaster 2002). The sample of these 'human capital investors' is constituted by 201 units working in 190 different companies, which are typically of large size and distributed in a wide variety of industries.

TABLE 3.1 *Operationalization of human capital governance mechanisms*

Governance mechanisms	Dimensions
Reward rights	Incidence of residual rewards contingent on individual, group, and firm performance
Residual decision rights (at the institutional level)	Managerial representation in boards, managerial shareholding and ownership
Residual decision rights (at the work level)	Autonomy in work, location of work, incidence of teamwork
Work effort	Work hours per day, time pressure of external requests, and control over work (percentage of work time self-managed)
Work content	Relative importance of professional interest, social relations, power/prestige, innovativeness
Investments in human capital	Relative investment by individuals and by firms
Human capital mobility	Average stay in each firm in years
Governance of mobility	From market-like circulation to quasi-internal labor markets

In order to control the extent of possible deviation between the views of these managers—possibly representing a relatively young and dynamic group—and managers which are considered critical human capital providers by the firms employing them, we constructed another sample consisting of 'high potential' managers from three major Italian firms. Each firm distributed the questionnaire to the internal managers that they define as 'high potentials' (HP). This sample includes 60 cases.

A sample of financial investor representatives (BM) has been constructed by contacting the first 200 Italian firms and gathering one questionnaire per firm compiled by a chief board member (CEO or president). This sample consisting of 63 valid questionnaires. Those firms are also dispersed in various sectors and are not concentrated in any particular setting.

The questionnaires were constructed on eight variables, operationalizing the mechanisms discussed above and summarized in Table 3.1. The questionnaire for human capital providers asked respondents first to describe the configuration of governance mechanisms *as they are* in the firms where they work ('as-is' in the following tables); second to rank *desired mechanisms* according to preference ('would-be' in the following tables). The questionnaire for board members asked respondents to rank according to preference only the desired (would-be) configuration.

Results: General Configuration of Actual and Preferred Mechanisms

Tables 3.2 and 3.3 report the descriptives (mean and standard deviations) obtained by the governance variables 'as they are' (firms' actual policies),

TABLE 3.2 *Descriptive statistics of actual (as-is) and preferred governance mechanisms (would-be): Part I*

	Mean (standard. deviation)				Scales				
	Managers (MGR) (as-is)	Managers (MGR) (would-be)	Financial investor representatives (BM) (would-be)	Managers large firms (HP) (would-be)	1	2	3	4	5
Base pay (fixed compensation)	4.52 (1.11)	3.20 (1.12)	3.67 (0.62)	3.78 (0.68)	<20%	21–40%	41–60%	61–80%	81–100%
Compensation contingent on individual/group performance	1.50 (0.7)	3.24 (1.20)	2.56 (0.89)	2.78 (0.95)	<10%	10–25%	26–40%	41–60%	>60%
Compensation contingent on corporate results	1.23 (0.68)	2.1 (1.0)	2.19 (0.80)	1.95 (0.65)	<10%	10–25%	26–40%	41–60%	>60%
Average job tenure	2.39 (0.87)	2.97 (1.2)	3.93 (0.82)	3.88 (0.93)	<2 yrs	2–3 yrs	4–5 yrs	6–7 yrs	>7 years
Autonomy	3.45 (1.15)	3.40 (0.9)	3.25 (1.00)	4.08 (0.80)	<20%	20–40%	41–60%	61–80%	>80%
Team work	3.30 (1.15)	3.97 (0.90)	3.83 (0.99)	4.27 (0.88)	<20%	20–40%	41–60%	61–80%	>80%
Work time	3.34 (0.85)	2.5 (0.94)	3.19 (0.59)	2.81 (0.69)	7 hours	8 hours	9–10 hours	11–12 hours	>13 hours
Work pressure	4.06 (0.80)	4.11 (0.88)	3.89 (1.10)	4.20 (0.60)	<20%	20–39%	40–59%	60–79%	>80%
Proportion of managers on the board	2.85 (1.58)	3.47 (1.09)	2.43 (1.27)	2.07 (1.32)	<10%	10–25%	26–39%	40–50%	>50%
Employee shareholding	2.01 (1.39)	3.66 (0.98)	1.62 (0.67)	2.0 (0.72)	<5%	6–10%	11–25%	25–49%	≥50%
Firm investment in training	1.98 (1.06)	3.27 (1.11)	2.19 (0.67)	2.20 (0.63)	<5%	6–10%	11–20%	21–30%	>30%

TABLE 3.3 *Descriptive statistics of actual (as-is) and preferred governance mechanisms (would-be): Part 2*

	Mean (std. dev.)				Scales	
	Managers (MGR) (as-is)	Managers (MGR) (would-be)	Financial investor representatives (BM) (would-be)	Managers large firms (HP) (would-be)	Least important 1	Most important 3
Mobility governance mechanisms (1,2,3 importance index—on selected three items)						
Curriculum ('external labor market')	1.62 (1.05)	1.63 (0.99)	1.58 (1.25)	1.36 (1.25)		
Headhunter (brokered market)	0.92 (0.88)	1.40 (0.98)	1.37 (0.66)	1.70 (1.0)		
Internal network (former co-employees)	1.07 (1.18)	0.86 (1.17)	1.45 (1.20)	1.10 (1.18)		
External network (former business partners)	0.66 (1.47)	0.80 (1.15)	1.15 (1.31)	1.56 (1.12)		
Social-primary network (friends, circles, studies, relatives)	1.62 (1.22)	1.38 (1.27)	0.64 (1.12)	0.40 (0.77)		
Work content (1, 2, 3 importance index on each item)					Marginal benefit 1	Core benefit 3
Fit with competencies	1.61 (0.83)	1.97 (0.95)	1.66 (1.09)	2.37 (0.72)		
Status	1.06 (1.09)	1.39 (1.08)	1.03 (1.01)	1.71 (0.94)		
Innovativeness	2.27 (0.92)	2.29 (0.86)	2.21 (0.81)	2.55 (0.59)		
Sociability	1.50 (1.04)	1.18 (1.22)	0.93 (0.91)	1.64 (0.90)		
Leadership	1.41 (1.01)	1.67 (0.93)	1.95 (1.00)	2.03 (0.91)		

'as they should be' in our proxy human capital providers' most preferred configuration, and 'as they should be' in board members' preferred configuration and 'as they should be' in the view of internally selected 'high potential managers' in very large and established firms.

As hypothesized, preferred reward structures for everybody are 'mixed' and transfer moderate, but non negligible risk to managers. Managers themselves do not maximize fixed compensation, but their average preferred mix is of about 55 per cent of base wage, 30 per cent of compensation contingent on personal or small group performance, and some 15 per cent contingent on firm performance. An interesting feature of the results is the closeness between the preferred reward structures by *all* actors and their gap with the current, realized governance structure.

The issue of human capital mobility is more competitive. As expected, managers prefer short-tenure jobs, while board members (and co-opted managers) envisage careers in a more firm-specific long-term fashion. The actual average length of stay of managers in each firm is low in this relatively young, 'emerging', cohort of managers (three–four years), but it is in line with the value we found for the older but 'innovative', and probably more mobile than average, population of managers who have entered new-economy firms in top positions (Grandori *et al.* 2002) as well as for the average firm tenure in relatively 'mobile' countries (like the US). However, the managers studied here would be willing to extend their firm tenure to some extent (by one year or so). On the other hand, managers accompany this willingness to stay with a demand for more intensive investments in the development of human resources through training: those investments are at present divided almost equally between managers and firms and amount to about 10 per cent of the whole manager's compensation for each part. Managers are willing to maintain their 10 per cent investment but would like firms to raise their investments by between 10 per cent and 20 per cent; while BM would like to maintain firm investments in human capital development below 10 per cent. It may seem untenable that firms should invest significantly in training and accept a high turnover. However, as discussed, this may be the only way to realize innovative projects, with firm-specific components which should be developed by the firm and used only in those projects. Managers may themselves cover the long-term and less firm-specific components of investments in the development of their human capital.

On the grounds of decision and property right diffusion, the hypothesis of convergence of interests and of practices toward a high degree of discretion and self-determination in work fits with the high levels of autonomy declared and the slightly higher level demanded by our managers. More consistent increases, with respect to what is currently practised, are demanded in terms of teamwork and collegiality. The 'co-opted high potential managers' group shows a peak of utility for autonomy and for teamwork. This signals that the type of decision rights they look for is different from those preferred by the younger and more mobile managers.

On corporate democracy, in fact, the two managerial sub-samples differ even more markedly, from one another and from the board members, as expected. Managers would like a more substantial 'share' of representation in boards (40 per cent) than it is actually conceded and than BM would like to see (25 per cent). The current average representation share is around 30 per cent—not negligible. A similar configuration of preferences (with lower values) holds for the desired incidence of employee shareholding by MGR (25 per cent), although property rights in this sense are less diffused in practice (less than 10 per cent) and an even lower level is desired by BM.

These configurations of preferences on the allocation of decision rights give some signal that the hypothesized differentiation between two different populations of managers—one more 'agent-like' and another more 'principal-like'—actually exist. This conjecture is further tested by means of the cluster analysis conducted in the next section.

On human capital mobility governance mechanisms, differences in evaluations are not marked, but are in the predicted direction. Everyone, but especially MGR, praises a mix of governance mechanisms, including the currently extensively applied social network and market-like governance mechanisms. However, everyone would like to increase the importance of brokers' markets and professional networks (Table 3.3), as expected. The differentiation of actors' preferences are also in the predicted direction, as BM are more favorable to quasi-internal labor markets (networks of former employers and co-employees) while young and mobile managers are more favorable toward 'private' social networks.

Among intrinsic rewards (job content), firms do provide innovative tasks, and that is considered to be, and wanted to remain, a 'major reason for doing the work' they are in, basically in agreement with boards' heads (Table 3.3). As expected, work effort is an issue of over-stress rather than of shirking. Firms do not seem to exert significant pressure on how managers allocate their effort: managers declare that the allocation of their attention and effort to tasks is self-determined for a mean percentage of 70 per cent, and both managers and BM are happy with this situation. However, actual working times are extremely extended (averaging around eleven hours a day) and BM would like to maintain this level of effort, while all managers would like to reduce it (Table 3.2).

Commenting generally on Tables 3.2 and 3.3, we can note the following. First, a notable pattern is that the preferences of 'human capital investors' and those of the closest representatives of financial capital investors (board presidents and CEOs) are much closer to one another than is usually thought; moreover, they rank high those governance arrangements that are reasonably close to theoretically efficient configurations. A second counter-intuitive, interesting finding of this study is that 'managers may be more Catholic than the Pope': managers' preferred policies seem even more aligned with firms' theoretical interests than are the preferences of financial investors, and certainly far more than firms' actual policies are. In fact, a third, striking, result is that firm actual policies—especially on reward—are dominated and inefficient with respect to both actors' preferences and theoretically efficient solutions. In other words, they are solutions that nobody wants.

To explain why and how this apparent 'social dilemma' situation has come about is beyond the scope of this chapter. Actual firm incentives structures may be close to the preferences of other actors not included in this survey: for example the (usually 'concentrated') financial owners themselves (who might differ from those of their BM delegated representatives). Or they are devised to respond to imaginary (or extinct) managers whose risk-aversion is much greater than that of actual managers. Alternatively, the current situation may be trapped in 'structural inertia' and/or 'institutional isomorphism' effects (Hannan and Freeman 1984; Powell and Di Maggio 1991): none of the key actors likes current solutions, but they are inherited from the past and are difficult to change as there are legal and institutional constraints that reinforce them. But whatever the explanation, the identified gaps between existing arrangements and superior configurations (both in theory and in parties' preferences respects) clearly suggest directions for improvement.

Second, the preferred governance arrangements are, as expected, hybrid combinations of mechanisms: high decentralization of decision rights, high incidence of 'team-like' governance, intermediate levels of 'high-powered incentives' (residual rewards); in addition, residual decision and control rights that are unbundled and shared in various degrees among actors rather than allocated as a bundle to just one type of actor.

This general picture can be refined by analyzing whether actors cluster around more than one configuration, that is, whether sub-groups of MGR and BM can find superior agreements on different packages. A cluster analysis is performed to this purpose.

Are There Coalitions? A Negotiation Analysis of Superior
Governance Arrangements

Do clusters of actors meet around more than one superior solution? Cluster analysis is employed to find those matches between preference functions that minimize distances between utility functions.

A two-group cluster analysis in presented in the Appendix. Figure 3.1 reports the cluster means of the two clusters across the governance variables. It also includes the mean for the actual structures (as-is).

With the exception of the variable 'autonomy' (on which there are basically no differences) the differences between the two clusters are statistically significant.

Cluster 1 is composed almost fifty-fifty of board members (BM) and managers (MGR), even though this means that almost three-quarters of all BM and one-quarter of all MGR are included in it. In contrast, Cluster 2 is composed almost exclusively of managers (see Appendix). This analysis

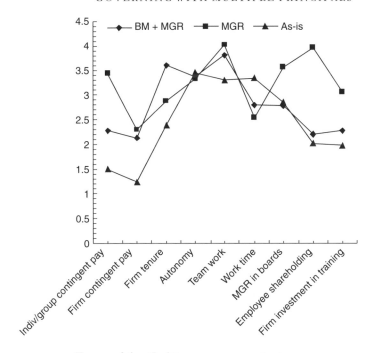

FIGURE 3.1 *Coalitions on governance structures.*
Note: Cluster analysis of preferences. Scores are the preference values 1–5 given
in Table 3.2. BM: Board members. MGR: Managers. As-is: Mean for actual
structures.

is conducted only on the master alumni sample (as co-opted high-potential
managers have actually and already found an agreement package, and it is
very close to what BM offer). The two clusters converge on three variables
(Fig. 3.1): autonomy, group work, and work effort. As in the overall sample,
high levels of discretion and teaming are generally efficient for everyone;
and work effort is not a conflict issue.

Where there are differences, as expected, is on incentive structures, mobility and investments in training, and corporate-level democracy (managerial
representation in boards, employee shareholding).

Cluster 1 represents a MGR/BM coalition around the following levels of
those governance variables:

- lower incidence of rewards contingent on individual and group
  performance;
- longer job tenures;
- symmetric and moderate investments in human capital; and
- lower levels of managerial representation in boards and ownership.

This combination of mechanisms is characterized by extensive 'delegation of
power' and a decentralized and team-like internal organization, but a limited

diffusion of residual decision and control reward rights. In other words, wide managerial discretion is coupled with protection from risk but relatively low involvement in ownership and firm-level decision making. Theoretically, the form can be conceived as a (relatively traditional) 'principal-agent hierarchy' (Grandori 1997a)—a decentralized form of hierarchy based on an agency relation rather than on an authority relation. However, some original features are worth noticing. As an agency relationship is founded on a 'delegation of the power to decide', even though in the interest of a principal, the essential component of this agreement, especially for agents, resides in the extent and credibility of delegation in the first place. The results of this research confirm that the extent of delegated power and managerial autonomy are essential, for both motivational and information-processing effectiveness reasons. High discretion is not complemented by significant investments in either incentives or monitoring—as agency theory would predict—but rather by high intrinsic motivation and peer control. The theoretical reasons identified here for this combination reside in the limits to both effective monitoring and significant risk transfers in complex, uncertain activities.

Almost all BM sustain this arrangement, but only a minority (albeit not negligible) of managers. In fact, the preferences of the control group of 'high potential managers' as defined by major firms are much closer to this cluster than to the following Cluster 2.

Cluster 2 is a group of 'managers in search for investors'. In fact, few of the investors' representatives of large Italian firms would rank the deal sought by these managers high. The preferred governance mix is characterized by:

- an acceptance of more significant risk-bearing;
- a demand for decision rights also at the corporate level and for diffused ownership; and
- higher levels of human resource mobility and of firm investments in human capital development.

Coupled with decentralized and team-like internal organization that everyone supports, this arrangement includes a more democratic allocation of firm-level decision and property rights with high flexibility and mobility of human capital. It is quite an unexpected cluster of mechanisms if traditional conceptual lenses are used. It calls for a system that is able to govern shifting resources, enabling them to participate fully to firm governance in the short term. However, these requirements are in fact consistent with the now recognized needs of a creative, innovative, and temporary association (Meyerson, Weick, and Kramer 1996). What seems to be inconsistent can actually be explained: it is a (rather innovative) 'swift' form of multiple principals 'democracy', wherein the possibility of generating firm-specific services rests on ad hoc investments in training, titles to participation should be formally recognized for being quickly exercised, willingness to bear risk and the preference for immediate distribution of performance gains are stronger, and significant residual decision and control rights at the firm level are demanded.

Conclusions

The codification of the two observed forms and of their differences suggests that they belong to a wider portfolio of possible forms. In fact, they enrich the traditionally envisaged 'principal-agent' and 'principal-principal' governance forms. In fact, the typical 'principal-agent' governance arrangement is conceived as a short-term contract, based on clear performance parameters, involving significant risk transfers and subject to a market discipline (the prototype of managers in an 'agent' position being, say, franchisees or insurance agents). By contrast, multiple principal governance is conceived as a long-lasting partner-specific association of stakeholders (the prototype being the professional partnership). The two solutions we have discovered combine in a different way the two dimensions of governance that have emerged as critically important in this study: *democracy* and *time*. One arrangement is a 'principal-agent hierarchy' but is long-term and more firm-specific. The other arrangement is a 'multiple principal democracy' but is short-term and less firm-specific.

A first general contribution produced by this study is the identification of new effective combinations of governance mechanisms, new governance structures to add to the available portfolio. It has been argued that they are effective where 'managers' (a quite ample category to be treated as a homogeneous group) are responsible for highly complex and/or innovative activities, as those conditions jeopardize both the conventional 'incentive and control' approaches and 'marriage-like partnership' solutions. The new forms identified suggest that the two dimensions of democracy and time can usefully complement the current focus on just one core dimension of governance, namely, accountability.

Second, the study has shown that unbundling 'property rights' and assigning them to different actors in various degrees—rather than treating 'ownership' as a unitary concept or a package of rights that cannot be separated—is indeed possible and useful.

Third, the study emphasizes the tight complementarities between property rights and 'governance mechanisms' in the usual narrow sense of the term—involving the allocations of 'residual control and reward rights'—and 'organization rights and mechanisms'—intended as allocations of decision, control, reward, action, and information rights of residual and non residual types (in fact, the two classes of rights and mechanisms largely overlap). Hence, a discussion on 'corporate governance' which does not pay attention to the internal organization of the firm is rather incomplete, and possibly dangerous.

Finally, the study has treated the preferences and utility of key actors as matters on which we have to advance testable hypotheses as opposed to making assumptions. The approach revealed interesting differences between the actual utility functions of both human capital providers and financial capital providers and the utility functions conventionally assumed in organizational economic models. In particular, if managers see the 'benefit side' of risk and effort (rather than seeing them in a 'cost and loss' frame), and principals see the 'benefit side' of managerial discretion (rather than just agency costs)—as seems to be the case—different solutions to the 'corporate governance problem' may be found. And after all, in many cases, policies based on frequent actual behaviors are wiser than policies based on the theoretical possibility of very unlikely behaviors.

Appendix: Cluster Analysis

Composition of clusters

	Number of cases	Sub-groups within clusters	Share of the total samples
Cluster 1	113	51% board members 49% managers	92% board members 27% managers
Cluster 2	143	99% managers 1% board members	70% managers 3% board members

Analysis of variance between two clusters

Variables	F (variance)	p (significance)
Indiv./group contingent pay	73.15	0.00
Firm contingent pay	84.19	0.00
Firm tenure	23.65	0.00
Autonomy	0.19	0.66
Team work	3.65	0.05
Work time	5.35	0.02
MGR in boards	29.48	0.000000
Employee shareholding	226.19	0.000000
Firm investment in training	31.13	0.000000

Cluster descriptives

Cluster means	Cluster 1	Cluster 2
Indiv./group contingent pay	2.28	3.43
Firm contingent pay	2.13	3.29
Firm tenure	3.60	2.88
Autonomy	3.38	3.33
Team work	3.80	4.03
Work time	2.81	2.55
MGR in boards	2.79	3.57
Employee shareholding	2.21	3.97
Firm investment in training	2.28	3.06

References

Alchian, A. and Demsetz, H. (1972). 'Production, Information Costs and Economic Organization', *American Economic Review*, 62: 777–95.

Barney, J. (1991). 'Firm Resources and Sustained Competitive Advantage', *Journal of Management*, 17: 99–120.

Bazerman, M. (1986). *Judgment in Managerial Decision Making*. New York: Wiley.

Becker, G. (1964). *Human Capital: A Theoretical and Empirical Analysis, with Special Reference to Education*. New York: Columbia University Press.

Blair, M. (1995). *Ownership and Control: Rethinking Corporate Governance for the 21st Century*. Washington, DC: Brookings Institution.

—— (1996). *Wealth Creation and Wealth Sharing: A Colloquium an Corporate Governance and Investments in Human Capital*. Washington, DC: Brookings Institution.

Bloom, M. and Milkovich, G. (1998). 'Relationships Among Risk, Incentive Pay, and Organizational Performance', *Academy of Management Journal*, 41/3: 283–97.

Coles, J., McWilliam, V., and Sen, N. (2001). 'An Examination of the Relationship of Governance Mechanisms to Performance', *Journal of Management*, 27: 23–50.

Demsetz, H. (1991). 'The Theory of the Firm Revisited', in O. Williamson and S. Winter (eds.), *The Nature of The Firm: Origins, Evolution and Development*. Oxford: Oxford University Press.

Fama, E. and Jensen, M. (1983). 'Separation of Ownership and Control', *Journal of Law and Economics*, 26: 301–25.

Grandori, A. (1991). 'Negotiating Efficient Organization Forms', *Journal of Economic Behavior and Organization*, 16: 319–40.

—— (1997*a*). 'Agency, Markets and Hierarchies', in A. Sorge and M. Warner (eds.), *International Encyclopedia of Business and Management: Handbook of Organizational Behaviour*. London: Routledge.

—— (1997*b*). 'Governance Structures, Coordination Mechanisms and Cognitive Models', *Journal of Management and Governance*, 1: 29–47.

—— (2001*a*). *Organization and Economic Behavior*. London: Routledge.

—— (2001*b*). 'Methodological Options for an Integrated Perspective on Organization', *Human Relations: Millennium Special Issue*, 54/1: 37–47.

——, Solari, L., Usai, A., and Bagdadli, S. (2002). 'The Governance of Human Capital: Lessons from Emerging Industries'. Invited paper, Harvard Business School conference 'The evolution of careers', London, 13–14 June.

Hannan, M. and Freeman, J. (1984). 'Structural Inertia and Organizational Change', *American Sociological Review*, 49: 149–64.

Hansman, H. (1996). *The Ownership of Enterprise*. Cambridge, MA: Harvard University Press.

Hart, O. (1995). *Firms, Contracts and Financial Structure*. Oxford: Oxford University Press.

—— and Moore J. (1990). 'Property Rights and the Nature of the Firm', *Journal of Political Economy*, 98: 19–58.

—— —— (1994). 'A Theory of Debt Based on the Inalienability of Human Capital', *The Quarterly Journal of Economics*, 109: 841–79.

Hatchuel, A. (2001). 'Towards Design Theory and Expandable Rationality: The Unfinished Program of Herbert Simon', *Journal of Management and Governance*, 5/3/4: 260–73.

Jensen, M. and Meckling, W. (1976). 'Theory of the Firm: Managerial Behavior, Agency Costs and Ownership Structure', *Journal of Financial Economics*, 3: 305–60.

Karpik, L. (1989). 'L'économie de la qualité', *Review Française de Sociologie*, 30/2: 187–210.

Luce, R. and Raiffa, H. (1958). *Games and Decisions.* New York: Wiley.

Meyerson, D., Weick, K., and Kramer, R. (1996). 'Swift Trust and Temporary Groups', in R. Kramer and T. Tyler (eds.), *Trust in Organizations: Frontiers of Theory and Research.* Thousand Oaks, CA: Sage.

Milgrom, P. and Roberts, J. (1992). *Economics, Organization and Management.* Englewood Cliffs: Prentice-Hall.

——— (1995). 'Complementarities and Fit: Strategy, Structure and Organizational Change in Manufacturing', *Journal of Accounting and Economics*, 19: 179–208.

Miller, G. (1992). *Managerial Dilemmas: The Political Economy of Hierarchy.* Cambridge: Cambridge University Press.

Osterloh, M., Frey, B., and Frost, J. (2001). 'Managing Motivation, Organization and Governance', *Journal of Management and Governance*, 5/3/4: 231–39.

Ouchi, W. (1979). 'A Conceptual Framework for Design of Organizational Control Mechanism', *Management Science*, 25: 833–48.

Penrose, E. (1959). *The Theory of the Growth of the Firm.* New York: Wiley.

Piore, M. (2001). 'Thirty Years Later: Internal Labor Markets, Flexibility and the New Economy', *Journal of Management and Governance*, 6: 271–9.

Powell, W. and Di Maggio, P. (eds.) (1991). *The New Institutionalism in Organizational Analysis.* Chicago: University of Chicago Press.

Simon, H. (1951). 'A Formal Theory of the Employment Relationship', *Econometrica*, 19: 293–305.

Useem, M. (1996), 'Corporate Restructuring and the Restructured World of Senior Management', in P. Osterman (ed.), *Broken ladders: Managerial Careers in the New Economy.* Oxford: Oxford University Press.

Uzzi, B. and Lancaster, R. (2002). 'Social Embeddedness and Price Formation in the Large Law Firm Market', paper delivered at an international conference 'Perspectives on competition and Cooperation', University of Umea, 5–7 May.

Varian, H. (1990). 'Monitoring Agents with Other Agents', *Journal of Institutional and Theoretical Economics*, 146/I: 153–74 (special issue on The New Institutional Economics).

Williamson, O. (1979). 'Transaction Cost Economics: The Governance of Contractual Relations', *Journal of Law and Economics*, 22: 233–61.

4

Corporate Governance in International Joint Ventures: Toward a Theory of Partner Preferences

JOHN CHILD AND SUZANA B. RODRIGUES

The formation of joint ventures (JVs) has become an increasingly popular means for companies to realize their strategic objectives (Doz and Hamel 1998). As a result, the field of study known as cooperative strategy came into fashion during the 1990s, following the attention that had been accorded to competitive strategy during the 1980s (Faulkner and de Rond 2000). The crossing of organizational boundaries through partnership was regarded as a particularly promising way for companies to secure a competitive advantage through enhancing market power, realizing economies, overcoming market entry barriers, achieving technological synergy, or other benefits (Dussauge and Garrette 1999). Many joint ventures today also cross national boundaries, being formed between partners from different countries (Beamish and Killing 1997).

JVs have been characterized as 'hybrid' organizations (Borys and Jemison 1989) in the sense that both their ownership and their management are typically shared between two or a small number of partner firms. This complication introduces a new theoretical challenge (Parkhe 1993) that has elicited a response from many perspectives (Ramanathan, Seth, and Thomas 1997; Faulkner and de Rond 2000). Important contributions to the analysis of JVs have come from market power theory, transaction-cost economics, agency theory, increasing returns theory, game theory, strategic management theory, and organizational theory (Child and Faulkner 1998). Yet, despite the scope of this list, one significant aspect of this organizational form continues to be almost totally neglected, namely, the corporate governance of JVs.

The significance of corporate governance for JVs is indicated by the fact that their relatively high failure rate is usually ascribed to a breakdown in relations between their owning partners (Singh and Mitchell 1996). The governance of *international* JVs (IJVs) formed between partner firms from different countries is likely to be even more precarious due to cultural differences and to potential dissonance between the governance regulations of the host country location and the governance preferences of one or more partners. A common form of IJV is that established between an international company and a local domestic company in the country where the venture operates. This arrangement is frequently found in emerging economies, and it serves as a potentially important vehicle for the transfer of technology and knowledge that can contribute to the development of such economies. The discussion to follow has this form of IJV particularly in mind and concentrates on the IJV governance preferences of the international ('foreign') partner. This is partly to provide focus to the analysis and partly to highlight the implications that such partners' governance preferences have for the ability of IJVs to promote economic development through knowledge transfer to local partners.

The aim of this chapter is to suggest key elements in a theory of corporate governance in international joint ventures. Given the nature of IJVs as a subject, it is appropriate to adopt a relatively broad definition of corporate governance as the process of control over and within the firm (that is, the IJV) that aims to reduce risk to its owners and to ensure that its activities bring a stream of acceptable returns to those owners in the long term. This definition draws attention to the behavioural and internal aspects of governance in addition to the purely structural and external aspects that have historically commanded most attention in the governance literature (such as Monks and Minow 2001).

The following section identifies the areas of risk that a company investing in an IJV can face with regard to financial, resource, and market requirements. These risks are seen to derive from two main sources: the institutional and economic context in which the IJV is located and the special condition of multiple agency that pertains in joint ventures. The chapter then offers an analytical framework that links the nature and sources of risk to the expected governance preferences of foreign IJV partners. These expectations are expressed in the form of propositions that are offered as a guide to further reflection and investigation. The chapter concludes with the implications of foreign partners' governance preferences for the capacity of IJVs to transfer knowledge to emerging economies.

Areas of Risk

Three areas of risk for IJV partners concern finance, resource deficiency, and lack of market opportunity. IJV partners can incur a *financial risk* over and above normal commercial uncertainties. The additional financial risk stems largely from the possibility that their investment could be eroded by specific administrative factors in the host country that reduce the level of return on the investment or the ease of repatriating it, and even threats to their ownership rights. These risks are liable to be greater in emerging economies because of their institutional limitations. These include less adequate legal regulations and provisions for the protection of intellectual property, as well as greater political risk (Peng 2000). Moreover, the risks attaching to the asset specificity of investment may be increased by the absence of well-developed secondary markets for the disposal of assets in the event of IJV termination. Additional financial risk can also result from governmental actions such as devaluation and changes in interest rates. For example, the uncertainty created by such actions discouraged foreign investment into Brazil before the stabilization reforms of the 1990s (Barros 1993). Fraudulent or other opportunistic behavior on the part of other IJV partners can pose a further financial risk.

A *resource-deficiency risk* arises if the resources available to an IJV are inadequate for it to operate as a viable business, including the inability to make best use of some resources due to skill or motivational deficiencies. Again, this risk is more likely to arise for an IJV based in an emerging economy than in a developed country (Rodrigues and Child 2001). In an emerging economy, resources may be in short supply and the relevant markets imperfect; it is also more likely that local partners lack important capabilities and resources.

Market-opportunity risk arises from the possibility that firms may enter new markets with an inaccurate appraisal of the opportunities these offer for achieving an acceptable return on the investment incurred. This is a particular risk for companies lacking international experience, which may underestimate the strength of local competition or the advantages already enjoyed by first-mover entrants (Lieberman and Montgomery 1988). Local partners may fail to deliver the market access they promised, perhaps because their distribution networks are too local or ineffective. This has been a common complaint of foreign-investing firms in China (EIU 1999).

Sources of Risk

There are two main sources of financial, resource, and market risk facing a foreign IJV partner. One is the local institutional and economic context in which the IJV is located. The risks arising from this context may therefore be called *contextual risks*. The other source of risk derives from the special condition of multiple agency that characterizes joint ventures, in which the local partner(s) also acts as an agent for the foreign partner (and vice versa). The risks arising from this source may be called *agency risks*. Following Dunning (1998), the first set of risks involve relationships between the venture and the local environment and are linked to 'locational' features, while agency risks stem from relationships intrinsic to the IJV itself. Moreover, we shall note how contextual conditions can moderate the level of agency risk. Table 4.1 summarizes the forms of financial, resource and market risk that can derive from contextual and agency sources.

TABLE 4.1   *Risks facing (foreign) IJV partners*

Source of risk	Area of risk		
	Financial	Resource	Market
Context			
Institutional	• limits to majority control	• underdeveloped intermediate institutions (business support services)	• restrictions on business, land use, and other licenses
	• inadequate minority owner protection		• informal local protectionism
	• poor contract enforcement		
	• poor accounting standards		
	• inadequate protection of intellectual property		
Economic	• inadequate working capital and liquidity	• lack of capital	• low rate of growth and GNP per capita
		• inadequate managerial and technical expertise	• instability of economy
Agency			
Partner(s) as agent	• partner engages in fraudulent or other opportunistic behavior	• deficiencies in partner's capabilities and resources	• partner cannot or will not deliver access to domestic market
	• exploitation of minority interests	• loyalty of managers and staff from partner is limited	

Contextual Risks

The impact of the *institutional context* on partner risks becomes particularly apparent in the international context where many IJVs are formed between multinational corporations (MNCs) and local firms. Here the effectiveness of the host location's legal system and the attitude of regulatory authorities are crucial.

For instance, the level of protection afforded to corporate investors has been found to vary significantly between countries (La Porta, Lopez-de-Silanes, and Shleifer 1998). Protection can be assessed in terms of various measures including legal recourse for the non-fulfillment of contracts, mechanisms to safeguard minority shareholders, risk of expropriation of assets, and accounting standards. In so far as many IJVs are vehicles for technology transfer, the extent to which intellectual property is effectively protected from the risk of leakage is another major concern to 'foreign' investors.

Local regulations, as well as norms of custom and practice, will define the formal corporate governance options that are available to IJV partners. These institutional features are likely to be 'cultural' in the sense of being historically embedded, and thus to display a high degree of path dependence (North 1990). At the same time, as Porter's analysis (1990) suggests, institutional and legal development is itself a function of the level of economic development and progress towards modernization. National institutions are expected to moderate both the possibilities of choice among corporate governance structures for firms located there and the corporate governance preferences of local owners and other local stakeholders. Thus, the possible choices of governance in strategic alliances are shaped by institutional factors through the mediation of national regulations and formats for corporate governance. An example is the shift toward a policy of economic liberalization in Brazil during the 1990s, which was reflected in changes in rules governing business ownership, including privatization. This in turn encouraged the formation of majority foreign-owned IJVs as well as outright acquisitions.

Some countries continue to impose legal restrictions on the share of IJV equity that can be taken up by foreign partners (at least in certain sectors), and hence limit the ability of those partners to protect their investment and resource provision through normal governance mechanisms such as holding a majority on the JV's board of directors. This remains the case in China, which is now the world's largest recipient of foreign direct investment, much of it leading to the formation of IJVs. China also provides an example of how an immature legal system and unpredictable behavior on the part of government agencies have created additional risks for foreign investors in IJVs (Child and Tse 2001). Even when, as in China, World Trade Organization (WTO) membership now places limits on institutional restrictions, they will remain in force for some time to come in strategic sectors of the economy (Nolan 2001).

Some of the institutional restrictions found in situations like China are applied informally, such as when local government agencies refuse business licenses to foreign-funded ventures in order to protect local firms from competition, or when product piracy and leakage of technology on the part of local IJV partners are condoned as 'patriotic acts'. Informal institutional behavior of this kind can clearly present a risk both to the achievement of market opportunities and in terms of agency costs. It impacts upon agency risk in that opportunism on the part of a local partner and/or local managers might be encouraged by a legal system that failed to support redress or an administrative regime that protected such behavior on the part of local actors. In this way, institutions can lend different degrees of support for trust between local and foreign partners (Child and Möllering 2003).

The extent to which intermediate institutions have developed impacts on the risk of deficiency in the resources required to operate an IJV successfully. Such institutions supply necessary business support services. If, for example, banking, legal, market research, technical consulting, and basic utility services are not readily available or are unreliable, this will either hamper the efficiency of the IJV directly or incur additional costs of supplying these resources from outside the country or region.

In these ways, the institutional context in which an IJV operates has a direct bearing on the level of risk incurred by an IJV partner, especially the 'foreign' investor from outside the host country, in respect of finance, resource deficiency, and market opportunity.

The *economic context* in which IJVs are located also impacts on the level of risk in each of these three areas. A shortage of working capital and liquid funds within the economy can add to the financial risk that an IJV faces. Similarly, if the instability of the local economy places an IJV's local partner under financial stress, this is likely to encourage opportunistic behavior on its part. For example, the high level of inflation that characterized the Brazilian economy in the 1980s encouraged companies there to engage in opportunistic behavior which exploited profits from price rises rather than from efficient production. Major shifts in government policy in respect of exchange rates, taxation, interest rates, or governance regimes both increase the level of risk and encourage defensive behavior of an opportunistic kind. A relatively low level of economic development, combined possibly with a lack of experience in joint-venture partnering, is also likely to limit the capabilities of a local partner to act as an effective agent for the other partner to achieve the objectives it seeks from the IJV.

The major risk impacts of the economic context are, however, likely to fall in the areas of resource deficiency and market opportunity. While many IJVs have been formed to provide MNCs with access to cheap labor, as in central and eastern Europe and parts of south-east Asia, a lack of other local resources such as working capital, managerial and technical expertise, and business support services can pose a threat to an IJV's viability. At the same time, resource deficiency in the local context can provide an opportunity for foreign partners to dominate IJV governance though funding a larger share of equity and providing other assets. Such dominance may also be regarded as essential to overcome inadequacies of experience and even trustworthiness among the local partner's managers. In line with the 'resource dependency' analysis of external organizational control (Pfeffer and Salancik 1978), the more dependent an IJV is on the resources provided by one of its partners, the greater the power one would expect that partner to have in its governance.

Another significant aspect of the economic context lies in the market opportunities that it offers. Its combination of high growth rates and a huge population is the prime reason why China has attracted so much foreign direct investment despite the other contextual difficulties that have operated there in the past. Market risk in China has arisen mainly as a result of institutional constraints, such as difficulties of securing licenses for distribution, rather than from insufficient or volatile market demand. In other countries such as Argentina, by contrast, uncertainties regarding the stability of the market per se have presented the greater risk. The instances mentioned of how institutional intervention over licenses or access to local sources of capital can impact on economic conditions serve to remind us that, in practice, economic and institutional contexts interact.

Agency Risks: Multiple Agency

Agency theory is concerned with the ability of 'principals' to ensure that their 'agents' are fulfilling their objectives. Within the Anglo-Saxon tradition of corporate governance, equity owners are regarded as the principals. Their vulnerability stems from their position as residual claimants in the sense that their returns depend upon all other contractual claims that have to be satisfied first (Shleifer and Vishny 1997). This means that self-serving or ineffective agents could respectively appropriate or dissipate such returns. Agency theory assumes that agents cannot necessarily be trusted and that this creates a serious risk for principals when there is an asymmetry of information in favor of their agents. It is therefore concerned with the governance mechanisms that limit agents' self-serving behavior (Berle and Means 1932; Jensen and Meckling 1976; Eisenhardt 1989).

The agency issue can also involve relations between shareholders themselves. Ideally, dominant shareholders will have regard for the interests of the minority, and managers will look after the interests of both. Evidence provided by some authors, such as La Porta, Lopez-de-Silanes, and Shleifer (1998) and Claessens et al. (1999), suggests, however, that wherever there is a dominant shareholder there is a tendency for minority shareholders to be sidelined. Lazonick and O'Sullivan (1996, 2000) also suggest that institutional investors will emphasize short-term returns at the expense of those investors who seek to develop the intrinsic worth of their companies through, for example, investing in innovation.

Multiple agency refers to a situation in which there is more than one party in agency relationships, as principals, or agents, or both. The formation of equity joint ventures is an important instance of multiple agency. This form of strategic alliance involves a pooling of ownership assets and usually a degree of joint management between partner firms.

The multiplicity of agency relationships in equity joint ventures arises from three of their salient characteristics. First, there are only a few owners, often only two. They have to be regarded as multiple principals because each has its own rationale for entering into the alliance and each is sufficiently salient to require its interests to be respected. Thus, if one partner decides to withdraw, the alliance normally breaks down. Second, because the owner-partners usually contribute complementary tangible and intangible assets to the joint venture (Geringer 1991), they also in effect become agents for each other in ensuring its viability. In other words, a joint venture cannot survive without the contributions of each partner, which places one partner in the role of acting as an agent for the fulfillment of the objectives that the other(s) invests in the venture. Third, the managers of the joint venture act as agents for its owners. Their agency role is often complicated by the presence of multiple owners, when each places its own expectations upon venture managers. Further problems can arise if the joint venture is managed by a mix of personnel who are supplied or appointed by the different partners, especially if they come from different national cultures and traditions of management practice (Shenkar and Zeira 1992).

The property rights over a joint venture, including rights of ultimate control, legally belong to the partners who contribute key assets to it on a contractual basis, especially in the form of equity (Hansman 1996). In practice, IJVs also depend on other assets that are provided by the partners outside of equity and often on a non-contractual basis: usually less tangible assets such as expertise, operating systems, and training. Non-contractual assets of this kind are essentially knowledge assets (Boisot 1998), and it is more difficult to safeguard property rights over them. Foreign IJV partners are in fact often concerned to protect the knowledge assets they provide to an IJV from leakage or misapplication. They can do so by allocating their own personnel to take charge of the assets and control their use, and the presence in an IJV of such staff may in any case be necessary for the assets to be used effectively. For reasons such as these, the provision of non-contractual knowledge assets by a partner has been found to predict its level of control in IJVs, especially over operational decisions (Child and Yan 1999).

In IJVs between international companies and partners from emerging countries, it is normally the former who are in a position to provide advanced knowledge assets. While it is consistent with corporate governance principles for control to go to those who provide assets (of whatever kind), if a foreign partner chooses to exercise tight and restrictive control over the knowledge assets it provides to an IJV, the effectiveness of the venture as a vehicle for knowledge transfer is likely to be compromised.

The strong potential for conflict between joint venture partners is a complicating factor. Even when the partners have completely compatible objectives, issues of fairness often arise with respect to the relative contributions to and benefits from the joint venture on the part of each partner. These problems are exacerbated if one partner is able to tip this cost-benefit balance in its favor through, for example, acquiring an advantage over the other partner in technology and other knowledge through superior learning (Hamel 1991). Uncertainty about how an alliance will evolve in terms of satisfying partner interests is likely to be high for the 'foreign' partner in an IJV if it lacks knowledge and experience of the host location, and of the local partner's capabilities and power to exercise leverage within that location. It may also fear the leakage of key knowledge assets through the IJV.

Moreover, each partner may be uncertain about the long-term intentions of the other toward their partnership.

Agency risk is therefore a broad category referring to a range of possible moral, legal, and managerial failures in an IJV relationship that can give rise to non-delivery, even default, on agreements or expectations. It arises if other partner(s) or IJV managers are either not competent or are not willing to meet a partner's formal and informal expectations. Competency limitations are more likely to arise when the host location of an IJV is an emerging economy. Opportunistic behavior by another partner is always a danger in joint ventures, including attempts to expropriate key resources from the first partner purposely, to overtake it or to drive it from the market (Doz and Hamel 1998). In emerging economies, institutional authorities sometimes condone opportunistic behavior by local IJV partners and managers (in their role as agents for the 'foreign' investor), which is justified on the grounds of catching up with an economically privileged partner. MNCs can themselves demonstrate opportunistic behavior toward local companies, using various devices to enhance their power such as placing key departments under their own managers even when they only have a minority holding. In order to prevent opportunistic behavior by either party, some countries like Brazil have devised shareholders' agreement instruments that define the special powers of the partners.

IJV owners have to face additional types of agency risk. A partner with a minority holding can be more vulnerable wherever the governance system favors concentration without appropriate protection of minority investors. If the proportion of equity held by an owner is large enough to ensure control of the company, there is incentive for that owner to reduce the return to the minority partners (La Porta, Lopez-de-Silanes, and Shleifer 1998; Valadares and Leal 2000). A further common problem of agency in IJVs concerns the loyalty of its managers. IJVs involve partners of different nationalities and cultural identities. Even when a foreign owner nominates them, local managers can feel their loyalty divided between demands of this principal on the one hand and the local partner and community on the other.

The degree of agency dependence between partners can be asymmetric if one of them possesses superior resources and capabilities. MNCs typically possess superior technological and managerial capabilities that provide them with sufficient influence to exercise considerable control, especially in the early years of IJVs with local firms (Child and Yan 2003). MNCs can also benefit from an accumulation of political capital if they are early entrants or are willing to locate in priority areas designated by host governments (Frynas, Mellahi, and Pigman 2003). Nevertheless, in contexts where government involvement in the conditions for doing business (such as the granting of land, the right to access working capital, and trading licenses) remains high, a local JV partner may retain considerable influence if it enjoys substantial political capital in that context (Boddewyn and Brewer 1994; Peng 2000).

Risks and Partner Preferences for IJV Governance

A range of risks therefore attaches to a partner's investment in an IJV. These risks are likely to cause that partner to seek control over those IJV activities and decisions where the risks are concentrated or, if that is not possible, to minimize its exposure. In practice, a number of accommodations are possible. For example, a weaker partner has the possibility over time of progressively securing greater control through learning faster than the other partner(s) (Makhija and Ganesh 1997). In some cases, a partner may be content with the share of return to which it is legally entitled and to leave the initiative in running the JV to the other partner because of its superior capabilities. Nevertheless, despite these possibilities, it is reasonable to assume that, in the main, partners will be concerned to reduce their risk through appropriate IJV governance arrangements. This section identifies the forms of IJV control that are likely to be favored to deal with contextual and agency sources of risk. The following section then offers an analytical framework for IJV governance preferences and supports this with propositions to guide future research.

The focus of most discussion about corporate governance has been on what the OECD (1999) has characterized as the 'outsider' system of governance. Here, owners have to rely on external levers and mechanisms, such as boards of directors, in order to ensure that their agents will act in accord with their interests. Organization theorists have referred to this as 'strategic control', which is concerned with 'the means and methods on which the whole conduct of an organization depends' (Child 1984: 137). The key assumption in the governance literature—that owners or their supervisory agents have the capacity to make sure that companies are conducted to serve their interests—is, however, premised on the assumption that such control extends to the use of resources and the conduct of operations. This means ensuring a level of operational effectiveness that will provide a good return to shareholders and a way of conducting operations that will not jeopardize proprietary rights over technologies, brands, or other assets. Operational control is therefore also vital to protect owners from risks, and has to be included within the scope of corporate governance. For 'control loss' within organizations means that corporate intentions may not be realized (Williamson 1970). These considerations call for attention to 'insider' controls that complement and support 'outsider' governance.

This broader perspective can be used to indicate the IJV governance and control mechanisms available to a partner for the purpose of limiting the risks it faces. Some elements of financial risk can be reduced through taking a majority share of IJV equity so as to control the use of surplus funds and other strategic decisions through having a majority of IJV board members. The active presence of a partner's own managers within the IJV may also help to reduce those financial risks arising from misadministration of accounts, and this is the prime reason why many MNC partners insist on appointing the chief financial officers of their local IJVs (Child 2000). Even in circumstances where an IJV partner can secure only a minority equity share, recommendations have been made on ways in which influence over financial and other strategic decisions might be secured through other means such as the appointment of able people to the IJV board and informed preparation before board meetings (Schaan 1988). Time spent by a partner's senior executives in the IJV's host country may further reduce financial risk if this leads to closer informal relations with officials in the host country, which in turn reduce the uncertainties attending their application of regulations to the IJV.

The reduction of resource-deficiency risk through the provision of compensatory resources of a physical, informational, and human kind to an IJV also carries control implications. Consistent with the resource dependency perspective, it has been found that an important source of influence over IJVs can arise from the authority and goodwill attaching to the partner who provides such key resources (Child and Yan 1999). While it is unlikely that resource provision will be made primarily with the enhancement of IJV control in mind, this is a useful by-product. Similarly, market opportunity risk can be mitigated by a partner taking control over key IJV appointments concerned with developing market research, distribution, product promotion, and other activities essential for securing market penetration. Market opportunity risk often arises when a local IJV partner lacks relevant market knowledge or marketing skills even in its 'home' market, possibly because its distribution has been effected only through middlemen or has been purely local in scope.

Agency risk, as we have noted, takes on a multiple nature in IJVs. It extends both to the possible failure of other partners to deliver on their commitments to an IJV and to the risk that its managers may be self-serving or serve primarily other partners' interests. The primary 'external' control that a partner can exercise over agency risk is that applying to all companies, namely, having sufficient equity for an effective voice in the board of directors. Also, through the IJV's board, the partner can endeavor to control the appointment, and removal if necessary, of its key managers. These managers in turn are then in a position to exercise control down through the organization through personal involvement and supervision. Thus, the monitoring of middle managers and employees is a further governance-support mechanism open to an IJV partner who has a sufficient equity stake and supplies key members of the IJV's management. This can be complemented by the training of local managers and employees with the aim not only of enhancing their competencies (thus reducing resource-deficiency risk) but

TABLE 4.2   *Forms of IJV control aimed at reducing different categories of risk*

	Control via equity share and IJV board majority	Control via key appointments and direct involvement of partner's personnel in the IJV	Control via non-equity resource provision (e.g. systems, training)	Control via managerial monitoring
Contextual risks				
Financial risk	✓	✓	✓	
Resource risk			✓	
Market risk		✓	✓	
Agency risks				
financial, resource, market	✓	✓	✓	✓

also of socializing them to the culture and objectives of the IJV partner. Many MNCs use training in this way as a support for their governance of foreign affiliates, including IJVs (Rudman 2003). If the other partner(s) fails to provide the access to markets that was expected of it, the foreign partner can adopt the generally more expensive option of developing its own marketing and distribution systems and appointing sales agents for the IJV. This move places marketing under its own control.

These postulated methods of reducing different categories of IJV risk are depicted in Table 4.2. The overall argument that IJV governance can in these ways be enhanced by measures to strengthen 'internal' control gains supports from investigations among Sino-foreign IJVs. These indicated that a foreign partner's share of IJV equity was particularly significant for securing strategic control and hence reducing financial risk, whereas the provision of non-contracted resources, systems, and personnel to the IJV was significant for the enhancement of operational control (Child and Yan 1999).

Risks and Partner Preferences for IJV Governance Modes

Analytical Framework

A review of risks, their sources, and partner preferences for IJV governance modes suggests the analytical framework depicted in Fig. 4.1. For purposes of simplicity, the framework focuses on IJV governance from the standpoint of a 'foreign' partner, typically an international company, rather than the host country IJV partner(s). It also takes account of the fact that the options available for IJV governance will be constrained by institutional provisions in the host country, including regulations about permissible governance formats.

The left-hand side of Fig. 4.1 depicts the sources of risk potentially facing a foreign IJV partner. Contextual risks arise because a country's institutional

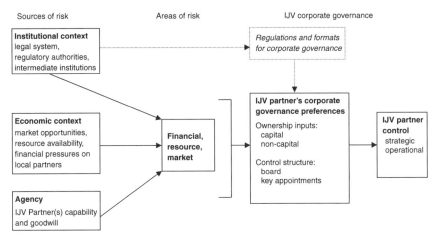

Sources of risk   Areas of risk   IJV corporate governance

FIGURE **4.1**   *Analytical framework for corporate governance in IJVs.*

and economic context establishes certain conditions that generate the level of uncertainty prevailing in an IJV's host environment. These were discussed in the second section. Institutional factors impact on the risks faced by foreign IJV partners primarily through the legal system, the attitude of regulatory authorities, and the adequacy of intermediate business support institutions. Macroeconomic factors bear upon the risks faced by IJV partners in areas such as market opportunity, resource availability, and the financial pressures that influence the behavior of local partners. Agency risks arise from the nature of the local IJV partner(s). They comprise the multiple agency risks arising from the dependence of an IJV partner on the other's competence and goodwill. Although the relationship between partners is a micro-level feature, the available choice of local partners in the first place, and their capabilities, reflect the host country macro context, notably the scale and level of development of its economy.

The level of risk in different areas (financial, resource, and market) is expected to impact on partners' policies on the equity capital and non-capital inputs to invest in an IJV, and the control deriving from these, as well as policies on structuring control through board membership and key appointments (see third section above). The corporate governance provisions established for IJVs, especially equity share, are seen to reflect an assessment of risks and opportunities in the host environment (Pan 1997), though the degree of choice may be limited by host government policy and regulations. Such regulations and approved formats become templates for governance at the firm (IJV) level. This limitation is indicated by the dotted line through 'regulations and formats for corporate governance' to 'IJV partner corporate governance policies'.

The formal ownership structure of an IJV, in terms of partner equity share and appointment of directors, is seen to impact directly upon the strategic control each IJV partner actually exercises, in line with the legal rights of corporate governance. We have noted, however, that there are other control levers available to owners or managers additional to the equity rights stressed in legal theory and in most discussions of corporate governance. Thus, the provision by an IJV partner of non-capital and even non-contractual support may well enhance its operational control. The availability of competent managers who can be trusted by one or more IJV partners may also facilitate the delegation of operational control and even of some influence over IJV strategy. The interplay between these levers is likely to give rise to a range of control solutions at the micro level.

The framework presented in Fig. 4.1 is not intended to be either static or to imply contextual determinism. Thus, over time IJV partners may be able to take collective action to develop and shape institutional policies in the host country. Also, a policy of technology and knowledge transfer can enhance the level of managerial competencies available in the local environment and so reduce one of the economic foundations for resource-deficiency risk.

Propositions on IJV Partner Governance Preferences

The strands of the argument we have advanced are now brought together in a set of ten propositions intended to provide guidelines for further investigation. The propositions refer to the main sources of risk that have been identified and postulate their implications for the preferences likely to be held by *foreign* partners for IJV governance modes. The sources of risk are categorized into context and agency related. The rationale for each proposition draws upon previous discussion in this chapter, and is therefore summarized only. Propositions are identified by a capital 'P' and the summary rationales by a capital 'R'.

Contextual Risk: Institutional

P1.   The lower the level of legal protection for contract fulfillment, the lower will be the level of capital and other contractual investment in an IJV by a foreign partner, and hence the greater the probability of that partner being in a minority equity position.

R1.   Lack of adequate legal protection raises financial risk, thus discouraging significant commitment of capital, technology, or other contracted resources. This reduction of financial risk is traded against weaker governance rights, and this may therefore limit the foreign partner's capacity to deal with agency risk.

P2.   The lower the protection for minority equity holders, the more importance will a foreign IJV partner attach to holding a majority share of IJV equity.

R2.   This proposition may counteract P1. If it is decided to form an IJV in a context that offers low protection for minority shareholdings, a foreign partner is likely to favor offsetting this risk by securing majority control.

P3.   In situations where regulatory restrictions prevent foreign majority equity holding, the lower the level of legal protection for minority IJV shareholders, the more importance that the foreign partner will attach to using non-equity forms of control.

R3.   Faced with risks to equity and restrictions on IJV governance through conventional external mechanisms, a foreign IJV partner can only resort to the non-equity based approaches to governance noted in Table 4.2 (making key appointments and direct involvement of its personnel, non-equity resource provision, and managerial monitoring). It will thereby attempt to retain some control over at least the implementation of IJV strategy through building up its operational control by these means.

P4.   The lower the protection for intellectual property, the more importance will a foreign IJV partner attach to securing a majority share of IJV equity and to involving its own personnel in the management of the IJV.

R4.   The significance of intellectual property varies between sectors and even firms. On the assumption, however, that proprietary rights over hard technology (such as products and processes) and/or soft technology (such as brand names and software systems) are an important issue for the foreign IJV partner, then, if the host context offers inadequate protection for those rights, the partner will be motivated to secure direct strategic control over the IJV's technology policy via a majority on the IJV board, and to appoint its own managers and experts to monitor the operational use of the technology.

P5.   The less developed are intermediate institutions in the host country, providing support for business, the more will a foreign IJV partner be obliged to supply this support itself, thus enhancing its operational control in the areas of IJV activity concerned.

R5.   Intermediate institutions supply business support services such as market research, education and training, consultancy, and technical advice. If the foreign partner is obliged to supply these directly, or from abroad, rather than securing them from within the host country, it will assume the initiative in the activities concerned through non-equity resource provision. This should enhance its governance over the IJV in terms of operational control.

Contextual Risk: Economic
P6.   The more limited the availability of investment capital in the host country, the more likely is the foreign IJV partner to become a majority equity shareholder in order to provide adequate capitalization for the venture.

R6.   This proposition suggests that limited external resource availability can have direct consequences for IJV governance arrangements. When opportunities exist for rapid growth, as in China, the inability of local partners to finance their share of capital expansion has often provided an opportunity for foreign partners to increase their equity shares and thus to take strategic control.

P7.   The more limited the availability of managerial resources in the host country, the more likely is the foreign IJV partner to supply people to key appointments, offer non-equity resources such as management systems, and hence to gain operational control of the venture.

R7.   Like R5, this proposition suggests that, when the economic context presents a resource-deficiency risk in terms of capable management for the IJV, the foreign partner is likely to compensate in a way that also strengthens its operational control.

P8.   The greater the market opportunities open to the IJV, the greater will be the foreign partner's preferred level of involvement in IJV governance.

R8.   Good market opportunities are a major driver encouraging substantial foreign investment. They increase the attraction of taking up a large share of IJV equity in order to secure the right to a corresponding share of the expected favorable returns on investment. This larger stake will in turn enhance the foreign partner's formal rights to govern the IJV through a majority on its board and thus to assume strategic control.

Agency Risk

P9.   The lower the local partner's managerial and technical capabilities, the greater will be the foreign partner's preferred level of involvement in IJV governance.

R9.   This proposition is consistent with the reasoning behind P5 and P7. The more that the local IJV partner lacks managerial and technical capabilities necessary for the success of the venture, the less reliable it is to serve as an agent for the foreign partner to attain its objectives through the partnership. The foreign partner will be encouraged to reduce this agency risk through taking on wider responsibilities and assuming greater operational control of the IJV.

P10.   The higher the opportunism displayed by the local partner, and the lower the trust invested in it, the greater will be the foreign partner's preferred level of involvement in IJV governance.

R10.   In circumstances of suspected opportunism by the local partner and low trust in its goodwill, it is rational for the foreign partner to respond in several ways, all of which enhance its control of IJV governance both strategically and operationally. For example, it may decide to protect its interests through insisting on a larger equity share, on the right to determine key IJV appointments, and on mutually signed contractual safeguards. It may also decide to invest additional person-hours in social contact with the local partner's personnel, in training and development, in the formulation of IJV normative and control systems, and in other activities intended to promote trustworthiness (Child and Möllering 2003). This additional involvement in the internal affairs of the IJV amounts to a centralization of control by the foreign partner with the aim of enhancing its overall influence in the governance process.

A Typology of IJV Partner Governance Preferences

The above propositions suggest that different types of IJV governance preference are likely to arise from the partners' perceptions of different levels of contextual and agency risk. Figure 4.2 identifies four broad categories of IJV governance preference, again with reference to *foreign* partners. The four are (i) concentrated personal governance, (ii) concentrated specialized governance, (iii) delegated managerial governance, and (iv) delegated financial governance. These four types are located with reference to the interaction between contextual and agency risk.

Preference for a *concentrated personal* form of governance is likely if the institutional and economic contexts present high risk and there is a high level of agency risk from the local partner(s) as well. The expectation in this case is for a foreign IJV partner to favor concentrated personal control based on a majority equity position and accompanied by a strong presence of its own appointed staff within the IJV. This would mean that the foreign partner tends to control both strategic and operational decisions. The concentrated personal type of IJV governance is common in Sino-Western joint ventures, where foreign partners view both contextual and agency risks as high (Vanhonacker 1997; Child and Yan 1999).

A *concentrated specialized* form of IJV governance is likely to be preferred when the institutional and economic contexts provide sufficient protection and opportunity for the foreign investor, but when at the same time the

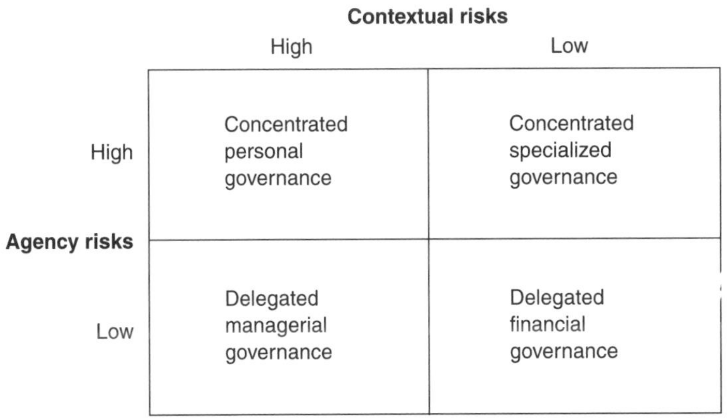

	Contextual risks	
	High	Low
Agency risks High	Concentrated personal governance	Concentrated specialized governance
Agency risks Low	Delegated managerial governance	Delegated financial governance

FIGURE 4.2   *A typology of IJV partner governance preferences associated with level and source of risk.*

local partner(s) are perceived to generate high agency risk through lack of capability or suspected opportunism. In other words, the local partner cannot be relied upon in respect of its capabilities to manage certain activities and/or its trustworthiness not to behave opportunistically in regard to such activities. For this reason, the foreign partner is likely to seek to retain close control over what it considers to be key IJV activities from the point of view of its interests, allowing discretion to the local partner in other areas. The result is that the IJV partners specialize their areas of control. The control the foreign partner endeavors to reserve to itself is intended, for example, to maintain its ability to prevent technology leakage, to maintain quality standards, and to protect the integrity of its international brands. This effectively confines knowledge transfer in such areas within limits that are specified by contracts and by the partner's managerial discretion. In these cases the local partner may maintain control over areas where the foreign partner has little experience or proprietary interest, such as liaising with government officials and managing the workforce.

Preference for a *delegated managerial* form of governance increases when there is relatively high contextual risk, but where the IJV partners' strategic intentions are complementary, the local partner can offer good managerial competencies, and the quality of relations between them is good. The high level of contextual risk means that the foreign partner may prefer to limit the size of its investment in the IJV and hence its share of equity. This may reduce its influence over the IJV's strategy. Moreover, the foreign partner can have some confidence in leaving the management of many IJV activities to its local partner, including those that concern dealing with contextual risk. The local partner may even supply the general manager of the IJV, though this is less likely when the foreign partner possesses superior managerial expertise and technologies. Examples of this form of IJV governance have been found in China, in which the foreign partner has only 50 percent of IJV ownership, governance rights are balanced, and both partners agree on the choice of the chief executive officer to ensure unified control (Child 2002*a*). It is distinguished from the concentrated personal type in that the influence of the foreign partner is mostly maintained through the IJV board and the general manager, who may be the only foreigner in the venture. This form of IJV control requires sufficient willingness on the part of local managers to accept the priorities of the foreign partner as a necessary condition for its willingness to delegate discretion to them.

Foreign IJV partners may be obliged to accept delegated managerial control in situations where national regulations do not allow a foreign majority equity share in certain sectors. It can also be favored in countries such as Brazil where institutional rules allow the local partner to enjoy influence disproportionate to its equity share through granting specific control rights to holders of preferential shares (Leal, Carvalhal da Silva, and Valadares 2001).

Delegated financial governance by the foreign partner focuses on the monitoring of financial returns from its IJV investment. It is likely to be preferred when contextual and agency risks are both low. The institutional environment may present low risk because of effective regulations and ease of repatriating funds; the economy may offer adequate resources (including managerial skills); and the quality and trustworthiness of local partners may not pose significant agency problems. This mode of governance may also be preferred by a foreign partner when the IJV is not highly integrated with its core activities or strategically very significant, when opportunities for growth in the local market are limited, or when it is engaging primarily in the IJV as a financial or speculative investment. In general, this kind of investor is concerned with the maximization of shareholder value and does not necessarily have a long-term interest in the venture. This can result in unfocused and sporadic governance because the foreign partner can withdraw from the business if it becomes financially advantageous to do so. From the local investor's point of view, the foreign investor fulfills the role of fund-raiser rather than supplier of technology or source of learning.

The prime distinction between the concentrated and the delegated forms of IJV governance preference lies in the degree of control that the foreign partner seeks to maintain. If the contextual risk is greater than the internal agency risk, the foreign partner is expected to prefer forms of control that are focused on strategic issues and resources. It may not consider significant personal control through the direct involvement of its managers and staff to be necessary. If the contextual risks are less than the internal risks, preference will be for monitoring activities closely and personally, even extending control to routine operations. If risk is high both externally and internally, a concentration of authority will be preferred, involving extensive forms of strategic and operational control and the personal intervention of foreign managers. When both external and internal risks are low, then it is expected that foreign partner preferences will be for forms of control that are occasional and focused on written reporting rather than close personal contact.

A preliminary comparison of IJV governance in Brazil and China suggests that this typology has sufficient utility to warrant its exploration in further research (Rodrigues and Child 2001). Contextual and agency risks are generally higher in China than in Brazil. It was found that in China most foreign partners tended to exercise concentrated personal governance with an active involvement in operational decision-making. Brazil, by contrast, appears to be in transition primarily from a concentrated specialized model toward greater delegated financial governance in which local managers are accorded more responsibilities in the venture. The more effective institutional context for corporate governance in Brazil, and the greater sophistication of managerial competencies in that country, would appear to provide some explanation for the contrasts between the two countries in line with the argument we have presented.

The typology also suggests that different modes of IJV governance can suit different types of foreign investor, subject always to prevailing environmental conditions. For instance, if the foreign investor adopts a long-term horizon and intends to expand to markets in which the economic and institutional environment provides low risk, it may prefer to move beyond an initial phase of concentrated specialized governance toward delegated financial governance. In other words, the IJV would develop into a semi-autonomous subsidiary managed locally and monitored by its economic results. However, it can be problematic to apply this mode to those emerging economies that are characterized by instability and limited managerial competencies. If, on the other hand, the foreign investor's interest lies in the generation of rapid and high returns, the favored initial approach might be one of delegated financial governance that permits easy withdrawal if either the external or the internal environment becomes unfavorable. The delegated financial mode requires an environment that is less prone to contextual risk than is the case in many contemporary developing economies.

Given the impact that environmental contexts are likely to have on the exercise of foreign partner preferences for IJV governance, it is not surprising that international bodies such as the IMF and the WTO are exerting pressures for the creation of favorable regulatory environments for foreign direct investment, or that the OECD is urging the worldwide adoption of the shareholder value principle. Both these policies would create a more propitious, less risky terrain for the free flow of financial capital. If they are implemented, IJVs are likely to become even more important vehicles for the internationalization of financial shareholdings.

Conclusion: IJV Governance Preferences and Economic Development

This chapter has indicated that, for an understanding of IJV governance, it is not sufficient merely to take into account the property rights attached to formal equity ownership. The possession by an IJV partner of key non-equity and non-contractual assets, especially knowledge assets, can also provide a significant level of de facto control, especially over operational matters. In the case of IJVs formed between internationally experienced companies and local partners in emerging economies, the former are likely to supply most of the IJVs' necessary knowledge assets. Indeed, in such economies, partnership with MNCs and other companies from developed countries has been regarded as a significant channel for the inward transfer of knowledge and technology to aid economic development. One of the particular benefits attributed to IJVs is the facilitation of tacit knowledge transfer through the interaction of staff appointed or seconded by their partners (Büchel et al. 1998; Inkpen 2000).

A number of factors can, however, militate against this policy objective because they lead foreign IJV partners to retain a level of control that inhibits knowledge transfer. First, investing companies from developed countries generally perceive that they face high contextual and agency risks when forming IJVs in emerging economies. Emerging economies tend to have high scores in country risk tables. Their legal and other institutional systems are typically immature and foreign investing companies are therefore exposed to problems such as corruption, counterfeiting, and a variable application of laws and regulations. Many emerging countries are prone to economic variability as well, which adds to risk in areas such as exchange rates and availability of working capital. Working with local partners who are inexperienced in international practices and who may act opportunistically, for reasons such as economic exigency, cultural antipathy or low trust, often creates a high level of agency risk. According to the analysis we have offered, high contextual and agency risks are likely to lead foreign IJV partners to aim for concentrated personal governance. Second, if the local environment is resource-deficient, and if the local IJV partner is also lacking in capability and resource, the foreign partner will be obliged to provide extensive tangible and intangible assets, and hence adopt a high and extensive level of IJV control. Third, most MNCs, especially those of American origin, have an a priori preference for strong and integrated control over their foreign affiliates, and have institutionalized this into their norms for foreign direct investment (Rudman 2003). Indeed, many of them regard IJVs as merely a stepping-stone towards acquiring complete ownership and control. Fourth, even if local IJV partners are granted access to the knowledge assets that their foreign partners bring to IJVs, they do not necessarily have the understanding or the motivation to transfer such knowledge to their other operations or to disseminate the knowledge effectively. Local partners can resist the introduction of new practices into IJVs by their foreign partners, if they perceive new knowledge and practices as a threat to their social identity (Child and Rodrigues 1996). However, the opportunity to participate in control should eventually reduce such resistance.

Paradoxically, the possession of superior tangible and intangible assets by foreign IJV partners, the transfer of which should be facilitated by IJVs, can actually create barriers to that transfer because the risks perceived by such partners encourage them to adopt restrictive forms of IJV corporate governance. The transfer of technology and expertise to local firms in emerging economies is jeopardized when they have limited power within an IJV and when their participation in sensitive activities is restricted. A degree of shared control and openness between IJV partners and their staff is necessary for knowledge to be transferred between them, especially knowledge of a less codified and more tacit nature.

The issue of IJV partner governance preferences is not therefore just a gap in the corporate governance discourse that needs to be filled. It also has wider implications for the role of international firms in economic development. What Stiglitz (2003) has argued at the macro level applies equally at the level of the firm: the key ingredients in a successful development strategy are local ownership and participation. Policies and practices imposed from outside are unlikely to be implemented, at least as intended. Moreover, failure to permit participation in the governance of their overseas affiliates actually spells danger to the long-term future of international firms (Child 2002*b*). While MNCs are making a major positive contribution to economic development through their investments and employment generation, their lack of accountability to local interests, including local partners, is generating resentment. Some of the most hostile opposition to MNCs is to be found in developing countries and experience suggests that if this resentment leads to conditions that pose greater country risk, foreign direct investment by corporations to the region concerned could dry up. It is therefore a matter of some urgency to find new ways of IJV corporate governance that can at the same time reduce perceived risk and permit the participation of local partners in control.

References

Barros, O. (1993). *Estudo da competitividade da indústria brasileira: oportunidades abertas para o Brasil face aos fluxos globais de investimento de risco e de capitais financeiros nos anos 90*. Campinas, São Paulo: UNICAMP.

Beamish, P. and Killing, J. P. (eds.) (1997). *Cooperative Strategies: Asian Pacific Perspectives, European Perspectives, North American Perspectives* (3 volumes). San Francisco: New Lexington Press.

Berle, A. and Means, G. (1932). *The Modern Corporation and Private Property*. New York: Macmillan.

Boddewyn, J. and Brewer, T. (1994). 'International-Business Political Behavior: New Theoretical Directions', *Academy of Management Review*, 19: 119–43.

Boisot, M. (1998). *Knowledge Assets: Securing Competitive Advantage in the Information Economy*. Oxford: Oxford University Press.

Borys, B. and Jemison, D. (1989). 'Hybrid Arrangements as Strategic Alliances: Theoretical Issues in Organizational Combinations', *Academy of Management Review*, 14: 234–49.

Büchel, B., Prange, C., Probst, G., and Rüling, C.-C. (1998). *International Joint Venture Management: Learning to Cooperate and Cooperating to Learn*. Singapore: Wiley.

Child, J. (1984). *Organization: A Guide to Problems and Practice*. London: Harper & Row.

——(2000). 'Occupying the Managerial Workplace in Sino-Foreign Joint Ventures: A Strategy for Control and Development?', in M. Warner (ed.), *Changing Workplace Relations in the Chinese Economy*. London: Macmillan.

——(2002*a*). 'A Configurational Analysis of International Joint Ventures Drawing upon Experience in China', *Organization Studies*, 23: 781–815.

——(2002*b*). 'The International Crisis of Confidence in Corporations', *Academy of Management Executive*, 16/3: 145–7.

——and Faulkner, D. (1998). *Strategies of Cooperation*. Oxford: Oxford University Press.

——and Möllering, G. (2003). 'Contextual Confidence and Active Trust Development in the Chinese Business Context', *Organization Science*, 14: 69–80.

—— and Rodrigues, S. (1996). 'The Role of Social Identity in the International Transfer of Knowledge through Joint Ventures', in S. Clegg and G. Palmer (eds.), *The Politics of Management Knowledge*. London: Sage.

—— and Tse, D. (2001). 'China's Transition and its Implications for International Business', *Journal of International Business Studies*, 32: 5–21.

—— and Yan, Y. (1999). 'Investment and Control in International Joint Ventures: The Case of China', *Journal of World Business*, 34: 3–15.

—— and Yan, Y. (2003). 'Predicting the Performance of International Joint Ventures: An Investigation in China', *Journal of Management Studies*, 40: 283–320.

Claessens, S., Djankov, S., Fan, J., and Lang, L. (1999). 'Expropriation of Minority Shareholders in East Asia'. Working paper, World Bank, www.econondev.forumone.com

Doz, Y. and Hamel, G. (1998). *Alliance Advantage: The Art of Creating Value through Partnering*. Boston: Harvard Business School Press.

Dunning, J. H. (1998). 'Location and the Multinational Enterprise: A Neglected Factor?', *Journal of International Business Studies*, 29: 45–66.

Dussauge, P. and Garrette, B. (1999). *Cooperative Strategy: Competing Successfully through Strategic Alliances*. Chichester: Wiley.

Eisenhardt, K. (1989). 'Agency Theory: An Assessment and Review', *Academy of Management Review*, 14: 57–74.

EIU (Economist Intelligence Unit) (1999). *China Hand*. Hong Kong: EIU.

Faulkner, D. and de Rond, M. (2000). 'Perspectives on Cooperative Strategy', in D. Faulkner and M. de Rond (eds.), *Cooperative Strategy: Economic, Business and Organizational Issues*. Oxford: Oxford University Press.

Frynas, J. G., Mellahi, K., and Pigman, G. (2003). 'First Mover Advantages in International Business and Firm Specific Political Resources'. Unpublished working paper, Birmingham Business School, University of Birmingham, UK.

Geringer, J. (1991). 'Strategic Determinants of Partner Selection Criteria in International Joint Ventures', *Journal of International Business Studies*, 22: 41–62.

Hamel, G. (1991). 'Competition for Competence and Inter-Partner Learning within International Strategic Alliances', *Strategic Management Journal*, 12: 83–103.

Hansman, H. (1996). *The Ownership of Enterprise*. Cambridge, MA: Harvard University Press.

Inkpen, A. (2000). 'Learning Through Joint Ventures: A Framework of Knowledge Acquisition', *Journal of Management Studies*, 37: 1019–43.

Jensen, M. and Meckling, W. (1976). 'Theory of the Firm: Managerial Behavior, Agency Costs, and Capital Structure', *Journal of Financial Economics*, 3: 305–60.

Killing, P. (1983). *Strategies for Joint Venture Success*. London: Croom Helm.

La Porta, R., Lopez-de-Silanes, F., and Shleifer, A. (1998). 'Law and Finance', *Journal of Political Economy*, 106: 1113–55.

Lazonick, W. and O'Sullivan, M. (1996). 'Organization, Finance and International Competition', *Industrial and Corporate Change*, 5: 1–49.

—— —— (2000). 'Maximizing Shareholder Value: A New Ideology for Corporate Governance', *Economy and Society*, 29: 13–35.

Leal, R., Carvalhal da Silva, A., and Valadares, S. (2001). 'Ownership, Control and Corporate Valuation of Brazilian companies'. Working Paper, COPPEAD, Federal University of Rio de Janeiro, Brazil.

Lieberman, M. and Montgomery, D. (1988). 'First-mover Advantages', *Strategic Management Journal*, 9/Summer: 41–58.

Makhija, M. and Ganesh, U. (1997). 'The Relationship between Control and Partner Learning in Learning-related Joint Ventures', *Organization Science*, 8: 508–27.

Monks, R. and Minow, N. (2001). *Corporate Governance* (2nd edn.). Oxford: Blackwell.

Nolan, P. (2001). *China and the Global Economy*. New York: Palgrave.

North, D. (1990). *Institutions, Institutional Change and Economic Performance*. Cambridge: Cambridge University Press.

OECD (1999). *Corporate Governance: Effects on Firm Performance and Growth*. Paris: OECD.

Pan, Y. (1997). 'Influences on Foreign Equity Ownership Level in Joint Ventures in China', *Journal of International Business Studies*, 27: 1–26.

Parkhe, A. (1993). '"Messy" Research, Methodological Predispositions, and Theory Development in International Joint Ventures', *Academy of Management Review*, 18: 227–68.

Peng, M. (2000). *Business Strategies in Transition Economies*. Thousand Oaks, CA: Sage.

Pfeffer, J. and Salanzik, G. (1978). *The External Control of Organizations*. New York: Harper & Row.

Porter, M. (1990). *The Competitive Advantage of Nations*. Basingstoke: Macmillan.

Ramanathan, K., Seth, A., and Thomas, H. (1997). 'Explaining Joint Ventures: Alternative Theoretical Pespectives', in P. Beamish and J. Killing (eds.), *Cooperative Strategies: North American Perspectives*. San Francisco: The New Lexington Press.

Rodrigues, S. and Child, J. (2001). 'Corporate Governance and International Joint Ventures: Insights from Brazil and China'. Working Paper 2001–14, Birmingham Business School, University of Birmingham, UK.

Rudman, S. (2003). 'Controlling Interests: Management Control Processes Employed by US Multinational Corporations within their China Affiliates'. Unpublished Ph.D. Thesis, University of Cambridge.

Schaan, J-L. (1988). 'How to Control a Joint Venture even as a Minority Shareholder', *Journal of General Management*, 14: 4–16.

Shenkar, O. and Zeira, Y. (1992). 'Role Conflict and Role Ambiguity of Chief Executive Officers in International Joint Ventures', *Journal of International Business Studies*, 23: 55–75.

Shleifer, A. and Vishny, R. (1997). 'A Survey of Corporate Governance', *The Journal of Finance*, 52: 737–83.

Singh, K. and Mitchell, W. (1996). 'Precarious Collaboration: Business Survival After Partners Shut Down or Form New Partnerships', *Strategic Management Journal*, 17/Summer: 99–115.

Stiglitz, J. (2003). 'Towards a New Paradigm of Development', in J. Dunning (ed.), *Making Globalization Good*. Oxford: Oxford University Press.

Valadares, S. and Leal, R. (2000). 'Ownership and Control of Brazilian Companies'. Working paper, COPPEAD, Federal University of Rio de Janeiro, Brazil.

Vanhonacker, W. (1997). 'Entering China: An Unconventional Approach', *Harvard Business Review*, 75/2: 130–40.

Williamson, O. (1970). *Corporate Control and Business Behavior*. Englewood Cliffs, NJ: Prentice-Hall.

5

Information Intermediaries' Incentives and Corporate Strategy Choices in the US

PATRICK MORETON AND TODD ZENGER

Introduction

Significant changes in managerial compensation and the market for corporate control have focused CEOs on strategies that they view as responsive to capital markets. One of the apparent drivers behind this shift is the substantial increase in the sensitivity of managerial compensation to stock price performance. Hall and Liebman (1998), for example, document a threefold increase in the elasticity of CEO compensation relative to shareholders' wealth between 1980 and 1994. They attribute this change to an increase in the stock and stock options holdings of CEOs. An unprecedented level of takeover activity during the 1980s and 1990s (see Holmstrom and Kaplan 2001 and the literature cited there) also encouraged managers to restructure public corporations to increase shareholder value.

On the face of it, tightening the alignment between shareholder and managerial interests has significantly reduced agency problems that undermined effective corporate governance during the 1960s and 1970s. With the revised compensation structure and pressure from outsiders, CEOs now face much stronger incentives to pursue strategies that increase stock prices and, presumably, shareholder wealth. Since share prices are fundamentally *perceptions* of value, CEOs now also seek to influence these perceptions by effectively *marketing* their strategies to those possessing capital or those influencing its distribution. Indeed, CEOs of public corporations today devote an expanding portion of their time to this activity—meeting with institutional shareholders, large investors, and sell-side financial analysts, those employed by financial intermediaries to assess the value of equity shares of publicly traded firms. In the extreme, this new, perhaps unintended, incentive has led to CEO behavior that the courts of the United States may ultimately find to be criminally fraudulent.

Criminal or not, the need for CEOs to market their strategies may have unanticipated negative welfare consequences because strategies that sell well in equity markets need not be welfare maximizing, even when the product

113

or service markets in which the firm operates are perfectly competitive. In particular, a strategy tailored to the tastes of financial analysts may reflect the incentives that the financial analyst faces within the investment banking community. These incentives need not be the same as those that an omniscient social planner would impose, and as a result CEOs will not necessarily choose strategies that generate the largest economic surplus. Rather, it is possible that some CEOs must choose between a strategy that maximizes the discounted present value of the firm's cash flows but does not attract a large analyst following, and one that analysts prefer but sacrifices the total wealth generated by the firm. For this reason, we think it is imperative that researchers carefully examine the role that financial analysts play in the formation of the firm's strategy.

As strategy researchers, we are primarily interested in management's response to the financial analysts. Ideally, we would like to directly test the following hypothesis: *Analysts' capacity to influence stock prices induces managers to pursue strategies that analysts prefer rather than strategies that maximize long-term discounted cash flows.*

A direct test of this hypothesis would require observing the set of strategies considered by management, appraising the expected operating profitability of each and the likely reception they would receive among financial analysts, and then demonstrating that management picks a strategy that maximizes the firm's stock price rather than the firm's economic value. Ambitious? Absurdly so, of course, but we think it is useful to state what a direct test of the hypothesis would look like in order to make the case for our more modest and incremental approach.

Clearly, it is infeasible to objectively appraise either the economic value or the analyst community's reaction to all strategies considered by a management team. Therefore, we propose to simply confirm that the necessary conditions hold for our hypothesis to be true. To wit, we confirm the existence of analysts' preferences for some strategies, a necessary condition for management to face a constraint in its choice of strategies. We then assert, supported by economic theory, that these preferences are likely to constrain the manager's choice of strategy to the degree that there is less strategy experimentation than is socially optimal.

To identify the existence of analyst preferences we specify a simple, conceptual model of the relationships between managers and analysts in which each player maximizes his or her individual utility. By assumption, a manager's compensation is tied to the performance of the firm's equity shares and, thus, managers choose strategies that maximize the performance of the firm's equity shares rather than the performance of the business itself. We justify this assumption by pointing to the growing literature examining the evolution of CEO compensation and corporate governance over the last twenty years, which shows a decided trend toward closer alignment between managers' and shareholders' interests.

Within this basic model, we argue that uncommon strategies have the potential to yield different results in terms of stock performance and business performance. Specifically, unfamiliar strategies—those rarely observed in the data—have the potential to give the firm a monopoly over whatever cost or product performance benefits the combined businesses impart to the firm, and hence to generate greater cash flows for the firm. Our argument is in concordance with recent theoretical work (MacDonald and Ryall 2002) that has identified relative rarity as a necessary condition for a strategy to impart a competitive advantage on the firm.

Uncommon strategies are also, however, inherently unfamiliar, and hence more difficult for investors and analysts to understand. Therefore, they require greater effort by analysts to evaluate. We argue that, at the margin, some analysts will deem the extra effort unattractive and elect not to cover the firm's stock, reducing the amount of information in the market about the firm and increasing uncertainty about the prospects for its equity shares. Among risk-averse investors, this greater uncertainty yields a lower willingness to pay for the firm's stock and the potential for underperformance relative to the stocks of firms with more familiar strategies even though these strategies yield inferior results for the businesses. At the heart of our claim is the fact that investors' preferences for equity securities are two-dimensional, encompassing return *and* risk. As a result, if the forecasts for unfamiliar strategies are unavoidably noisier because they attract fewer analysts, then firms with these strategies will trade at a discount relative to their more familiar peers. This effect may actually be at the heart of the diversification discount found in several studies (see, for example, Lang and Stulz 1994; Berger and Ofek 1995). A manager seeking to maximize shareholder wealth may then find it optimal to pursue more familiar strategies (and more focused strategies) with lower expected returns because their stock market valuation is higher.

We look for analysts' preferences for familiar strategies in a cross-sectional dataset containing information on the primary and secondary Standard Industrial Classification (SIC) codes for approximately 10,000 publicly traded firms in Disclosure's SEC Database. With this dataset, we develop simple measures of the frequency of occurrence of particular strategies—defined as the fraction of firms that list a given pair of SICs among their primary and secondary SICs. The familiarity of a particular firm's strategy is then measured as the fraction of firms with identical SIC combinations among its peer set, generally defined as firms with the same primary SIC. We then use this data and a number of control variables in a reduced-form regression on the number of analysts covering a firm. Our results indicate that, after controlling for the size, complexity, and predicted stock performance of a firm, firms that have strategies that are similar to other peer firms with the same primary SIC receive more analyst coverage than firms that have strategies that are not as similar.

These results are broadly consistent with work by Zuckerman (2000) that offers empirical evidence that firms divest unrelated businesses in order to make their business models conform to those preferred by the analyst community. We also confirm earlier results by Bhushan (1989) that the sheer number of SICs in which a firm operates has a negative effect on the number of analysts its stock attracts, suggesting that the bias against diversified firms is not strictly a sociological tendency towards isomorphism in strategies, as suggested by Zuckerman (1999), but is instead at least partly due to the greater costs imposed on the analyst by more complex strategies.

The welfare implications of our results could be quite significant if it turns out that managers are indeed constrained in their strategy choices by the need to attract analysts. Entrepreneurs and managers create value by organizing firm resources in unique and novel ways. Often the unique configurations implemented by the entrepreneur create value by bridging the boundaries between previously separate or seemingly unrelated industries. If analysts are assigned to cover firms according to pre-existing industry classifications, then the entrepreneur or manager attempting to create value in this way will have difficulty communicating the value of these strategies to analysts who are trained and rewarded to think in terms of extant industry structures. We think that this narrowing of the strategies considered by managers is likely to grow in importance as publicly traded firms increase the intensity of the stock-price-based incentives they use with senior managers.

The remainder of this chapter is organized as follows. In the second section we outline a stylized, conceptual model of the relationship between firm strategies and stock prices and use it to identify four conditions that must hold in order for it to be the case that managers are constrained in their strategic choice by the need to attract analyst coverage. We then use the existing literature in finance, accounting, and strategy to make the case that three of the four conditions are likely to hold, leaving the fourth—that analysts prefer familiar to unfamiliar strategies—as needing empirical investigation. The third section then describes our dataset and the methodology we use to examine analysts' strategy preference, and the fourth section presents the results of our preliminary regressions. The final section concludes with a brief summary and some directions for future research.

Firm Strategy, Analyst Coverage, and Stock Prices

We model the linkage between a firm's corporate strategy—its choice of industries in which to operate—and its stock price as a three-stage process. First, managers choose corporate strategies, which we define as the mix of SICs in which their firms operate and locate these strategies along a continuum between commonplace and unique. Commonplace strategies are those that are observed frequently among the firms in an industry while unique strategies are those that are rarely observed in an industry. Second, analysts observe firm strategies and then choose whether or not to cover a firm. For those firms that they choose to cover, they issue a report available to at least a subset of the investors in the market. For each analyst, there is a positive probability that he or she will discover some information that other analysts do not discover so that, the more analysts cover a firm, the more information there is about a firm. In the final stage, investors in the market review the reports issued by analysts and then submit buy and sell orders to a market maker, who sets a market-clearing price.

This process is akin to a three-stage product market value chain in which publicly traded firms 'manufacture' equity investments for sale to investors through retail brokers. These equity investments are complex products that investors have difficulty evaluating, and hence investors are willing to pay more for the equity securities if they are sold through intermediaries—the retail brokers—that provide a more precise assessment of the value of the product. The retail brokers employ financial analysts for the purpose of enhancing the value of the equities they sell to their clients and these analysts must make decisions on the brokerage firms' behalf regarding which equities to 'stock' by choosing whether or not to cover a firm's equity issue. Issuers of equity then have an incentive to cultivate the attention of analysts who both increase the distribution of the firm's equity and enhance its value by reducing the amount of uncertainty that investors have about its performance prospects.

Within this value chain, a manager's choice of strategy plays two critical roles in determining the 'quality' of the firm's equity product and the analysts' willingness to cover the security. First, it dictates the stochastic function that determines the mean and variance of the operating performance prospects of the firm, and in this regard determines the underlying value of the firm's equity as an investment. That is, it determines the mean and variance of the firm's cash flows. Second, the firm's strategy also determines the degree of uncertainty that investors have regarding the performance prospects of the stock, and hence the firm-specific risk associated with investing in the firm's stock. Note that this uncertainty is in addition to the general cash flow variance that stems from the stochastic nature of firm performance. It is a measurement error that is inherently higher for unfamiliar strategies, but it can be reduced through additional effort by analysts. Therefore, its contribution to the value of the firm's equity is a function of the total effort that the analyst community expends on understanding the firm's strategy. Specifically, more coverage by the analyst community reduces the forecast error regarding a firm's performance prospects, reducing the overall uncertainty of the stock's performance and increasing its value to risk-averse investors in a market in which it is not possible to diversify away all firm-specific risk, a feature of many models of rational trade in financial securities (see, for example, Hellwig 1980).

Given this process, there are four general conditions that must be met in order for managers to face an analyst-imposed constraint on their strategic decisions.

1. Managers seek to maximize the equity market's *appraisal* of the underlying value of their firms' activities, not the actual *cash flows* generated by these activities.
2. The market's appraisal of the firm's underlying value increases with the number of financial analysts who cover the firm so that, *ceteris paribus*, a manager prefers more to less coverage by analysts.
3. The underlying economics of the firm's business must, on average, be better when the strategy is unique than when it is commonplace.
4. The net benefit—compensation less effort—that an analyst receives from covering a firm must decline as the firm's strategy becomes more unique.

We support each of these conditions in the discussion below.

Managers' Objectives

Since the pioneering work of Berle and Means (1968), there has been a general concern that managers are in a position to exploit their private knowledge about the firms they manage and, as a result, pursue strategies that are in their interests but not always in the interest of their shareholders. In particular, research in the 1970s and early 1980s provided a sound theoretical basis for arguing that there were decided economic costs associated with using non-owner managers to direct the operations of public corporations (Jensen and Meckling 1976). Subsequent empirical research, both anecdotal (see, for example, Donaldson 1984) and more formal cross-sectional and longitudinal studies (Murphy 1985; Jensen and Murphy 1990) indicated that managerial compensation was only tenuously tied to shareholder wealth maximization, a condition that is hypothesized to lead managers to pursue strategies for their private benefit. The conclusion generally drawn by these researchers and many commentators in the area of corporate governance has been that managers of public corporations are largely unconcerned with the stock price consequence of their strategic decisions and instead take actions primarily to increase their power and control (Jensen 1986) and size-based compensation (Murphy 1985), or to reduce their employment risk (Amihud and Lev 1981; Shleifer and Vishny 1989).

Recent work by Hall and Leibman (1998), however, casts serious doubts on the applicability of these conclusions for the late 1990s. Using the best data currently available on CEO compensation, they find that the median elasticity of CEO compensation relative to the stock price performance increased twofold between 1982 and 1994, from 1.6 to 3.3.[1]

---

[1] Even without the increase over time, Hall and Leibman's (1998) estimate of the sensitivity of CEO compensation to changes in shareholder wealth is an order of magnitude greater than earlier estimates by Jensen and Murphy (1990). Perhaps more importantly, Hall and Leibman (1998) show that the wealth increase a CEO can obtain by improving firm performance is easily in the range of several million dollars, not the $50,000 increases that Jensen and

As Holmstrom and Kaplan (2001) observe, the performance sensitivity of CEO compensation for public corporations is now of the same order of magnitude as the performance sensitivity for managers at private leveraged buyout firms in the late 1980s. Since managers of these highly leveraged private firms have generally been assumed to have incentives more closely aligned with the interests of equity holders (Jensen 1986), the same conclusion of close alignment seems appropriate for managers and shareholders of public corporations at this time.

Holmstrom and Kaplan (2001) also highlight the positive effects on corporate governance produced by the substantial improvements in information technology and the increasing concentration of equity ownership in the hands of institutional investors. The two trends simultaneously lowered the cost of and increased the benefits to investors from monitoring managers and thereby encouraged the market for corporate control that was used to dismantle and restructure poorly performing public companies in the 1980s and 1990s. In turn, the advances in the market for corporate control seem to have also induced managers to act pre-emptively to restructure their firms before outsiders did, and thereby secure for them a portion of the value created.

This is not to say that managers do not continue to pursue their own wealth maximization when they make strategic choices. Rather, we contend there is a compelling case for our claim that, in the late 1990s, the time frame we are considering in our empirical analysis, both the incentives managers face and the monitoring they receive from the financial markets make stock price performance the key objective used in decision-making. Thus, we believe that changes in CEO compensation and the evolution of the financial markets have substantially narrowed the disparity between management's objectives and the objectives of shareholders, and therefore we assume that a strategy that increases the firm's stock price is preferred by managers to one that does not, regardless of its effect on the firm's underlying cash flows.

Analyst Coverage and Share Prices

The finance and accounting literature provides a substantial empirical and theoretical basis for believing that managers care about analyst coverage and desire more rather than less of it. Empirically, Amir, Lev, and Sougiannis (1999) have shown that earnings forecasts by analysts explain between 12 per cent and 40 per cent of the above-normal returns earned by investors from publicly traded stocks, suggesting that analysts do indeed provide information that is valuable to the markets. Moreover, they find that

Murphy (1990) found, even in the early 1980s. The differences in the two estimates stem primarily from the better data that Hall and Leibman (1998) have, which provides a much more complete measure of CEO stockholdings.

the contribution of analysts is particularly large when the firms operate in high-tech and R&D-intense industries, are in financial distress, or have more volatile fluctuations in performance, settings in which publicly available financial information is less informative about the performance prospects of the firm. Finally, Zuckerman (1999) has shown that a firm's share price is lower when fewer analysts cover it.

The theoretical case for the importance of financial analysts is also quite strong. A standard result of modern finance is that, when investors are risk-averse and are unable to eliminate all firm-specific risk through diversification strategies, the market discounts the values of higher risk firms (see, for example, Merton 1987). Thus, informational uncertainty about a firm's strategy increases the investor's firm-specific risk from owning the firm's stock and thereby diminishes the security's price. Given this effect, the firm's management has an incentive to attract more coverage by analysts in order to increase the amount of information possessed by investors and to raise the stock prices of the firms they manage.[2]

Unique Strategies and Firm Performance

From a theoretical standpoint, all firm strategies that yield above-normal returns—that is, impart a competitive advantage to the firm—must involve some scarce resource or capability that is not competitively available to all buyers, suppliers, and competing firms in the firm's industry. In this respect, a firm that operates in a unique combination of businesses is in a position to exploit any unique value-creating resources or capabilities that come about through its combination of diverse businesses. There is, of course, a large variety of resources and capabilities that can confer a competitive advantage to a business unit, many of which, such as possessing scarce capacity for example, do not necessarily entail combining different types of businesses. Nonetheless, creating such advantages at the *corporate* level frequently requires choosing the business lines in which the corporation will operate.

The choice of which businesses to enter or exit necessarily entails using some private information that the firm has about the value that two previously separate businesses will create when combined. Specifically, the decision requires that the firm's management identify non-obvious synergies between two heretofore unrelated businesses. These synergies must be non-obvious in order for the firm to earn rents from the decision to

---

[2] Even when investors do not care about firm-specific risk, managers may still have an incentive to cultivate a larger following of analysts. Fishman and Hagerty (1989), for example, have shown that firm managers have a positive incentive to increase analyst coverage in order to overcome a downward bias in the manner in which the market evaluates investments by the firm.

integrate the two. If the synergies are obvious, the market for business units—a strategic factor market as defined in Barney (1986)—will incorporate these synergies in the price the firm pays for these business units. In essence, these synergies will be competed away as other firms with similar resource endowments recognize the synergies and bid for the acquisitions or resources. For this reason, we think it is reasonable to hypothesize that *ceteris paribus* rent-generating diversification strategies will be unique rather than common.

Uniqueness is, however, only a necessary, not a sufficient, condition for above-normal returns (MacDonald and Ryall 2002). A strategy must also add value in the sense defined by Brandenburger and Stuart (1996), which requires that the strategy create more value than that of its rivals by either improving the firm's products or lowering its costs. Clearly, unique strategies can be either good or bad from a corporate cash-flow perspective, and many have argued that corporate diversification is value destroying rather than value creating.[3] In particular, there is a substantial body of literature in the finance area suggesting that diversified firms trade at a discount in the capital markets relative to focused firms (Lang and Stulz 1994; Berger and Ofek 1995; Servaes 1996).[4] These results are interpreted to imply that firms with unique strategies, which by definition are more diversified relative to their peers than firms with common strategies, trade at a discount because they are expected to be poorer performers. In essence, diversification is taken by the market as a signal of significant agency costs that reduce the value of the firm to shareholders.

Such a conclusion, however, rests upon the assumption that the capital market's valuation of the firm is an unbiased estimate of the firm's underlying value (that is, based on its operating profitability). We will argue below that there are compelling reasons to believe that the market's valuation of firms with unique strategies is biased downward because they attract less analyst coverage. Hence, a diversification discount is actually consistent with our hypothesis. If diversified firms do indeed attract less analyst coverage, then we would expect Tobins q, a common measure used to detect the diversification discount, to be lower for diversified firms than for their more focused peers. Therefore, we think it is premature to conclude that

---

[3] The theoretical argument that diversification destroys value rests primarily on the hypothesis that managers use their information advantage over investors to pursue projects that are in their own private interests rather than the shareholders'. Among the hypothesized benefits that managers pursue through diversification are a reduction non-diversifiable employment risk (Amihud and Lev 1981; Jensen 1986; Shleifer and Vishny 1989).

[4] Note that the agreement about the presence of a diversification discount is far from unanimous. The best studies to date, which correct for a number of sample selection biases and problems in reported data, find very small negative and even positive 'discounts' (see Villalonga 2003 for a recent survey of this literature).

the diversification discount indicates that diversification strategies are value destroying.

Note that there is also a significant body of literature that indicates that diversified firms are *more*, not less profitable on an accounting basis than focused firms. These studies, dating from Rumelt (1974), indicate that firms that are diversified in a 'coherent' or 'related' fashion have higher returns on invested capital (Rumelt 1982), have higher price-cost margins (Rhoades 1973, 1974), and higher returns on sales (Palepu 1985). More recent work using better, more comprehensive data at the plant level indicates that diversified firms are also generally more efficient than less diversified firms, as measured by total factor productivity (Schoar 2002). The implication is that, on average, diversification is a good rather than a bad thing for value appropriation by the *firm*, as distinct from value appropriation by *shareholders*. Overall, we think that there is no clear basis to conclude that diversification is systematically value destroying rather than value creating at the firm level, in particular in the current era when managers face much stronger incentives to maximize share prices.

Analyst Coverage and Strategy Uniqueness

Analysts face a number of different incentives when deciding whether or not to cover a firm. Although the current dialogue in the popular press has focused almost exclusively on the benefits analysts receive by helping their investment-bank employers earn underwriting fees on equity securities,[5] we are primarily concerned with the cost side of their coverage decisions. These less scandalous *disincentives* to cover firms reflect the additional effort that is required to investigate a costly-to-analyze firm. An analyst's report pushing for the break-up of Monsanto's portfolio of related businesses reveals some of these incentives:

Proper analysis of Monsanto requires expertise in three industries: pharmaceuticals, agricultural chemicals and agricultural biotechnology. Unfortunately, on Wall Street, particularly on the sell-side, these separate industries are analyzed individually because of the complexity of each. This is also true to a very large extent on the buy-side. At PaineWebber, collaboration among analysts brings together expertise in each area. We can attest to the challenges of making this effort pay off: just

---

[5] The *New York Times*, for example, reports that Jack Grubman, a highly influential analyst who is now under criminal investigation for his buy recommendations of several now-bankrupt telecommunications companies, received compensation of nearly $20m a year (18 July 2002) during a period when his employer, Citigroup, was generated over $800m in underwriting fees in that industry (25 April 2002). More recent accounts of the perquisites received by Mr Grubman for his role in Citigroup's efforts to sell underwriting services to AT&T border on the farcical—in his efforts to gain admission for his children to a prestigious Manhattan preschool, Mr Grubman allegedly received help from Sanford Weill, the CEO of Citigroup, in exchange for an upgrade in his recommendation regarding the stock of AT&T.

coordinating a simple thing like work schedules requires lots of effort. While we are willing to pay the price that will make the process work, it is a process not likely to be adopted by Wall Street on a widespread basis. Therefore, Monsanto will probably have to change its structure to be more properly analyzed and valued.[6]

The foregoing quotation highlights the presence of increasing returns to specialization in the production of financial analysis. Such specialization leads investment banks to organize their financial analysis along existing industry lines and makes it more difficult for analysts to assess the prospects of an entrepreneurial firm whose strategy combines businesses in unique ways and diverges significantly from those of its industry peers. There is already some empirical support for this conclusion. Bhushan (1989), for example, shows that the number of analysts covering a security declines as the total number of SICs in which a firm operates increases. The explanation provided is that, as the number of business lines increases, the analysts' costs of acquiring information about the security increases more rapidly than the benefits of the information gained, leading analysts to elect not to cover highly diversified firms. In our empirical analysis we seek to refine this result by looking for evidence that, after controlling for the sheer number of business lines, firms with unique strategies systematically receive less coverage.

To summarize, we think that it is reasonable to assume that managers evaluate strategies at least in part based on the effect the strategy will have on the price of their firms' equity shares and that, as a result, they must consider analyst coverage in their strategy choice. The existing literature on the relationship between stock prices and analyst coverage indicates that greater coverage should increase the price of a firm's shares and thus managers have an incentive to increase the number of analysts following their firms. We also think that the case can be made, at least at a theoretical level, that managers who seek to maximize their firm's future cash flows prefer unique strategies to commonplace strategies because the former meet the necessary condition for above-normal returns while the latter do not. Therefore, if we can show that analysts prefer commonplace strategies to unique strategies, we can provide evidence that is at least consistent with our hypothesis that financial markets do indeed constrain manager's corporate strategy in ways that may be inconsistent with maximizing long term operating performance.

Data

For our analysis we construct a dataset from information about firms and their analyst following using the I/B/E/S Detailed History Dataset[7] and

---

[6] PaineWebber, Research Note, 2 November 1999.

[7] I/B/E/S International Inc. is a unit of Thomson Financial and collects analysts' estimates and research for institutional investors. It is available to researchers through the Wharton Research Data Services.

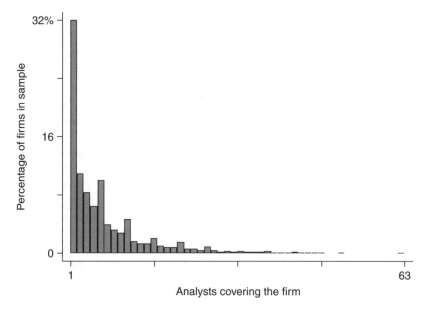

FIGURE 5.1   *Percentage of firms in sample with a given level of coverage.*

Disclosure's SEC Database. We limit our initial investigation to firms listed in both datasets for the calendar year 1999. Future research explores a ten-year time series with which we will use changes in firm and analyst behavior to identify the interaction between analysts and managers.

The I/B/E/S Detailed History file for 1999 contains more than 165,000 firm-forecasts-date observations. In this data, we identify 7,731 unique firms, 4,517 unique analysts, and approximately 46,000 unique firm-analysts pairs. Among these firms, approximately 850 are not covered at all. Among the remaining 6,900 firms, the mean number of analysts per firm is approximately 6.8, with a standard deviation of 7.2. The maximum number of analysts per firm is 63 (America On-line). At the other extreme, there are approximately 1,400 firms covered by only one analyst each (see Fig. 5.1 for a histogram of analysts per firm). For each firm in our I/B/E/S dataset, we have stock price as at the end of January 1999, actual earnings per share, and the firms' shares outstanding.

To measure the market's general assessment of the future prospects of the stock, we calculate the absolute value of the ratio of the firm's earnings to its stock price (EP), the inverse of the standard price-to-earnings ratio that is frequently quoted in the financial markets.[8] We take the absolute value of

---

[8] We use the inverse of the traditional price-to-earnings ratio to avoid the discontinuity that occurs as earnings fall to zero. Thirty-nine firms in our dataset report zero earnings.

the earnings-to-price ratio because the relationship between this ratio and the number of analysts following the firm is apt to be non-monotonic. If we hold earnings constant, a high stock price relative to earnings generally implies that the market believes that the firm's future earnings will exceed its current earnings. Therefore, when earnings are positive, a low earnings-to-price ratio implies that the firm's future prospects are considered good by the market, making the firm more attractive to analysts as a coverage target. The implication is that there should be a negative relationship between the earnings-to-price ratio and the number of analysts covering a firm. When earnings are negative, however, the reverse logic applies. High prices, again imply a small earnings-to-price ratio in an absolute sense. But the ratio is now more negative for firms with low prices, so that a comparison between the earnings-to-price ratio and the number of analysts covering a firm will be positive. Using the absolute value of earnings per share corrects for this non-monotonicity so that lower values of our variable, EP, correspond to firms with higher stock prices, regardless of whether earnings are negative.

The 1999 Disclosure SEC Database contains 9,579 firms with at least a primary SIC listed. We match 5,050 of the firms in our IBES dataset to their primary and secondary SICs in the Disclosure dataset. Among these firms were 365 that were not covered by any analysts, a considerably smaller fraction than that found in our original I/B/E/S sample (7 per cent versus 18 per cent). On average, those that are not covered in our combined database are smaller, have negative earnings, and higher sign-adjusted earnings-to-price ratios, suggesting that new or distressed firms may be over-represented in the subpopulation of firms without analyst coverage.

Measuring the rarity of a firm's strategy presents several challenges. First, a firm in our dataset can report up to five SICs. Therefore, the most specific manner in which to characterize the rarity of its strategy is to calculate the frequency of occurrence of its individual monadic, dyadic, triadic, tetradic, or pentadic strategy. Such a measure uses all the available information regarding which SICs the firm has chosen to report. It may also overemphasize firm heterogeneity, however, to the point of characterizing each firm as *sui generis*. Perhaps more importantly, this definition also implies that the uniqueness of the firm's strategy stems from complementarities among all its SICs. It is quite possible that the benefits of a unique strategy require only that the firm engage in a novel SIC dyad, the minimum level of interaction. Indeed, Teece *et al.* (1994) has shown that, although firms that operate in many SICs tend to have less coherence in an absolute sense—they consist of many dyadic SIC combinations that are very uncommon in the market as a whole—they tend to maintain a relatively high and constant level of coherence when only the most salient SIC combinations are included in the coherence measure.

In Teece *et al.* (1994), a dyad's salience is determined by (*a*) its relative frequency in the population as a whole, that is, the relatedness of two SICs, and (*b*) its inclusion in a network that maximizes the firm's aggregate relatedness while linking each of the firm's *m* activities together through *m*-1 dyadic relationships. Implicit in this methodology is the notion that firms expand their scope through a chain of extensions from one SIC to another, an approach that is broadly consistent with the resource-based view of the firm first proposed by Penrose (1959) and developed later by others (Rumelt 1984; Teece 1984; Wernerfelt 1984). For the present analysis, we assume that this type of extension into new businesses is precisely the type of strategy for which the underlying economics of the firm and the incentives of the analyst will diverge. That is, from the firm's perspective expansion into a new SIC that is not commonly associated with any of its current SICs satisfies the necessary condition of uniqueness, while from the analyst's perspective such an expansion raises the cost of analysis because its novelty requires the analyst to expand the scope of his or her efforts into a new domain.

Having selected the dyad as the most meaningful unit of analysis, the question remains as to the basis upon which to measure the relative rarity of each dyad. At the most general level, rarity can be measured using the entire population as a basis. Implicit in this choice is the notion that each analyst considers all firms in the market as potential targets for analysis. An alternative measure of rarity would entail ascertaining the frequency of the firm's strategy within the subpopulation of firms in its 'industry'. We place the term industry in quote marks to emphasize that the concept is not defined in an absolute sense but instead has meaning only in the context of the questions one is asking. In the present case, we are concerned with an analyst's view of an industry, which, we argue, is defined by the current markets and technologies of the firms that he or she would consider covering.

Choosing the consideration set for approximately 4,500 analysts and calculating the rarity of the strategies of 5,000 firms for each consideration set presents substantial analytical and computational challenges. We defer this task until we have at least confirmed (or disconfirmed) the existence of a relationship between the rarity of a firm's strategy and the number of analysts covering it. To this end, we propose the following, relatively straightforward examination of the data using the firm as the unit of analysis.

Consider the following stylized model of analyst behavior. Define X_i as a vector of non-industry specific aspects of firm i such as shares outstanding and the sign-adjusted price-to-earnings ratio that have been identified as factors that affect the analyst's decision to cover a firm. Define R_{ik} as the rarity of firm i's strategy relative to the strategies of the other firms considered for coverage by analyst k. Finally, define

$$U_{ik} \equiv \beta_0 + \beta_1 X_i + \beta_2 R_{ik} + u_{ik}$$

as the net benefit that analyst k obtains when covering firm i, in which u_{ik} is a disturbance term that incorporates analyst k's idiosyncratic benefit from covering firm i. With this specification, analyst k covers firm i whenever

$U_{ik} > 0$ and we have a multivariate discrete choice problem. Assume for simplicity that, $u_{ik} = \varepsilon_i + v_k$ and is uncorrelated both within and across indices. We can then summarize U_{ik} across all k to obtain the average benefit that an analyst will obtain from covering firm i:

$$U_i \equiv \beta_0 + \beta_1 X_i + \beta_2 E_k[R_{ik}] + \varepsilon_i \qquad (1.0)$$

If we assume that the firm-specific disturbance term ε_i is i.i.d. across i with some known distribution $F(\varepsilon_i)$, then the probability that firm i is covered by an analyst is:

$$\Pr(\varepsilon_i > -\beta_0 - \beta_1 X - \beta_2 E_k[R_{ik}]) = 1 - F(\beta_0 + \beta_1 X + \beta_2 E_k[R_{ik}]) \qquad (2.0)$$

If there are K analysts in the population, then we can use Equation (2.0) to generate

$$n_i = K(1 - F(\beta_0 + \beta_1 X_i + \beta_2 E_k[R_{ik}])),$$

the number of analysts that find it attractive to cover firm i. With this simple specification, it is relatively straightforward to estimate the parameters in $\beta = (\beta_0, \beta_1, \beta_2)$ using a Poisson or negative binomial count model in which the number of analysts is our dependent variable.

In this specification, the variable $E_k[R_{ik}]$ is a measure of the average rarity of firm i's strategy, with the average taken across all analysts. In our Disclosure SEC data, we observe 930 unique, four-digit SICs among approximately 9,500 firms. Only 10,000 out of the 432,000 possible dyads are actually observed, a strong indicator of the degree of clustering by firms in their strategy choices. In the analysis, we make no distinction between whether the SIC is listed as a primary SIC or a secondary SIC, and thus treat each dyad as equally important to the firm's strategy and the analyst's decision regarding whether or not to cover it. To give a few illustrative examples, our most frequent dyad is 6712 (bank holding companies) and 6022 (commercial banking), which occurs 414 times or among 2 per cent of the 20,000 dyads observed. At the other extreme, approximately 80 per cent of all dyads occur only once.

Each firm can have between 0 and 10 dyads characterizing its activities. To obtain a firm-level measure of the rarity of the firm's activities, we simply calculate the arithmetic mean of the frequency of its dyads. Higher values then correspond to more common dyad-based strategies. Note that such a variable is not defined for firms that focus their activities in a single SIC. Assigning them a value of zero would imply that their strategies are rarer than the rarest dyads, which occur with strictly positive probability. Alternatively, assigning them a value of one would imply that their strategies occur approximately two orders of magnitude more frequently. There are a number of ways to address this issue. One is to simply exclude the focused firms from the analysis and concentrate on diversified firms. Another is to treat the focused strategy as observationally equivalent to a strategy dyad and recalculate the frequency of all dyads among this enlarged population. The resulting variables, POPDEN and POPDENF, respectively, are equal to the density of each strategy relative to the total population of observed strategies. Higher values of each are then associated with more common strategies.

One problem with this measure of uniqueness is that it is strongly linked to the size of the industry (measured as number of firms) in which a firm competes. Firms competing in industries with a large number of participants are more likely to have common strategies (that is, to share common dyads) than firms competing in industries with a small number of participants. Firms in industries with numerous participants are likely to be composed of small firms, each with a relatively few equity shares, low trade volume, and thus limited incentive for analyst coverage. Consequently, contrary to our hypothesis, firms in these 'large' industries will tend to have both more common strategies and less analyst coverage. We control for this effect by including the variable, INDSIZE, which measures the number of participants that share the same primary SIC code.

The fact that the analyst community tends to cluster by industry raises further concerns about our broad specification of uniqueness. In particular, our assumption that the disturbance term in equation 2.0 is additively separable into uncorrelated firm-specific and analyst-specific components is at odds with this description of an analyst community clustered by industry. Clearly, if the effort expended by an analyst is higher when investigating non-standard firms than standard firms, as we hypothesize, then the analyst's idiosyncratic benefit, u_{ik}, will generally be higher for the set of firms i that are covered by analyst k since u_{ik} will be picking up the unobserved characteristics shared by these firms. In particular, to the extent that an analyst considers only firms in industry j, u_{ik} should be higher for firms that are more similar to the typical strategy of industry j. For both reasons listed above, we calculate a second set of variables measuring the rarity of a firm's strategy among the population of firms that are active in industry j.

The primitives for these variables are the conditional probability of observing a firm active in SICs h and j among all firms that are active in industry j. More formally, if SIC_{ih} as an indicator value takes on the value of 1 when firm i is active in industry h, then the conditional probability of observing a firm in h and j among firms active in j is:

$$Pr(h \mid j) = \frac{\sum_i SIC_{ih} {}^* SIC_{ij}}{\sum_i SIC_{ij}}$$

With this measure, large values of $\Pr(h|j)$ imply that the majority of firms that are active in j are also active in h. That is, the strategy hj is relatively common. By contrast, small values of $\Pr(h|j)$ imply that strategy hj is relatively uncommon among firms in industry j. If we define $I = \{h\text{:SIC}_{ih} = 1\}$ as the set of industries in which firm i is active, then we can calculate the rarity of firm i's strategy relative to its peers in industry j by taking the arithmetic average of $\Pr(h|j)$ for all $h \in I$. Again, we are presented with the issue of how to treat focused firms, so we adopt the same approach as that which we used for the population-level measures of firm strategy—we calculate these variables using only the population of diversified firms, SICDEN, and the larger population of firms that includes focus as a possible strategy, SICDENF. For these variables we face the additional choice of assigning each firm to a particular industry. As a first pass, we use the firm's self-reported primary SIC as its industry.

Results

All our regressions were run using Stata's preprogrammed negative binomial regression routines. We obtained equivalent results using a Poisson count model, but we can reject at a very high confidence level the null hypothesis of equal mean and variance, making the Poisson model inappropriate. In each regression we include three firm-specific control variables that we do not expect to vary across analysts—the log of shares outstanding (LSO), the sign-adjusted earnings-to-price ratio (EP), and the number of SICs in which the firm is active (NOSIC). We include this last variable to control for the absolute complexity of the analyst's task and expect the sign of its coefficient to be negative. The implication is that firms with more business lines require more analytical effort, regardless of how similar the business lines are to those covered by the analyst. Tables 5.1 and 5.2 present summary statistics for all variables used in our regressions for data consisting of only diversified firms and all firms, respectively.

The coefficients for all three of the control variables are statistically significant at standard confidence levels and of the expected sign in all of our specifications (Column 1 of Tables 5.3 and 5.4). Larger firms and firms with higher stock prices relative to their earnings (low values of EP) received more coverage by analysts. The relationship between shares outstanding and analyst coverage is quite pronounced, to the point of being readily apparent in a simple plot of LSO against the number of analysts following the firm (Fig. 5.2 in Appendix). A similar pattern is also visible in a plot of EP against the number of analysts (Fig. 5.3 in Appendix). We also found that more focused firms (low values of NOSIC) received greater analyst coverage. Although our NOSIC variable is a relatively coarse-grained measure of firm diversification, the negative sign on its coefficient is consistent with the hypothesis that more diversified firms are harder to analyze. It also suggests

TABLE 5.1a *Summary statistics for diversified firms*

Variable	Mean	Std. dev.	Min.	Max.
A	7.359	8.159	...	51.000
EP	0.118	0.470	...	11.000
LSO	16.945	1.430	12.904	23.009
NOSIC	2.920	1.101	2.000	5.000
SICDEN	0.209	0.169	0.001	1.000
SICDENF	0.187	0.158	0.001	1.000
POPDEN	0.003	0.005	...	0.020
POPDENF	0.002	0.004	...	0.018
INDSIZE	118.631	193.702	1.000	557.000

$N = 3,254$.

Note: EP is the absolute value of the earnings to price ratio. LSO is the log of the number of outstanding shares. NOIC is the number of Standard Industrial Classification (SIC) codes listed by the focal firm. SICDEN measures, for the focal firm's primary SIC code, how common the focal firm's combination of SIC codes is within the population of diversified firms listing the same primary SIC as the focal firm. SICDENF is a similar measure based on a population of firms that also includes firms in only a single SIC (focused firms). POPDEN measures the overall uniqueness of the focal firm's SIC combinations relative to the entire population of diversified firms, irrespective of their primary SICs. POPDENF is a similar measure based on a population that also includes focused firms. INDSIZE measures the number of firms that share the focal firm's primary SIC.

TABLE 5.1b *Summary statistics for both diversified and focused firms*

Variable	Mean	Std. dev.	Min.	Max.
A	7.163	7.805	...	63.000
EP	0.119	0.454	...	11.000
LSO	16.906	1.350	12.337	23.009
NOSIC	2.377	1.272	1.000	5.000
SICDEN	0.150	0.171	...	1.000
SICDENF	0.206	0.151	0.001	1.000
POPDEN	0.002	0.004	...	0.020
POPDENF	0.002	0.004	...	0.018
INDSIZE	108.668	176.933	1.000	557.000

$N = 4,538$ firms.

that the diversification discount observed in earlier studies may be due in part to the poorer coverage received by these firms.

Our results also confirm that firms competing in industries with numerous other participants, as measured by INDSIZE, receive less analyst coverage (see Column 3 of Tables 5.2 and 5.3). These 'large industries' are composed of many small firms, each of which appears to support only a limited number of analysts, if any.

TABLE 5.2   *Regression results: number of analysts covering a firm in a sample composed of all diversified firms*

Variable	(1)	(2)	(3)	(4)
EP	−1.25***	−1.28***	−1.28***	−1.28***
	(0.33)	(0.33)	(0.33)	(0.33)
LSO	0.54***	0.54***	0.54***	0.54***
	(0.01)	(0.01)	(0.01)	(0.01)
NOSIC	−0.04***	−0.04***	−0.05***	−0.05***
	(0.01)	(0.01)	(0.01)	(0.01)
SICDEN	0.09	0.16*	0.10	0.15*
	(0.07)	(0.07)	(0.07)	(0.08)
POPDEN		−9.01***		−6.93
		(2.56)		(5.87)
INDSIZE			−0.0002***	−0.0001
			(0.00)	(0.00)
C	−7.29***	−7.20***	−7.20***	−7.20***
	(0.17)	(0.18)	(0.18)	(0.18)
Log Likelihood	−8612.04	−8607.62	−8608.10	−8607.55

Notes: All results are negative binomial regressions with $N = 3,254$.
Huber-White Robust Standard Errors in parentheses.
*$p < .10$, **$p < .05$, ***$p < .01$, two-tailed t-tests.

TABLE 5.3   *Regression results: number of analysts covering a firm in a sample composed of both diversified and focused firms*

Variable	(1)	(2)	(3)	(4)
EP	−1.26***	−1.28***	−1.29***	−1.29***
	(0.25)	(0.26)	(0.26)	(0.26)
LSO	0.53***	0.53***	0.53***	0.53***
	(0.01)	(0.01)	(0.01)	(0.01)
NOSIC	−0.04***	−0.04***	−0.04***	−0.04***
	(0.01)	(0.01)	(0.01)	(0.01)
SICDENF	0.09	0.17*	0.12*	0.13
	(0.07)	(0.07)	(0.07)	(0.08)
POPDENF		−7.90***		−0.64
		(2.49)		(5.59)
INDSIZE			−0.0002***	−0.0002
			(0.00)	(0.00)
C	−7.09***	−7.04***	−7.02***	−7.02***
	(0.15)	(0.15)	(0.16)	(0.16)
Log likelihood	−12051.77	−12047.94	−12047.04	−12047.03

Notes: All results are negative binomial regressions with $N = 4,538$.
Huber-White Robust Standard Errors in parentheses.
*$p < .10$, **$p < .05$, ***$p < .01$, two-tailed t-tests.

Our results from examining the rarity of the firm's strategy were somewhat mixed. The coefficients for POPDEN and POPDENF are both negative and statistically significant in the Column 2 specification, suggesting that more common strategies actually attract *less* analyst attention rather than more, when rarity is measured relative to the whole population of firms under consideration. However, this result appears to be driven by the effect of INDSIZE. The correlations between the variables POPDEN and POPDENF and INDSIZE across the two samples range from 0.82 to 0.89 (Tables 5.4a and 5.4b in Appendix). Thus, when INDSIZE is added to the regressions, the coefficients for POPDEN and POPDENF become insignificant (Column 4). On the other hand, the coefficients for SICDEN and SICDENF are positive as expected in all specifications, but significance varies with model specification.

Conclusions

Our results provide evidence that analysts (or the firms which govern their behavior) make coverage decisions that are based on the costs and benefits associated with initiating and maintaining coverage. We find that more diverse firms—those with more lines of business—receive less analyst coverage. Similarly, firms competing in industries with numerous participants receive less coverage. Presumably, the benefit to the analyst in initiating coverage is limited in such industries.

Our primary empirical objective was to demonstrate a negative relationship between the uniqueness of a firm's strategy and the level of analyst coverage. Using a very simple specification, we have indeed demonstrated such a relationship. However, the result is not highly robust, suggesting the need for further study. We encourage the development of a finer-grained measure of the rarity of a strategy. Future research should also seek greater structure in the estimation procedures. Most importantly, a thorough analysis of this question demands multiyear panel dataset, which would allow us to more precisely test our hypotheses. In particular, we could examine how changes in uniqueness, changes in industry structure, and changes in diversification alter the scope of analyst coverage.

Appendix

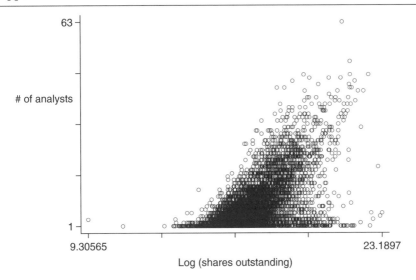

FIGURE **5.2**   *Plot of analyst coverage and shares outstanding.*

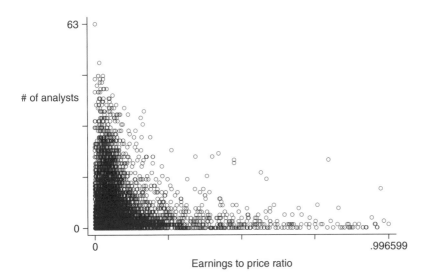

FIGURE **5.3**   *Plot of analyst coverage and earnings to price ratio.*

TABLE 5.4a *Correlations among regression variables for diversified firms*

	A	EP	LSO	NOSIC	SICDEN	SICDENF	POPDEN	POPDENF	INDSIZE
A	1.000								
EP	−0.107	1.000							
LSO	0.736	−0.060	1.000						
NOSIC	0.229	−0.051	0.360	1.000					
SICDEN	−0.012	0.001	−0.038	−0.172	1.000				
SICDENF	−0.030	−0.016	−0.063	−0.156	0.979	1.000			
POPDEN	−0.118	−0.032	−0.253	−0.308	0.352	0.414	1.000		
POPDENF	−0.118	−0.032	−0.253	−0.308	0.352	0.414	1.000	1.000	
INDSIZE	−0.103	−0.040	−0.237	−0.311	0.147	0.204	0.886	0.886	1.000

$N = 3,254$.

TABLE 5.4b *Correlations among regression variables for all firms*

	A	EP	LSO	NOSIC	SICDEN	SICDENF	POPDEN	POPDENF	INDSIZE
A	1.000								
EP	-0.115	1.000							
LSO	0.714	-0.067	1.000						
NOSIC	0.176	-0.036	0.268	1.000					
SICDEN	0.013	-0.003	-0.003	0.269	1.000				
SICDENF	-0.005	-0.002	-0.025	-0.240	0.614	1.000			
POPDEN	-0.090	-0.028	-0.207	-0.038	0.429	0.300	1.000		
POPDENF	-0.082	-0.021	-0.184	-0.236	0.211	0.415	0.796	1.000	
INDSIZE	-0.076	-0.033	-0.185	-0.150	0.163	0.200	0.816	0.877	1.000

$N = 4,538$.

References

Amihud, Y. and Lev, B. (1981). 'Risk Reduction as a Managerial Motive for Conglomerate Mergers', *Bell Journal of Economics*, 12: 605–17.

Amir, E., Lev, B., and Sougiannis, T. (1999). 'What Value Analysts?', Tel Aviv: The Recanati Graduate School of Management. Tel Aviv University.

Barney, J. (1986). 'Strategic Factor Markets: Expectations, Luck, and Business Strategy', *Management Science*, 32: 1231–41.

Berger, P. and Ofek, E. (1995). 'Diversification's Effect on Firm Value', *Journal of Financial Economics*, 37: 39–65.

Berle, A. and Means, G. (1968). *The Modern Corporation and Private Property*. New York: Harcourt Brace & World.

Bhushan, R. (1989). 'Firm Characteristics and Analyst Following', *Journal of Accounting and Economics*, 11/2/3: 255–74.

Brandenburger, A. and Stuart, J. (1996). 'Value-Based Business Strategy', *The Journal of Economics and Management Strategy*, 5: 5–24.

Donaldson, G. (1984). *Managing Corporate Wealth*. New York: Praeger.

Fishman, M. and Hagerty, K. (1989). 'Disclosure Decisions by Firms and the Competition for Price Efficiency', *The Journal of Finance*, 44: 633–46.

Hall, B. and Liebman, J. (1998). 'Are CEOs Really Paid Like Bureaucrats?', *Quarterly Journal of Economics*, 113: 653–91.

Hellwig, M. (1980). 'On the Aggregation of Information in Competitive Markets', *Journal of Economic Theory*, 22: 477–98.

Holmstrom, B. and Kaplan, S. (2001). 'Corporate Governance and Merger Activity in the U.S.: Making Sense of the 1980s and 1990s'. Working paper, University of Chicago and MIT.

Jensen, M. (1986). 'Agency Costs of Free Cash Flow, Corporate Finance, and Takeovers', *American Economic Review*, 76: 323–9.

—— and Meckling, W. (1976). 'Theory of the Firm: Managerial Behavior, Agency Costs and Ownership Structure', *Journal of Financial Economics*, 3/4: 305–60.

—— and Murphy, K. (1990). 'Performance Pay and Top-Management Incentives', *Journal of Political Economy*, 98: 225–64.

Lang, L. and Stulz, R. (1994). 'Tobin's q, Corporate Diversification, and Firm Performance', *The Journal of Political Economy*, 102: 1248–80.

MacDonald, G. and Ryall, M. (2002). 'How Do Value Creation and Competition Determine Whether a Firm Appropriates Value?' Working paper, Olin School of Business. St Louis, MO, Washington University in St. Louis.

Merton, R. (1987). 'A Simple Model of Capital Market Equilibrium with Incomplete Information', *The Journal of Finance*, 42: 483–510.

Murphy, K. (1985). 'Corporate Performance and Managerial Remuneration: An Empirical Analysis', *Journal of Accounting and Economics*, 7: 11–42.

Palepu, K. (1985). 'Diversification Strategy, Profit Performance and the Entropy Measure', *Strategic Management Journal*, 6: 239–55.

Penrose, E. (1959). *The Theory of the Growth of the Firm*. New York: Oxford University Press.

Rhoades, S. (1973). 'The Effect of Diversification on Industry Profit Performance in 241 Manufacturing Industries: 1963', *The Review of Economics and Statistic*, 55: 146–55.

—— (1974). 'A Further Evaluation of the Effect of Diversification on Industry Profit Performance', *The Review of Economics and Statistic*, 56: 557–9.

Rumelt, R. (1974). *Strategy, Structure, and Economic Performance*. Cambridge, MA: Harvard University Press.

—— (1982). 'Diversification Strategy and Profitability', *Strategic Management Journal*, 3: 359–69.

—— (1984). 'Toward a Strategic Theory of the Firm', in R. Lamb (ed.), *Competitive Strategic Management*. Englewood Cliffs, NJ: Prentice-Hall.

Schoar, A. (2002). 'Effects of Corporate Diversification on Productivity', *Journal of Finance*, 57: 2379–403.

Servaes, H. (1996). 'The Value of Diversification During the Conglomerate Merger Wave', *The Journal of Finance*, 51: 1201–25.

Shleifer, A. and Vishny, R. W. (1989). 'Management Entrenchment: The Case of Manager-Specific Investments', *Journal of Financial Economics*, 25: 123–39.

Teece, D. (1984). 'Economic Analysis and Strategic Management', *California Management Review*, 26/3: 87–110.

——, Rumelt, R., Winter, S. and Dosi, G. (1994). 'Understanding Corporate Coherence: Theory and Evidence', *Journal of Economic Behavior & Organization*, 23: 1–30.

Villalonga, B. (2003). *The Diversification Discount*, Cambridge, MA: Harvard Business School.

Wernerfelt, B. (1984). 'A Resource-Based View of the Firm', *Strategic Management Journal*, 5/2: 171–81.

Zuckerman, E. (1999). 'The Categorical Imperative: Securities Analysts and the Illegitimacy Discount', *The American Journal of Sociology*, 104: 1398–438.

—— (2000). 'Focusing the Corporate Product: Securities Analysts and De-Diversification', *Administrative Science Quarterly*, 45: 590–621.

PART II

Beyond 'Control and Alignment': Non-economic Objectives and Relational Governance

6

Economy, Society, and Worker Representation in Corporate Governance

MICHAEL J. PIORE

This chapter represents an attempt to rethink the role of worker representation in corporate governance. It focuses on the United States and developments in other countries are considered only as they enter into American debates. This focus is dictated by my own background and knowledge. I believe that much of what I have to say is of at least some relevance to other countries, especially those at comparable levels of economic development. But I am not really in a position to work out the relationship between developments in the United States and those abroad.

The chapter is written against the background of the rise in the last twenty-five years of shareholder value as the normative standard against which corporate governance is judged, and the reaction to that standard, whose dimensions are still unclear, which has emerged in the wake of the recession that began at the end of the 1990s and the corporate accounting scandals that emerged shortly thereafter. The reaction has at least three distinct, although interrelated, elements. First is a concern with the relationship between existing governance arrangements and true shareholder value and/or the relationship between the latter and economic efficiency. The second is nostalgia for the older institutions that were replaced by the governance arrangements instituted in the name of economic efficiency and shareholder value. In the United States, these older institutions grew out of the reforms of the New Deal in the 1930s; they are associated with the welfare state and specifically designed to adjust or constrain governance structures in a way that aligns them with worker welfare. Third, there has been a movement in reaction to both the older model and the new normative standard to replace shareholder with stakeholder value. In addition to the shareholders, the principal stakeholders are workers and the local community.

The argument of the chapter is developed in four sections. The first section defines the underlying problem that worker voice in corporate governance tries to address as a clash between two realms of activity and two opposing frameworks for thinking about evaluating behavior within them. One is an economic realm that we have learned from economic theory to think about in terms of autonomous individuals interacting in a competitive market. The second is a social realm, understood in terms of the collective nature of human endeavor and exemplified by our capacity to generate language and our need to understand and realize ourselves within a linguistic community. The clash is captured by the framework of analysis developed by Karl Polanyi in *The Great Transformation* (1944). That framework is particularly powerful in capturing the tensions surrounding the issue of labor market flexibility which has come to the fore in the policy debates of the last several decades, and both the shareholder value model and the stakeholder model which has been proposed as an alternative can be understood in its terms.

Polanyi's framework is not, however, helpful in understanding the governance structures that the shareholder model replaced. These grew out of a very different understanding of the nature of industrial society. The second section of the chapter tries to lay out, by contrast with Polanyi, what that alternative model was and the perceptions of the dilemmas of economic efficiency upon which it was based. The third section of the chapter explains how this alternative understanding, and the perceptions which rendered it plausible, were progressively undermined by economic events in the course of the last thirty years, rendering Polanyi's framing of the problem increasingly plausible and bringing the debate between shareholder value and the stakeholder models to the fore.

In the fourth section, however, we argue that, as a complete understanding of the changes that undermined the old institutional structures and as a guide to what might constitute an alternative, Polanyi's framework is also limited. The limits lie in the way it treats the social structure as a black box, a passive restraint upon the dynamic forces inherent in the economy. As a result, it leads us to ignore the way in which the structure of society, even more perhaps than the structure of the economy, has evolved in the course of the last thirty years and the way in which that evolution, quite separately from the evolution of the economy, has undermined the old institutions of corporate governance.

We conclude in the last section, however, that, once one begins to recognize the independent role of social forces in the evolution of institutional structures and the way in which they influence their operation, the economist's case for the shareholder value model also begins to degenerate. The argument leads to a fairly conclusive case for separating issues of corporate governance from those of worker welfare and for pursuing the latter through a distinct and more direct set of public policies. But, on the issue of corporate governance itself, the implications are less conclusive: They point to the need to rethink these issues, but leave no clear indication as to where that process might lead.

Some Conceptual Issues

The debate about corporate governance has come to be framed by the shareholder value model, and hence it is from this model that any argument must proceed. But this point of departure presents problems. The shareholder value model rests on a highly articulated theory of individual behavior within a competitive market economy. Neither the stakeholder model nor the models that underlay the New Deal welfare state reforms are as fully developed. And once one accepts the shareholder value model as a point of departure, it is difficult to formulate the problem in a way that these alternatives have any legitimate place. A starting point, however, is to pose as a central problem of economic organization the relationship between the economic and social realms of human activity. This is itself a difficult problem to formulate, let alone resolve. The very idea of there being two distinct realms of activity is itself a strong assumption. But there is a long tradition in Western sociological thought which argues that the separation of realms is critical to the process of economic development, especially in a capitalist economy. The argument is developed with particular force by Max Weber (1958), but is generally carried forward in contemporary economic sociology (Sahlins 1976; Bell 1976). The two realms are distinguished by the principles that govern behavior within them and by normative standards by which behavior and the outcomes it produces are different as well; principles of rationality and efficiency in the economic realm, but affective, charismatic, and/or dynastic principles in the social realm. The standards by which one judges behavior in the two realms may not only be different, they may also be incommensurate, raising the question of how one even talks about the conflicts between them.

In modern industrial society, economic behavior is invariably understood and analyzed in terms of conventional economy theory. The shareholder value model is rooted in that theory. The principal characteristic of the theory is that it is individualistic. Its analytical and normative starting points are the values which the individual holds internally and can think about and compare in his or her own head. It generally assumes that individuals do this in isolation from each other, but that is not integral to the theory. What is integral is that our relationships with other people are introduced into this personal and individualistic calculus. To care about and relate to other people is for them to enter into our own personal calculus, either because we 'feel for them' (their utility enters into our utility function) or because they provide us with resources or information, which we then use in the pursuit of our own welfare. This way of thinking almost invariably leads one to resolve problems of social organization by increasing competition and hence the ability of prices to effectively guide individual decisions toward economically efficient outcomes, or through adjustment in the distribution of income, after these decisions have played themselves out, through taxes and transfers. Adjustments in governance structures that give workers a voice in the operation of the enterprise as separate and distinct from the 'voice' they achieve by the companies' attempts to minimize costs in the face of competitively determined wages are not compatible with this way of looking at the world (but see Freeman and Medoff 1984; Hirschman 1970).

There are, however, some things which cannot be thought about in this way. For me, the best examples are language and, by extension, personal identity. The neoclassical model wants to reduce language either to a means (people learn a language like they acquire an occupation) or an end (people are so attached to their language that they are willing to sacrifice higher incomes in order to remain in their language community). But when language is associated with identity, it takes on a different meaning. It becomes fundamental to our condition as human beings, a sine qua non for everything else. Without language we would be unable to be what we are. This makes language a social good that is incommensurate with individualistic calculations. It precedes our individuality. In the shareholder value model, you would not be able to correct the calculations or their outcomes through taxes or transfers. Instead, you would have to make the shareholder value calculation first and think outside that framework for what it means for the social values represented by language. The one social scientist who has come closest to formulating the problem in these terms is Karl Polanyi, and this formulation, as developed in *The Great Transformation*, provides a starting point for our discussion here (Polanyi 1944).

Polanyi sees the principal problem in contemporary economic organization as the clash between the competitive market and the social nature of human beings. Because we are social creatures, meaningful life is possible only in a community—a set of stable relations with others—and communities are in turn rooted in a particular historical time and, above all, *place*. An efficient competitive market, however, can function only by treating both labor and land as commodities which are bought and sold freely in the marketplace and respond readily to variations in demand and supply as reflected in prices and wages. This ability of labor and land to respond to the exigencies of the market is captured by the term 'flexibility' around which the current debate about labor policy revolves. There is, Polanyi's argument suggests, an inherent conflict between the flexibility required by an efficient economy and the stability needed for meaningful human life. An economy governed by the market is thus completely 'unnatural': it is in conflict with the communal nature of humankind. The movement toward a market economy is, Polanyi argues, the artificial product of efforts beginning in the late eighteenth century to reorganize society in conformity with the economist's model. Modern labor market regulation from its inception in the nineteenth century is understood by Polanyi as an attempt to reassert, in the face of this endeavor, the value of community by limiting the commoditization of land and labor (and hence their flexibility).

Contemporary versions of the stakeholder model are readily understood in precisely these terms—a less rigid, more dynamic way of introducing the value of community into economic decisions. The shareholders' interest is in economic efficiency signaled by the competitive market—the competitive market for the firm's inputs and outputs as reflected in the competitive market for its shares. The other stakeholders, representing the workers and the local community, temper the pursuit of economic efficiency with the recognition of the cost of excessive turnover and mobility (Jacoby 1985; Weiss 2003; Clarkson 1998).

Other Interpretations of Industrial Society

Polanyi's formulation of the relationship between the social and the economic realms, however, is better at capturing the stakeholder model than it is the model underlying the welfare states. It is a convenient starting point, and it is helpful in sharpening the analytical issues, but the other models of corporate governance are not readily understandable in these terms.

Until relatively recently, at least, Polanyi was alone among contemporary commentators in seeing this conflict as central to the evolution of modern society. Others saw industrial society as moving progressively away from competitive markets governed by variations in prices toward large, bureaucratic enterprises that were stable, enduring and well-defined, and whose behavior was governed by the decisions of technocratic managers. Gains by adjustments to market prices on the margin in the technocratic decisions were swamped by the gains to be had by organizing the technology and the marketplace. This view was most forcefully expressed by Karl Marx, but one can find different versions in a diverse group of social scientists, from Max Weber and Joseph Schumpeter (1950) to John Kenneth Galbraith (1972) and Oliver Williamson (Williamson and Winter 1993), but its most forceful recent exponent is Alfred Chandler (1977). In many of these writers, but especially in Chandler, this view becomes linked to the technological trajectory of mass production. In a certain sense, therefore, the current dilemmas of corporate governance and worker welfare emerge in the transition from a world in which Polanyi's model was not particularly plausible to one in which it seems increasingly relevant. So we can begin to think through the issues here by asking how the old industrial economy managed to escape from Polanyi's dilemma and why that dilemma seems to have come back to the fore.

My own understanding of the answers to these questions draws heavily upon the argument that I developed with Charles Sabel in *Second Industrial Divide* (Piore and Sabel 1984). It rests on the nature of mass production as an approach to industrial development. The essential idea of mass production, especially in the context of Polanyi's formulation of the problem, is that economic efficiency comes to be highly dependent on stability. It does so because technological progress in mass production is about the development of highly specialized resources dedicated to the production of a single make and model of a particular good. The resources are so specialized that they cannot switch to alternative uses, and hence they become fixed investments. The efficiency of producing in this way then comes to depend on the ability to keep these specialized resources fully employed. Any variability in the demand for the final product, in the supply of inputs to the production process, or in the regularity of work becomes a threat to economic efficiency. In other words, the technology of mass production makes economic efficiency dependent on the very rigidities which Polanyi (and the neoclassical economists) saw as inimical to a competitive market. Conversely, the variability of the parameters of economic decisions in a market economy becomes inimical to economic efficiency. And it is precisely because of this conflict with a competitive market that the economy is reorganized progressively around large bureaucratic enterprises as mass production develops and spreads. The rigidity that Polanyi attributed to society comes to reside under mass production in the technology. The fact that it does so, and the increasing importance of stability to efficiency that this entails, eliminates the conflict between the society and the economy which Polanyi foresaw. Of course, not any social structure, not any community, is consistent with economic efficiency. Pre-industrial communities needed to be reorganized around the structures of mass production, but once that reorganization has taken place and the community has re-emerged in a new form, the stable commitments which it entails are actually a boon to the production process. Given this construction, it is easy to see how labor rights would become linked to the mass production enterprise.

The old regime of corporate governance was essentially the regime of managerial capitalism which grew up around mass production. In the context of the debate about shareholder value, the key feature was the way in which management was insulated from the pressures of the capital market by a cushion of retained earnings. Managerial careers were bureaucratic (even ecclesiastical). But, because the technological trajectory was so clear, the role of the manager was essentially a technical one and the requisite skills could be acquired and perfected through internal career trajectories.

Strong trade unions developed in the United States only after these corporate organizations with their highly articulated structures and procedures were already in place. The unions emerged out of a spontaneous social movement, and there was a period of experimentation with a variety of participatory schemes when the movement was at its peak. In this period, the trade unions' goals were arguably in conflict with mass production and economic efficiency. But as the system was consolidated and institutionalized in the immediate postwar period, unions came to participate in corporate governance in a highly restrictive way (Sahlins 1976). A sharp distinction was made in law and in practice between labor and management. The canon of US labor relations was: 'management acts, the union reacts'. Collective bargaining let the union place constraints upon managerial action, but it did not permit the unions to propose alternatives or even to discuss and evaluate alternatives proposed by others. Unions were relegated to an essentially passive role, which preserved the essential features of managerial capitalism.

The US welfare state grew up around these mass production enterprises as well. Public benefits were made largely conditional on employment and financed through payroll taxes. The public system was supplemented by private pensions, medical insurance, unemployment benefits, and so on, each negotiated on a company-by-company basis by unions in collective bargaining, and thus predicated on the stability and durability of the corporate entity.

In sum, then, the dilemma between the society and the economy which Polanyi foresaw was resolved through mass production, in two ways. First, the requirements of an efficient production process involved the kind of stability which was necessary to preserve society. In this sense, one could say that the conflict between the economy and society was reproduced within the economy itself in terms of a conflict between the flexibility of the marketplace and exchange and the stability of production; and under mass production the gains to be had from accommodating the requirements of the production process outweighed those to be had from accommodating the market. But the second way in which the conflict was reduced was that the social system in the workplace was adjusted to the requirements of production so that the two systems essentially came to coincide.[1]

The End of the Old Regime

The old regime of mass production, managerial capitalism and collective bargaining unraveled in the course of the last three decades of the twentieth century, and it is in that context that the debates about corporate governance and worker welfare must be understood. But the challenge emerged in a series of stages, and our understanding of the institutions which might effectively address it has shifted as those stages have unfolded. The stages roughly correspond to the different decades of which the periods were composed.

In the 1970s, the principal challenge came from the instability of the business environment. The instability appeared to be associated with a series of discrete events: the failure of the Russian wheat harvests and its impact on the world market for basic foodstuffs; the Arab oil boycott and then other destabilizing events in the Middle East; the shift from a regime of fixed to flexible exchange rates; macroeconomic mismanagement leading to stagflation; and ending in very high inflation and unprecedented interest rates, and so on (McCracken 1984). One might believe that, once these events had played themselves out, the economy would stabilize once more and the basic institutional structures could be preserved. In Europe, at the beginning of the decade, there was also considerable labor unrest which was interpreted as a reaction to the alienation of work under mass production, a long-term and permanent trend which stimulated a series of innovations

---

[1] Polanyi anticipated some of this in his discussion of Robert Owen's reforms in the nineteenth century, but it is an aspect of his argument which is not developed analytically.

in work organization (Boltanski and Chiapello 1999). But social unrest in the United States in this period took a form that was associated with racial unrest and protests against the war in Vietnam, provocations which had nothing to do with the organization of work and which grew out of conditions that would be corrected with time, eliminating the threat that they posed to the efficiency of mass production as an approach to industrial development.

As the instability continued into the 1980s, however, it was increasingly more difficult to dismiss it as the product of temporary aberrations. Moreover, in the 1980s it was compounded by other difficulties. Structural crises in several industries threatened the viability of major companies in steel, coal, and automobiles. The heavy welfare burdens attached to the enterprises in the form of private pensions, unemployment insurance, and medical care, moreover, complicated the adjustment process and led to perverse effects. The less efficient companies had the oldest labor forces, which imposed the greatest burdens in terms of pensions and medical care, but the desire to preserve these benefits led both government and unions to resist rationalizing the productive structure; and instead of closing the least efficient enterprises and preserving the most modern and up-to-date facilities, they prolonged the adjustment process through wage concessions which kept the older enterprises in business (Hoerr 1988).

More important in terms of the debate about corporate governance was the challenge to US manufacturing which came from competitors abroad, principally from Germany and Japan. In retrospect, much of this competitive challenge appears to reflect an overvaluation of the dollar, which was corrected in the course of the decade. But at the time, the competitive problems of American business were widely attributed to the superior quality of foreign products and to the greater variety of different versions of the same product which foreigners were able to produce efficiently. The ability of Germany and Japan to compete along these dimensions was thought to reflect, in turn, differences in the organization of production, and American management moved to adapt new practices modeled on these foreign systems (Dertouzos, Lester, and Solow 1989; Smith and Alexander 1999). These efforts had several effects. First, they clashed with the social system of the workplace which had grown up around older forms of mass production and hence encountered strong resistance from trade unions. That resistance increased opposition on the part of management to trade unions and to the legal arrangements which secured their place in corporate governance. But second, it led to a search for models of the workers' place in corporate governance which were more consonant with their new place in the productive process. On the whole, these involved much closer collaboration between labor and management, a reduction in hierarchy and greater horizontal communication, and an elimination of the extreme division between conception and execution. In Germany and Japan, these seemed to involve a more active participation of the workers through collective organization in areas which in the United States had previously been reserved for management. In Germany this took the form of works councils; in Japan, of company unions. Non-union US companies were freer to move in this direction and provided the most influential domestic models for the new institutions forms (Kochan, Katz, and McKersie 1986; Jacoby 1985). But there was also some movement in this direction within the framework of collective bargaining, and this had the flavor of the stakeholder value model. Workers and their representatives became involved in management decisions of a kind and at a level from which, under the New Deal system of collective bargaining, they had been excluded. The most prominent and far-reaching of these new arrangements was the Saturn Company created within General Motors in close collaboration with the United Automobile Workers union. There were also efforts at a form of worker ownership in which the labor force through its unions acquired stock in the company and obtained seats on the boards of directors. Such arrangements were particularly prominent in the airline industry, where they were actually as much of a response to the structural crisis in the industry as to the new forms of production (Rubinstein and Kochan 2001; Gittell 2003).

In terms of the Polanyi framework and the conflict between the social and the economic realms which it highlights, these arrangements reflected a view of the relationship between the economy and society that was very similar to that which underlay mass production. Production was still embedded in social arrangements and the importance of those arrangements to efficiency outweighed the importance of accommodations to the market, but the social arrangements in the new production systems were different from those under mass production, and different governance structures were required to effect them.

This was not of course the only, or even the predominant, response to the pressures of the 1980s. It was in this period that the market model rose to dominance in managerial thinking and business practices, leading to the era of hostile takeovers, leveraged buyouts, and a shift in managerial compensation, especially for top managers, toward incentive-based systems, including increasingly extensive stock options. It led as well to an opposition to trade unions which was rooted in both ideology and in the competitive pressure which management was under and which was completely separate from any reluctance the unions might have felt toward accepting the new production techniques.

Other themes in the 1980s were increasing globalization and the new information technologies. The latter facilitated the flexibility of the production process and had an important impact on both quality and product variety. Globalization was reflected in the structural crisis of steel and automobiles and in the competitive pressures emanating from Germany and Japan. These forces became even more prominent and took a different role in the 1990s, which proved even more threatening to models of corporate governance in which workers played a prominent role.

In the 1990s, the focus shifted from the production process to the generation of new products, and new technologies, particularly in information, communication, and biology, came to the fore. This had two effects upon thinking about corporate governance and its relation to worker welfare and community. The first effect of these new technologies was the inter-penetration of previously separate and distinct industries. The most prominent examples are in information and communication technologies, where firms like IBM, Kodak, Xerox, and AT&T, which had previously operated in completely separate domains, came into direct competition with each other and with other new firms in telecommunications and software. In the process, the focus of the company became less obvious; whereas before, the domain in which the company operated had hardly seemed to require a decision, it now was open to alternative interpretations, and shifted radically depending upon who exactly was directing the enterprise. As the focus of the company shifted, the linkage between the company and any particular set of occupational skills or a production community was broken. At the same time, occupational and skill sets became more open and diffuse. Production—now more the generation of new products than the reproduction of products through mass production—was still dependent on close collaboration among a group of workers in a kind of work community, but the particular types of skills, and hence the members of that community, were no longer stable or predictable. At the same time, there has been a tendency for that part of production which remained relatively stable and routine to be moved abroad, and hence to become increasingly irrelevant to governance arrangements in the United States. Finally, there was a growing importance of new firms and the processes through which they were created and the structures that evolved as they grew.

One can argue that these arrangements have a strong social component which competitive economic theory fails to comprehend. We return to this point below. But it is no longer obvious that the community at stake here is coincident with the borders of the firm or that it is represented in any meaningful sense by the workforce of the firm at any moment of time. The new models of worker participation in management which were developed in the 1980s were clearly and decisively rejected in the 1990s. Symptomatic of this change was the decision of General Motors and the United Automobile Workers *not* to expand Saturn or extend the innovations in labor relations there to the rest of the company (Rubinstein and Kochan 2001).

A Model of Society

But the notion of what the economy should look like was only one part of the model upon which the institutions coming out of the 1930s were built, and the factors leading to its demise are only one of the sets of forces which must be taken into account in constructing a viable replacement. The postwar institutional structures also reflected an implicit model of the structure of society. In this, the vision was not so much different from Polanyi, but it was definitely more elaborate. For Polanyi, the structure of society was a black box: Its essential characteristic in his construction was its stability or its need for stability, but he never went beyond that to discuss the form and substance of the social structure. The social model underlying the New Deal reforms had a definite form (Piore 2004). It envisaged a radical separation between the economy and society: each operating according to its own values and each with its characteristic structures and institutions. If the dominant institution in the economy was the corporate enterprise, the dominant institution in the society was the family. The family, like the enterprise, was stable, enduring, and well-defined. It was also headed by a single, male wage earner—the family breadwinner. The breadwinner represented the family in the economy. Given this construction, all conflicts between the economy and the society could be resolved by adjustments in the wage of the male breadwinner and the terms and conditions of his employment in the enterprise. This is a construction very close to that of economic theory in which adjustments in the wage can compensate for any cost, monetary or non-monetary. But it is not exactly the same. Since the family existed outside the workplace, an adjustment in the wage might solve most of its problems. But the workplace itself was also a social environment, one in which the worker spent most of his day, and it was not obvious that wage adjustments alone could compensate for problems encountered there. Thus, the bargain in the workplace had to take explicit account of what in American labor law are termed *other* terms and conditions of employment.

The final piece of this construction was the trade union. The union became the representative of the workers and, once it did so, any conflict between the social and economic realms was resolved by negotiations between the union and the enterprise.

This construction was of course a kind of ideal type. There were a variety of other institutions in each realm of activity as well as family enterprises in which the two realms were not sharply distinguished. In many families women and children worked as well as the male head. But these complications were thought to be exceptional, vestiges of an earlier era that were destined to disappear as the modern industrial economy matured, and with rising incomes women withdrew into the household and children to school. The secondary sector and the informal economy which we tend now to view either as a symptom of the incomplete nature of the efforts to impose a structure on the labor market or a perverse reaction to the efforts were not unanticipated at the time.

The collapse of the trade union movement effectively spelled the end of this construction of the relation between the economic and social realms.

In two decades, the percentage of the private-sector labor force represented by trade unions fell from almost a fourth of the labor force to under a tenth. But the collapse of the postwar model reflected as much changes in the organization of American society as it did the collapse of the union movement or the changes in the organization of the economy which we have just reviewed. Chief among these social changes is the steady rise of female labor force participation over the postwar period, the increasing commitment of women to work as a career, and the growing importance of their earnings as a component of family income. The increase in female labor force participation has been accompanied by a rise in the divorce rate, increasing numbers of children born out of wedlock, and an increase in female-headed households. At the same time, a number of other family members have moved out of the family to form their own households, a movement facilitated by the growing importance of the welfare state that provides income independent of the labor market. The aged are the most prominent of this group, but disabled people and unmarried mothers constitute other important categories. These developments have marked the end of the family as a stable, enduring, and well-defined social unit, in much the same way that changes in the economic climate have undermined these characteristics of the corporation as an economic unit.

An important body of social science commentary in recent years has viewed the social changes as leading to a kind of individualism which one might think of as the social complement to the individualism of economic theory (Putnam 2000; Baron, Field, and Schuller 2000; McLean, Schultz, and Steger 2002). But, at least in terms of the social forces important in the labor market and the economy, what seems to be happening is very different. With the blurring of the boundaries of the enterprise and of jobs and occupations, economic identities have become increasingly weak and lost their power as a fulcrum of social mobilization. But social identities which originated outside the economy—identities associated with race, sex, ethnicity, age, physical disability, sexual orientation, and the like—have become stronger, serving as the major axis of social mobilization in their place. As the social and the economic realms have become increasingly blurred, and economic identities increasingly ambiguous, social identities have invaded the economic. The focus of these newly emergent groups is not confined to the economy, but workplace issues are one of its purviews. Identity-based organizations have emerged in almost every professional association and in a number of major corporate enterprises. Identity-based social movements are also increasingly important at the local level, where they are beginning to generate significant economic regulations as well (Fine 2003). We have been studying the role of these identity groups in a series of studies at MIT: They seem to serve a variety of purposes in the eyes of their members. But, among these, they operate as networks of contacts for facilitating movement in the labor market, and they are used in this way not only by members looking for jobs but also by employers looking for workers. Adherence to them thus reflects in part (although it is hard to say how much relative to other motives) the weakened attachment to particular enterprises and well-defined occupations in career mobility. These groups and social mobilization around their concerns have been the driving force in a new system of labor market regulation built around employment rights generated by federal and local laws, court decisions, and administrative regulation.

The New System and the Old

In the United States, this emergent regime of employment rights sheds an ironic new light on the system of collective bargaining, which it replaced. The attack on the old collective bargaining system focused on its lack of flexibility, but in point of fact, through collective bargaining, the rules of the workplace could be tailored to the peculiarities of each employment situation and changed through negotiation in response to radical changes in the environment in which the company operated. The new system involves employment rights which are universal in character and can be adjusted only through a cumbersome legal or bureaucratic process.

A major difference between the new employment rights system and the old collective bargaining system is the disarticulation between the economic and the social structures. In a way, therefore, Polanyi's dilemma re-emerges. The new identity groups make demands on the economy and on particular economic institutions but, because their organization is orthogonal to the structure of the economy, there are no inherent mechanisms for reconciling the demands of particular groups with the needs of the economy or the total-ity of demands with the economic resources required to meet them. The new groups are active both within the enterprise and outside it. In the enterprise, their demands take a variety of forms, some of which are basically symbolic with political overtones. African-American groups have, for example, been active in pressing major corporations to boycott South Carolina because of its aggressive display on the state flag of a Confederate symbol associated with slavery and white supremacy; gay and lesbian groups similarly placed pressure upon companies to boycott Colorado because of a statewide refer-endum banning local legislation protecting against discrimination on the basis of sexual orientation. But other demands these groups make at the enterprise level involve economic resources: paid family leave, day care, facilities for handicapped workers, or domestic partner benefits. When attached to the enterprise, these benefits introduce the same distortions in the competitive position of the enterprise and their ability to adjust efficiently to the eco-nomy that collectively bargained benefits introduced under the old system. But because the demands are made piecemeal and each case is relatively trivial (although in the aggregate their cost may be substantial) the impact on the economic viability of the enterprise is not as meaningful a constraint as it was in collective bargaining, where contract negotiations constituted a moment when the overall balance was periodically redrawn.

The major impact of these groups has not, however, been at the enterprise level but rather through political mobilization, where it has taken the form of laws, administrative regulation, or court orders. The problem of overburdening the system with multiple and conflicting demands presents itself as a problem of political governance, not corporate governance.

The political demands are nonetheless having a major impact on managerial procedures and structures. Employers trying to manage an environment where they are subject to multiple, often ambiguous, regulations from overlapping jurisdictions have shaped a response through the human resource management movement (HRM) (Dobbin and Sutton 1998). Two aspects of that response are of note. One is the spread of explicit personnel codes—essentially a detailed employment contract. These codes enable the employer to prove that its treatment of employees follows general and impersonal rules that thus become a defense against charges of employment discrimination and harassment against particular social groups. They also constitute a defense against breach of contract suits which the courts have, in a reversal of historic practice, been increasingly willing to entertain. A second response has been to create internal grievance procedures ending in arbitration to adjudicate claims by employers arising out of the new employment law and the internal personnel codes. The arbitration process, once of dubious legality, has recently been sanctioned by the courts (Supreme Court 2001; Stone 1996). Together these HRM practices introduce many of the inflexibilities of the old collective bargaining system but, again, without the accompanying contract negotiations which provided an escape valve, a way of circumventing or eliminating the rigidities when they became too burdensome.

While the emergence of these groups seems to regenerate the Polanyi problem with respect to labor, it should be noted that contemporary developments undermine his point about the market for land. In the United States, at least, many of these groups are ethnic minorities; they grow out of the immigration process. They create communities and organizations that span geographical barriers. The ethnic identities associated with these groups do have certain geographical roots. And to some extent those roots are embodied in institutions which govern the economy; an example would be the Philippine Nurses Association which negotiates contracts for immigrant workers with US hospitals. But the bi-national (or multinational) character of these communities means that disruptions in any particular location do not necessarily threaten the community as a whole. In the United States, moreover, the importance of particular geographical origins tends to decline as the immigrants assimilate, not necessarily into a broader mass culture as was once assumed, but at least into broader identities no longer directly rooted in a particular place, such as for Asians or Latinos. Finally, Polanyi's assertion has been further undermined by developments in information and communication technologies that create the possibility of so-called virtual communities; indeed, the web and the Internet make his assertions about the relationship between place and community seem quaint and anachronistic.

Social Restraints on the Economy in the Aftermath of the 1990s

A very different set of concerns has begun to emerge as we review the experience under the shareholder value models of corporate governance in the 1990s. Attention in the popular press has focused upon the way in which accounting practices have obscured the financial condition of the enterprise and hence make it difficult (or impossible) for shareholders to make the judgments which the model presumes will force the enterprise towards efficiency. But a recent study of the CEO selection process by Rakesh Khurana (2002) raises a different and potentially more serious problem. In the 1980s and 1990s, as the managerial model of the enterprise was abandoned and the shareholder value model came to predominance, control over the selection of CEOs shifted from the existing managerial hierarchy to the corporate board of directors. As it did so, the criteria in the selection of the CEO shifted as well. The practice of the promotion of internal candidates was replaced by the recruitment of executives from outside the enterprise, even from outside the industry, and the choice among these external candidates, Khurana argues, became dominated by a single selection criterion: the ability of the candidate to provide *charismatic* leadership. In addition, the pool of candidates from which these presumed charismatic candidates were drawn became extremely narrow. Both the criterion for selection and the pool were the product, he shows, of the social relations which developed among a small and relatively isolated group of people from which the boards of the large companies involved are generally constituted. The conflict which Polanyi identifies between social relations and economic efficiency in the large thus emerges even in the narrow confines of the managerial elite and even in the period when the competitive pressures associated with the shift toward a shareholder orientation are most acute.

Khurana is an economic sociologist and extremely sensitive to the social dimensions of economic activity. But the solutions he proposes to the problem of CEO selection are basically economic solutions designed to push the board through competitive pressures to break out of their narrow social circle and the restraints it places on their ideas of viable action. One might imagine, however, a set of social solutions to the problem; the stakeholders model could be reinterpreted in this light. The addition of worker representatives to the board, or representative of the local community, might break the social cohesion of the clique from which the board is drawn and open a debate about a different candidate pool and different criteria for selection. In the current environment, the one factor pushing the board in this direction is the legal requirement to find women and minorities to add to their candidate lists.

But the basic problem with Khurana's analysis is that it offers no way of judging whether this type of solution would really work. He identifies the role of cohesive social groups but not the underlying process through which they emerge. We therefore cannot say whether new representatives to the board drawn from a different arena would act independently or would instead be drawn into the existing 'corporate executive board' culture. Nor does Khurana examine the way in which social structure and cohesion may themselves contribute to economic efficiency in management just as we have seen that they do (or did) in production. One can imagine that the standards of the corporate elite inhibited even greater abuse in the era of the 1990s than actually took place; or that the remedy for those abuses will depend less upon legal reforms than upon new social standards (perhaps a response to the reforms and the political climate which produces them) embodied in these groups.

Ultimately, one is led to conclude that our intellectual framework for thinking about these problems is too weak; or, rather, that the conceptual framework of the competitive market model and rational choice decision-making is overdeveloped relative to our understandings of social problems. It is overdeveloped relative to a second set of issues, closely related but too complex to be treated in detail here: rational decision-making assumes a sharp separation between ends and means; an ability to identify these ends and means; and a well-defined model which connects the latter to the former and enables us to 'solve' the rational choice problem. Where does all this come from; where do our ends come from; how do we distinguish ends from means; and above all, how do we come to understand the underlying causal relations between them? Our economic models, and the shareholder value model in particular, just assume all of this. But the missing pieces must be connected to social processes. Khurana's claim concerning the corporate boards' mistaken beliefs about the kind of CEO they should be searching for suggests that, in at least his particular case, the social group is the underlying source of the problem.

Such considerations lead one to wonder whether the demise of managerial capitalism reflects more than anything else a change in our belief systems. We thought in an earlier era that we knew how to manage business effectively. We have come to doubt these beliefs. But in place of a new set of substantive beliefs and conventions about the direction business should be taking, we have substituted a set of procedures based on the competitive market model.

To say this is not to resolve the relationship between society and the economy. The two may not be neatly separated as they were under the structure of mass production and the New Deal labor regime, or as economic theory would like to assume. But they do represent distinct sets of forces which must be reconciled for an effective, functioning socio-economic system. The one conclusion that emerges clearly from the experience of the last thirty years is that both social structures and economic structures have evolved in ways which make the old arrangements basically untenable. And whatever its limits, worker representation in a shareholder value model is unlikely to resolve the dilemmas that have emerged in this process.

References

Baron, S., Field, J., and Schuller, T. (2000). *Social capital: Critical perspectives*. Oxford, New York: Oxford University Press.

Bell, D. (1976). *The Cultural Contradictions of Capitalism*. New York: Basic Books.

Boltanski, L. and Chiapello, E. (1999). *Le Nouvel Esprit du Capitalisme*. Paris: Gallimard.

Chandler, A. (1977). *The Visible Hand: The Managerial Revolution in American Business*. Cambridge, MA: Belknap Press.

Clarkson, M. (1998). *The Corporation and its Stakeholders: Classic and Contemporary Readings*. Toronto, Buffalo, NY: University of Toronto Press.

Dertouzos, M., Lester, R., and Solow, R. (1989). *Made In America: Regaining The Productive Edge*. Cambridge, MA: MIT Press.

Dobbin, F. and Sutton, J. (1998). 'The Strength of a Weak State: The Rights Revolution and the Rise of Human Resources Management Divisions', *American Journal of Sociology*, 104: 441–76.

Fine, J. (2003). 'Community Unions in Baltimore and Long Island: Beyond the Politics of Particularism'. Ph.D. dissertation, Dept. of Political Science, MIT.

Freeman, R. and Medoff, J. (1984). *What Do Unions Do?* New York: Basic Books.

Galbraith, J. (1972). *The New Industrial State*. New York: New American Library.

Gittell, J. (2003). *The Southwest Airlines Way: Using the Power of Relationships to Achieve High Performance*. New York: McGraw-Hill.

Hirschman, A. (1970). *Exit, Voice, and Loyalty: Responses to Decline in Firms, Organizations, and States*. Cambridge, MA: Harvard University Press.

Hoerr, J. (1988). *And the Wolf Finally Came: The Decline of the American Steel Industry*. Pittsburgh, PA: University of Pittsburgh Press.

Jacoby, S. (1985). *Employing Bureaucracy: Managers, Unions, and the Transformation of Work in American Industry*. New York: Columbia University Press.

Khurana, R. (2002). *Searching for a Corporate Savior: The Irrational Quest for Charismatic CEOs*. Princeton, NJ: Princeton University Press.

Kochan, T., Katz, H., and McKersie, R. (1986). *The Transformation of American Industrial Relations*. New York: Basic Books.

McCracken, P. (1984). *On Key Economic Issues*. Washington, DC: American Enterprise Institute.

McLean, S., Schultz, D., and Steger, M. (2002). *Social Capital: Critical Perspectives on Community and 'Bowling Alone'*. New York: New York University Press.

Piore, M. (2004). 'Reconfiguration of Work and Employment Relations in the United States at the Turn of the Century', in J. Geile and E. Holst (eds.), *Changing Life Patterns of Western Industrial Society*. Oxford: Elsevier.

Piore, M. and Sabel, C. (1984). *The Second Industrial Divide: Possibilities for Prosperity.* New York: Basic Books.

Polanyi, K. (1944). *The Great Transformation.* Boston, MA: Beacon Press.

Putnam, R. (2000). *Bowling Alone: The Collapse and Revival of American Community.* New York: Simon & Schuster.

Rubinstein, S. and Kochan, T. (2001). *Learning From Saturn: Possibilities for Corporate Governance and Employee Relations.* Ithaca, NY: ILR Press.

Sahlins, M. (1976). *Culture and Practical Reason.* Chicago: University of Chicago Press.

Schumpeter, J. (1950). *Capitalism, Socialism, and Democracy.* New York: Harper & Row.

Smith, D. and Alexander, R. (1999). *Fumbling the Future: How Xerox Invented, then Ignored, the First Personal Computer.* New York: toExcel.

Stone, K. (1996). 'Mandatory Arbitration of Individual Employment Rights: The Yellow Dog Contract of the 1990s', *Denver University Law Review*, 73: 1017–50.

Supreme Court of the United States (2001). *Circuit City Stores, Inc., Petitioner* v. *Saint Clair Adams*, No. 99-1379, 532 U. S. ___. 21 March.

Weber, M. (1958). *The Protestant Ethic and the Spirit of Capitalism.* New York: Scribner.

Weiss, J. (2003). *Business Ethics: A Stakeholder and Issues Management Approach* (3rd edn.). Mason, Ohio: South-Western/Thomson Learning.

Williamson, O. and Winter, S. (1993). *The Nature of the firm: Origins, Evolution, and Development.* New York: Oxford University Press.

7

Corruption, Fraud, and Corporate Governance: A Report on Enron

PAUL WINDOLF

> The United States has the best corporate governance, financial reporting, and securities markets systems in the world.
>
> (Business Roundtable, *Principles of Corporate Governance*, 2002)

Accounting Fraud

Enron, WorldCom, Adelphia Communications, and Arthur Andersen are company names that have in the early twenty-first century become metaphors for falsified balance sheets, corruption, and fraudulent bankruptcy.[1] Some commentators have referred to these scandals as a 'Watergate' in the world of business and have prophesied a long-term loss of trust in the American financial markets. An extensive history could be written about each of these bankruptcies, but the intention here is to summarize the most important charges and to illustrate them with examples primarily but not exclusively from the Enron case. Above all, this analysis of the empirical evidence should answer three questions:

First, are the bankruptcies of Enron or WorldCom the result of deceptive strategies for which certain *individual* executive managers are responsible? If

A first German version of this chapter has been published in *Leviathan*, 32 (2003), 185–218. The research for this article was supported by a grant from the *Volkswagen-Stiftung*. It was completed during the summer 2002 while I was guest of the Hoover Institution, Stanford. I gratefully acknowledge the support of both institutions. I thank R. Buxbaum, R. Dore, N. Fligstein, B. Frey, P. Gourevitch, S. Kalleberg, and J. Lampel for helpful suggestions on earlier versions of the chapter.

[1] Enron filed for Chapter 11 protection on 2 December 2001; Adelphia Communications on 25 June 2002; Sunbeam on 6 February 2001; Global Crossing on 28 January 2002; WorldCom on 21 July 2002 (the largest bankruptcy claim in US history). Arthur Andersen was the accounting firm for Enron, WorldCom, Sunbeam, Waste Management, Global Crossing, and Qwest. Each of these firms has been charged with forging the financial reports. Arthur Andersen was found guilty of obstructing justice (15 June 2002); the firm ceased to be an auditor on 31 August 2002 (*New York Times*, 31 August 2002, p. B3).

so, then the actors in the Enron drama would only be particularly greedy specimens of the species *homo economicus*, and their behavior could be explained by citing a quote from David Hume ([1741] 1994*b*: 59): 'Avarice, or the desire of gain, is an universal passion, which operates at all times, in all places, and upon all persons.'

Second, are these cases of fraud rather the result of institutional failures? In this case, the bankruptcies would have to be explained by the structure of the economic *institutions* in the United States.

Finally, what motives should we attribute to the actors in order to make their behavior comprehensible? Is greed 'an universal passion' or perhaps a *culturally specific* pattern of behavior?

The first two questions are used to present two competing hypotheses. The third question is posed in an effort to link the perspective of the actors (the defrauders) with the level of institutions. In the end, the aim is to explain and understand a *singular* event (Enron) by applying the methods and theories of social science.

First, let us summarize the most important charges.[2]

Accounting fraud. By using complex procedures that made it extremely difficult for an outsider to follow, the companies falsified their balance sheets. Arthur Andersen is accused of having supported and covered up the fraud. The purpose was almost always to fulfill the profit expectations of the financial markets. The actors 'tweaked' the books as much as was necessary to ensure that the earnings per share would correspond down to the penny to the expectations of the analysts.

[Enron's] executives conceived a plan to take advantage of a group of power plants under construction in the Midwest.... If Enron could sell contracts tied to the output of some of the plants well in the future, the company could book the long-term profits immediately, even if it did not receive a dime up front. But when no energy company could be found to participate in such a deal, Enron turned to its banker, Merrill Lynch, which operated its own energy trading unit.... The plan was to create a kind of mirror swap in which Enron would purchase energy contracts from Merrill and Merrill would simultaneously purchase energy contracts from Enron. (*New York Times*, 8 August 2002: C12)

Even though Arthur Andersen and Merrill Lynch were troubled by the structure of the deal, it was completed within 10 days. 'Enron executives benefited tremendously from the deal. Because Enron met its profit targets, dozens of top executives collected millions in stock and bonuses' (*New York Times* 2002: C12).

---

[2] A brief summary of Enron's 'accounting gimmicks and deceptive transactions' is given in Senator Levin's 'Opening Statement: The Role of the Board of Directors in Enron's Collapse' (Permanent Subcommittee on Investigations 2002).

Special purpose entities.   Enron set up numerous special purpose entities (SPEs). The creation of such off-balance-sheet entities is a strategy that facilitates falsified balance sheets and fraud. Debts can be removed from the books of the corporation and 'transferred' to the books of a subsidiary company. The corporation then (apparently) has less debt. Very risky investments and business transactions can also be transferred out through the SPEs. Should the executive managers miscalculate the risk, the losses resulting from their mistakes can be 'hidden' for a while in the SPE. 'By the time of the collapse, Enron held almost 50% of its assets off its books.'[3]

In March 1998, Enron acquired a $10 million block of shares in *Rhythms NetConnections*, a high-speed Internet service provider. Enron was not allowed to sell these shares until the end of 1999. In April 1999, Rhythms went public and its stock soared to where Enron's investment was now worth $300 million. Because [Enron] could not sell the shares for several months, it wanted to get insurance against a significant decline in Rhythms.[4] The standard way to acquire such insurance is through the purchase of a put option. Enron's problem was that [Rhythms] was so risky that there was no one on Wall Street willing to provide this insurance. Fastow's[5] solution was to create a company [SPE] that he would run *that used Enron stock as its capital* to sell the insurance on Rhythms stock to Enron . . . . Because Enron was essentially insuring itself . . . there really wasn't any insurance. (Fusaro and Miller 2002: 133–4, emphasis added)

This is clearly a violation of all accounting procedures and principles, and apparently one that Arthur Andersen approved . . . . It led to a $1.1 billion reduction in Enron's equity and a $700 million reduction in earnings. These same people knew that a partnership run by [Fastow] was benefiting greatly from these transactions. All of them, and an unquestioning Board of Directors, did nothing. (Committee on Energy and Commerce 2002: Part 3)[6]

Self-enrichment.   A company that fulfills the expectations of the financial markets can count on rising share prices. The falsified balance sheets of Enron fulfilled these expectations and enabled Enron top managers to increase their yearly personal income to $100m or more, chiefly through stock options.

---

[3] Permanent Subcommittee on Investigations (2002: 8, pdf-version). The transfer of money-losing assets to SPEs allowed Enron to make itself appear more attractive to Wall Street investment analysts and credit-rating agencies.

[4] *Rhythms NetConnections* filed for Chapter 11 protection on 2 August 2001.

[5] Andrew Fastow was the Chief Financial Officer of Enron and the 'villain of the piece'. On 3 October 2002, Fastow was indicted for fraud, money laundering, and conspiracy before a US court.

[6] The loss to which the Committee refers came mainly from the SPEs called 'Raptors', a name inspired by the dinosaurs in the movie *Jurassic Park*.

Before the Permanent Subcommittee on Investigations, Dr Charles LeMaistre (chairman of the Compensation Committee of Enron's Board of Directors) testified that the total income of Kenneth Lay for the year 2000 was $141m, of which $131m—93 per cent of total income—came from stock options. Andrew Fastow collected $30m in side payments from Enron on the fraudulent insurance on Rhythms stock.[7]

Corruption. Enron, an energy trader, was only able to expand so quickly because the market for electricity in the United States was deregulated. In this liberalized market, Enron organized numerous ostensible transactions, which led to an artificial shortage of electricity in California and to a dramatic increase in the price of electricity.[8] During the course of this energy crisis, Enron was able to increase its profits by several billion US dollars. Therefore, the company had a direct interest in the deregulation of the energy market. The following three examples[9] show that many politicians received contributions from Enron:

1. 'Of the 248 senators and House members on the committees investigating Enron's collapse and its accounting practices, 212 have received contributions from Enron or Arthur Andersen, its auditor, since 1989.'
2. Managers from Enron contributed $1,836,865 to Republicans and $175,699 to Democrats in the period between 1989–2001; roughly 44 per cent of these contributed funds came from Mr and Mrs Kenneth Lay.
3. The energy industry in the United States is one of the economic sectors that spends the most on political lobbying ($159.1m in 2000). (By comparison, the drug industry spent $73.3m on lobbying in 2000.)

Conflict of interests (cf. Saunders 1985). On the one hand, accounting firms are supposed to guarantee that the balance sheets they audit reflect a realistic portrait of the financial situation of the company in question; on the other hand, these accounting firms are being paid by the companies themselves for

---

[7] Kenneth Lay was CEO of Enron until 23 January 2002. LeMaistre (2002); Powers Report (2002); *New York Times*, 8 August 2002, p. C12. See also transcript of the interview with the wife of Kenneth Lay at www.msnbc.com/news/695478.asp# BODY (February 2002).

[8] On 6 April 2000, Enron moved electricity from California to Oregon and back from Oregon to California. Enron dealers repeated this phony transaction *seven times on that day* (*Wall Street Journal*, 16 September 2002, p. A8). For a detailed description of similar practices see: *New York Times*, 7 May 2002, p. A11, and 8 May 2002, p. C1, C6. Cf. also Hogan (2002: 126).

[9] Center for Responsive Politics, data from the Federal Election Commission at: www.NYtimes.com/Enron (August 2002) and *New York Times*, 19 September 2002, p. C2; www.opensecrets.org/news/enron/andersen_totals.asp

the audit.[10] Not infrequently, accounting firms are pressured by their clients to confer legality upon a business transaction that is only semi-legal. Such procedures are known as 'creative accounting' among professionals, that is, 'standards which are so flexible that profits can be called losses or vice versa to suit the client's needs' (Buckley and O'Sullivan 1980: 7).

The analysts of the major investment banks also find themselves faced with a similar conflict of interests: On the one hand, they are supposed to provide an 'objective' evaluation of the future development of a company whose shares they recommend to the public. On the other hand, the analysts are paid by the investment banks, and their income is often determined to a certain percentage on the number of shares the investment bank can sell to the public.[11] The following example shows what sanctions are leveled against analysts who think that their first responsibility is to *shareholders*.

Chung Wu, an analyst at UBS Paine Webber, sent an e-mail containing this warning to 73 of his clients: 'Financial situation is deteriorating in Enron . . . . I would advise you to take some money off the table.' A copy of the e-mail landed at Enron. Wu was fired the same day. (Fusaro and Miller 2002: 72–3)

This brief account illustrates that the Enron managers were integrated into a network of collaborators[12] without whose help they could not have realized their goals: Arthur Andersen had to approve the booking of virtual profits as real profits; Merrill Lynch had to cooperate in the dubious energy swap trans- actions; the California Independent System Operator (ISO), which monitors California's electricity network, had noticed Enron's fraudulent energy trade but declined to pursue criminal prosecution against the company;[13] the California Public Employees Retirement System (CalPERS) cooperated in several of the Special Purpose Entities organized by Enron;[14] Enron's Board of Directors neglected to audit the company's accounting books closely; and so forth. It was the *convergence* of these various 'institutional failures' that enabled Enron to commit fraud 'on a grand scale.'

---

[10] For auditing and consulting services, Arthur Andersen received about $52m from Enron in 2000 (*Business Week*, 12 Aug. 2002, pp. 52–5). See also Bazerman, Morgan, and Loewenstein (1997).

[11] Some contracts promise 3% to 7% of all the investment banking revenues that analysts help to generate. The investment bank Salomon Smith Barney raised about $24.7bn for WorldCom. Salomon's fees then totaled $140.7m. Jack Grubman, chief analyst of Salomon, recommended the stock of WorldCom until 22 April 2002 ('buy'); in July 2002 WorldCom went bankrupt (*Business Week*, 13 May 2002, pp. 39–40 and 5 Aug. 2002, p. 36).

[12] Gourevitch (2002: 1) points to a 'collusion among "reputational intermediaries" (accountants, bond and stock analysts, banks, lawyers).'

[13] 'On July 20 [2001] ISO caught Enron and Sempra Energy collecting fees for relieving congestion without moving any power' (*Wall Street Journal*, 16 September 2002, p. A8).

[14] The name of the SPE was Joint Energy Development Investments (JEDI). The joint venture with CalPERS provided pension fund money for financing Enron's energy deals.

The Spirit of Capitalism

In *The Protestant Ethic and the Spirit of Capitalism*, Max Weber writes ([1905] 2002: 152):

The 'pursuit of profit' has actually nothing to do with capitalism.... Such striving has been found, and is to this day, among waiters, physicians, chauffeurs, artists, prostitutes, corrupt civil servants, soldiers, thieves, crusaders, gambling casino customers, and beggars. One can say that this pursuit of profit exists among 'all sorts and conditions of men,' in all epochs and in all countries of the globe.

Up to this point, this passage could also have come from David Hume. But then Weber makes a major distinguishing point: 'A fully unconstrained compulsion to avarice cannot be understood as synonymous with capitalism, and even less as its "spirit". On the contrary, capitalism can be identical with the *taming* of this irrational motivation, or at least with its rational tempering.'

Irrational greed is transformed into a rational aspiration for monetary gain through the institutions of capitalism.[15] The 'spirit of capitalism' cannot be reduced to 'avarice' but is the result of a process of rationalizing and modernizing Western societies. Unbridled greed is not only irrational, it is also inefficient, because the success of capitalist enterprise is based on continuous and calculable profitability.

For Hume ([1741] 1994a: 55), 'passions' are the spur of the capitalist economic process: 'Avarice, the spur of industry, is so obstinate a passion ...' This view places him squarely in the tradition of Adam Smith, who considered 'interests' to be the motor of capitalism. The 'invisible hand' causes the pursuit of individual interests eventually to serve the general welfare.[16]

In the case of Enron, the 'invisible hand' evidently failed. Yet Enron is not an isolated case. The historical development of American capitalism has experienced recurring waves of fraud and corruption.[17] Enron is an example of the unavoidable transaction costs of a system whose dynamics are spawned by market competition that is little regulated by institutions.

With illustrations from the Enron case, the 'institutional failures' are to be discussed in greater detail in the following sections. For the moment, the analysis is succinctly presented in six theses. The first two theses can be labeled as 'push factors' while the rest refer to the opportunity structure for fraud and corruption.

---

[15] For Max Weber, such rational tempering was naturally the work first and foremost of the religious institutions of Protestantism.

[16] The relationship between passions, interests, and institutions cannot be discussed in detail here. See Hirschman (1977: 17): 'The idea of harnessing the passions of men, of making them work toward the general welfare ... was put forward [already] by Bernard Mandeville.'

[17] 'If early capital formation in an economy could be explained only by Marx or fraud, there is no doubt to which camp the American evolution of 1870–1910 would belong' (Buxbaum 1979: 244). See also Perrow (2002); McCormick (1981).

Push factors

1. 'Socially deviant behavior [is] just as much a product of social structure as conformist behavior' (Merton 1968: 175).
2. Intensified *competition* forces companies to operate in the gray area between the 'legally permissible' and the 'criminal'. In the professional terminology of public accountants, this is called 'aggressive accounting', meaning the use of accounting practices that push the law to its limits.

Pull factors (opportunity structure)

3. Each information asymmetry between two market actors which is based on economically usable knowledge improves the opportunity structure for fraud.
4. The 'economics of intangibles' has further intensified the information asymmetry between insiders and outsiders and has improved the opportunity structure for (fraudulent) manipulation in the financial markets.
5. Stock options for corporate executives create a systematic incentive to manipulate the balance sheets, to exploit insider knowledge, and to selectively give preferential treatment to analysts who evaluate the company as 'positive'.
6. Corruption facilitates the colonization of the political system by the major corporations and reduces the autonomy of political institutions.

In the following section, we will define corruption and fraud. Afterward, these six theses will be discussed.

Corruption and Fraud Defined

Perrow (2002: 14) offers this description of the 'legal' regulation of the railways in the state of New York at the end of the nineteenth century: 'If one [railroad] had bribed a judge for a favorable ruling, the other [railroad] could quickly travel to an otherwise remote county, and purchase another ruling, and send it back instantly by telegraph . . . . once the railroad made it easy to go from one county judge to another, the railroads could shop for a judge that would give them the best verdict.' This example illustrates well what corruption is.

Modern societies are divided into subsystems, and in every subsystem exchange processes are transmitted by a specific 'medium'. In the political system the medium is (legitimate) 'power'; in the economic system, it is 'money'; in the legal system, it is 'justice'; and in the scientific system it is 'truth.' The *autonomy* of a subsystem is upheld through the use of only one specific medium—the one constitutive of the system operations of a subsystem—as the *legitimate* 'currency' to transmit exchange processes. The 'operations' in the scientific system are based on the code 'true/untrue', in the legal system 'legal/illegal', in the economic system 'profitable/unprofitable' (Luhmann 2000).

Corruption is defined as an exchange between subsystems in which the specific code of a system is violated. Firms that buy 'justice' or 'politics' and politicians who use power in order to force scientists to produce a politically useful truth violate the code of each respective system.[18]

On the system level, corruption blurs the differentiation within a social system by causing subsystems to lose a degree of their autonomy. On the values level, corruption leads to a loss of legitimacy for specific operations and, on the functional level, to the collapse of system operations. If enterprises buy politicians, the political system is being 'colonized' by business: political decisions lose their legitimization, and the difference between economics and politics tends to disappear.

Fraud is a breach of trust. If I do not trust a person, it will be hard for this person to cheat me. Financial markets become a 'market for lemons' (Akerlof 1970) once investors lose their trust in them. It was also a loss of trust that led to the demise of the firm Arthur Andersen, one of the five largest accounting firms in the world.

After he resigned his job as CEO of Arthur Andersen, Joseph Berardino expressed the point in this way: '*Andersen sells trust!*'[19] Unfortunately for the firm, this insight came too late. Enron was not the first case of manipulated accounting and bankruptcy in which Andersen was involved. Waste Management, Sunbeam, and Baptist Foundation of Arizona had all previously been down that same road. First a massive accounting fraud was uncovered, then came bankruptcy. In each of these cases, Andersen had been the auditor.[20]

Fraud is a zero-sum game played among the actors *within* a system. What the insider wins on the stock market, the outsider loses. The profits bagged by Enron executives have to be set against the losses suffered by the employees and stockholders.

Social Structure and Deviant Behavior

In a classic article written in the 1930s, Merton argues (1968: 175) that 'Socially deviant behavior [is] just as much a product of social structure as

---

[18] Cf. Parsons (1969: 342): 'At various points in the societal system, power is exchanged both for other generalized media, notably money and influence, and for intrinsically significant rewards.' (Given the context of fraud and corruption being analyzed here, Parson's statement is ambiguous.)

[19] Speech at the Commonwealth Club, San Francisco, 4 June 2002. www.commonwealthclub.org/archive/02/02–06berardino-audio.html

[20] 'Andersen was under an injunction reached as part of a settlement in the Waste Management case, which prohibited the firm from engaging in future wrongdoing and significantly increased the penalties if it was found to have done so' (*New York Times*, 8 May 2002, p. C6).

conformist behavior'. He goes on, 'Some social structures exert a definite pressure upon certain persons . . . to engage in non-conforming conduct' (1968: 186). To answer the question of the conditions under which a specific social structure 'pressures' individuals to behave in a deviant manner or at least insinuates that such behavior would be a rational adaptational reaction, Merton refers to a structural conflict. If the main cultural values of a society are success, wealth, and upward mobility,[21] but the legal means to fulfill these aims are available only to a minority, then deviant behavior is a rational adaptational strategy. Especially relevant to the topic under discussion, Merton believed that this conflict was particularly pronounced in American society: 'Contemporary American culture appears to approximate the polar type in which great emphasis upon certain success-goals occurs without equivalent emphasis upon institutional means' (1968: 190).

What Merton had in mind when he wrote the first version of this article in 1938 were the high crime rates in cities like Chicago or New York; of lesser concern to him were such exclusive managerial circles as are being discussed here. At any rate, it cannot be argued that a 'lack of institutional means' is what drove the corporate executives to commit fraud. The problem was rather an overabundance of 'institutional means' (opportunity structure).

Therefore, we modify Merton's thesis by introducing two further assumptions. First, not until a dominant set of values (wealth and success) *connects* with the *competitiveness* that permeates all aspects of life does there emerge the 'pressure' that Merton identifies as the cause of deviant behavior. The 'villains' in the Enron drama were top managers from the highest executive levels. In such positions, competition does not decrease, it increases exponentially. And competition not only dominates business life but also affects private lifestyles.[22] A former manager of an energy company is on record as having said:

I swear, my voice mail machine was jammed every day with bankers trying to pitch me something. They'd come in with their Power-Point slides telling us why we needed to buy this or that and how if we didn't we'd be left in the dust by the guys down the street who were doing a deal a minute. (*New York Times*, 21 August 2002, p.16)

---

[21] Cf. Kalberg (2001: 310): 'the pursuit of wealth is extolled.'

[22] 'L. Dennis Kozlowski, 55, the son of a Newark police officer who as chief executive helped build Tyco into an international conglomerate . . . is accused of using the money [of Tyco] to pay for everything from an apartment on Park Avenue and homes in Boca Raton, Fla., to jewelry from Harry Winston and Tiffany's. [He] is also accused of having the company pick up half the cost of a multi-million-dollar 40th-birthday party on the Italian island of Sardinia for his wife, a former waitress at a restaurant near Tyco's headquarters in New Hampshire' (*New York Times*, 13 September 2002, p. A1). 'Conspicuous consumption' is not only openly displayed as a manifestation of the American ideology on 'from rags to riches' success, it becomes a social *obligation* in the social circles of those whose income is published in the Forbes' rankings.

Both Enron and WorldCom grew almost exclusively by buying up other companies. In a matter of only a few years, for example, WorldCom bought sixty-five telecommunications companies.[23] The investment bankers who conducted these transactions earned fortunes through the 'deals'. The energy trader articulated the competitive pressure to which executives in the market for corporate control are exposed: either buy or be bought.

Another example should further clarify this point. Arthur Andersen compiled a 'risk profile' for each of the 2,500 firms it audited. The firms (clients) were then divided into four categories: 'Maximum, high, moderate, and low risk'. Enron was one of some 50 clients deemed 'maximum risk' while 700 more were considered 'high risk' (*Business Week*, 12 August 2002, p. 53). 'High risk' companies are those that stretch their accounting practices to the limits of what is legally permissible, that is, they engage in 'aggressive accounting'.

Why do executives take the risk of teetering on the edge of legality? There is one explanation that at first has nothing to do with 'avarice': the more a company is exposed to competition in the market for corporate control—meaning the greater the danger that the company will be bought up and thereby lose its autonomy—the more important the share price of the company becomes. High share prices offer a relative protection from (hostile) takeovers. Among other factors, the share price is determined by what the executive managers publish in their *financial statements*.

Not until the specific values of a culture (for example, extolling the pursuit of wealth) link up with a pervasive competitiveness in all aspects of life do those dynamic effects emerge, the 'fallout' of which we can observe in the Enron case.

Our second modification of Merton is the observation that the cultural values that Merton assumes are not equally distributed throughout society. Individuals for whom wealth and a high income are very important will attempt to secure positions in the *economic system* and will reject positions in the scientific or welfare systems because these offer relatively few opportunities for substantial income earning.[24] Such *self-selection* is intensified by the selection process in hiring. The 'assessment centers' of companies ensure that only those applicants are hired who indicate that a large income is important to them. If the personnel of a company were indifferent to the idea of earning a lot of money, the company's incentive system could not work (for example, stock options). In other words, through a process of selection and self-selection, those individuals who aggressively pursue large incomes

---

[23] 'For WorldCom, acquisitions were behind its rise and fall' (*New York Times*, 8 Aug. 2002, p. A1).

[24] This process of selection and self-selection operates already at the level of college education (preference for a particular university subject: for example, history versus business administration). It can be seen here that the generalized mediums of exchange (truth, justice, money) can be interpreted as patterns of preferences internalized during the socialization process (Windolf 1995).

congregate in the economic subsystem.[25] Within the economic system, they gather foremost in those companies offering particularly ample opportunity due to their rapid growth. Enron belonged to this group of companies.[26]

This modification of Merton's thesis has two advantages. First, it avoids the assumption that *all* members of a society have internalized the pattern of values Merton postulates: that is, we assume that 'avarice' is not equally distributed among social subsystems. Second, certain value patterns do not automatically produce deviant behavior; not until they are 'unleashed' in a specific institutional structure do they develop these dynamics (competition).

Even if individuals are willing, however, to seek large incomes with aggressive and (in borderline cases) criminal means, it does not mean that they are successful. They need a certain 'opportunity structure' in which they can test their talents. This is the topic of the following section.

The Opportunity Structure for Fraud

Cloward and Ohlin argue that every society has a dual opportunity structure at its disposal. There are legal and criminal careers. 'We believe that each individual occupies a position in both legitimate and illegitimate opportunity structures' (1960: 150).

If someone wants to successfully (that is, professionally) rob a bank, this person needs access to a specific opportunity structure, meaning information, social networks, technical training, and so on. Most bank robbers (fortunately) are dilettantes.

What does the opportunity structure for (accounting) fraud look like? With the help of the two following examples—information asymmetries and the increasing importance of 'intangible assets'—we will see how economic structural change clearly improved the conditions to successfully use accounting to defraud.

Information Asymmetries

During the 1990s, the catchwords 'knowledge society' and 'knowledge worker' have been used to point to the increasing impact of science and technology on almost all facets of life (Neef 1998; Kleinman and Vallas 2001). In many studies two developments are emphasized: the amount of knowledge available to society has grown exponentially, and the knowledge that individuals have at their disposal is becoming increasingly diversified.

[25] Cf. Etzioni's typology of compliance relations within organizations (1961: 12–17): The processes of selection and self-selection are likely to produce a congruent type of compliance in large organizations, that is, the motivation of organization members (calculative) is congruent with the power resources of the organization (remunerative).

[26] 'Enron preferred to recruit its employees straight out of school so that they would know only the Enron way of doing things' (Fusaro and Miller 2002: 147; see also 48–51).

Society 'knows' more and more, but the intersection of *common* knowledge shared by all individuals is becoming smaller and smaller.

A medical specialist may know a great deal about a rare disease, but she probably knows almost nothing about the future prospects for the development of a certain technology. In turn, a stock analyst who specializes in this area knows a great deal about this technology, but almost nothing about the chances of success for a certain therapy. The relationship between the doctor and the analyst is characterized by a strong information asymmetry.

Should the stock analyst become ill, he is 'at the mercy' of the doctor, while the doctor will be able to judge the value of the analyst's advice in matters of financial investment only after the fact (that is, when it's too late). For this reason, most professions have a 'code of ethics.'

Thesis 1: Each information asymmetry between two market actors which is based on economically applicable knowledge improves the opportunity structure for fraud.

Thesis 1 is plausible only if an additional assumption is introduced. There has always been an information 'asymmetry' between doctor and patient, but that is not to say that patients are constantly being cheated. Yet here it is being *additionally* assumed that the process of individualization has weakened the codes of ethics of the professions. Only when the members of a profession view their code of ethics as no longer or only marginally binding can they transform the information asymmetries into market opportunities and income generators. Arthur Andersen is a particularly impressive example of 'creative accounting' in which the code of ethics of the profession was violated and the victims were the (uninformed) Enron shareholders and employees.[27]

Thesis 2: The opportunity structure for fraud improves the more market relations become detached from social relations (disembeddedness), the less 'tacit knowledge' exists in economic relations, and the more market actors are forced to rely on abstract and generalized knowledge (Polanyi 1997).

A bank that grants a company credit knows the management of this firm personally, and often a bank executive sits on the supervisory board of the company. In addition, the bank is integrated into networks in which information is circulated about this company. However, an investment fund in Luxembourg, relying on Standard and Poor's ratings, will purchase shares in a Korean company although it has never seen this company and does not know its management.

---

[27] The 'code of ethics' not only prohibits the (fraudulent) exploitation of information asymmetries, it also regulates the competition between members of the profession. See the Registered Public Accountants' Association Code of Ethics: www.rpaa.org/ethics.htm; Carey (1969: 3).

In communication processes, we can distinguish between digital and ana-log codes (Watzlawick 1967). 'Hard facts' are transmitted through digital code. The testimony of a witness in court or the financial statements of a company are considered to be 'hard facts'. Through analog code, information is transmitted that qualifies the digital statements: whether they are meant seriously or only lightly; whether a person harbors a hostile or friendly atti-tude. A great deal of information is transmitted through analog code that enables us to judge the *trustworthiness* of a person.

The information defined here as 'tacit knowledge' is that which is derived from social contexts, which is often communicated through analog code, and which cannot be formalized and standardized and is therefore unsuitable for dissemination worldwide. The hypothesis presented here is that an extensive loss of tacit knowledge has occurred in connection with the globalization of the financial markets, and that this loss has improved the opportunity structure for fraud.[28]

Intangible Assets

A conveyor belt, an office building, or a truck belonging to a transport business are all 'tangible' assets. The value of these assets is measurable and can be credited according to the standard rules of Generally Accepted Accounting Principles (GAAP). The *business idea* behind amazon.com, the Universal Mobile Telecommunications System (UMTS) *licenses* that Telecom (Germany) purchased for € 8.5bn, the *brand name* of Coca-Cola, the insider knowledge of an energy trader at Enron are all examples of 'intangible' assets. More and more, the assets of companies that are a part of the 'new economy' are not tangible assets but intangible ones. The new economy is a knowledge economy (Lev 2001).

Yet another distinction needs to be made in order to underscore the relevance of intangible assets to the problem being discussed. How do we determine the 'value' of a commodity? There are two different definitions.

Under the first definition, 'The value of any commodity is determined by the amount of labour socially necessary for its production' (Marx [1867] 1970: 39). This is the definition found in the labor theory of value, which dates back to Ricardo and Marx. In an updated version, we can say that the value of a commodity is determined by the production costs. This definition bases the value on the costs incurred during production (that is, *past* costs) and therefore the value can be measured with relative precision.

---

[28] Charles Tyson Yerkes, the traction magnate in Chicago who was involved in the fraud-ulent bankruptcy of the National Bank of Illinois (1905), was considered by Marshall Field to be 'not safe' (Tarr 1966: 454). It is this kind of 'tacit knowledge' that is lacking in globalized, standardized, and professionalized forms of knowledge (for example, a balance sheet).

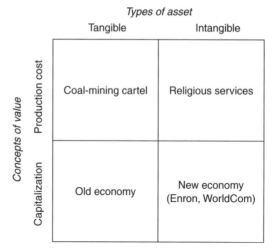

FIGURE 7.1   *Assets and values.*

Under the second definition, the value of a commodity is determined by the sum of the future earnings that can be expected with this commodity (capitalization). In this case, a commodity is considered to be an investment commodity. What counts is not its concrete value in use but only its ability to generate income in the future. This definition bases value exclusively on *future* events and developments, which cannot be predicted at all or only with great uncertainty (for example, earnings per share two years hence).

In Fig. 7.1, the two pairs of terms are matched up, thus creating four possible combinations. In the coal-mining cartel existing prior to the First World War, the price (value) of coal was determined by the productions costs and what was considered a reasonable profit.[29] The value of a company in the new economy is marked by a double dose of uncertainty. For one, it is not clear what assets a company actually possesses (intangibles); for another, the value determination of these assets is strapped with a high degree of uncertainty. It is easy to credit the UMTS licenses purchased by Telecom for € 8.5bn as an 'asset' worth the price the company paid. At the same time, however, it is obvious that the value of these assets is totally fictitious according to the first definition of value (production costs) and is extraordinarily uncertain according to the second definition (capitalization).

If the value of intangible assets is so uncertain and if the earnings that can be made with these assets cannot be rationally calculated, it is understandable why the new economy has improved the opportunity structure for fraud. Companies whose share prices increased tenfold on the stock market within

---

[29] The *regulated* electricity markets provide another example for Panel (1): Tariffs were designed to recover the operating and fixed costs of the power plants (Joskow 2000: 123).

a short period of time could assert that their intangible assets deserved to be valued so highly. When stockholders became suspicious and asked to see and 'touch' these assets, they were informed that the wealth of the company was 'intangible'.

From this we can derive two hypotheses. First, the opportunity structure for fraud becomes more favorable as the following three indicators increase: the percentage of firms in a country that are financed through the stock market (and not through bank credit), the percentage of companies whose value is based primarily on intangible assets, and the degree to which share prices are influenced by predictions of expected earnings on intangible assets.

Second, under highly uncertain conditions, the demand for predictions grows. The gurus of the stock market are charismatic prophets who predict events during periods of great uncertainty that cannot be predicted through *rational* calculation. Whether the prophets are really swindlers can usually be determined only after the fact.[30]

A Final Round in a Prisoner's Dilemma Game

The CEO of Enron, Kenneth L. Lay, earned a total annual income of $103,559,793 in 2000 (one year before Enron filed for bankruptcy).[31] The average family income in the United States equaled roughly $48,950 in 1999 (Mishel, Bernstein, and Schmitt 2001: Table 1.1). To simplify the math, we will assume that a family is in a position to earn this income over a period of forty years. Thus, the life income of this family would equal $1,958,000. This means that in 2000 alone Kenneth L. Lay earned about fifty-three times as much as the average American household would over a lifetime.

If an executive can earn such an income just over a period of a few years (the 'average' American would be happy to earn it even just *once*), it is rational to weigh the consequences of fraudulent bankruptcy against the chance to make such exorbitant sums of money. Often the opportunity costs of bankruptcy are relatively small *for the executive*[32] who is playing in the final round of a prisoner's dilemma game, in which the dominant strategy is defection.

---

[30] Prophecies are well remunerated in the financial markets: Jack Grubman, chief analyst of Salomon Smith Barney, 'was paid handsomely for his efforts, earning an average of $20 million a year' (*Wall Street Journal*, 16 August 2002, p. A4).

[31] *New York Times*, 18 June 2002, p. C1; LeMaistre testified that K. Lay earned $141m in 2000 (LeMaistre 2002). In the following calculation the lower figure of the *New York Times* is used.

[32] The opportunity costs of a (fraudulent) bankruptcy is the loss of reputation in the market for managers. On 26 June 2003 the US Department of Labor sued K. Lay for 'mismanagement of two of Enron's main pension plans'. K. Lay has been sued for 'mismanagement', but not for fraud! Source: www.dol.gov/_sec/media/speeches/20030626_Enron_Lawsuit.htm

In the 1990s, all CEOs of the 500 largest US firms received stock options. In 1992, the value of these options equaled about 25 per cent of an executive's annual income; by 1998, this had risen to 40 per cent (Hall and Murphy 2000: 1). Thus, an ever-growing percentage of executive incomes is determined by stock options. This has at least four consequences, all of which are usually ignored by the advocates of the principal-agent theory.

First, the incentive influencing the behavior of corporate executives is not linked to a continuous (internal) growth of the company, but solely to the share price. The stock market is volatile, and the volatility has increased during the past decade. In boom periods this leads to excessive income increases; in bust periods the stock options lose their incentive effect. Second, the income gap between the 'average' American and top executives has increased dramatically. 'The real wage of the median CEO rose 62.7% during 1989–99, helping the average CEO to earn 107 times more than the typical worker' (Mishel, Bernstein, and Schmitt 2001: 5). Third, stock options offer a permanent incentive to falsify balance sheets. Since share prices are influenced by what the company managers publicize in the financial statements, and since executive incomes are significantly dependent on the share price of company stock, then there exists a constant temptation to manipulate the accounting books.[33] Fourth, if top executives can successfully earn incomes resembling lottery winnings for a few years, then their commitment to the long-term development of the company becomes secondary. These managers have already earned incomes to secure them for their lifetime.

Side Note: What Are Stock Options?

Since the Enron debacle, many critics have demanded that stock options be defined as 'costs'.[34] However, stock options are not costs. A stock option is the right to purchase shares of stock during a defined period at a price that is specified in the option (the 'exercise price'). The actual impact of such options is that they water down the equity value later on.

In October 1999, Kenneth Lay received Enron stock options totaling several hundred thousand. At this point, the price of Enron shares stood at about \$38, which also happened to be the exercise price.[35] By 24 January 2000, the share price had risen to \$65. Kenneth Lay sold 143,704 Enron

---

[33] 'Instead of figuring out their sales and subtracting expenses to calculate the profit, [companies] work backward, starting with the profit investors are expecting and manipulate sales and expenses to make sure the numbers come' (*New York Times*, 29 June 2002, p. B1).

[34] Gary S. Becker: 'The value of the options given in any year should be deducted from revenue in that year' (*Business Week*, 5 August 2002).

[35] 'One of the most striking facts about executive stock options is that the exercise *price* of virtually all options is set equal to the current stock price at the grant date' (Hall and Murphy 2000: 1).

shares that day and thereby earned $9,340,760. Where do shares come from like those that Lay sold? They are *newly issued shares* (capital stock increase). For his options, Lay had to transfer to Enron $38 for each of the 143,704 shares for a total of $5,460,752.[36] His profit consisted of the difference between the 'exercise price' ($38) and the stock market price on the day of sale ($65).

Stock options do not incur costs when they are issued. At this point they are nothing more than a contract between the company and the executive involved. (This is what makes stock options so attractive for newly established companies: they can 'pay' their employees with self-issued paper money.) When the executive exercises the option, meaning when he receives the (new) shares from the company and then sells these on the stock market, the 'costs' are still hidden. At this point, the share price has risen (that is, the market price of a share is higher than the exercise price) and indicates that the demand for such shares is greater than the supply.

The costs to shareholders become obvious only during a period when the market price is falling. At this point, an increased supply of shares (the supply is increased by the number of exercised options) become available to a weak market, and the shareholders pay for the executive options with a considerable drop in share prices.[37] But this need not worry the company executives: they have already sold their shares.[38]

Lack of Countervailing Powers

Falsified balance sheets and other forms of fraud drove Enron into bankruptcy and destroyed thousands of jobs. Did anyone in the management ranks become suspicious and attempt to warn their superiors? This question

[36] This is the 'amount of consideration to be received by the issuer for the issuance of shares of its stock' (Kraus 2002: 2–16,§2.03). Lay did not transfer this amount to Enron, but exchanged 98,062 Enron shares back to his company (on 25 January) to cover this consideration and taxes (*New York Times*, 8 August 2002, p. 12). Some managers received this consideration as a company loan; later they saw to it that their company redeemed the loan: 'Former CEO of Tyco, D. Kozlowski, has misappropriated millions of dollars of company money through unapproved and undisclosed loans' (*New York Times*, 12 September 2002, p. C1).

[37] 'The stockholders pay for [stock options] by suffering some dilution in equity values, but the cash or other properties of the enterprise itself are not consumed as they are by the payment of other types of compensation, such as salaries' (Kraus 2002: 2–11,§1.06).

[38] The executive managers at Enron encouraged their company's employees to invest their pension funds in Enron stock, yet the managers did this at a point when they themselves were beginning to sell their own Enron stock on a massive scale (*Wall Street Journal*, 1 March 2002: 'Pension practices used by Enron'). 'Mr. Lay went so far as to tout the stock as a good investment for his own employees—even after he had been warned that a wave of accounting scandals was about to engulf the corporation.' Quote from the indictment of the US Department of Labor: www.dol.gov/_sec/media/speeches/20030626_Enron_Lawsuit.htm

is particularly poignant in connection with the board of directors, who were responsible for the supervision of Enron's management. Did not one board member closely examine the company's tampered books?

To answer the first question: Sherron Watkins, vice president of corporate development, was one of the few Enron employees who was willing to testify before the Subcommittee on Oversight and Investigations of the Committee on Energy and Commerce early in 2002. Before being hired by Enron, Watkins had worked eight years at Arthur Andersen. Therefore, she knew how to prepare balance sheets (and how to manipulate them). Watkins was convinced that the accounting books at Enron were falsified, and she feared for the future of the company. Likewise, she feared for her job and therefore dared not express her concerns outwardly at first. 'I was not comfortable confronting either Mr. Skilling or Mr. Fastow with my concerns. To do so I believed would have been a job terminating move.' On 14 August 2001, she wrote an *anonymous* letter to Kenneth Lay, in which she described several cases of accounting fraud. She summarized her views by stating: '*We're such a crooked company.*' Later on, Lay met Watkins. When Fastow found this out, he is reported to have said: 'He wanted to have me fired. He wanted to seize my computer' (Committee on Energy and Commerce 2002: Part 3).

Further reference is found in the records of the congressional hearings: 'Ms. Watkins is still an Enron employee, and because of this fact has reques-ted a subpoena compelling her testimony today'.[39] At the point when a Committee of the House of Representatives was investigating the Enron case, Ms Watkins still appears to have feared she would be fired. For this reason, she requested the Committee to subpoena her in order to force her to testify what she knew.

The hearings throw light on the internal balance of power in US corpora-tions. In only a few firms are trade unions strong enough to be able to protect critical employees from losing their jobs. The fate of the analyst Wu at UBS Paine Webber, who warned clients about Enron, has already been mentioned: 'Wu was fired the same day.' American newspapers have reported a number of similar incidents.[40] Policies of 'union busting' and 'hire and fire' often deter company employees from exercising their 'voice' option.

---

[39] Senator J. Greenwood (Pennsylvania), Committee on Energy and Commerce (2002: Part 3).

[40] Bradley P. Farnsworth was Dynegy's chief accounting officer. When he refused 'to "shave" the value of losses in the gas market' he was fired (*New York Times*, 5 August 2002, pp. C1, C6). When Joseph Mulder alerted his superiors to what he said were serious violations of Securities and Exchange Commission rules, he was fired by Donaldson, Lufkin, & Jenrette. When Owen Cheevers refused to comply with the request of investment bankers at his firm to make his cautionary notes on the radio industry more 'glowing', he was fired by the Bank of Montreal in New York (*New York Times*, 20 June 2002, p. C1). Roy L. Olofson, finance executive at Global Crossing, was fired after he questioned the use of [fraudulent] capacity swaps (*New York Times*, 25 Sept 2002, p.C4).

Those who do not want to work in a '*crooked company*' quit (exit option), but they don't protest.

To answer the question whether any board members scrutinized the company's books, it is necessary to examine the membership of the board of directors at Enron more closely. In September 2001, the board consisted of the following sixteen members.

- Two medical doctors who had contributed outstandingly to cancer research at the M. D. Anderson Cancer Center in Houston (C. LeMaistre, J. Mendelsohn).
- Two directors dependent on Enron (J. Foy, K. Harrison). Harrison had a cross-interlock with Lay. Harrison was the CEO from Portland General Electric, a complete subsidiary of Enron; Lay, the CEO of Enron, sat on the Board of Directors of Portland General Electric. So Harrison was to monitor Lay and Lay was to monitor Harrison.
- A professor for accounting at Stanford University (Robert K. Jaedicke) and the dean of the Anderson School of Business, University of California, Los Angeles (Bruce G. Willison).
- Three directors from businesses outside the United States: R. Chan (Hong Kong), P. Pereira (Rio de Janeiro), J. Wakeham (London).
- An executive manager of the United States Olympic Committee (N. Blake).
- Two directors employed in the energy industry, whose appointments to the board could be questioned as having been a violation of the Clayton Act (R. Belfer, J. Duncan).[41]
- In addition, there was a former member of the U.S. Commodity Futures Trading Commission (W. Gramm), the chairman of Tektronix (J. Meyer), and the chairman of Alliance Capital Management (F. Savage).[42]

C. LeMaistre and J. Mendelsohn are two renowned cancer researchers at the University of Texas (Austin). It is not surprising that they did not see through the technical details of the financial statements. R. Jaedicke is a professor emeritus for *accounting* at the Stanford Graduate School of Business. He was the chairman of the audit committee of Enron (until 2001)

---

[41] Section 8 of the Clayton Act restricts the use of interlocking directorates by competing corporations (Murray 1984).

[42] '. . . 10 of the 15 most recent outside directors had conflicts of interest including contracts with Enron, common bonds to charities, and memberships on the boards of other companies doing business with Enron. Some examples: charities close to some of the directors were supported heavily by Enron and its officers. Two directors had earned more than $6.5 million in consulting fees from Enron since 1991. One director served on the board of a company that in 1999 signed a $1 billion energy management agreement with an Enron affiliate.' Permanent Subcommittee on Investigations (2002): Statement of Chairman J. Lieberman, 7 May 2002. One of the charities mentioned by J. Lieberman is the M. D. Anderson Cancer Center (see below).

and therefore presented with the balance sheet for examination and signed approval.

Jaedicke's assertion that he knew 'nothing' about the accounting fraud is hardly credible.[43] In order to understand his behavior, we need to analyze more closely the situation in which Jaedicke found himself as an Enron director.

In October 2001, Andrew Fastow was questioned during a meeting of the Board of Directors. One of the directors welcomed Fastow by saying: 'We very much appreciate your willingness to visit with us.' Carl Levin, Senator of Michigan, commented on the behavior of the Enron directors by noting: 'You can't get much more deferential and obsequious' (*New York Times*, 8 May 2002, p. C7). Why does a seventy-year-old director act in a 'deferential and obsequious' manner toward a forty-year-old financial executive from Enron, whose financial transactions the director is supposed to be monitoring?

A report published regularly by the Stanford Graduate School of Business makes available information on donations to the school. Roughly 50 per cent of the Business School's expenditures are covered by sponsors. These include, for example, Hewlett, Packard (Foundations) and Pfizer, which have each donated more than $500,000 and are labeled as 'principal investors'. Goldman and Sachs, Intel, Charles Schwab, and several other companies have donated between $100,000 and $499,999. This is followed by a long list of 'lead investors' that have each donated between $50,000 and $99,999 and include such firms as Eli Lilly,[44] Morgan Stanley Dean Witter, and Sun Microsystems. The Business School has 52 'endowed professorships', meaning professors whose positions are financed completely or partially by sponsors for a limited period. 'As dean, Jaedicke became a champion fundraiser. Under his leadership the School received 13 endowed professorships, including the Philip H. Knight deanship, which Jaedicke was first to hold.'[45]

It is *not* being asserted here that the sponsors 'paid' Robert K. Jaedicke to neglect his responsibility as an Enron director to closely examine the company balance sheet. Such an assertion would be absurd. However, the Business School is dependent on corporate donations. If a portion of the sponsors were to cease or even reduce their donations, the Business School

---

[43] Carl Levin, Senator of Michigan and Chairman of the U.S. Senate Permanent Subcommittee on Investigations (2002: 56), listed a few 'red flags' that the Board Members must have noticed: 'In February 1999, the Board's Audit Committee was told by Arthur Andersen directly that Enron's accounting practices were high risk and pushed the limits.' 'By October 2000, the Board knew that Enron had $27 billion in assets—almost half of its assets—off its balance sheet.'

[44] Kenneth L. Lay had a seat on the Board of Directors of Eli Lilly.

[45] Source: Stanford University Graduate School of Business, *Report to Investors* (several years); www.gsb.stanford.edu/news/faqs.html# financials; http://gobi.stanford.edu/facultybios/bio.asp?ID=187. The endowed deanship was established in 1985 by Philip H. Knight (MBA '62), president of Nike Corporation.

would no longer be able to function fully. We call this the *colonization* of the scientific system by business. The former dean was well aware of these facts, and they acted like an automatic censor in his head. Jaedicke was forced to think twice about being critical of business practices while sitting on the board of directors at Enron.

Jaedicke was aware that management always knows a great deal more than the directors (information asymmetries).[46] Outspoken criticism of 'creative accounting' can backfire should it be proven later that such criticism was unfounded. When information is not fully available, it is risky to criticize a management whose strategies were praised by a Harvard professor as recently as mid-2001 for being the 'hotbed of entrepreneurial activity and an engine of growth' (*Business Week*, 17 December 2001, p. 34). For a seventy-year-old professor emeritus, it no longer pays off to take great risks at that point. Faced with the choice between the 'voice' option and the 'keep quiet' option, he chose the latter. This was all Enron's managers expected from him.

Corruption has become subtle. Senator Levin, who strongly attacked the Enron directors during the hearings,[47] overlooks the constellation of interests and the dependency that limited the perception and critical faculties of Robert Jaedicke.

In 1874, Collis P. Huntington, the president of Southern Pacific Railways, could bribe the members of the US Congress with a check for $200,000 and thereby hope that Congress would pass a law benefiting his railway (see below). In 2001, a (clever) company no longer chooses this path. Energy corporations do not bribe elected officials directly in order to block environmental legislation. Instead, they sponsor the research of climatologists who come to the conclusion that global warming is not taking place.

Companies finance universities and research centers and hope that the professors, who are then appointed to the board of directors, will be 'deferential and obsequious' in their behavior. Dr Charles LeMaistre, the former president of the M. D. Anderson Cancer Center (Houston, Texas) was chairman of Enron's Compensation and Management Development Committee for almost seventeen years. When he was president of the M. D. Anderson Cancer Center, Enron donated $600,000 to this Center (*Wall Street Journal*, 25 September 2002, p. C12). *Honi soit qui mal y pense!*

---

[46] In his testimony, R. Jaedicke repeatedly claimed that 'without full and accurate information, an Audit Committee cannot be effective' (Jaedicke 2002).

[47] 'You're the board. You're the captain of the ship that went down, and you're denying any responsibility. There were plenty of things you were told and that you knew which should have triggered much stronger action on your part' (*New York Times*, 8 May 2002, p. C7). It has to be taken into account that the Hearings are often used by US senators to enhance their own public relations profile. The statement that the board members are 'the captain of the ship' is nonsense. A director has to make sure that the executive managers meet their fiduciary duties.

The composition of the board of directors at Enron also indicates another reason why none of the directors chose to exercise the 'voice' option. In 2001, Enron was one of the ten largest corporations in the United States. As a rule, the boards of directors at these extremely large companies are comprised of executives from other major enterprises and the banks.[48] Because they hold positions of *equal* rank, these top executives can be expected to possess the necessary authority and critical judgment. It is therefore striking to find that not one of the directors on the board at Enron was from a firm among Standard and Poor's top-500 rankings or from one of the major banks. This offers another explanation why the Board never posed any (critical) questions to management: 'An unquestioning Board of Directors did nothing' (Committee on Energy and Commerce 2002: Part 3).

In summary, it can be said that corporate governance failed in the case of Enron. There are no institutions in American firms that can protect employees when they attempt to defend themselves against (criminal) manipulation. Even the board of directors failed in the Enron case. In selecting the board members, Enron obviously chose people from whom the company expected little resistance.

In the next section, we will explain in greater detail the colonization of the *political* system by business.

The Opportunity Structure for Corruption: A Market for Law

Collis P. Huntington and David D. Colton were co-owners of the Southern Pacific Railways. In 1874, Huntington wrote to Colton:

Friend Colton: Scott is prepared to pay, or promises to pay, a large amount of money to pass his bill, but I do not think he can pass it, although I think this coming session of Congress will be composed of the hungriest set of men that ever got together...I believe with $200,000 I can pass our bill, but I take it that it is not worth that much to us. (Quoted from Perrow 2002: 146–7)

Thomas Scott was president of the Pennsylvania Railroad, and we can describe the relationship between Scott and Huntington as 'competitors in corruption': 'In a market for special interest legislation, legislation is "sold" by legislators and "bought" by winning coalitions that outbid their rival seekers' (Butler 1985: 130).

In a study on donation practices and lobbying by US firms, Ansolabehere, Snyder, and Tripathy (2002) pose the provocative question: 'Why is there so little money in U.S. politics?' The authors discovered that in 2000 the energy industry only donated $34m to political candidates and parties, while the Department of Energy distributed more than $1.7bn in subsidies to energy

---

[48] Cf. Windolf (2002: 32–3): Interlocking directorates of the 480 largest US firms in 1997 (Tables 2.1 and 2.2).

companies that year. Thus, a relatively minor investment of capital leads to enormously high rates of profit in the 'market for special interest legislation'. From these findings, the authors conclude that 'exceptionally high average rates of return... imply that more firms and industries should enter the political marketplace' (Ansolabehere, Snyder, and Tripathy 2002: 3).

The point here is not to criticize the authors' *data* but the *terms* they use in analyzing the political system. If political institutions are understood to be a 'market for special interest legislation' and elected officials are depicted as the 'salespeople of legislation', the choice of terms makes it appear that the difference between politics and economics does not play a role in this analysis. In this vein, politics is nothing more than a market in which specific commodities (legislation) are offered. This type of 'economic' institutional analysis reduces institutions to strictly market operations.

North (1990) maintains that markets cannot function without institutions. This argument makes sense only if there is a *difference* between the markets and institutions. If this difference is obliterated, what is left is a market that functions as the energy market did in California in 2000.[49]

Corruption has been defined as an exchange between systems that violates the specific code of a system. The practice of selling laws in exchange for money from special interests violates the code of the political system and obliterates the difference between politics and economics. It is questionable whether corruption can be defined at all within the terminological apparatus used by Ansolabehere, Snyder, and Tripathy (2002) in their analysis. It appears as if money is a legitimate medium of exchange in *all* social systems.

Special interest legislation not only violates the code of the political system, it also confronts the courts with a difficult problem: when these laws are later 'interpreted' in judicial rulings, the courts must stick to the wording of the law (in which, as a rule, the 'intention' of the legislators cannot be discerned). 'It is often beyond the capacity of the courts to delve into the legislatures' actual motives when construing pure special interest group legislation' (Macey 1984: 3). Since the courts are not in a position to reconstruct the history of corruption behind the genesis of the law, they are often forced to legitimize special interest legislation in the rulings they hand down.

In conclusion, it can be said that the concept of a 'market for law' violates the fundamental contractual principles of state: 'the rules of order are, and must be, selected at a different level and via a different process than the decisions made within those rules...'(Buchanan 1977: 11). Buchanan

---

[49] 'Fat boy', 'death star', and 'get shorty' were the nicknames that Enron traders gave the complex trading strategies they employed (*New York Times*, 8 May 2002, p. C1). Dynegy (one of the largest US energy traders) was also engaging in 'round-trip trades'. On 24 September 2002, it agreed to pay $3m to settle the accusations of the SEC. The accounting firm for Dynegy was *Arthur Andersen* (*New York Times*, 25 September 2002, p. C5).

selects the terms 'different level' and 'different process' in order to distinguish between politics and economics. In the context discussed here, this passage can be interpreted as a defense of the autonomy of the legal and political system.

Dworkin (1986: 176, 225) makes a similar argument when he emphasizes *integrity* and autonomy as important prerequisites for the ability of the legal system to function:

We have two principles of political integrity: a legislative principle, which asks lawmakers to try to make the total set of laws morally coherent, and an adjudicative principle, which instructs that the law be seen as coherent in that way, so far as possible . . . According to law as integrity, propositions of law are true if they figure in or follow from the principles of justice, fairness, and procedural due process.

The External Effects of Fraud

Williamson (1985) argues that rational actors do not pursue their interests in the market solely with legal means, but that they also use fraud and guile to pursue their ends when the opportunity arises. Therefore, special institutional and contractual regulations are necessary to protect market actors from fraud and breaches of contract. Williamson (1985: 64) does *not* assume that *all* market actors are unprincipled opportunists and cheaters: 'To the contrary, I merely assume that some individuals are opportunistic some of the time and that differential trustworthiness is rarely transparent *ex ante*. As a consequence, *ex ante* screening efforts are made and *ex post* safeguards are created.'

A similar argument was made in connection with the Enron case, namely, that the vast majority of American firms and executive managers are law-abiding. They don't cheat, they pay their debts, and they fulfill their contractual obligations. The problem lies in an information asymmetry: we do not know *ex ante* which companies breach their contracts and which do not or which use other fraudulent methods and which do not. (Only the cheaters know for sure . . .)

Following the bankruptcy of Enron, the US Congress passed laws with amazing speed to prevent the falsification of balance sheets and fraud in the future. For instance, the Sarbanes-Oxley Act (2002) established a 'Public Company Accounting Oversight Board' that is to supervise accounting firms in the future. Section 101 states:

The Board will have five financially-literate members, appointed for five-year terms. Two of the members must be or have been certified public accountants, and the remaining three must not be and cannot have been CPAs [Certified Public

Accountants]. The Chair may be held by one of the CPA members, provided that he or she has not been engaged as a practicing CPA for five years. The Board's members will serve on a full-time basis.[50]

Additional measures included in this law stipulate that thenceforth every company must change its external accounting firm every five years, that CEOs must add their signatures in authorizing the financial statements of the company, and so on. It was argued that these laws will make the financial markets more efficient in the future. Here it is argued, however, that most of these laws will raise the transaction costs of the financial markets. This point can be illustrated by the following.

Every year, several hundred million passengers are scanned, searched, and interrogated at airports. Here too exists a problem of an extreme information asymmetry. In order to identify (or deter) a dozen individuals who are willing and able to commit a terrorist act, millions of passengers must be searched. We know that these measures are necessary, but it is not very reasonable to maintain that they increase the 'efficiency' of air travel.

The (negative) external effects of fraud and corruption can now be more precisely defined: these are the '*ex ante* screenings'[51] and '*ex post* safeguards' that are growing in number. The increasing mass of laws, regulations, authorities, and guards incurs transaction costs that are far greater than the immediate damage done by the criminals and defrauders.

The Oversight Board is one example of the 'bureaucratic vicious circle' that Crozier (1963) describes in an analysis of French bureaucracy. When rules are broken, orders disobeyed, and instructions ignored in large organizations, *new* rules and monitoring agents are introduced in order to limit the 'degree of freedom' of the organization's members. The Oversight Board itself, for example, will be monitored by the Securities and Exchange Commission (SEC), thereby creating the following bureaucratic chain of supervision: SEC→Oversight Board→accounting firm→(say) Enron. The basic principle behind the measures is to police the police of the police.

Crozier goes on to show that the actors then develop new strategies to circumvent the new rules or to make them ineffective. This, in turn, leads to even more new rules. However, social behavior cannot be controlled completely through rules and regulations. However strict or tight the rules become, there always remains a degree of freedom to make strategic

---

[50] The Oversight Board will be financed by assessments on accounting firms and public companies.

[51] The following report illustrates this point: 'The nation's major corporations, facing a tide of public suspicion and investor mistrust, are responding by vetting candidates for top positions as never before, looking into all aspects of their professional and private lives with an intensity usually reserved for major criminal investigations' (*New York Times*, 19 August 2002, p. A1).

decisions (opportunity structure for fraud).[52] All that is certain is that these regulations will increase the transaction costs of the financial markets.

Obviously, the *intention* of the five-year-rotation rule is to prevent accounting firms from identifying their interests too closely with those of the company they are auditing, that is, to prevent conspiracy between the two. The *unintended consequence* of this rule could become a greater mistrust in the financial markets and possibly a greater risk of fraud. Why? As pointed out above, 'tacit knowledge' is gained through direct social relationships. Such knowledge is often important in judging the trustworthiness and reliability of a contractual partner. It is unlikely, however, that from now on accounting firms will incur the costs needed to attain such tacit knowledge about their clients when they know that this knowledge will be worthless in five years at most.[53]

Conclusions

Fraudulent bankruptcies are almost always the outcome of irresponsible individual decisions, if not criminal behavior. In the case of Enron, a relatively small group of top managers pushed the law to its limit and, in many cases, acted beyond this limit. Nevertheless, the analysis of 'push' and 'pull factors' and the description of the opportunity structure for fraud presented above has shown that Enron's managers developed their strategies within the framework of a particular institutional structure and that their strategies could not have been successful without the support of this institutional framework. Enron is an example not only of individual failure, but also— and perhaps even more so—of *institutional* failure. In this concluding section, two questions will be asked. Was Enron so different? How can we interpret the results from a comparative perspective (the varieties-of-capitalism debate)?

Was Enron So Different?

Arthur Andersen compiled a 'risk profile' for 2,500 of its clients. Fifty of these were classified as 'maximum-risk' enterprises, including Enron, and 700 as 'high-risk' ones. This relatively large sample of US corporations enables us to draw the following conclusion. Andersen suspected that 30 per cent

---

[52] Cf. Largay (2002: 154): 'I doubt there is a group of standard setters on this earth that can enumerate enough rules to contain those who are intent on circumventing full and fair disclosure.' James A. Largay III has been the Arthur Andersen & Co. Alumni Professor of Accounting at Lehigh University since 1982. (It must be hard these days to be an Arthur Andersen & Co. Alumni Professor.)

[53] The unintended consequence of the signatures (that the CEOs must add in authorizing the financial statements of their companies) will probably be an increase in the premium of the professional liability insurance (which is paid by the company). Cf. C. Parsons (2001).

of its clients belonged to the category of firms which Marshall Field would have characterized as 'not safe'. Enron was only one of many companies that pushed the law to its limits.

Agnew Fastow is considered to be the 'villain' in the Enron drama. It seems that he only 'adjusted' strategies and financial techniques that he learned at the Business School at Northwestern University (which were characterized as a 'hotbed of entrepreneurial activity and an engine of growth') to a 'new territory'. A quick glance at the educational background of the top Enron managers indicates that they were not a small group of desperados but a highly educated team of young professionals, similar to those found in other businesses.

The energy transactions that Enron conducted transgressed the borders of legality (for example, energy from California was exported to Oregon and then re-imported an hour later). However, Enron was not the only company to earn billions in dubious energy transactions. Dynegy (one of the largest US energy traders) was also engaging in such 'round-trip trades'.

In 2000, Kenneth Lay earned about $140m. This is nothing unusual for a CEO in the United States. The total personal income of John Reed (Citigroup) equaled $293m. Charles Wang (Computer Associates) earned in the three years between 1998 and 2000 roughly $682.2m, even though the share price of this company plummeted by 63 per cent during this period. The value of the stock options owned but not yet exercised by Lawrence Ellison (Oracle) was estimated to be $3.4bn (*Business Week*, 16 April 2001, pp. 77–9). Kenneth Lay does not appear to have been unusually greedy compared with his fellow CEOs.

Varieties of Capitalism

Institutional structures vary between countries and, therefore, the opportunity structure for fraud and corruption varies between them. The question to be addressed here is *not* whether a bankruptcy like Enron could have happened in other countries but whether such cases occur *more frequently* in the United States than in countries with a higher level of market regulation.[54]

Chandler (1990) distinguishes different types of capitalism. The United States is an example of what he calls 'competitive capitalism' while Germany is an example of 'cooperative capitalism'. We believe that the former type can be characterized by Schumpeter's notion of 'creative destruction' while

---

[54] The following example illustrates the point: 'The incarceration rate in the United States in 2000 was 686 per 100,000 population, compared with rates of 105 in Canada, 95 in Germany, and only 45 in Japan' (Uggen and Manza 2002: 778). The question to be answered is not whether there is a country with a zero-crime-rate but why the incarceration rate in the US is about fifteen times higher than in Japan.

the latter type is an example of a coordinated market economy in which a strong institutional structure limits the excesses of pure market competition.

For Schumpeter (1942) the 'spirit' of capitalism lies in the process of 'creative destruction': again and again, that which has just been created is destroyed through market competition. This does not apply to material commodities and production plants alone, but also to institutions and cultural creations. Technical innovations not only create new markets for entrepreneurs but also destroy the income opportunities linked to obsolescent technologies. The many hostile takeovers which restructured the corporate economy of the United States during the 1980s are a prominent example of creative destruction.

Hall and Soskice (2001: 38–9) make a distinction between radical and incremental innovation. Radical innovation 'entails substantial shifts in product lines, the development of entirely new goods, or major changes to the production process', while 'incremental innovation [is] marked by continuous but small-scale improvements to existing product lines and production processes'. Radical innovations are very hard to implement in highly institutionalized markets; they are more successfully introduced into 'liberal market economies', that is, in those countries that have a low level of market regulation. Radical innovations—a notion almost synonymous with creative destruction—are particularly important in fast-moving technology sectors with short-term product cycles.

The history of Enron illustrates a process of creative destruction. The corporation was undoubtedly an innovator in the deregulated energy market. It created new forms of energy trade that have since been adapted to other economic sectors. Only a few years later, though, the company crumbled in a process of criminal destruction.

It was argued above that the *irrational* compulsion of greed is controlled by the institutions of capitalism and is transformed into the *rational* pursuit of gains. The 'spirit of capitalism' expresses itself in the tempered pursuit of profit within the framework of continuous, rational, capitalist enterprise. If we reinterpret Weber's 'spirit of capitalism' from a comparative perspective, it seems that the puritan ethic can provide only part of the explanation. Perhaps as important is the 'force of traditions' embodied in the institutions of different countries which limit the excesses of creative destruction and of pure market competition.[55]

We complete this conclusion with two observations. First, the less market competition is restrained by institutions—that is, the more economic exchanges are coordinated by pure market competition—the more opportunities there are for the implementation of radical innovations and processes of creative destruction. Yet the comparative advantages of one economic

---

[55] A more detailed picture of differences in the traditions and institutions of various countries is given in *The Three Worlds of Welfare Capitalism* (Esping-Anderson 1990).

system have to be weighed against its specific transaction costs. Enron illustrates the transaction costs of an economic system in which radical innovations do not encounter much resistance. Stagnation and a low level of innovation exemplify the transaction costs of an alternative form of economic organization that Hall and Soskice (2001: 38) have termed the 'coordinated market economy'.

Second, Lindblom (2001) points to the relationship between economic and political institutions. The more economic exchanges are coordinated by the market, the larger, *ceteris paribus*, social inequality is. He argues that extreme forms of social inequality threaten political democracy and prevent citizens from effectively controlling political and economic elites. 'If genuine democracy requires at least a rough equality of political influence or power among citizens in their attempts to control elites, then any significant economic inequality among citizens is an obstruction to democracy' (2001: 236). The side payments made by Enron to political representatives are not only to be condemned as 'corruption' but also as an 'obstruction to democracy'.

References

Akerlof, G. (1970). 'The Market for Lemons', *Quarterly Journal of Economics*, 84: 488–500.

Ansolabehere, S., Snyder, J., and Tripathy, M. (2000). *Are PAC Contributions and Lobbying Linked? New Evidence from the 1995 Lobby Disclosure Act*. Boston: Department of Political Science, MIT (PDF version).

—— (2002). *Why Is There So Little Money in U.S. Politics?* Boston: Department of Political Science, MIT (PDF version).

Bazerman, M., Morgan, K., and Loewenstein, G. (1997). 'The Impossibility of Auditor Independence', *Sloan Management Review*, 38/summer: 89–96.

Buchanan, J. (1977). *Freedom in Constitutional Contract*. College Station: Texas A&M University Press.

Buckley, J. and O'Sullivan, P. (1980). 'Regulation and Public Accounting: What Are the Issues?', in J. Buckley and F. Weston (eds.), *Regulation and the Accounting Profession*. Belmont, CA: Lifetime Learning Publications.

Butler, H. (1985). 'Nineteenth-Century Jurisdictional Competition in the Granting of Corporate Privileges', *Journal of Legal Studies*, 14: 129–66.

Buxbaum, R. (1979). 'The Relation of the Large Corporation's Structure to the Role of Shareholders and Directors: Some American Historical Perspectives', in N. Horn and J. Kocka (eds.), *Law and the Formation of the big Enterprises in the 19th and Early 20th Centuries*. Göttingen: Vandenhoeck & Ruprecht.

Carey, J. (1969). *The Rise of the Accounting Profession*. New York: American Institute of Certified Public Accountants.

Chandler, A. (1990). *Scale and Scope*. Cambridge, MA: Harvard University Press.

Cloward, R. and Ohlin, L. (1960). *Delinquency and Opportunity*. New York: Free Press.

Committee on Energy and Commerce (2002). US House of Representatives (107th Congress), Subcommittee on Oversight and Investigations of the Committee on

Energy and Commerce, Hearing on the Financial Collapse of ENRON, Parts 1–4. Washington, DC. www.access.gpo.gov/congress/house

Crozier, M. (1963). *Le phénomène bureaucratique*. Paris: Seuil.

Dobbin, F. (1999). *Forging Industrial Policy: The United States, Britain, and France in the Railway Age*. New York: Cambridge University Press.

Dworkin, R. (1986). *Law's Empire*. Cambridge, MA: Harvard University Press (Belknap).

Esping-Anderson, G. (1990). *The Three Worlds of Welfare Capitalism*. Princeton, NJ: Princeton University Press.

Etzioni, A. (1961). *A Comparative Analysis of Complex Organizations*. New York: Free Press.

Fusaro, P. and Miller, R. (2002). *What Went Wrong at Enron?* Hoboken, NJ: Wiley & Sons.

Gourevitch, P. (2002). 'Collective Action Problems in Monitoring Managers: The Enron Case as a Systemic Problem', *Economic Sociology (European Electronic Newsletter)*, 3/3: 1–17.

Hall, B. and Murphy, K. (2000). *Optimal Exercise Prices for Executive Stock Options*. Cambridge, MA. National Bureau of Economic Research (Working Paper No. 7548).

Hall, P. and Soskice, D. (2001). *Varieties of Capitalism*. Oxford: Oxford University Press.

Hirschman, A. (1977). *The Passions and the Interests*. Princeton: Princeton University Press.

Hogan, W. (2002). 'Electricity Market Restructuring: Reforms of Reforms', *Journal of Regulator Economics*, 21: 103–32.

Hume, D. ([1741] 1994a) 'Of Civil Liberty', in K. Haakonssen (ed.), *Political Essays*. Cambridge: Cambridge University Press.

—— ([1742] 1994b): 'Of the Rise and Progress of the Arts and Sciences', in K. Haakonssen (ed.), *Political Essays.*. Cambridge: Cambridge University Press.

Jaedicke, R. (2002). Statement of Dr Robert K. Jaedicke before the Permanent Subcommittee on Investigations. The Committee on Government Affairs, US Senate, 7 May. www.senate.gov/~gov_affairs/050702jaedicke.htm

Joskow, P. (2000). 'Deregulation and Regulatory Reform in the U.S. Electric Power Sector', in S. Peltzman and C. Winston (eds.), *Deregulation of Network Industries*. Washington, DC: AEI-Brookings Joint Center.

Kalberg, S. (2001). 'Should the "Dynamic Autonomy" of Ideas Matter to Sociologists?', *Journal of Classical Sociology*, 1: 291–327.

Kleinman, D. and Vallas, S. (2001). 'Science, Capitalism, and the Rise of the "Knowledge Worker": The Changing Structure of Knowledge Production in the United States', *Theory and Society*, 30: 451–92.

Kraus, H. (2002). *Executive Stock Options and Stock Appreciation Rights*. New York: Law Journal Press (Release 14).

Largay, J. (2002). 'Lessons from Enron', *Accounting Horizons*, 16: 153–6.

LeMaistre, C. (2002). Statement of Dr Charles A. LeMaistre before the Permanent Subcommittee on Investigations. The Committee on Government Affairs, US Senate, 7 May. www.senate.gov/~gov_affairs/050702lemaistre.htm

Lev, B. (2001). *Intangibles: Management, Measurement, and Reporting*. Washington, DC: Brookings Institution Press.

Lindblom, C. (2001). *The Market System: What It Is, How It Works, And What To Make Of It*. New Haven: Yale University Press.

Luhmann, N. (2000). *Die Politik der Gesellschaft*. Frankfurt: Suhrkamp.

Macey, J. (1984). 'Special Interest Groups Legislation and the Judicial Function: The Dilemma of Glass-Steagall', *Emory Law Journal*, 33: 1–40.

Marx, K. ([1867] 1970). *Capital, Vol. I*. New York: International Publishers.

McCormick, R. (1981). 'The Discovery that "Business Corrupts Politics": A Reappraisal of the Origins of Progressivism', *American Historical Review*, 86: 247–74.

Merton, R. (1968). *Social Theory and Social Structure*. New York: The Free Press.

Mishel, L., Bernstein, J., and Schmitt, J. (2001). *The State of Working America 2000/2001*. Ithaca, NY: Economic Policy Institute, Cornell University.

Murray, J. (1984). 'The Definition of Competitors under Section 8 of the Clayton Act', *Washington and Lee Law Review*, 41: 135–53.

Neef, D. (1998). *The Knowledge Economy*. Boston: Butterworth-Heinemann.

North, D. (1990). *Institutions, Institutional Change and Economic Performance*. Cambridge, MA: Cambridge University Press.

Parsons, C. (2001). 'Managerial Liability, Risk and Insurance: An International View', *International and Comparative Corporate Law Journal*, 3: 1–31.

Parsons, T. (1969). *Politics and Social Structure*. New York: Free Press.

Permanent Subcommittee on Investigations (2002). US Senate, Permanent Subcommittee on Investigations, Committee on Governmental Affairs: The Role of the Board of Directors in Enron's Collapse. Washington, DC, 7 May. www.senate.gov/~gov_affairs/hearings.htm

Perrow, C. (2002). *Organizing America: Wealth, Power and the Origins of Corporate Capitalism*. Princeton NJ: Princeton University Press.

Polanyi, M. (1997). 'The Tacit Dimension', in L. Prusak (ed.), *Knowledge in Organizations*. Boston: Butterworth-Heinemann.

Powers Report (2000). Report of Investigation by the Special Investigative Committee of the Board of Directors of Enron Corp. Chairman: William C. Powers, Jr. Austin, Texas. 1 February. http://news.findlaw.com/wp/docs/enron/specinv020102rpt3.pdf

Saunders, A. (1985). 'Conflicts of Interest: An economic view', in I. Walter (ed.), *Deregulating Wall Street*. New York: Wiley.

Schumpeter, J. (1942). *Capitalism, Socialism and Democracy*. New York: Harper & Broth.

Tarr, J. (1966). 'J. R. Walsh of Chicago: A Case Study in Banking and Politics, 1881–1905', *Business History Review*, 40: 451–66.

Uggen, C. and Manza, J. (2002). 'Democratic Contraction? Political Consequences of Felon Disenfranchisement in the United States', *American Sociological Review*, 67: 777–803.

Watzlawick, P. (1967). *Pragmatics of Human Communication: A Study of Interactional Patterns, Pathologies, and Paradoxes*. New York: Norton.

Weber, M. ([1905] 2002). *The Protestant Ethic and the Spirit of Capitalism* (trans. S. Kalberg). Los Angeles: Roxbury.

Williamson, O. (1985). *The Economic Institutions of Capitalism.* New York: Free Press.

Windolf, P. (1995). 'Selection and Self-selection at German Mass Universities', *Oxford Review of Education,* 21: 207–32.

—— (2002). *Corporate Networks in Europe and the United States.* Oxford: Oxford University Press.

8

Corporate Governance for Crooks? The Case for Corporate Virtue

Margit Osterloh and Bruno S. Frey

Double Trouble with Managerial Behavior: Exorbitant Salaries and Scandalous Fraud

In recent times, the media have been full of accounts of managerial mis-behavior. For some considerable time, the often exorbitant salaries of CEOs and other top managers have made the headlines. This is not surprising if one takes into consideration that some managers were able to amass huge incomes in the form of bonuses, stock options, and many different forms of fringe benefits and perks. A pertinent example is General Electric's Jack Welch, who in 1998 received US$261.5m in stock options, $7.2m in bonuses and a base salary of $2.8m. Another example is Disney's Michael Eisner who, in the same year, received $107.2m, $5.0m, and $0.8m respectively. On average, the income of the top managers of ten widely known US companies, such as American Express, Boeing, Coca-Cola, Chevron, or Merck, amounted to $76m in stock options, $3m in bonuses and $1.3m in base salary (*The Economist* 1999: 4). As a consequence, the imbalances in income distribution have deteriorated significantly. In 1970, an American CEO earned, on average, twenty-five times as much as an industrial worker. Twenty-six years later, in 1996, the average CEO earned about seventy-five times as much, if we take only base salaries and bonuses into account. If we look at income including exercised stock options, the income differential reaches an almost incredible level. The ratio rises from a factor of twenty-five in 1970 to a factor of 210 in 1996 (Murphy 1999: 2553). The prospect of such huge salaries has led some top managers to act in ways that are detrimental to their firms. In particular, they have jacked up short-term profits instead of focusing on long-term opportunities, and they have neglected paying out

We wish to thank Margaret Blair, John Child, Ronald Dore, Anna Grandori and Siegwart Lindenberg for helpful comments during the preparation of this chapter and Rosemary Brown for checking the English.

dividends to their shareholders (Lambert, Lanen, and Larcker 1989). In his authoritative survey on 'Executive Compensation' in the *Handbook of Labour Economics*, Kevin Murphy (1999: 2555) has this to say: 'Although there is ample evidence that CEOs (and other employees) respond predictably to dysfunctional compensation arrangements, it is more difficult to document that the increase in stock-based incentives has led CEOs to work harder, smarter, and more in the interest of shareholders.'

Corporate scandals are reflected in fraudulent accounts. Well-known examples are WorldCom, Xerox, and Enron. In some cases, the CEOs who fiddle the accounts are the same persons who receive exorbitant compensations, for example, Enron's Kenneth Lay and WorldCom's Scott Sullivan (Cassidy 2002). These scandals cause an enormous amount of damage, not only to the companies affected but also to the market economy as a whole. Many observers argue that the drop in stock prices has gained added impetus as a result of such misbehavior. Investors have lost trust in managers.

However, major contributors to agency theory tend to defend the existing corporate governance system. But most of them admit major weaknesses in the approach. An example is Holmstrom and Kaplan (2003: 2), who state: '... while parts of the U.S. corporate governance system failed under the exceptional strain of the 1990's, the overall system, which includes oversight by the public and the government, reacted quickly to address the problems'. Jensen (*The Economist* 2002b: 66) accepts that the existing system of managing compensation, especially by the use of stock options, is seriously deficient; he argues that it has proven to be 'managerial heroin', encouraging a focus on short-term highs, with destructive long-term consequences. But he believes that the system can be salvaged by better-designed share options.

Politicians and some scholars reacted in line with this orthodox view of agency theory. They suggest more monitoring and sanctioning of management, first at the level of the board of directors and second at the level of legal regulations. On the board of directors, a higher number of 'independent' directors are expected to curb managerial discretion. In addition, the members of the board themselves should be recompensed with performance-related compensation in order to induce them to exercise more effective control. In the United States, by means of the Sarbanes/Oxley Act, Congress forced the top managers of firms with a turnover exceeding $1.5bn to take an oath promising not to fiddle their accounts. If caught breaking the regulations, the CEOs risk serious personal consequences, including imprisonment. Clearly, the public no longer trusts their corporate leaders to be honest without the threat of prison doors slamming behind them.

We argue that these efforts will create a structure encouraging *governance for crooks*. Corporate governance, when based on the principles of monitoring and sanctioning, tends to worsen the very problem it is designed to solve. The apparent remedy raises the incentives by managers and other employees to take advantage of the firm they are supposed to care about. Instead of stricter monitoring and sanctioning, we suggest that the conditions which led to the breeding of crooks have to be taken into account, as Argyris (1964) stated forty years ago.

The second section argues that the basic problem of corporate governance is the existence of a social dilemma, causing self-interested individuals to neglect the common good of the firm. Corporate virtue is one of the most important common goods in firms. Social dilemmas cannot be solved by still more privatizing, but rather by putting more emphasis on employees' intrinsic motivation to contribute to the common good of the firm. In the third section, we explain the difference between extrinsic and intrinsic motivation and its relevance for mitigating social dilemmas. The fourth section presents theoretical and empirical findings for the crowding-out and crowding-in effects, suggesting that the preferences of the employees are influenced by the way corporate governance is run. Drawing on these insights, the fifth section explains why traditional agency theory does not provide adequate answers to the current problems of corporate governance. The sixth section suggests alternative measures, based on motivation crowding theory. The last section concludes.

What Has Gone Wrong?

It seems that the whole corporate sector has been infiltrated by malpractice, greed, and distrust. This happened even though most companies were governed by boards composed of outstanding people. Nor has a larger proportion of outside directors had much effect. Some of the most extreme cases of malpractices occurred in corporations with a majority of outside directors, such as Enron (80 per cent outside directors), Tyco (65 per cent) and WorldCom (45 per cent) (Tosi, Shen, and Gentry 2003). A meta-analysis of fifty-four studies of board dependence showed no statistical relationship between board independence and firm financial performance (Dalton *et al.* 1998). Moreover, the firms were often audited by well-established lawyers, bankers, and accountants. Thus, Enron's auditing committee was chaired by a distinguished accounting professor (*The Economist* 2002a: 50). How can these facts be explained?

In companies, activities are characterized by a high degree of complex interdependencies (Thompson 1967; Grandori 1997, 2000). Simon (1991: 33) makes this point very clear in his important paper on organizations and markets:

In general, the greater the interdependence among various members of the organization, the more difficult it is to measure their separate contributions to the achievement of organizational goals. But of course, intense interdependence is precisely what makes it advantageous to organize people instead of depending wholly on market transactions.

However, particularly intensive interdependencies create a special kind of governance problem. Their outcome cannot be attributed to any particular actor. Therefore, incentives for free-riding arise (Osterloh, Frost, and Weibel 2002). In this situation, there is immediate danger of a social dilemma.

Thus, social dilemmas are at the heart of a firm's activities, in contrast to competitive markets (Miller 1992; Frey and Osterloh 2002). Social dilemmas arise if the actions of self-interested individuals do not lead to socially desirable outcomes. This kind of conflict between individual and collective rationality is modeled in the prisoner's dilemma game. Dawes defines social dilemmas as situations in which '. . . a) each individual receives a higher payoff for a socially defecting choice (e.g. using all the energy available, polluting his or her neighbors) than for a socially cooperative choice, no matter what the other individuals in society do, but b) all individuals are better off if all cooperate than if all defect' (Dawes 1980: 169). Self-interested individuals do not consider the externalities their actions impose on others when choosing their course of action, leading to either overuse (in the case of external costs) or undersupply (in the case of external benefits) of the collective goods in question. In firms, social dilemmas arise whenever a group of people jointly use or produce some resources without having the possibility of attributing the value of their consumption or production to the individuals of this group. Such a situation has been called the 'tragedy of the commons' (Hardin 1968). Today, the most important 'commons' in companies are not only accumulated organizational knowledge or absorptive capacity, corporate culture, and common organizational routines, as widely discussed within the knowledge-based theories of the firm (for example, Grant 1996; Kogut and Zander 1996; Nonaka and Takeuchi 1995). Rather, we argue that a crucial 'commons' consists of *corporate virtue*. This entails a generally shared notion of what business honesty is about and behaving honestly, even when not being watched. Corporate virtue, similar to corporate reputation, is a public good within the firm. As is the case with all public goods, the characteristics of non-rivalry and non-excludability cause a problem of undersupply unless formal sanctions or informal mechanisms such as peer pressure raise costs (Kandel and Lazear 1992) or the common good enters into the preferences of the employees (Sen 1974). Efforts to solve this social dilemma by offering private incentives are doomed to failure if employee's contributions are not measurable, as is the case with intensive interdependencies. Under such circumstances, market failures are imported into the firm (see, for example, Vining 2003).

The scandals demonstrate that such undermining of corporate virtue has indeed taken place due to individual incentives. In the case of Enron, people were paid like entrepreneurs. Short-term thinking and, at the same time, performance distortion were encouraged (Spector 2003). They were even induced to resort to illegal actions. Dishonest behavior was by no means restricted to top management, but filtered down through many layers within the corporation. With Enron, for instance, it was revealed that the whole board, including its president and vice president, knew about the malpractice. It was also general knowledge among the firm's employees. In the case of WorldCom, dishonesty was not confined to the accounting department; the sales staff also falsified the accounts.

What has gone wrong is a general deterioration of *intrinsic motivation* to contribute to the corporate virtue. We refer to a distinction between two kinds of motivation: extrinsic motivation and intrinsic motivation.

Extrinsic and Intrinsic Motivation

In order to distinguish between extrinsic and intrinsic motivation and to study their interdependence, various authors (Deci, Koestner, and Ryan 1999; Frey 1997; Osterloh and Frey 2000) offer a new way of mitigating social dilemmas.

Extrinsic motivation works through indirect satisfaction of needs, most importantly through monetary compensation. This kind of motivation dominates in conventional economics. The extensive use of pay for performance schemes has focused the attention of both principals and agents in the firm on extrinsic motivation. As a result, employees have been conditioned to perceive the money received as being an overriding incentive. Extensive research accumulated over recent decades has established the importance of a very different kind of motivation in the firm, namely *intrinsic motivation*. In this case, an activity is valued for its own sake and is self-sustained. The work content itself provides satisfaction or utility.[1]

Intrinsic motivation is indispensable when external incentives cannot solve the problems of social dilemmas, either because behavior is not observable or because the outcomes are not attributable to individuals. If there is an intrinsic motivation to work and to cooperate, contributing to the common good ceases to become a social dilemma. This is true not only in the case of contributing to common knowledge but also in the case of incorporating norms of honesty and corporate virtue in firms. Sanctioning of norm-violators in firms is efficient only when there is a certain amount of intrinsic motivation on the part of the one doing the sanctioning as well as on the part of the norm violator. On the part of the one doing the

---

[1] In economics, with the exception of Frey (1997), and more recently Benabou and Tirole (2002) and Sliwka (2003), only a few authors deal with intrinsic motivation. Examples are implicit contracts (Akerlof 1982) or norms (Kreps 1997). Some economists admit the existence of intrinsic motivation, but then leave it aside because it is difficult to analyze and control (for example, Williamson 1975), even if they agree that the assumption of solely extrinsically motivated people is an 'extreme caricature' (Milgrom and Roberts 1992: 42). These authors believe that institutions should be designed as if people were entirely selfish. But this has consequences for the crowding-out effect of intrinsic motivation.

sanctioning, psychological costs arise while sanctioning the norm violator, because colleagues usually tend to avoid open conflicts. On the norm violator's part, sanctions are more efficient if this person feels shame when it is disclosed that he or she has been free-riding. A precondition for feeling shame is at least some minimal intrinsically motivated commitment to the rules. Purely extrinsically motivated persons do not feel any shame (Elster 1999; Orr 2001).

A useful distinction can be made between two types of intrinsic motivation (Lindenberg 2001):

- *Enjoyment-based* or *self-actualization-based* intrinsic motivation refers to a satisfying flow of activity (for example, Csikszentmihalyi 1975), such as playing a game or reading a novel for pleasure. This is the incentive focused on by Deci, Koestner, and Ryan (1999).
- *Obligation-based* or *pro-social* intrinsic motivation was introduced into economics by Frey (1997) as a further important form of incentive. It is crucial in accounting for the existence of corporate virtue.

A wealth of empirical evidence demonstrates that many people are indeed prepared to contribute to the common good of their company and society. They exhibit *obligation-based* or *pro-social intrinsic preferences* (Frey and Meier 2002). Important instances can be found both in the public sphere (tax morale and environmental ethics, see Frey 1997) and in the business sphere. In business, three major instances have been discussed in the literature:

1. According to research in 'Organizational Citizenship Behavior', employees provide voluntary inputs, so-called extra-role behavior, going far beyond the duties stipulated in their employment contracts and the lack of which cannot be punished (Organ 1988; Organ and Ryan 1995). 'Organizational Citizenship Behavior' is thought of as a 'willingness to cooperate', and accounts for the relatively low amount of free-riding in organizations, compared with what orthodox economists would expect (Simon 1991). Of particular interest with respect to the solution of social dilemmas are helping behavior, organizational compliance, and civic virtue, which all include subduing individual interests for the sake of the whole organization.

2. In one of the most innovative industries, software production, a very successful form of so-called open-source software production has become a serious competitor to Microsoft. Software, like Linux, is produced voluntarily as a common good. This is done to a large extent without any monetary compensation and private property. Instead, this production is, to a large extent, based on a gift relationship (Raymond 2000; Osterloh, Rota, and Kuster 2003).

3. More generally, careful laboratory research in economics and psychology reveals that a large number of people voluntarily contribute to public goods (see the surveys by Rabin 1998 and Ostrom 1998).

These instances show that the social dilemma can be overcome if intrinsically motivated pro-social behavior exists. If the love of work and the good of the community enter into the preferences of the actors, the social dilemma is transformed into a coordination game in which there is no social dilemma.

The reason why corporate virtue—which patently exists in the corporate sector—has weakened can be located in motivation crowding theory. This is discussed in the next section.

Why has Corporate Virtue been Undermined? Motivation Crowding Effects

Intrinsic and extrinsic motivation are not additive. Rather, there is a dynamic relationship between the two. This dependence has been proved to exist in a large number of experiments (Deci 1975; Deci, Koestner, and Ryan 1999), as well as in field research (for example, Barkema 1995; Frey, Oberholzer-Gee, and Eichenberger 1996; Gneezy and Rustichini 2000*a*, 2000*b*). These relationships between intrinsic and extrinsic motivation are called *crowding effects* (Frey 1997). These effects show that preferences are influenced by outside intervention. This relationship has important consequences for corporate governance. In the case of fraudulent accounts and exorbitant pay, external intervention took the form of employees' conditioning on monetary incentives.

The crowding theory of motivation (Frey 1997; Frey and Osterloh 2002) analyzes the systematic dynamic relationship between extrinsic and intrinsic motivation. Crowding effects can be subdivided into a crowding-out effect and a crowding-in effect. We discuss each of these effects in turn.

Crowding-out Effect

According to self-determination theory (Deci and Ryan 1985, 2000), crowding out can take place *first*, because perceived self-determination suffers from external interventions in the form of monetary incentives. As a result, individuals shift their 'locus of causality' from inside to outside. Their attention shifts from the activity itself to the monetary reward. The content of the activity loses its importance. In the case of civic virtue, intrinsically motivated honesty was undermined by the presumption that agents act solely in the interests of the shareholders if they are paid enough. It was overlooked that exactly that conditioning on monetary compensation reduces the voluntary commitment to the firm and its shareholders. Such commitment is necessary when behavior and outcomes cannot be monitored or attributed to a particular individual. A precondition for crowding-out to occur is that the individuals concerned have intrinsic motivation, which can then be undermined.[2]

There is much empirical evidence supporting this conclusion (for a comprehensive overview of empirical evidence, see Frey and Jegen 2001). It is impossible to summarize the results here of the large number of *laboratory experiments* on the crowding effect. Fortunately, no fewer than five formal meta-empirical studies of crowding theory are available. Rummel and Feinberg (1988) carried out forty-five experimental studies from 1971 to 1985; Wiersma (1992) carried out twenty studies from 1971 to 1990; and Tang and Hall (1995) carried out fifty studies from 1972 to 1992. These meta-analyses essentially support the findings that intrinsic motivation is undermined.[3] Deci, Koestner, and Ryan (1999) conducted an extensive meta-analysis. The sixty-eight experiments reported in fifty-nine articles span the period from 1971 to 1997 and refer to ninety-seven experimental effects. It turns out that tangible rewards undermine intrinsic motivation for interesting tasks (that is, tasks in which the experimental subjects show an intrinsic interest) in a highly significant and very reliable way. Such undermining is particularly true for monetary compensation. The crowding-out effect is stronger with monetary than with symbolic rewards. The crowding-out effect is also larger with expected than with unexpected rewards. When the problems in question are complicated, the negative relationship between reward and performance is stronger than when the problems are simple (see Deci and Ryan 1985; Heckhausen 1991: ch. 15). In all cases, the behavior was initially perceived to be interesting and therefore intrinsically rewarding.

These laboratory experiments all consider effects of external interventions on enjoyment-based intrinsic motivation. But there are also experiments which focus on obligation-based norms, such as perceived obligations of reciprocity. The experiments by Fehr and Gächter (2002) and Irlenbusch and Sliwka (2003) produce an unexpected result from the point of view of traditional agency theory. A treatment with effort-dependent variable compensation leads to lower effort inputs than a treatment with fixed compensation.

The relevance of the crowding-out effect is also supported by numerous *field studies*. The corresponding econometric results are consistent with circumstantial evidence proposed by McGregor's (1960) theory X and theory Y.

---

[2] In situations where no intrinsic motivation exists in the first place, monetary rewards can increase performance, like simple jobs working on an assembly line: see, for example, Lazear (1999).

[3] This view was challenged by Cameron and Pierce (1994) and Eisenberger and Cameron (1996), who concluded that the undermining effect is largely 'a myth' on the basis of their own meta-analysis of studies published in the period 1971 to 1991. Deci, Koestner, and Ryan (1999) conducted an extensive study to show that these conclusions are unwarranted and that the crowding-out effect is a robust phenomenon under specified conditions.

Another real-life case of the crowding-out effect is provided by blood donors, as argued by Titmuss (1970). Paying donors for giving blood undermines the intrinsic motivation to do so. Though it is difficult to isolate the many different influences on blood supply, in countries where most of the blood is supplied free of charge paying for blood is likely to reduce total supply (Upton 1973). The crowding-out effect has also been shown to exist in econometric analyses for the so-called not-in-my-back-yard (NIMBY) syndrome (Frey and Oberholzer-Gee 1997; Frey, Oberholzer-Gee, and Eichenberger 1996). In a carefully designed survey for a community located in central Switzerland, more than half the respondents (50.8 per cent) agreed to have a nuclear waste repository built in their community. When compensation (in monetary terms) was offered, the level of acceptance dropped to 24.6 per cent. Baumol and Oates (1979), Hahn (1989) and Kelman (1981) observed that, under certain conditions, the introduction of environmental charges has little effect. When the penalty for environmental pollution is perceived to be very controlling, people are no longer so motivated to protect the environment for intrinsic reasons. Stukas, Snyder, and Clary (1999) show that voluntary contributions to unpaid helping activities are higher when external pressure is low. Gneezy and Rustichini (2000*a*) found in a field study that fining parents for picking up their children late from a childcare center had an adverse effect. The fine led to a significantly lower level of punctuality. When the fine was discontinued, punctuality remained at the lower level. Obviously the parents' obligation to norms of good conduct was undermined by the external monetary intervention. In a second study, the same authors (Gneezy and Rustichini 2000*b*) analyzed the behavior of school children collecting money voluntarily, that is, without monetary compensation (for example, for cancer research or disabled children). The children reduced their efforts by about 36 per cent when they were promised a bonus of 1 per cent of the money collected. Their effort to collect for the good cause could be significantly raised again only when the bonus was increased from 1 per cent to 10 per cent of the money collected, but they did not reach the initial collection level again.

This field experiment shows clearly that there are two countervailing forces affecting behavior: the first is the standard *relative price effect*, suggesting that an increase in payment increases effort. This is shown in Fig. 8.1, which illustrates the well-known supply curve of work effort.

The second countervailing force affecting behavior is the *crowding-out effect*, suggesting that an increase in payment reduces effort. In our example, both experimental and field studies indicate that children begin to lose interest as a result of the bonus. As shown in Fig. 8.2 the supply curve shifts to the left from S to S'. As a result, children's efforts fall to A_3.

There is, however, one essential prerequisite: intrinsic motivation must have been present at the outset, otherwise there would be nothing to undermine. In the case of straightforward activities, for instance, where

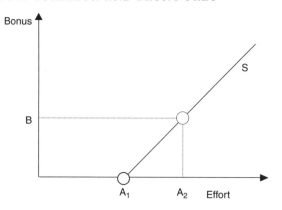

FIGURE 8.1   *The price effect.*
With no bonus, children put in effort A_1. Provided there is no crowding-out
effect, a bonus with the value of B will increase their effort from A_1 to A_2. This is
the pure price effect.

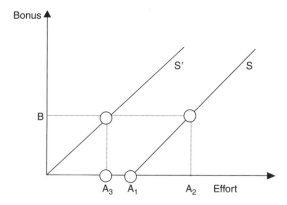

FIGURE 8.2   *Net outcome of the price effect and a strong crowding-out effect.*
In this instance, the price effect from A_1 to A_2 is outweighed by the crowding-out
effect from A_2 to A_3. However, this need not necessarily be the case. As
illustrated in Figure 8.3, it very much depends on the intensity of the crowding-out
effect. In this case, the crowding-out effect shifts the supply curve for effort from
S to S ''. The bonus now increases effort from A_1 to A_4. Thus, the crowding-out
effect can be seen to counteract the price effect. It is difficult to forecast whether
the price or crowding-out effect will predominate in any
particular case.

intrinsic motivation is often scarce, there will be no discernible crowding-out
effect.

A *second* reason for the decrease in intrinsic motivation is the feeling of
being exploited by others. This helps to explain why whole firms, and not
only the top management, were subject to all-pervading greed and malpractice. Empirical evidence shows that many individuals contribute voluntarily

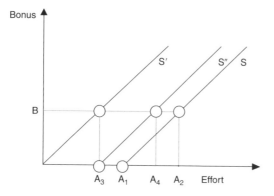

FIGURE 8.3   *Net outcome of the price effect and a weak crowding-out effect.*
Figure 8.3 represents the situation which occurred when the children were
promised the much higher bonus of 10 per cent. While there are no empirical
studies so far analyzing the effect of monetary compensation on managerial
behavior, one can safely assume that the crowding-out effect carries over to the
huge monetary compensations recently administered in firms.

to public goods in social dilemmas as long as a relevant number of other
individuals also contribute. They are conditional cooperators (Levi 1988;
Ostrom 2000; Fischbacher, Gächter, and Fehr 2001). On the other hand,
many people are conditional defectors. As a consequence, intrinsic motivation is crowded out if too many people free ride. Employees' honesty is
undermined if they see that their superiors feather their own nests at the
expense of their employees. They are no longer prepared to contribute voluntarily to the common good of honesty and to blame their colleagues
if they fail to do so. Therefore, institutional mechanisms must be put in
place hindering such exploitation. Corporate governance rules are needed
which impose on managers what Hansmann (1980) calls the non-distribution
constraint, which is a major precondition for voluntary donations to organizations: voluntary contributions cannot be redistributed among those in
charge of the organization.

The exorbitant salaries received by top management thus crowded out
intrinsically motivated corporate virtue in two ways. First, the honesty of
the managers themselves was damaged in many cases. Second, the ensuing
malpractices and excessive wages at the top undermined the honesty at lower
levels because they felt like suckers. As conditional defectors, they also fell
prey to all-pervading greed, and were no longer prepared to contribute to
the common good. This exacerbates the social dilemma.

Crowding-in Effect

A positive effect on intrinsic motivation of an external intervention or institution is called *crowding-in*. This effect has been investigated much less than

the crowding-out effect (but see Deci and Ryan 2000). The most important condition for crowding-in intrinsic motivation is perceived autonomy, but perceived competence and social relatedness also matter. Thus, in Fig. 8.2, the crowding-in effect shifts the supply curve to the right. A pay rise, accompanied by supportive feedback, reflects appreciation of one's work and thus tends to increase work morale.

The need for *autonomy* refers to the need for personal causation. People, as suggested by DeCharms (1968), have a basic desire to experience themselves as causal agents. They would like to see themselves as initiators of action rather then as 'pawns'. However, this sense of internal locus of causality can be reduced. In contrast, contextual conditions can support this sense of autonomy if the agent is given choice and if using initiative is encouraged (for example, Zuckerman et al. 1978).

People also share the need for *competence*: that is, they want to control outcomes and experience efficacy. Each individual seeks to master his or her own way of dealing with the environment. A context in which feedback is provided enhances feelings of competence. Being informed influences one's perceived competence and strengthens the feeling of internal control.

Although autonomy and competence have been found to be the most powerful influences on intrinsic motivation, *social relatedness* also plays a role. As this need has only quite recently been incorporated into self-determination theory, not much empirical research has been done so far. However, a promising avenue of research into this area has been the work of Tyler and others (Tyler 1999; Tyler and Blader 2000), who express the need for social relatedness in the so-called group value model. This model tries to explain why people care about fairness and participation. Both aspects convey information on social standing, which in turn defines a person's status in a group and helps shape the person's self-worth (Tyler and Lind 1992). The precise conditions for this to happen are explored in the organizational justice literature, where procedural and interactive fairness have been analyzed for more than twenty years now (for example, Greenberg 1990; Lind and Tyler 1988).

The next section will show the consequences that can be inferred for corporate governance.

Why Agency Theory is Incomplete

Agency theory suggests three methods of counteracting the misuse of power by management: intensive monitoring and sanctioning, pay for performance, and corporate control by hostile takeovers. All three have proven to be ineffective (Daily, Dalton, and Canella 2003; Sundaramurthy and Lewis 2003).

Monitoring and Sanctioning

In an econometric study of 116 managers in medium-sized Dutch firms, Barkema (1995) found that the number of hours worked in the company decreased under intense supervision on the part of the superiors. This study underlines what Argyris (1964) suggests: strict control has a paradoxical effect. It leads to a never-ending and continuously expanding need to increase control. In view of the intensive interdependencies which characterize firms, this is a futile endeavor. Moreover, such an exercise seriously affects the loyalty of employees to their firms. In laboratory experiments, it was shown that negative sanctions crowd out intrinsically motivated trust (Bohnet, Frey, and Huck 2001; see Fehr and List 2002, who find similar results). Low levels of legal contract enforcement crowd in trustworthiness. Thus, more order results from less law.

Pay for Performance

Pay for performance does not lead to the expected alignment of the interest of managers with those of shareholders. Experience in recent years has shown that performance pay, by linking salaries to stock options, led to an explosion of compensations due to the stock market boom. This trend has, in many cases, simply continued, even under changed economic conditions. Management compensation has often increased even more, despite the fact that share prices have plummeted. This suggests that, in reality, the compensation of managers has little to do with performance. Rather, the reason for the steady increase in compensation is due to the fact that managers are able to exert considerable control over the amount of money they get (see, for example, Benz, Kucher, and Stutzer (2002). Most importantly, they can do so by producing short-term increases in share prices or by re-pricing their stock options. Some managers even resorted to unlawfully misrepresenting their firms' accounts in order to raise their private incomes. Looking back, it is possible to state that agency theory has obviously neglected the possibility of managers distorting their own standards of performance: '. . . much of agency theory . . . unrealistically assumes that earnings and stock prices cannot be manipulated. That is a major weakness of the theory . . . (Becht, Bolton, and Röell, forthcoming: 47). These shortcomings have not been overcome by the board of directors, which proves unable to effectively control the managers. They would be made worse by the proposal of agency theorists to compensate board members according to performance. This provides board members with the same incentives as the management to manipulate performance standards. This might explain why equity compensation of board members is not positively associated with firm performance (Daily, Dalton, and Canella 2003), as agency theorists have claimed (Jensen 1993).

Control by Takeovers

Corporate control by hostile takeovers has received a great deal of attention from agency theorists. It has also proven to be far from effective from that point of view.[4] Even in the US and the UK, it is seldom used and, in most other countries, it is almost non-existent. Managers are obviously able to mobilize anti-takeover defenses, such as super-majority amendments or poison pills (for a description, see Becht, Bolton, and Röell, forthcoming). Moreover, managers successfully supported regulatory interventions, making takeovers more difficult, or preventing them altogether (Romano 1993).

It may be concluded that the fundamental problem of 'who watches the watcher' is not solved by existing agency theory. In contrast, crowding theory provides strong arguments that the measures posed by the agency theory *reinforce* the very pro-self extrinsic motivation of managers that it is supposed to defeat. The dynamics between intrinsic and extrinsic motivation must therefore be introduced into an evolving theory to provide a better model of corporate governance and to overcome the problems ensuing from the misuse of management power. Empirical evidence suggests that stricter control and the threat of negative sanctions tend to decrease loyalty to the firm. Therefore, other approaches should be considered.

What to Do?

We advance three propositions for the design of corporate governance, taking heed of the insights gained from crowding theory.

Selection of Management

Selection processes should favor employees with pro-social intrinsic preferences. Selection criteria should not be restricted to purely efficiency-oriented aspects, as was the case with many of the scandalous firms. At Enron, with respect to managers, an executive admitted: 'I never heard a discussion about a person's teamwork or integrity or respect' (Spector 2003: 215). This is important, because a higher number of intrinsically motivated, honest organization members increases conditional cooperation. Intrinsic motivation to behave honestly tends to be crowded out all the more if a large number of other members of the firm are acting in a dishonest way (Blair and Stout 2001*b*). Human Resources seem to be well aware of the importance of protecting the company from malefactors on the shop floor. In his book on wage rigidity, Bewley (1999) reports many instances in which the

---

[4] From the point of view of directors as mediators of the interests of different residual claimants, anti-takeover provisions make sense. They give directors the leeway to find solutions serving not only the shareholders but also other actors making firm-specific investments in particular employees (see Blair and Stout 2001*a*: 422).

most important criterion when workers had to be dismissed was weeding out bad characters. But this insight was obviously not applied to management.

More Emphasis on Fixed Salaries

Selecting pro-socially motivated managers does not guarantee that they always act in an appropriate way. According to North (1990: 43), there is a downward sloping demand curve for moral concerns. The more costly it gets, the less people contribute. Conversely, if a low-cost-decision for each individual is at stake, many of them contribute small amounts to the common good so that the total amount of contributions rises considerably. As a consequence, it is important to look for institutions favoring low-cost-decisions (Kirchgässner 1992). An important means to design low-cost situations to overcome the social dilemmas in a firm is to give *fixed salaries* more prominence again. Four empirical results support such a change in policy.

First, a recently published review on different types of variable pay suggests that even small percentages of monetary incentives—often as low as 3 per cent of a person's total pay—increased performance appreciably. It appears that the actual amount of incentive pay as a proportion of fixed pay can be quite small and still be effective (Bucklin and Dickinson 2001). It can be argued that such small monetary rewards are perceived mainly as a feedback which supports crowding in rather than as an external control.

Second, public governance teaches us that politicians, public officials, and judges receive fixed salaries because those persons who set the regulations should not be given an incentive to manipulate the corresponding criteria in their own favor (Frey 2003). In management, the exact opposite took place: the top executives were given the opportunity to manipulate the criteria by which they were evaluated and compensated.

Third, people behave more cooperatively when they are told to do so. In experiments, subjects behave more pro-socially when the experimenter suggests that they should do so, even without external incentives (Blair and Stout 2001*b*). Over the last decade, principal-agency theorists prompted managers and directors to think that performance without incentive pay is irrational. This certainly had an effect on their behavior. As Paul Volker, the former Chairman of the Federal Reserve Board remarked: 'Traditional norms didn't exist. You had this whole culture where the only sign of worth was how much money you made' (Cassidy 2002).

Fourth, there is strong empirical evidence that even honest people are subject to an unconscious 'self-serving bias'. In situations characterized by ambiguity or discretion, it is typical that managerial decision-making judgments of what constitutes fairness conflates with what is beneficial for oneself. Unlike conscious corruption, such conflation cannot be deterred by sanctions (Babcock and Loewenstein 1997; Bazerman, Loewenstein, and

Moore 2002). Instead, it can be reduced by lowering the incentives to take care of one's own interests. This can be achieved by attributing more importance to fixed wages for managers as well as for board members. With respect to the self-serving bias, it is most important not to compensate the board members according to the same criteria (for example, stock prices) as the management, because the self-serving bias would unconsciously undermine the willingness to control.

Managers must be paid a fair market wage in exchange for their overall performance, thus reducing the temptations to cheat the firm, consciously or unconsciously. According to crowding theory, greater emphasis on fixed salaries reduces crowding out of pro-social intrinsic preferences, for two reasons. As we have argued, excessive short-term pay for performance, by means of bonuses and stock options, under identifiable conditions undermines the loyalty voluntarily offered to the company by inducing a switch to a purely calculating mode. As a consequence, a contract including pro-social motives is changed into a purely selfishly motivated contract (Lindenberg, Chapter 9, this volume). Moreover, most people cooperate only as long as others do so too. Therefore, when top management lines its pockets, many employees also start maximizing their monetary incomes by whatever means, including fraudulent bookkeeping. Employees are no longer prepared to oppose the wrongdoings of their bosses. They no longer feel obliged to support corporate virtue.

Participation and Increased Self-Governance of Employees

The decision-making process of firms must strengthen participation and self-governance as a part of corporate governance. It promotes self-monitoring and sanctioning in an informal way by the corporate community and therewith reduces the breaking of rules. As monitoring and blaming colleagues and superiors carry at least psychic costs (and sometimes ruin one's career), civic virtue is needed. Extensive experimental and field research shows that civic virtues are strengthened by procedural utility. Anyone breaking the rules is more easily identified by colleagues than by superiors, and is informally admonished. This has the expressive function of ensuring that others are doing their part in using the common good wisely. Experiments show that sanctions perceived as pro-socially motivated enhance cooperative behavior, whereas sanctions serving the punisher's self-interest crowd it out (Fehr and Rockenbach 2003). This is important because making people feel shame works only if employees feel at least some minimal intrinsically motivated obligation to follow the rules and to contribute to the common good. Purely rational egoists do not experience any shame (Elster 1999; Orr 2001); this again underlines the importance of intrinsically motivated corporate virtue. This conclusion is empirically supported by evidence in the literature on organizational citizenship behavior (Organ 1988), procedural utility (Frey and Stutzer 2002), and procedural justice (Tyler and Blader 2000).

Conclusions

The reactions of principal-agent theorists and politicians to the malpractices and excessive compensations of top management by intensifying monitoring and sanctioning tend to worsen the very problems they are designed to solve. The apparent remedy raises the incentives of managers and other employees to take advantage of the very firm they are supposed to care about. The conditions leading to '*a governance of crooks*' have to be taken into account. Instead of stricter monitoring and sanctioning, we suggest three alternatives. First, the selection of managers should emphasize pro-social intrinsic preferences to ensure the conditional cooperation of other employees. Second, care must be taken not to crowd out the corporate virtue based on the intrinsic motivation of managers and employees. We suggest that stronger emphasis should again be placed on fixed salaries to avoid the crowding-out effect and to reduce the temptation to cheat. Third, employees' willingness to contribute to corporate virtue by identifying and admonishing anyone resorting to fraudulent accounting must be strengthened by participation possibilities and self-governance.

These proposals clash with conventional wisdom but, based on existing research, they promise to yield better long-term results than governance structures made for crooks.

References

Akerlof, G. (1982). 'Labor Contracts as Partial Gift Exchange', *Quarterly Journal of Economics*, 84: 488–500.

Argyris, C. (1964). *Integrating the Individual and the Organization*. New York: Wiley.

Babcock, L. and Loewenstein, G. (1997). 'Explaining Bargaining Impasse: The Role of Self-Serving Biases', *Journal of Economic Perspectives*, 11: 109–26.

Barkema, H. (1995). 'Do Job Executives Work Harder When They Are Monitored?', *Kyklos*, 48: 19–42.

Baumol, W. and Oates, W. (1979). *Economics, Environmental Policy, and the Quality of Life*. Englewood Cliffs: Prentice-Hall.

Bazerman, M., Loewenstein, G., and Moore, D. (2002). 'Why Good Accountants Do Bad Audits', *Harvard Business Review*, 80/11: 97–102.

Becht, M., Bolton, P., and Röell, A. (forthcoming). 'Corporate Governance and Control', in G. Constantinides, H. Milton, and R. Stulz (eds.), *Handbook of the Economics of Finance*. Amsterdam: North Holland.

Benabou, R. and Tirole, J. (2002). *Intrinsic and Extrinsic Motivation* (Working Paper). Princeton: Princeton University, www.princeton.edu/~rbenabou/Intrinsic2.pdf

Benz, M., Kucher, M., and Stutzer, A. (2002). 'Stock Options for Top Managers—The Possibilities and Limitations of a Motivational Tool', in B. Frey and M. Osterloh (eds.), *Successful Management by Motivation: Balancing Intrinsic and Extrinsic Incentives*. Berlin, Heidelberg, New York: Springer.

Bewley, T. (1999). *Why Wages Don't Fall during a Recession*. Cambridge, MA: Harvard University Press.

Blair, M. and Stout, L. (2001a). 'Director Accountability and the Mediating Role of the Corporate Board', *Washington University Law Quarterly*, 79: 403–49.

———— (2001b). 'Trust, Trustworthiness and the Behavioral Foundations of Corporate Law', *University of Pennsylvania Law Review*, 149: 1735–810.

Bohnet, I., Frey, B., and Huck, S. (2001). 'More Order with Less Law: On Contract Enforcement, Trust, and Crowding', *American Political Science Review*, 95: 131–44.

Bucklin, B. and Dickinson, A. (2001). 'Individual Monetary Incentives: A Review of Different Types of Arrangements Between Performance and Pay', *Journal of Organizational Behavior Management*, 21: 45–137.

Cameron, J. and Pierce, W. (1994). 'Reinforcement, Reward, and Intrinsic Motivation: A Meta-Analysis', *Review of Educational Research*, 64: 363–423.

Cassidy, J. (2002). 'The Greed Cycle: How the Financial System Encouraged Corporations to Go Crazy', *The New Yorker*, 23 September.

Csikszentmihalyi, M. (1975). *Beyond Boredom and Anxiety*. San Francisco: Jossey-Bass.

Daily, C., Dalton, D., and Canella, A. (2003). 'Corporate Governance: Decades of Dialogue and Data', *The Academy of Management Review*, 28: 371–82.

Dalton, D., Daily, C., Ellstrand, A., and Johnson, J. (1998). 'Meta-Analytic Reviews of Board Composition, Leadership Structure, and Financial Performance', *Strategic Management Journal*, 19: 269–90.

Dawes, R. (1980). 'Social Dilemmas', *Annual Review of Psychology*, 31: 169–93.

DeCharms, R. (1968). *Personal Causation: The Internal Affective Determinants of Behavior*. New York: Academic Press.

Deci, E. (1975). *Intrinsic Motivation*. New York: Plenum Press.

—— and Ryan, R. (1985). *Intrinsic Motivation and Self-Determination in Human Behavior*. New York: Plenum Press.

———— (2000). 'The "What" and "Why" of Goal Pursuits: Human Needs and the Self-Determination of Behavior', *Psychological Inquiry*, 11: 227–68.

——, Koestner, R., and Ryan, R. (1999). 'Meta-Analytic Review of Experiments: Examining the Effects of Extrinsic Rewards on Intrinsic Motivation', *Psychological Bulletin*, 125: 627–68.

The Economist (1999). 8 May.

—— (2002a). 17 August.

—— (2002b). 16 November.

Eisenberger, R. and Cameron, J. (1996). 'Detrimental Effects of Reward: Reality or Myth?', *American Psychologist*, 51: 1153–66.

Elster, J. (1999). *Alchemies of the Mind: Rationality and the Emotions*. Cambridge: Cambridge University Press.

Fehr, E. and Gächter, S. (2002). *Do Incentive Contracts Crowd out Voluntary Cooperation?* (Working Paper No. 34). Zurich: Institute for Empirical Research in Economics, University of Zurich.

—— and List, J. (2002). *The Hidden Costs and Returns on Incentives—Trust and Trustworthiness among CEOs* (Working Paper Nr. 134). Zurich: Institute for Empirical Research in Economics, University of Zurich.

—— and Rockenbach, B. (2003). 'Detrimental Effects of Sanctions on Human Altruism', *Nature*, 422/13: 137–40.

Fischbacher, U., Gächter, S., and Fehr, E. (2001). 'Are People Conditionally Cooperative? Evidence from Public Good Experiments', *Economic Letters*, 71: 397–404.

Frey, B. (1997). *Not Just For the Money: An Economic Theory of Personal Motivation.* Brookfield: Edward Elgar.

—— (2003). *Corporate Governance: What Can We Learn from Public Governance?* (Working Paper). Zurich: Institute for Empirical Economic Research, University of Zurich.

—— and Jegen, R. (2001). 'Motivation Crowding Theory: A Survey of Empirical Evidence', *Journal of Economic Surveys*, 15: 589–611.

—— and Meier, S. (2002). *Pro-Social Behavior, Reciprocity or Both?* (Working Paper Series 107). Zurich: Institute for Empirical Economic Research, University of Zurich. www.unizh.ch/iew/wp/iewwp107.pdf

—— and Oberholzer-Gee, F. (1997). 'The Cost of Price Incentives: An Empirical Analysis of Motivation Crowding-out', *American Economic Review*, 87: 746–55.

——, —— , and Eichenberger, R. (1996). 'The Old Lady Visits Your Backyard: A Tale of Morals and Markets', *Journal of Political Economy*, 104: 193–209.

—— and Osterloh, M. (2002). *Successful Management by Motivation: Balancing Intrinsic and Extrinsic Incentives.* Berlin, Heidelberg, New York: Springer.

—— and Stutzer, A. (2002). *Beyond Outcomes: Measuring Procedural Utility* (Working Paper Series 63). Berkeley, CA: Berkeley Olin Program in Law and Economics, University of California. http://repositories.cdlib.org/blewp/art63

Gneezy, U. and Rustichini, A. (2000a). 'A Fine Is a Price', *Journal of Legal Studies*, 29: 1–18.

—— —— (2000b). 'Pay Enough or Don't Pay at All', *Quarterly Journal of Economics*, 115: 791–810.

Grandori, A. (1997). 'An Organizational Assessment of Interfirm Coordination Modes', *Organization Studies*, 18: 897–925.

—— (2000). *Organization and Economic Behavior.* London: Routledge.

Grant, R. (1996). 'Towards a Knowledge-based Theory of the Firm', *Strategic Management Journal*, 17: 109–22.

Greenberg, J. (1990). 'Organizational Justice: Yesterday, Today, and Tomorrow', *Journal of Management*, 16: 399–432.

Hahn, R. (1989). 'Economic Prescriptions for Environmental Problems: How the Patient Followed the Doctor's Orders', *Journal of Economic Perspectives*, 3: 9–114.

Hansmann, H. (1980). 'The Role of Nonprofit Enterprise', *Yale Law Journal*, 89: 835–901.

Hardin, G. (1968).'The Tragedy of the Commons', *Science*, 162: 1243–8.

Heckhausen, H. (1991). *Motivation and Action.* Berlin, Heidelberg, New York: Springer.

Holmström, B. and Kaplan, St. N. (2003). *The State of U.S. Corporate Governance: What's Right and What's Wrong?* (Working Paper Series 9613). Cambridge, MA: NBER.

Irlenbusch, B. and Sliwka, D. (2003). *Incentives, Decision Frames and Motivation Crowding Out—An Experimental Investigation* (Working Paper). Bonn: University of Bonn.

Jensen, M. (1993). 'The Modern Industrial Revolution, Exit, and the Failure of Internal Control Systems', *Journal of Finance*, 48: 831–80.

Kandel, E. and Lazear, E. (1992). 'Peer Pressure and Partnership', *Journal of Political Economy*, 100: 801–17.

Kelman, S. (1981). *What Price Incentives? Economists and the Environment*. Boston: Auburn House.

Kirchgässner, G. (1992).'Toward a Theory of Low-Cost-Decision', *European Journal of Political Economy*, 8: 305–20.

Kogut, B. and Zander, U. (1996). 'What Firms Do? Coordination, Identity, and Learning', *Organization Science*, 7: 502–18.

Kreps, D. (1997). 'Intrinsic Motivation and Extrinsic Incentives', *American Economic Review*, 87: 359–64.

Lambert, R., Lanen, W., and Larcker, D. (1989). 'Executive Stock Option Plans and Corporate Dividend Policy', *Journal of Financial and Quantitative Analysis*, 24: 409–25.

Lazear, E. (1999). 'Personnel Economics: Past Lessons and Future Directions', *Journal of Labor Economics*, 17: 199–236.

Levi, M. (1988). *Of Rule and Revenue*. Berkeley: University of California Press.

Lind, E. and Tyler, T. (1988). *The Social Psychology of Procedural Justice*. New York: Plenum Press.

Lindenberg, S. (2001). 'Intrinsic Motivation in a New Light', *Kyklos*, 54: 317–43.

McGregor, D. (1960). *The Human Side of Enterprise*. New York: McGraw-Hill.

Milgrom, P. and Roberts, J. (1992). *Economics, Organization and Management*. New Jersey: Prentice-Hall.

Miller, G. (1992). *Managerial Dilemmas: The Political Economy of Hierarchy*. Cambridge: Cambridge University Press.

Murphy, K. (1999). 'Executive Compensation', in O. Ashenfelter and D. Card (eds.), *Handbook of Labour Economics*. Amsterdam: Elsevier.

Nonaka, I. and Takeuchi, H. (1995). *The Knowledge-Creating Company*. New York, Oxford: Oxford University Press.

North, D. (1990). *Institutions, Institutional Change, and Economic Performance*. Cambridge: Cambridge University Press.

Organ, D. (1988). *Organizational Citizenship Behavior: The Good Soldier Syndrome*. Lexington: Lexington Books.

—— and Ryan, K. (1995). 'A Meta-Analytic Review of Attitudinal and Dispositional Predictors of Organizational Citizenship Behavior', *Personnel Psychology*, 48: 775–82.

Orr, S. (2001) .'The Economics of Shame in Work Groups: How Mutual Monitoring Can Decrease Cooperation in Teams', *Kyklos*, 54: 49–66.

Osterloh, M. and Frey, B. (2000). 'Motivation, Knowledge Transfer, and Organizational Firms', *Organization Science*, 11: 538–50.

——, Frost, J., and Weibel, A. (2002). *Solving Social Dilemmas: The Dynamics of Motivation in the Theory of the Firm* (Working Paper). Zurich: Institute for Research in Business Administration, University of Zurich.

——, Rota, S., and Kuster, B. (2003). *Open Source Software Production. Climbing on the Shoulders of Giants* (Working Paper). Zurich: Institute for Research in Business Administration, University of Zurich.

Ostrom, E. (1998). 'A Behavioural Approach to the Rational-Choice Theory of Collective Action', *American Political Science Review*, 92: 1–22.

—— (2000). 'Crowding Out Citizenship', *Scandinavian Political Studies*, 23: 3–16.

Rabin, M. (1998). 'Psychology and Economics', *Journal of Economic Literature*, 36: 11–46.

Raymond, E. (2000). *The Magic Cauldron*. www.tuxedo.org/~esr/writings/cathedral-bazaar/magic-cauldron/index.html

Romano, R. (1993). *The Genius of American Corporate Law*. Washington, DC: American Enterprise Institute.

Rummel, A. and Feinberg, R. (1988). 'Cognitive Evaluation Theory: A Meta-Analytic Review of the Literature', *Social Behavior and Personality*, 16: 147–64.

Sen, A. (1974). 'Choice, Orderings and Morality', in S. Körner (ed.), *Practical Reason: Papers and Discussions*. Oxford: Blackwell.

Simon, H. (1991). 'Organizations and Markets', *Journal of Economic Perspectives*, 5: 25–44.

Sliwka, D. (2003). *On the Hidden Costs of Incentive Schemes*. Bonn: University of Bonn.

Spector, B. (2003). 'The Unindicted Co-conspirator', *Organizational Dynamics*, 32: 207–20.

Stukas, A., Snyder, M., and Clary, E. (1999). 'The Effects of "Mandatory Volunteerism" on Intentions to Volunteer', *Psychological Science*, 10: 59–64.

Sundaramurthy, Ch. and Lewis, M. (2003). 'Paradoxes of Governance', *The Academy of Management Review*, 28: 397–415.

Tang, S. and Hall, V. (1995). 'The Overjustification Effect: A Meta-Analysis', *Applied Cognitive Psychology*, 9: 365–404.

Thompson, J. (1967). *Organizations in Action*. New York: McGraw-Hill.

Titmuss, R. (1970). *The Gift Relationship*. London: Allen and Unwin.

Tosi, H., Shen, W., and Gentry, R. (2003). 'Why Outsiders on Boards Can't Solve the Corporate Governance Problem', *Organizational Dynamics*, 32: 180–92.

Tyler, T. (1999). 'Why People Cooperate With Organizations: An Identity-Based Perspective', in R. Sutton and B. Staw (eds.), *Research in Organizational Behavior*. Greenwich, CT: JAI-Press.

—— and Blader, S. (2000). *Cooperation in Groups: Procedural Justice, Social Identity, and Behavioral Engagement*. Philadelphia: Psychology Press.

—— and Lind, E. (1992). 'A Relational Model of Authority In Groups', in M. Zanna (ed.), *Advances in Experimental Social Psychology*. Amsterdam: Academic Press (Elsevier).

Upton, W. (1973). 'Altruism, Attribution and Intrinsic Motivation in the Recruitment of Blood Donors'. Ph.D. dissertation. Abstract: *Dissertation Abstracts International*, 34B (12), 1974, 6260, Cornell University.

Vining, A. (2003). 'Internal Market Failure: A Framework for Diagnosing Firm Inefficiency', *Journal of Management Studies*, 40: 431–57.

Wiersma, U. (1992). 'The Effects of Extrinsic Rewards on Intrinsic Motivation: A Meta-Analysis', *Journal of Occupational and Organizational Psychology*, 65: 101–14.

Williamson, O. (1975). *Markets and Hierarchies: Analysis and Antitrust Implications: A Study in the Economics of Internal Organization*. New York: Free Press.

Zuckerman, M., Porac, J., Lathin, D., Smith, R., and Deci, E. (1978). 'On the Importance of Self-Determination for Intrinsically Motivated Behavior', *Personality and Social Psychology Bulletin,* 4: 443–6.

9

Myopic Opportunism and Joint Production: A Relational Approach to Corporate Governance

SIEGWART LINDENBERG

> The cost of mistrust has become painfully evident in very concrete ways during the last few years: reduced share prices, lost jobs, shrunken pension funds. At the same time, the potential competitive advantage of trustworthy companies is becoming clearer. Benefits include reduced costs of capital, retention of longer-term investors, distinctive brands and strong reputations.
> (Mark Moody-Stuart, 'The measure of a good company', *Herald Tribune*, 25–6 January 2003)

Introduction

Governance, notably also corporate governance, is mostly about reducing opportunistic behavior. The message of this chapter is that reducing opportunistic behavior is mainly a matter of relational effort and only for the smallest part a matter of control and interest alignment. Seen this way, corporate governance consists of three parts: (i) owners establishing a certain relationship with each other; (ii) owners establishing a certain relationship with their managers; and (iii) owners holding managers accountable for how they manage relations with stakeholders. Clearly, I will not have institutional designs ready for these three parts. However, I will argue that the relational approach will lead to a search for institutional designs for corporate governance that is different from the mode that presently dominates the design discussion.

Why such an emphasis on relations? The answer to this question comes from relatively new research on opportunistic behavior. The by now classical view of opportunistic behavior in the fields of organization studies and corporate governance comes from the principal-agent approach in which the principal attempts to increase control and, failing that, chooses incentives in such a way that the interests of the agent align with those of the principal. This has proved to be a powerful approach. Enriched with transaction cost theory, which drew specific attention to *ex post* problems with contract execution, it has permeated the views of what governance is all about.

More recently, research on combined motivational and cognitive influences on opportunistic behavior has introduced a new element into the discussion. First of all, there is a new conception of opportunistic behavior. In day-to-day conduct, opportunistic behavior consists mainly of responding to unanticipated *short-term* opportunities and pressures. This opportunism is not strategic but myopic.[1] For example, 'golden' opportunities present themselves, seemingly too good to let go, and yet they are against the contractual agreements or against agreed-to rules and principles. Similarly, problems often arise quite suddenly in an unexpected way and motivate 'cutting corners'. For example, time pressure to make use of a golden opportunity often also reduces the intensity of safety checks. Thus, at first blush, the books of the company that can be taken over for a good price (if one is quick) look acceptable. Why not skip the laborious procedure of a thorough check this time round? There are also unforeseen mishaps. For example, it might happen that many employees are ill just at a time when the delivery deadline approaches and everyone is under great stress. So why not skip quality control only this once, to get over this tight spot? Another important factor subject to myopic opportunism is intelligent effort. It is needed in so many modern jobs but it is difficult to gauge and thus difficult to monitor. Knowledge, needed for intelligent effort, is often also only tacit and its use can by definition not be enforced contractually.[2] For these reasons, higher-intensity intelligent effort often cannot even be informally monitored and short-term temptations to apply it to goals unrelated or even hostile to the principal's interests are great. For instance, managers may be tempted to put more intelligent effort into their own career than into the company's longer-term growth. Day-to-day myopic opportunistic behavior creates its own path dependencies and cumulative effects which, in turn, demand more short-term crisis management and thereby also myopic opportunism. For example, at a certain moment, the books may have to be 'adjusted' to cover up these cumulative effects, officials may have to be bribed, and further corners may have to be cut in quality control as the financial situation worsens. In addition, the accumulation of myopic opportunism in an organization is likely to normalize increasing margins of deviance, stretching the boundaries of what is acceptable and possibly blinding agents to danger signals. All this can happen with interest-aligning instruments in place. There does not seem to be much sinister, farsighted calculation (that is, strategic opportunism) involved in the bulk of corporate deviance.[3] The control and alignment instruments are

---

[1] By 'strategic opportunism' I mean the rational pursuit of longer-term self-interested goals in interaction with others without ethical constraints about lying, cheating, and so forth. By 'myopic opportunism', I mean the rational pursuit of short-term self-interested goals in interaction with others without ethical constraints about lying, cheating, and so forth.

[2] This point about tacit knowledge has been made by Osterloh and Frey (2000).

[3] See Vaughan 1999 for a review of these kinds of phenomena related to the cumulative effects of myopic opportunism that involve the normalization of deviance.

important and they do curb strategic opportunism, but they are too crude to deal with most of the short-term temptations and their cumulative effects, or with the subtle allocation of intelligent effort away from the principal's interests.

Second, myopic opportunism is the consequence of a combined motivational and cognitive process called 'framing' (see Lindenberg 1998). What happens is that a strong goal (the motivation) triggers cognitive processes in such a way that certain aspects of the situation are pushed into the foreground and others into the background. For example, a golden opportunity may lead to a situation in which a CEO is caught up in a strong feeling of loss by the thought of letting this opportunity slip away. Loss avoidance is a strong motivator and it is likely to lead to the salience of aspects that help avoid the loss. It is also likely to lead to a cognitive and motivational veiling of aspects that tell against taking advantage of the golden opportunity.

Myopic opportunism comes about through a process of framing, but the curbing of myopic opportunism does not lie in the suppression of the framing process (that will never work). Rather, as I will try to show, it lies in the use of the very same process of framing for cooperative purposes. The governance of myopic opportunism boils down to governing the framing process. In this chapter, I will elaborate on the framing process and its governance, and I will apply both to the question how corporate governance can be improved by taking these processes into account.

A Framing Approach to Sustainable Relationships

The term 'sustainable' is used in many different ways in the literature on corporate governance. The meaning attached to this term (in conjunction with relationships) in this chapter is equivalent to 'cooperative over time in situations of joint production', meaning that a relationship does not break up as long as it is potentially advantageous for both in the longer run. By 'gain-driven behavior' we mean behavior that is calculative (including opportunistic behavior for which lying, cheating, and manipulating are not excluded as possible strategies) and oriented towards the increase of one's control over scarce resources. *The basic idea of the framing approach is that even potentially profitable cooperative relationships are rarely sustainable over the longer term if they are not accompanied by a partial suspension of gain-driven behavior.*[4] The exception consists of situations in which behavior can easily be monitored and when

---

[4] This is different from but compatible with Osterloh and Frey's approach (Chapter 8, this volume) based on research on intrinsic motivation, but it contrasts with important contemporary approaches that have not (yet) incorporated research on myopic opportunism, especially with the 'self-interest' and social bonding approaches. The former are close to the control and align paradigms (including credible commitment approaches, reputation and learning approaches, and reciprocal altruism approaches, see for examples Buskens 2002; Raub and Weesie 2000; Williamson 1993). The latter are close to the 'social preference'

it involves little tacit knowledge and intelligent effort. Then the interaction partners can easily predict each other's behavior and can even deal *ex ante* with possible predictive failures. The relationships of the shareholders to each other and to the management of the corporation, and the relationships of the corporation to its stakeholders, are not of this kind. Rather, most of these relationships are riddled with uncertainties and difficulties of monitoring; they require much intelligent effort, and lead potentially to much damage when things have gone wrong.

As I have argued above, even when interests are broadly aligned, there is, in such relationships, much room for opportunism. Mutual dependability requires something in addition to knowledge of the other's constraints and interest alignment. It also requires the *alignment of commitment to the relationship*, which partially suspends the instrumental use of the relationship, creates trust, and directs intelligent effort towards joint goals. This is something of a paradox.[5] Certainly in the business world relationships should either be instrumental in reaching economic goals or be broken up. Yet, paradoxically, their instrumentality (in terms of economic gain) is enhanced if the interaction is *not* guided by the goal to maximize the instrumental value of the relationship. For example, in a recent study of the better dress sector of the apparel industry in New York, Uzzi (1997) found that manufacturers with long-term relations with contractors believed that the contractors would not act in their self-interest at the manufacturers' expense, and vice versa. This showed up in concrete actions such as resource pooling among partners and, when transactions had to be done fast, *post hoc* pricing. As one CEO put it, 'we do first and fix price after'; another CEO would say, 'the contractors know that they will not lose'. The partial suspension of gain-driven behavior was beneficial for both parties. Uzzi could also show that this was not true for all business relationships in this industry. Certain relationships were long-term with partial suspension of gain-driven behavior, but there also were transactions with changing 'arm's-length' (or pure market) partners, without any suspension of gain-driven behavior. Seemingly, the two served different purposes and possibly one influenced the other in the sense that the committed relationships were stabilized by the availability of arm's-length partners.

How does this kind of commitment alignment work? Where does the 'relational concern' come from? Very likely, relational concern derives from the mutual perception of the partners that they are engaged in a *joint production* (see, for example, Scott and Cherrington 1974). At times, it is assumed in the economic literature of organizations and management that an allocation is efficient only if it maximizes the total value of the parties involved and

---

approaches because they focus on stable changes in people's preferences (through liking, see for examples Lawler and Yoon 1993; Sabel 1993; Tyler and Degoey 1996).

[5] It has been called 'the by-product paradox' (see Lindenberg 1986).

that, under the assumption of efficient bargaining (for dividing the costs and benefits), the parties involved will behave so as to jointly maximize the total value (see, for example, Milgrom and Roberts 1992: 36 ff.). However, the whole point about opportunism is that 'efficient bargaining' cannot be assumed, not even with transaction cost-lowering instruments of interest alignment. The willingness to see the transaction as a cooperative effort, as a *joint* production, and to signal this perception to the other is the only way we can come even close to the maximization of total value. Principal-agent theory is based on the opposite assumption, namely, that principal's and agent's interests are in conflict unless the agent's interests are aligned with those of the principal as an act of governing his or her behavior. There is not even a place for the perception of joint production in principal-agent theory.

Relational concern is not a matter of stable preferences for being 'nice' to transaction partners. As we saw in Uzzi's research, the same manufacturers and contractors that had a relational commitment also had other business relations with pure (that is, blatantly gain-driven) market transactions. Nor was it pure 'prudence' of business partners to behave cooperatively in their own self-interest. Again, Uzzi found that relationally committed business partners helped each other far beyond the call of self-interest. For example, when there is a lull in the market, they would help each other out. In the words of a production manager, 'We will put a dress into work to keep the contractor going. We'll then store the dress in the warehouse.' By contrast, in the pure market relations the other would 'push the price down when the contractor tells of his production problems'. It is very likely that what is going on in the committed relationships is a partial suspension of gain-driven behavior. The sustainability of the relationship is not maintained by the partners deciding against being opportunistic (because they think it is prudent to do so), but *by their not even considering the strategically opportunistic alternatives*. With the help of cognitive psychology, one can trace how such a partial suspension of gain-driven behavior is possible (see Lindenberg 2000) and why is has the positive effect it is said to have.

Seemingly, there are overriding goals that govern how people 'frame' a situation, that is, how they perceive it, what alternatives they see, what aspects they consider important, what pieces of knowledge are being activated, and so on. The overriding goal 'frames' the situation in a particular way. For example, if the overriding goal is to make as much money as possible, the alternatives perceived are instrumental for this goal and they include what, from the point of view of a relational concern, would be called 'opportunistic' alternatives. The knowledge being activated includes information of opportunities that can be exploited, of the weaknesses of the other, of the probability of being found out. By contrast, if the overriding goal is a relational concern, the alternatives perceived pertain to the goal of sustaining the relationship, and the knowledge that is being activated includes information of opportunities to advance joint goals, of threats to the relationship, of possibilities to help, and so on (see also Kahneman, Knetsch, and Thaler 1986).

A frame is not a stable preference that keeps steering behavior in the same direction. It comes about through the situational dominance of a certain goal. If that goal is replaced by another, the frame switches, say, from making money to relational concern or the other way around. Thus, in the framing process certain concerns are pushed into the foreground and others into the background, but none vanishes. There is no fundamental change of preferences taking place. For example, in a market economy, the goal of making money will rarely be suspended altogether. It is essential for corporations to make money. However, the crucial question is whether relational concern as a goal is strong enough ever to push making money as a goal into the background. If it is, gain-driven behavior is, for the time being, partially suspended. How does it happen?

Foreground and background goals are dynamically interdependent. When people are in a certain frame, their actions may be so contrary to the background goal that the latter's salience (that is, its relative strength) increases to the extent that it becomes the new frame. For example, going after making as much money as possible, a person may do things that come step by step closer to hurting the other's legitimate interests and his own interest in keeping the relationship in good order. He may increase the price a bit more than is justified by inflation, put the customer's order on the back-burner in order to accommodate a new and well-paying customer, skip the quality control to save some time, and so on. If there is a relational concern in the background, the increasing violations in the person's pursuit of making money may strengthen it to the degree that it takes over as the new frame. In that frame, the alternatives for sustaining the relationship become prominent, and he may offer late payment, rapid delivery of the new order, and so on. Dyer (1997) reports from Japan that more than 75 per cent of the suppliers of large firms interviewed indicated that, if an inequity occurred in the present transaction, it would be 'remembered' and corrected in the future. Conversely, when the pursuit of the relational concern costs increasingly more money, the goal 'to make money' (in the background) will increase in relative strength and may displace relational concern as a frame. This seesawing of making money and relational concern in time to avoid great harm to either concern has been called *weak solidarity* (see Lindenberg 1998) to contrast it with the kind of solidarity found in tight-knit groups in which making money from the other is a good reason to break off the relationship altogether. This is to say that, in strong solidarity relationships, the relational concern is so strong that it is not displaced by concerns for making money. Similarly, in 'pure' market relationships, the concern for making money is so strong that it is not displaced by relational concerns. In such a relationship, even cooperation is perceived in terms of weakness rather than relational commitment (see Sattler and Kerr 1991). Weak solidarity can occur and be sustained only if relational concern and making money are not diametrically opposed. It takes an economy in which there are no strong in-group-out-group animosities that foster strong solidarity inside the group and pure opportunism between groups. In turn, such an economy can thrive only when the delivery of law does not much depend on being inside or outside a group.[6] In addition, as already mentioned, transactions must be complex enough to render pure power strategies ineffective. They are complex in this sense when performance in transactions cannot be easily monitored and when it involves much tacit knowledge and intelligent effort (see Lindenberg 2002, 2003). Making money and being concerned about the relationships with business partners are then compatible enough to allow weak solidarity but still incompatible enough in the short run to create problems that need special attention, as we will see in the next section.

Joint Production and Institutional Design

The application of the framing approach to institutions implies that institutions do not regulate behavior just by incentives but also by affecting frames (see Lindenberg 1992). In the case of institutions that govern cooperative relationships, this means that they must be designed to encourage weak solidarity by creating the preconditions for joint production as a guiding principle of interaction. This contrasts sharply with the major approaches to corporate control, in both the US and Europe. There are important differences between various institutional settings (such as whether there are one or two boards) but, by and large, they all are guided by the principal-agent paradigm of 'control and align', mostly in the US, somewhat less so in Europe. In the relational approach, control and interest alignment are not superfluous but they are secondary in institutional design that concentrates on establishing overlapping sets of 'joint productions'. We thus search for potentially relevant contexts of joint production in corporate governance.

Three such interrelated contexts stand out as obviously relevant (see Fig. 9.1). First, for the shareholders, the major task is corporate governance and it can be (but mostly is not yet) seen as joint production of all shareholders (within the framework of legal provisions which may itself be the target of shareholder activism). Second, even if we assume that profitability of investment is the major 'goal' of corporate governance, this goal

---

[6] Of course, even in advanced Western capitalism, in-group effects in the courts cannot be completely avoided (see Galanter 1974). However, relatively speaking, the system of law in most Western economies does not contribute much to the creation of strong in-group/out-group boundaries.

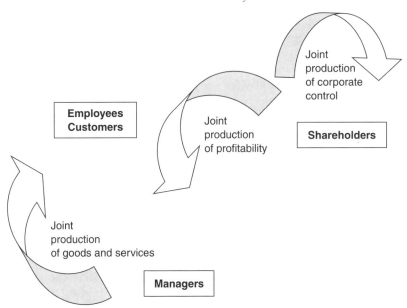

FIGURE 9.1 *Relationships between shareholders among themselves, shareholders and managers, and managers with other relevant stakeholders, all built on joint production (of corporate governance, profitability, and goods and services, respectively).*

cannot be achieved by the shareholders alone. Rather than viewing the relationship of shareholders (as principals) to managers (as agents) as one of control, this relationship could be seen as a joint effort to maximize sustainable profitability. Control (say, in terms of accountability of managers) and interest alignment between shareholders and managers are then only two instruments among a variety of other instruments to aid this joint effort. They are not the main target of institutional design, but flanking arrangements for joint production. Third, profitability, in turn, largely depends on how the corporation interacts with relevant stakeholders, such as employees and customers. Here too, potentially profitable relationships should not break down because of gain-driven behavior by the corporation. In fact, the production and distribution of goods and services can be seen as joint efforts by the management and employees on the one hand, and by the management and customers on the other. Shareholders would do well to hold managers accountable for their relational management with employees and customers, for two reasons. First of all, this relational management is important for sustainable profitability. Second, the relational management would also be a good indicator of a weak solidarity approach of the managers. In all likelihood, if managers treat employees and customers with relational concern, they will do the same with shareholders, which, in turn, would make joint production of profitability more likely.[7] Let me briefly go into each one of these contexts of joint production in more detail, even though I cannot offer worked-out suggestions for institutional design, nor do I go through a critical review of existing institutions and design suggestions. Rather, with the relational approach I will offer a heuristics for the search for institutional design and for the evaluation of existing suggestions.

One of the problems of corporate governance seen from the relational perspective is that the owners are not often 'partners' for the managers to establish a relationship with. In terms of institutional design, shareholders who wish to govern the managers of their assets would have to find a way to establish relationships with these managers. In the principal-agent paradigm, this was not necessary because, in this approach, control is so central that the owners can hire a controlling agent to sit on the board of the corporation and can add control and interest alignment measures (such as establishing an auditing committee and making the CEO and CFO personally responsible for the corporation's compliance with bookkeeping rules). But the first concern for institutional design is that, before shareholders can establish a relationship with managers, they would have to establish a relationship among themselves, and become a potential partner in joint production with the managers.

There are many obstacles to this endeavor because shareholders are often widely dispersed and ill-informed. There have been various suggestions on how to deal with these problems, ranging from giving institutional investors a larger say in governance issues to making it mandatory for institutional investors to attend the annual general meeting, to allow shareholders to vote remotely, or to allow proxy voting by advisory firms. From a relational point of view, making a difference between investors in terms of rights (for example, by giving institutional investors a larger say) is probably not a good idea. It makes it much more difficult to come to any conception of joint production.[8] Compulsory attendance of institutional investors at annual general meetings is also not a good idea, for the same reasons. The way to go is probably more in the direction analogous to informational systems for political voters (see, for example, Latham 2003) and communication and voting systems analogous to Internet communities. In addition, periodic opportunities for face-to-face meetings would offer the social basis for creating and maintaining an orientation of joint production of corporate

---

[7] For this reason, the behavior of managers towards the environment is also an indicator of the management's relational approach, extending the relational concern to future generations (also of employees and customers). From the literature on corporate deviance, we learn that corporations charged with non-minor violations (concerning the treatment of workers, product quality and agreement violations against customers, environmental violations) are mostly multiple offenders (see Clinard and Yeager 1980).

[8] There are other good reasons to doubt the wisdom of giving institutional investors a larger role in corporate governance. See, for example, Webb, Beck, and McKinnon (2003).

governance. These meetings would not be used for voting because that again would punish minority investors who are too dispersed to be able to attend.

Second, sustainable profitability can be seen as a joint effort between shareholders and managers, not just a task for managers. From a principal-agent point of view, a takeover threat is a strong form of managerial discipline (see Jensen 1986). From the point of view of joint production of profitability, hostile takeovers are destructive and have bad effects on the entire system of shareholder-manager relationships. Even before the takeover might take place, managers will take defensive measures, many of which are presumably against sustainable profitability. For example, managers may stagger the terms of directors and afford themselves golden parachutes or other forms of severance pay, and shield themselves from liability. In addition, the threat of a hostile takeover is likely to create mutual protection of various managers in an organization, a form of cooperation that will also aid in stretching the boundaries of what is deemed acceptable practice. If governments enact anti-takeover laws in order to protect firms from hostile takeovers, this may have the beneficial effect of reducing the defensive measures but it will do nothing against gain-driven (and therefore also opportunistic) behavior by managers. In order to check this behavior, voluntary or law-enforced restraints on takeovers would have to be flanked by increased rights by shareholders to underline the jointness of the production of profitability, for example by voting on directors and bylaws, by removing directors whose performance is below the acceptable level, to establish codes and require accountability and so on. Recently, Gompers, Ishii, and Metrick (2003) have shown that the combination of weak defensive measures by managers and participatory measures for shareholders has positive effects on profits and sales growth, and lowers capital expenditures.[9] Managers' accountability is a key element in making joint production possible. It can be used in control approaches and in joint production approaches, and in most cases it will have some measure of both. But their relative weight can differ. In the US, accountability is mainly phrased in control language (see, for example, the Sarbanes-Oxley law). By contrast, in Europe in recent times there has been an increase in codes that managers are expected to follow (such as the Combined Code in Britain, the Cromme-Kodex in Germany, the proposed Code-Tabaksblat in the Netherlands). They contain a new element of transparency and disclosure that boils down to 'comply or explain'. They offer managers the chance to provide good reasons for deviating from a 'best practice' because it is well-known that best practices are very sensitive to situation and context. Even though this accountability

---

[9] The authors provide some evidence that the causal direction is not the other way around. Note that to speak, as the authors do, in this case of the 'right' power balance between managers and shareholders is still using the imagery of control-and-align approaches, neglecting joint production with different but complementary tasks for achieving profitability.

measure is linked to supervisory boards, it can be interpreted as a first approximation to a shareholder-manager dialogue in the light of joint production. The British have gone one step further by making the board collectively responsible for the success of the corporation. These are beginnings of an institutional evolution away from the 'control and align' approach to the creation of the conditions for joint production of profitability with weak solidarity.

Third, sustainable profitability can never be guaranteed. However, there are certain ways managers can act that pretty much prevent sustainable profitability, if they behave opportunistically towards key stakeholders, especially shareholders, employees and customers. We have already discussed the relationship with shareholders. But in the relationships with employees and customers, gain-driven behavior has also to be partially suspended in order to prevent a break-up of potentially profitable relationships due to mistrust and opportunism. For this reason, corporate governance would advance in the right direction if managers were held accountable for their relational management towards employees and customers, and if the standard of judgment were weak solidarity. France has recently enacted a law that requires companies to disclose details of their social responsibility practice (effective 2004). The standards are not very exacting yet—they are along the lines of the Global Reporting Initiative (GRI 2000)—but the idea is that these social reports allow shareholders and financial markets to evaluate the company better, and, from a joint production point of view, this makes sense (see Spencer and Taylor 1987; Wood 1991). It is another matter whether such reporting should be required by law or be a matter of negotiation between shareholders and managers. For the creation and maintenance of an orientation of joint production, it would be better to leave this reporting to the voluntary initiative of shareholders and managers. Once such reporting is required by law, it may lose its signal value. Until now, companies that provided such reporting sent a signal to the investors by the very fact of offering social reports. As we will see in the following and final sections, signaling becomes especially important from a framing point of view because frames are precarious. They are not equivalent to stable preferences.[10] Governments thus should be careful not to interfere in this signaling. In the next and last sections, I will briefly deal with the question of what signals are particularly important in joint production.

---

[10] This strongly distinguishes the framing approach from approaches that work with types, some of which have social preferences and others not. The problem with types is that interaction partners want to know whether they are one or the other, and people either signal what type they are or try to fool the other, as the case may be. Once they have been found out, interaction partners don't have to worry. They know exactly what they can expect: social or egoistic preferences. By contrast, frames can change if they are not reinforced and it will thus always matter how people behave towards others.

Relational Signals

In a market economy, it is especially the relational frame that is precarious. It may easily be displaced by a gain (that is, money-making) frame without any guarantee to the partner that the relational frame will kick in in time. For this very reason, partners in a relationship will monitor each other's behavior for signs that the other is still in a frame that partially suspends gain-driven behavior. For the same reason, they will send *relational signals* to indicate to the other that they are still driven by relational concern (see Lindenberg 2000). Collective actors are not people but they are run by people and one can monitor whether these people give off the 'right' relational signals. For each context of joint production, these signals are important. For this reason, I will report in this section on the relational signals that have been worked out in the context of a project on monitoring social corporate performance.[11]

When parties are engaged in joint production, what signals are particularly important to convey partial suspension of gain-driven behavior and commitment to the relationship for its own sake?

First of all, there are *direct relational signals* that indicate the partial suspension of gain-driven behavior to the stakeholder. For example, the commitment to keep to agreements (even when it takes extra sacrifices) signals to the partner that the corporation partially suspends gain-driven (including opportunistic) behavior towards the other. Second, sustainable relationships need some reliable ground rules (*rights*) that shield the relationship from certain forms of gain-driven behavior, especially in the face of power differences. For example, certain power-related problems (such as non-sustainable agreements, exploitation, and suppression of complaints) undermine the sustainability of weak solidarity relationships and, therefore, a corporation that commits to ground rules that ban power-related problems signals to the partner in joint production that it is relationally committed and makes a serious effort to avoid opportunistic behavior due to power differences. Third, power differences do not just invite gain-driven behavior, they also lead to unintended negative side effects on the weaker party. For example, power differences create moral hazard problems. Without relational concern, the more powerful party can afford to pay little attention to negative side effects on the weaker party. Cumulative negative side effects undermine the sustainability of a relationship and thus need to be monitored and avoided. We call this *care*.

---

[11] This project of Groningen University, coordinated by Siegwart Lindenberg, consists of a social science group (Lindenberg and Steg) responsible for the social reporting part. It also contains a group of environmental scholars (Gerbens, Moll, and Schott-Uiterkamp), and a group of economists (Groot [Free University Amsterdam] and Van Witteloostuijn). The overall goal is to develop assessment tools for all three dimensions of corporate performance. See Steg *et al.* (2003).

In sum, the three kinds of relational signals are:

- *direct relational signals*: signaling partial suspension of gain-driven behavior;
- *granted rights*: signaling commitment to ground rules and to the avoidance of the gain-driven exploitation of power differences; and
- *care*: signaling commitment to the relationship by reducing or avoiding negative side effects of power differences.

I will briefly elaborate on each of them with regard to the specific signals and therefore the specific principles involved.

Direct Relational Signals

From the sociological and social-psychological literature about weak solidarity relationships, a number of direct relational signals can be extracted. This list may not be exhaustive but it is likely to contain the most important signals. Space does not allow a thorough discussion of each of these signals. Direct relational signals convey a dual message: (*a*) that one is not all out gain-driven in one's behavior because (*b*) one also values the relationship for its own sake (that is, not just as a resource). First, probably the most basic direct relational signal vis-à-vis the other is to be *open and honest in one's communication to the other* (in the context of corporate governance this is at times referred to as 'transparency and disclosure'). Failure to do so will quickly raise suspicion that information was withheld in order to manipulate the other in the pursuit of gain. This open and honest communication plays an important role in all three joint-production contexts. Examples are: disclosure of (proxy) votes among shareholders; disclosure of relevant information on various dimensions of corporate performance by the management towards shareholders and potential investors; open communication towards employees and customers about issues relevant to their well-being. Second, promises that are made for strategic reasons in the pursuit of gain are also expected to be broken for the same reasons. Commitment to *keep to agreed rules and promises* (even if that entails a sacrifice) is thus an essential relational signal. Deviation from rules and promises needs special and believable explanation (such as mishaps and accidents, see below), embedded in an open dialogue. For example, if employees' wages have to be cut while managers' wages and bonuses are grossly increased, it is difficult to find believable explanations. As a consequence, there may be stonewalling, which damages the relationship. In a relational approach, deviations that cannot be explained or compensated are a sign of gain-driven behavior. For this very reason, the 'comply or explain' clause of many new codes is a step in the relational direction. Third, when scarce resources have to be divided or distributed among the partners of a relationship, the *fairness* of the division or distribution is a strong relational signal. If one obviously tries to get more of the rewards and/or less of the costs than one's fair share, it is clear that one's gain-driven behavior is not suspended and that the value of the relationship was in any case not large enough to keep gain-driven behavior in check. This issue is mostly relevant to the relationships between managers and shareholders (for example, about management's claims to compensation, and about insiders' trading which leads to an unfair distribution of windfall gains), between managers and employees (for example, regarding wages), and between managers and customers (for example, regarding the sharing of rising or falling costs). Fourth, things can go wrong and look like gain-driven behavior although they are not. They happen because of mishaps, misunderstandings, accidents, wrong conceptions about the other's interests and constraints, and so forth. For this reason, the commitment to an *open dialogue* is a clear signal that the other's intentions and restrictions are taken seriously in their own right and seen as an essential part of the ongoing relationship. The possibility that such situations can arise can hardly be overestimated. Given the importance of relational signals, there is little that can damage a relationship so quickly as the wrong interpretation of signals. An open dialogue is important for all three contexts of joint production, but probably most important for shareholders and managers, and for managers and employees.

Granted Rights

Ground rules set the basic parameters of interaction. Like constitutions (see Buchanan 1990), they must be exempt from change through negotiation because, if they were open to negotiation, they would be in danger of being affected by power differences. Power differences can make partners agree to arrangements they find degrading or make them accept dictates without the right to be heard, both of which are incompatible with sustaining joint production.

What are the relevant ground rules for relationships engaged in joint production? First, every potential partner must have the right not to be excluded from joining the joint production on the basis of a characteristic that is functionally non-essential, such as gender, race, sexual preference, nationality, or status (*non-discrimination*). Second, a basic ground rule that must be granted in sustainable relationships is the right to have those norms observed that protect the other's moral identity. These are *general and local norms of decency*. For example, sexual harassment of employees goes against this basic right, as do attempts at corruption, or orders to lie or cheat. Power differences may render this non-negotiable right additionally important because people in desperate situations may be willing to waive norms of decency for certain rewards. Third, because things can go wrong, a relationship cannot be sustained if there is no basic *right to issue a complaint and be heard*. Again, without strong commitment, this right may be simply taken away by the more powerful actor or it may be bargained away by a weak partner. Either way, without this right, infractions against other basic rights and other such negative relational signals are likely to accumulate and undermine sustainability. For specific actors in joint production, there may be specific rights, such as the right not to be forced into labor service (this includes a prohibition of child labor under the assumptions that children up to a certain age cannot negotiate a labor contract for themselves). Another example is the right of employees to bargain collectively. Even though one is used to encounter these signals in discussions about management-employee relationships, they are just as relevant in the other contexts of joint production. We are just not used to looking at shareholders as jointly producing corporate governance and at shareholders and managers as being engaged in a joint effort to increase and sustain profitability. Therefore, issues of barring certain investors from being heard or orders to lie and cheat in supervisory boards are not often subject of deliberation regarding basic rights.

Care

Remember that the basic heuristics that guided our search for signals is weak solidarity. This does not contain charity in the sense of contributing to a worthy cause. 'Care' as used here is related only to cushioning the possible negative consequences of power differences. The more asymmetric the relationship of the one party to another, the more the sustainability of this relationship requires the more powerful partner to show care for the 'well-being' of the less powerful partner. If not, negative externalities of the power difference are likely to undermine the sustainability of the relationship. This asymmetry in power can, for example, be found in institutional investors vis-à-vis minority investors, or by employers vis-à-vis employees and customers. The most general signal of relational commitment via care is to show commitment to *decrease the power differences* by helping to advance the situation of the weaker partner. This can take different forms, depending on the partner. For shareholders, this would mean special institutional arrangements for representing minority investors' interests. For managers, it would mean offering employment and insurance security, job training, and career development to employees, and health and safety provisions to both employees and customers.

Informal Sanctions

Criminalizing deviant behavior by managers does not deliver the expected results of conformity to ethical standards. Criminalizing emanates from a control approach, such as the principal-agent approach. A scholar on criminal justice recently observed about criminalization of corporate crime: 'criminalization is uninformed by the empirical literature. It is "bad science" and therefore "bad policy"' (Simpson 2002: 159). By contrast, it has often been observed that informal sanctions may work much better than formal sanctions (see, for example, Grasmick and Bursik 1990; Nee 1998). When people can be shamed into conformity to norms of business ethics, when they care about their ethical reputation and identity, when they care about what significant others think of them, then behavior is sensitive to small informal mutual sanctioning and the disadvantages of a formal sanction system (it requires observability and fairly high standards of proof) can be avoided. However, there are rarely concrete suggestions on how one gets these informal sanctions to work and, if they work, how one can prevent them from having perverse effects. There are at least two prominent perverse effects of informal control. First, when people gossip behind your back or complain to higher-ups, it will lead to animosity and relational breakdown, lowering or preventing the potential advantages of informal sanctions (see Wittek, Van Duijn, and Snijders 2003). Second, informal control can lead to 'old-boy networks' or defiant sub-groups in which members help each other in reaching deviant goals which undermine organizational goals (Flache and Macy 1997). In this chapter, the answer to the question how to prevent the perverse effects from occurring can be found in relational signaling. As we have just seen, these signals are in part institutional commitments (such as basic rights) and in part signals in daily interaction (such as keeping to agreements), both premised on joint production and the alignment of relational commitment. The claim here is that whatever makes relational signals work will also make informal sanctions work because then informal sanctions become themselves relational signals.[12] If management and workers both perceive their interrelation as joint production, then the likelihood of perverse effects of informal sanctions among and between them is small.

Consistency

Relational signals convey a certain orientation towards partners in joint production. Because of framing effects, such an orientation also conveys what is in the foreground and what in the background of people's minds, what overriding goal is being pursued, what kind of alternatives are being considered, and so forth. For this very reason, an actor in joint production cannot afford to stand for some of the signals and neglect the others if he is committed to sustainability of the relationship. Partners will interpret the other's actions in the light of consistent relational signals. If, for example, a corporation keeps to agreed rules and promises but shows no commitment to basic rights or to standards of fairness, then it is likely that the employees will interpret the keeping to agreed rules and promises not as a relational signal but as a strategy that might change the moment it suits the corporation

---

[12] See Wittek (1999), which investigates the relation between relational signaling and informal control.

to do so. In other words, selective neglect of relational signals is likely to work against sustainability of relationships. Of course, not all detailed signals weigh equally heavily. For example, because of the asymmetry between gains and losses (see Kahneman and Tversky 1984), it is likely that failing to abstain from harming the other will be more damaging to sustainability than failing to reduce the power difference. If this relational approach is at least in part correct, then relational signals would have to be incorporated into codes of corporate governance in all three contexts of joint production. They would have to be monitored and made the basis of the dialogue between partners of joint production. In addition, they would lend themselves well as criteria for shareholders holding managers accountable for their relationship with employees and customers.

Conclusion

Corporate governance, as all governance, is to a large extent directed at reducing opportunistic behavior. The approach to corporate governance taken in this chapter is a relational one. It is based on new research on opportunism. In the principal-agent approach, opportunistic behavior is 'strategic', that is, in interaction it is farsighted and calculating and needs to be checked by control and interest alignment. By contrast, research on motivational and cognitive processes shows that people are often strongly guided by short-term interests, even if they thereby go against their longer-term interests ('myopic opportunism'). Thus, control and interest alignment are not enough by themselves to check opportunistic behavior. What is worse, the control approach often leads to an escalation of protective meas-ures (to avoid control) and increased control (to break through the protective measures) with increasingly adverse side effects of both. The same research on motivational and cognitive processes (that is, framing) that identified the power of 'myopic' opportunism suggests that the same mechanisms can be used against it. Framing effects combine dominant goals with processes of selective attention, pushing opportunity costs into the cognitive background. When a person's frame is linked to a dominant goal of gain (in terms of scarce resources, such as money and status) this person is unlikely to be able to sustain a cooperative relationship with others. Such a relationship depends on the partial suspension of gain-driven behavior and a clear interest in the relationship for its own sake. When this interest is strong enough, it can displace a gain frame in favor of a relational frame whenever the former becomes too incompatible with sustaining the relationship, and vice versa. People who are aware of being engaged in *joint production* can develop and sustain such relationships, given that they can convincingly signal their rela-tional concern through relational signals. When these signals work, informal sanctions will also work to keep the various parties focused on the joint tasks.

Having tools for the workings of informal sanctions in place becomes increasingly important as the limits of stronger controls and punishments (criminalization) become widely recognized. Governance in the sense of checking opportunistic behavior is then first and foremost the governance of framing processes that allow potentially advantageous relationships not to break up for reasons of mistrust and myopic opportunism. For corporate governance, this means a change in institutional design, away from control and alignment as the major emphasis, and towards joint production and the relational management that goes along with joint production. The three obvious and interrelated foci of joint production for corporate governance are the shareholders themselves, the relationship of shareholders with managers, and the relationship of managers with employees and customers. In order to establish a relationship with the managers, shareholders would first have to establish a context in which they see themselves jointly producing corporate governance. Second, profitability can be seen as a joint effort of shareholders and managers. Third, profitability depends to a large extent on the production and distribution of goods and services, and that can be seen as joint production of the corporation with relevant stakeholders (such as employees and customers). In all three foci, the overriding heuristics for institutional design would not be control and interest alignment but possibilities for joint production. There are some encouraging signs in some of the new European codes in the direction of joint production. But there is still a long way to go to get away from the old guiding idea that corporate governance is corporate control.

References

Buchanan, J. (1990). 'The Domain of Constitutional Economics', *Constitutional Political Economy*, 1: 1–18.

Buskens, V. (2002). *Social Networks and Trust*. Boston, Dordrecht, London: Kluwer.

Clinard, M. and Yeager, P. (1980). *Corporate Crime*. New York: Free Press.

Dyer, J. (1997). 'Effective Interfirm Collaboration: How Firms Minimize Transaction Costs And Maximize Transaction Value', *Strategic Management Journal*, 18: 535–56.

Flache, A. and Macy, M. (1997). 'The Weakness of Strong Ties: Collective Action Failure in a Highly Cohesive Group', *Journal of Mathematical Sociology*, 21: 3–28.

Galanter, M. (1974). 'Why the "Haves" Come Out Ahead: Speculations on the Limits of Legal Change', *Law and Society Review*, 9: 95–160.

Gompers, P., Ishii, J., and Metrick, A. (2003). 'Corporate Governance and Equity Prices', *Quarterly Journal of Economics*, 118: 107–55.

Grasmick, H. and Bursik Jr., R. (1990). 'Conscience, Significant Others, and Rational Choice: Extending the Deterrence Model', *Law and Society Review*, 24: 837–61.

GRI (Global Reporting Initiative) (2002). *Sustainable Reporting Guidelines on Economic, Environmental and Social Performance*. Boston, MA: GRI.

Jensen, M. (1986). 'Agency Costs of Free Cash Flow, Corporate Finance, and Takeovers', *American Economic Review*, 76: 323–9.

Kahneman, D. and Tversky, A. (1984). 'Choices, Values, and Frames', *American Psychologist*, 39: 341–50.

Kahneman, D., Knetsch, J., and Thaler, R. (1986). 'Fairness as Constraint on Profit Seeking: Entitlements in the Market', *American Economic Review*, 76: 728–41.

Latham, M. (2003). 'Democracy and Infomediaries', *Corporate Governance*, 11: 91–101.

Lawler, E. and Yoon, J. (1993). 'Power and the Emergence of Commitment Behavior in Negotiated Exchange', *American Sociological Review*, 58: 465–81.

Lindenberg, S. (1986). 'The Paradox of Privatization in Consumption', in A. Diekmann and P. Mitter (eds.), *Paradoxical Effects of Social Behavior: Essays in Honor of Anatol Rapaport*. Heidelberg/Vienna: Physica-Verlag.

—— (1992). 'An Extended Theory of Institutions and Contractual Discipline', *Journal of Institutional and Theoretical Economics*, 148/2: 125–54.

—— (1998). 'Solidarity: Its Microfoundations and Macro-dependence: A Framing Approach', in P. Doreian and T. Fararo (eds.), *The Problem of Solidarity: Theories and Models*. Amsterdam: Gordon and Breach.

—— (2000). 'It Takes Both Trust and Lack of Mistrust: The Workings of Cooperation and Relational Signaling in Contractual Relationships', *Journal of Management and Governance*, 4: 11–33.

—— (2002). 'Governance Seen from a Framing Point of View: The Employment Relationship and Relational Signaling', in B. Nooteboom and F. Six (eds.), *The Trust Process Within Organizations*. Cheltenham: Edward Elgar.

—— (2003). 'The Cognitive Side of Governance', *Research in the Sociology of Organizations*, 20: 47–76.

Milgrom, P. and Roberts, J. (1992). *Economics Organization and Management*. Englewood Cliffs: Prentice-Hall.

Nee, V. (1998). 'Norms and Networks in Economic and Organizational Performance', *The American Economic Review*, 88: 85–9.

Osterloh, M. and Frey, B. (2000). 'Motivation, Knowledge Transfer, and Organizational Form', *Organization Science*, 11: 538–50.

Raub, W. and Weesie, J. (2000). 'The Management of Durable Relations', in J. Weesie and W. Raub (eds.), *The Management of Durable Relations: Theoretical Models and Empirical Studies of Households and Organizations*. Amsterdam: Thela Thesis.

Sabel, C. (1993). 'Studied Trust: Building New Forms of Cooperation in a Volatile Economy', in R. Swedberg (ed.), *Explorations in Economic Sociology*. New York: Russell Sage Foundation.

Sattler, N. and Kerr, N. (1991). 'Might versus Morality; Motivational and Cognitive Bases for Social Motives', *Journal of Personality and Social Psychology*, 60: 756–65.

Scott, W. and Cherrington, D. (1974). 'Effects of Competitive, Cooperative, and Individualistic Reinforcement Contingencies', *Journal of Personality and Social Psychology*, 30: 748–58.

Simpson, S. (2002). *Corporate Crime, Law, and Social Control*. Cambridge: Cambridge University Press.

Spencer, B. and Taylor, G. (1987). 'A Within and Between Analysis of the Relationship between Corporate Social Responsibility and Financial Performance', *Akron Business and Economic Review*, 18: 7–18.

Steg, L., Vlek, C., Lindenberg, S., Groot, T., Moll, H., Schoot-Uiterkamp, T., and Van Witteloostuijn, A. (2003). *Towards a Comprehensive Model of Sustainable Corporate Performance*. Groningen: Departments of Economics, Environmental Sciences, Management Science, Psychology, and Sociology, University of Groningen.

Tyler, T. and Degoey, P. (1996). 'Trust in Organizational Authorities: The Influence of Motive Attributions on Willingness to Accept Decisions', in R. Kramer and T. Tyler, *Trust in Organizations*. Thousand Oaks: Sage.

Uzzi, B. (1997). 'Social Structure and Competition in Interfirm Networks: The Paradox of Embeddedness', *Administrative Science Quarterly*, 42: 35–67.

Vaughan, D. (1999). 'The Dark Side of Organizations: Mistake, Misconduct, and Disaster', *Annual Review of Sociology*, 25: 271–305.

Webb, R., Beck, M., and McKinnon, R. (2003). 'Problems and Limitations of Institutional Investor Participation in Corporate Governance', *Corporate Governance*, 11: 65–73.

Williamson, O. (1993). 'Calculativeness, Trust, and Economic Organization', *Journal of Law and Economics*, 36: 453–86.

Wittek, R. (1999). *Interdependence and Informal Control in Organizations*. Amsterdam: Thela Thesis.

Wittek, R., Van Duijn, M., and Snijders, T. (2003). 'Frame Decay, Informal Power, and the Escalation of Social Control in a Management Team: A Relational Signaling Perspective', *Research in the Sociology of Organizations*, 20: 355–80.

Wood, D. (1991). 'Corporate Social Performance Revisited', *Academy of Management Review*, 16: 691–718.

10

The Benefit of Doubt: Shadow Norms and Governance in Trust-based Organizations

JOSEPH LAMPEL

... homo fidelis is an endangered species.
(Ronald Dore, 'Trust and the Workings of Market Capitalism', 1999)

Major corporate scandals are reshaping the way that corporations are directed and controlled. Increasingly, we are witnessing a return to what may be called 'hard governance': governance based on rules, formal mechanisms, and stringent legal enforcement. By contrast, 'soft governance': governance based on loyalty, trust, and informal obligations is losing favor. The resurgence of hard governance and the decline of soft governance may to some extent be a product of headlines. There is a natural tendency whenever corporate governance is shown to be faulty to veer towards hard governance to deprecate soft governance if not to blame it outright for causing the crisis.

On a deeper intellectual level, however, the resurgence of hard governance at the expense of soft governance may be due to the fact that we have strong theories of hard governance but weak theories of soft governance. We are receptive to strong theories of governance because they provide clear guidelines on how we can effectively tackle underlying problems. By contrast, when scandals and crises are frequent we see weak theories of governance as strong on aspirations, but weak when it comes to ensuring execution.

This chapter is an attempt to reinforce the foundations of soft governance by probing the notion of trust-based organizations: organizational forms that put trust at the heart of the relationship between the organization and its key stakeholders (Sabel 1993; Bartlett and Ghoshal 1998). Over the past decade we have witnessed a proliferation of trust-based organizations. Major corporate scandals have generated doubts about such organizations. With trust egregiously betrayed, assumptions about such organizations have switched their emphasis from trust to distrust; from believing that, given the power to exercise their own initiative, managers will behave ethically, to an assumption that trust is more likely to be abused than reciprocated.

In this chapter I argue that, notwithstanding the current doubts, most trust-based organizing is robust and will endure precisely because their normative foundations are flexible. This flexibility operates at two levels, one overt and the other covert. The overt level is based on informal but widely acknowledged primary norms that regulate task performance and allocation of rewards. The covert level is based on secondary norm structures that evaluate violation of primary norms. I call these secondary norm structures 'shadow norms'.

I argue that obtaining the strategic advantages of trust-based organizing requires not only the evolution of norms but also the emergence of shadow norms. Without shadow norms trust is highly fragile and is prone to crisis and disintegration (Bendor, Kramer, and Stout 1991). Shadow norms provide what is arguably the subtext of trust—allowing not only those who are involved to make nuanced decisions about trustworthiness but providing a context for organizational bystanders to participate in norm enforcement.

My argument develops as follows. In the first section I suggest that trust-based organizing emerges directly from the strategic imperative of attaining flexibility in rapidly changing environment. I distinguish between structure and process flexibility, and argue that process flexibility depends heavily on increasing trust. In the second section I argue that in organizational terms sustaining trust depends on the existence of norms, while trustworthiness depends on conformity to norms. The problem with norms, however, is that they are not sufficiently flexible to deal with unforeseen contingencies that produce violation of norms. To prevent an inevitable breakdown of trust, organizations evolve shadow-norms to contain the potential damage and restore trust in the aftermath of random or unintended norm violation.

In the third section I look at the role of organizational bystanders in the process of sustaining norms. I argue that Axelrod's (1986) view that bystanders can be forced to participate in norm sustaining through sanctions by hierarchical authority is at odds with the realities of modern corporate life. Instead, bystanders are brought into the process by investing in legitimate meta-norms that provide bystanders with the security to exercise their moral preferences in an organizational context. The strength of these intervention meta-norms and, more generally, the density of norms in a given context define normative regimes that facilitate the process of norm sustaining. In the concluding section I examine and describe four normative regimes.

Flexibility and Trust

If one proposition in organization studies elicits unanimity today, it is that Taylorism, the paradigm that conceived of organizations as efficient machines, has been dismantled and replaced by a paradigm of organizations as flexible systems made up of knowledgeable and highly motivated individuals. The fall of Taylorism has made efficiency a suspect word, for some even a dirty word (see Mintzberg 1982). Flexibility, on the other hand, is a word with universally positive allure. But, though it resonates widely, it is far from a clear concept.

At present, flexibility has two distinct facets. The first is a macro facet that sees flexibility as the strategic relationship between organizations and their environments. The second is a micro facet that is concerned with flexibility as the product of the organization's internal structures and systems. Thinking about the two facets of flexibility has generally proceeded along distinct paths. Strategy researchers such as Harrigan and Hambrick (1985) and De Leeuv and Volberda (1996), focus on the first to the exclusion of the second. De Leeuv and Volberda (1996), for example, see flexibility from the perspective of control theory, defining flexibility as a function of a control relationship between the organization and its environment. Thus, an organization can be said to be flexible to the extent to which it has the ability to initiate or adapt to competitive change (Volberda 1996). This entails developing capabilities to effectively explore and exploit new opportunities as well as effectively responding to unexpected events.

Intrinsically, however, the two facets of flexibility cannot be separated. In organizations of even moderate size and complexity, macro flexibility will not develop without a corresponding growth in micro flexibility. To probe deeper into the relationship we have to distinguish between structure and process flexibility. The structural dimension of flexibility entails an increase in the autonomy and discretion of middle and first-line managers. In practice this means a reduction in the number of rules governing managerial activity and a willingness to waive existing rules under exceptional circumstances. It also entails a change in the authority relationship—primarily a more consultative style of interaction between superiors and subordinates.

Structural flexibility points directly to process flexibility. Process flexibility entails greater willingness to communicate, to share knowledge, to avoid hoarding of resources, and to coordinate activities. Process flexibility also implies greater initiative, a willingness to take risks, and, more generally, willingness to champion ideas and projects that are of benefit to the organization.

Process flexibility, I would argue, is the crucial link between micro and macro flexibility. The ability to take advantage and respond rapidly to environmental change depends on developing flexible communications and decisions processes. When organizations pursue structural flexibility—which is often the case when they try to improve macro flexibility—they do it with a view to improving their process flexibility. What they find in practice, however, is that organizational structure is a blunt instrument. Increasing structural flexibility may be easier to achieve—primarily because structure is more amenable to direct intervention. But by the same token the impact on process flexibility may be unpredictable. Structural flexibility increases autonomy and discretion, but this allows managers to pursue personal agendas. Such 'self-seeking with guile', to quote Oliver Williamson (1993), undermines the entire enterprise. As performance deteriorates organizations are forced to tighten formal controls and reintroduce greater monitoring of activities. Structural flexibility is compromised, and with it is lost the possibility of attaining greater process flexibility.

The weak link in the relationship between structural flexibility and process flexibility is clearly human motivation, or more precisely, the possibility of 'self-seeking with guile' of the type highlighted by Oliver Williamson. The way out of this dilemma is to turn managerial motivation away from 'self-seeking with guile' towards behavior that is consistent with the positive performance implications of process flexibility. Doing this, however, requires sharing the benefits of macro flexibility at the micro level. In other words, managers have to believe that eschewing self-seeking with guile in favor of good faith effort will yield positive returns for themselves as well as for the organization.

To forgo self-seeking with guile, managers need some sort of guarantee. The best guarantee would be a binding contract which meters and allocates returns. However, as Williamson has persuasively demonstrated, binding long-term contracts are difficult to draft and monitor. Operational feasibility dictates hierarchy as the only viable solution. In modern corporations, however, this solution is increasingly undermined by extensive reliance on professional and technical expertise. Crucial to the governance of modern corporations, therefore, is formation of implicit agreements between superior and subordinate, and between managers and their organization, which complements if not substitutes for hierarchical authority (Azariadis 1989).

Implicit agreements, however, are paradoxical, and never more so than in the present case. An implicit agreement is an undertaking by parties with the explicit awareness that such an undertaking is not backed by formal sanctions such as resorting to courts or the triggering of formal complaints to panels or committees charged with enforcing compliance with explicitly stated rules and regulations. Such agreements can function reasonably well when the actions stipulated are specific and clear. I agree to work on a weekend in return for your willingness to give me additional time off in January. I may have no formal recourse if you renege on the agreement, but at least there is little ambiguity about your non-compliance, regardless of the excuses you provide.

Implicit agreements that are meant to encourage process flexibility are expected to do the following: (*a*) encourage managers to fully apply their skills and competences; and (*b*) encourage managers to undertake initiatives with a significant risk of failure. In both instances it is impossible to stipulate with precision the actions that fulfill these expectations. In both instances, also, no agreement is possible unless managers are convinced (*a*) that they will be rewarded for applying their skills and competences and (*b*) that they will be rewarded for undertaking successful initiatives and not punished for those that fail.

An implicit agreement that meets all these conditions is manifestly a difficult proposition. It cannot be negotiated in the conventional sense, for all the reasons mentioned earlier; it can be created only by establishing trust: trust in the good faith of the parties involved and trust in the commitments made. This, however, moves the problem away from the overt issue of control to the deeper problem of trust itself.

Trust, Norms, and Shadow Norms

Uslaner (2002) calls trust 'the chicken soup of social life'. The metaphor is apt. Just as there are many recipes of chicken soup, there are also different versions of trust, though arguably they all have a common flavor. Ring and Van de Ven (1992: 488), for example, define trust as 'confidence in the other's goodwill'. Sitkin and Roth (1993: 368) conceptualize trust as a 'belief, attitude, or expectations concerning the likelihood that the actions or outcomes of another individual, group or organization will be acceptable'. The common flavor in these and other definitions is an emphasis on benevolent state of mind; on the psychology of good intentions as manifested in cooperative and supportive behavior. Here the chicken soup metaphor has added relevance. Much like soup, trust in most definitions comes across as a fluid social and psychological substance that can nourish interaction in ways that are at times inexplicable.

The inexplicability is due to the difficulty of linking trust to tangible social reality. Intuitively we understand trust as first and foremost an interpersonal and inter-subjective experience. But when it comes to trust at the institutional and organizational levels inter-subjective definitions are not adequate. We clearly cannot form an inter-subjective relationship with a collective entity in the same way we do with individuals. Nor can we speak of trust as an aggregation of individual interactions: the sheer variety and contingency of interactions in modern organizations makes this next to impossible.

Trust in modern organizations requires an external social reality that does not depend on inter-subjective processes of trust giving (Sunstein 1996). Such external reality, it has been argued, is created by structures that provide stable 'hinges' or focal points for social interaction more generally (Coleman 1990).

The emergence of focal points is closely related to the problem of coordination beset by uncertainty, especially where communication is physically or socially hampered. Who should call back when a telephone call is cut off? What should you do if you become separated from your friend in a shopping mall? Who should be the first to say goodbye, the host or the guest?

Rational choice theorists argue that stable solutions to the coordination problem arise when social systems have 'conventions'. Young (1996: 105) defines a convention as a 'pattern of behaviour that is customary, expected and self-enforcing. Everyone conforms, everyone expects others to conform, and everyone has good reasons to conform because conforming is in each person's best interest when everyone plans to conform'.

Conventions resolve the problem of inter determinacy in coordination without attributing a value to the solution: it does not matter who calls back if a telephone call is interrupted as long as contact is reestablished. It does not matter if you reconnect with your lost friend by going to the information counter or the last place you saw each other, as long as you reconnect. And it does not matter to social life if the guest takes leave or the host bids him goodbye, as long as everybody follows the rule.

Multiple conventions are possible in most situations, but only few tend to evolve in a given situation, and from the point of view of the social system it does not matter which. From the point of view of societal efficiency it does not matter whether people drive on the right or left as long as everybody follows the same rule. (From a legal point of view, as we point out below, this is a different matter.) By the same token, breaking a convention can lead to the collapse of coordination—sometimes with catastrophic consequences—but this has no direct bearing on trust. We do not trust people or organizations more because they conform to conventions. At most, we respect their driving competence or their social skills.

Some conventions, of course, are elevated to legal status. For example, driving on the left or the right in almost every country is a legal requirement, not simply a matter of personal choice. However, while conventions that are efficient for society are often legislated to reinforce conformity, this should not make us lose sight of the difference between conventions and laws. When we speak of conventions we speak of social institutions that regulate interactions through social sanctions not legal sanctions. The distinction is not always clear-cut. In the case of many conventions social sanctions often operate side-by-side with legal sanctions. For example, it is a social convention for house guests not to make costly long-distance phone calls without first obtaining permission from their host. In principle, violators of this social convention are subject to legal sanction, but with the rare exception most hosts prefer the sanction of refusing future hospitality to resorting to the courts. And overwhelmingly it is the force of conventions rather than the fear of legal action that leads guests to inform their hosts of their intentions.

Conventions often underpin trust, but conventions become truly crucial to trust when they are endowed by social systems with special moral significance, when, in other words, they are transformed into social norms. The transformation is context dependent, more a matter of anthropology than an expression of functional rationality. Thus the logic of social norms may be consistent, but the form can vary greatly. This is clearly manifest in the diversity of norms that we find not only in cultures but also in different organizational contexts.

For social conventions to function two conditions must prevail. First, we have to be sure all the parties to the interaction know the conventions (hence the popularity of courses in etiquette for expatriate managers). Second, we have to be reasonably certain that the parties are rational and that cooperation is in their interest. When norms function as social conventions they require no more than these conditions to operate successfully. However, norms are often called to do much more than simply facilitate coordination: they are called on to ensure coordination in situations where opportunism can be advantageous. It is at this point that trust enters the picture, and it is at this point that conformity to norms becomes an index for trustworthiness.

Conformity to norms, however, is uncertain evidence for trustworthiness. Organizations and individuals frequently espouse norms tactically, as a way of signaling trustworthiness, and they may conform to norms for the same reason—or for reasons that are entirely different. Thus, while both espousing and conforming norms reinforce trust, neither guarantees trust. This brings us to the heart of the dilemma of a norms-based view of trust: trust that is allocated or maintained on the basis of conformity to norms has an element of risk. There is always a gap between norm conforming and norm embracing, in part because neither the morality nor the intentions of the individuals involved can be directly verified, and in part because adverse circumstances often open a wide gap between norm conforming and norm embracing.

To conclude that trust contains irreducible risk is not in itself a revelation. Trust would not be truly trust, certainly not in the sense that the word has been used for centuries, without containing an irreducible risk even under ideal conditions. In this respect Barney and Hansen's (1994) definition of trust as vulnerability is accurate: trust cannot be said to exist without vulnerability and, correspondingly, without refusal to take advantage of vulnerability. The real question that arises is not how to eliminate risk entirely, but what happens to trust when norm violation gives evidence of increasing risk?

A strict construction of the notion of trust would see norm violation as sufficient grounds for terminating relationships and repudiating the individual or organizations involved. Betrayal may be too strong a word to describe the reaction, but rejection and rupture are probably quite accurate description of what normally ensues if norm violation is seen as a crisis that must be addressed with strong action.

Such crisis-oriented view of norm violation is inherently costly. If relationships are viewed as investments built over time, then writing off these investments requires evidence that is proportional to past history. Norms do not stipulate such proportionality rules, and yet without a doubt norms generate heuristics that evaluate the proportionality of their violation. I shall call these heuristics 'shadow norms' because in a manner of speaking they evolve in the shadow of norms—emerging through repeated interaction to become institutionalized through repeated espousal and use. They should not be mistaken for the fuzzy edges of norms in practice, that is, as a proxy for imprecision, but deal directly with consequences of non-conformity: Should a violation be viewed as minor, perhaps a result of random event, or should it be viewed as a major breach of trust?

The crucial issue here is one of intention, not the act or its consequence. We do not judge the violation of trust simply by the consequence of that violation but by the intention behind it. An employee that accidentally leaves a door open may be reproved for allowing thieves to get in, but this reproof will change fundamentally if a suspicion exists that the door was not left open by accident. The consequences of incompetence and fraud may be identical, but the judgment that is attached to each is intrinsically different. The first is human failure; the second is breach of trust.

Shadow norms have distinct historical and moral dimensions. Shadow norms regulate our ability to make sense of violation in the light of previous behavior. We allow friends more leeway when they behave inappropriately than people we have just met. By the same token, organizations are more tolerant of transgressions by members with long tenure. History provides us with a larger sample of past behavior, and shadow norms provide the heuristics by which violations can be related to the sample. And notwithstanding the fact that these heuristics are often biased (Lampel and Shapira 2001), the judgment of trust is strongly influenced by these heuristics.

Shadow norms, however, are not simply behavioral heuristics. They also have moral significance. The significance derives from the fact that norms are not only means of efficient coordination but have moral content. Violating a norm will usually trigger a web of significance that extends beyond the specific act and norm in question. This is rather obvious in religion, but arguably extends beyond to all ethical conduct.

As a matter of policy there is a tendency on the part of all normative systems to espouse the importance of principles without concession to proportionality. There are no caveats in the Ten Commandments. And yet norms in practice pose a dilemma that is well captured by Atkinson's (2002) musings on the complexity of applying the lessons of her convent education to adult life:

At convent school, adhering to the ten commandments was never easy. They had to be rote learned, which was difficult enough. But the details were then unpicked, with terrifying precision. The tiniest transgression might turn out to have been a mortal sin.

Stealing was a particularly difficult sin to pin down. You knew that you shouldn't pinch another pupil's purse or gym shorts, but failing to return a borrowed pencil was that really stealing? And poaching another's boyfriend? How many of the commandments did that break? Possibly all, bar killing, if you did it on a Sunday, against your parents' wishes, and accompanied by ripe biblical oaths in order to impress.

Because not all norms have the same force, it follows that some shadow norms extend further in what they allow than others. Proportionality heuristics exist even in environments where such proportionality is disavowed. This is one of the reasons why the fundamental texts of all religions are often supported by commentaries that seek to clarify nuance and context. In organizational contexts, however, norms may be espoused but commentary is usually informal, partly reflecting the attitude of top managers and, more often than not, evolving as the result of myriad interactions (Klein 1997).

Shadow Norms and Normative Regimes

Writing about the tendency of norms to decay over time, Axelrod (1986) argues that for norms to endure it is necessary for individuals and organizations to impose sanctions on those who tolerate the violation of norms. In effect, Axelrod rejects normative neutrality for practical not moral reasons: it may suit us to turn a blind eye to norm violation that has no direct input on us, but by doing so we are contributing to the ease with which norms are being violated. As far as Axelrod is concerned, there are no innocent bystanders when it comes to norm violation. At a deeper level, however, he is also pointing to the duality of norm enforcement. Norms are not only enforced by individuals and organizations that are directly involved in norm regulated action, but they are also enforced by individuals and organizations that are not involved in the action but nevertheless have a stake in the norms (see Bendor 1990).

The problem of norm enforcement springs directly from the different position of each group vis-à-vis norm violation. The first group is made up of organizational actors that are directly involved in norm-regulated interaction and thus have an incentive to invest in monitoring and deterrence. This group, however, is usually small compared with the second group of organizational actors, which is not directly involved in the norm-regulated interaction. The second group does not have the same incentives to become involved as the first, and thus is not likely to monitor either norm conformity or violation very closely.

For Axelrod (1986), the only way to bring the second group into the enforcement process is to create meta-norms that penalize neutrality on the part of those who do nothing about norm violation. In organizational terms this means delegating to authority the task of punishing individuals who turn a blind eye to norm violation. This prescription, however, runs counter to the reality of modern organizations. Not only are top managers constrained by lack of time and informational resources, but there are clear legal and political limits to their ability to engage in actions that can be easily perceived as adversarial if not persecuting in nature.

In practice, it is more likely that bystanders will become involved in upholding norms if they feel strongly about the norms and when they perceive norm violation as an affront (Coleman 1990: 282–6). The difficulty for bystanders, however, resides in knowing when to become involved. Bystanders do not regularly monitor the behavior of others. Hence they lack the information necessary for rigorous analysis. Bystanders are also concerned about the possibility of being manipulated through distorted or partial information disclosure, and hence are likely to shy away from punishing norm violation that benefits some at the expense of others. Shadow norms perform this function well by providing indices of norm violation that are inexpensive in terms of information, computationally undemanding, and politically tractable. And because shadow norms are sufficiently broad they require only selective interventions on the part of bystanders yet are sufficiently binding to make sure that such interventions will occur when it matters.

Objectively, shadow norms provide bystanders with the means for participating in norm enforcement, but subjectively there is still the question of their willingness to utilize these means. In the first instance this will depend on contextual knowledge of shadow norms—it is clearly risky to act in function of shadow norms without an organizationally appropriate knowledge. In the second instance this will depend on legitimacy, the sense that intervention is not only permitted but is also encouraged.

Society provides a baseline level of legitimacy: some actions attract active disapprobation regardless of where they occur. But there are other actions whose legitimacy or non-legitimacy is defined by the organizations rather than by the society at large. (Enron is a fascinating case study in this regard.)

As organizations become less centralized and more loosely coupled, legitimacy increasingly replaces direct control as a way of ensuring norm compliance. The most obvious way in which this tends to occur is through internalization, which encourages norm compliance by imposing psychological costs on norm violators. Unfortunately, populations are heterogeneous when it comes to internalizing norms. For legitimacy to function as an effective substitute to direct control it is necessary not only for violators to pay a price for non-compliance, but also for bystanders to be accorded the legitimacy to impose additional costs. This overt legitimacy, I would argue, operates at several interlocking levels. First, organizations invest legitimacy in certain norms, and by extension accord legitimacy to the upholding of these norms. Second, organizations associate norms with other norms, and by implication see norm compliance as systemic, that is, you do not pick and choose from different norms—you are meant to obey them all.

The density of norms within a given organization is a function of the importance of trust as regulating principle. In trust-based organizations, especially in organizations that rely on professional expertise, norm density imposes higher costs for norm enforcement through centralized control.

In response, organizations evolve what I shall call 'normative regimes': a set of norms and practices that regulate the organization's response to norm violations. Such regimes have strong influence on setting proportionality heuristics that define shadow norms. The influence is shaped by regime evolution. The legitimacy of expressing disapproval of a colleague's action will be determined by norms that govern the legitimacy of generally criticizing colleagues, by the degree to which the norm in question is strongly held, and by whether the action violates the associated shadow norm.

In total, this suggests a typology of regimes corresponding respectively to low/high norm density and weak/strong intervention meta-norms, as follows:

First, *bureaucratic regimes*. Bureaucracies are generally characterized by the predominance of rules and procedures over norms. And, by the same token, clear task definition and strong lines of authority tend to produce weak intervention meta-norms. The lack of bystanders' involvement in enforcing norms adds to the difficulty of developing trust-based organizing in bureaucracies, and under extreme conditions its absence shows itself in the tendency of norm violation to increase when bureaucracies become dysfunctional or pathological.

Second, *professional regimes*. Organizations that are run or dominated by professionals normally have high norm density. Professionals rely heavily on tacit knowledge in their practice and, by extension, this practice is usually regulated a complex body of norms. However, because professionals strive for autonomy they vigorously resist intervention in their practice, and this resistance constrains the growth of intervention meta-norms, which as a result are usually weak in professional regimes. The combination of normative density and weak intervention meta-norms tends to produce broadly defined shadow norms, but also promotes strong sanctions against violators of norms. Trust-based organizing is normally associated with these regimes at the individual level, and consists primarily of trust in the competence of the professionals involved.

Third, *missionary regimes*. Missionary regimes are characterized by low norm density and strong intervention meta-norms. The typical missionary regime will emerge in entrepreneurial firms with clearly articulated vision. The norms in these regimes are few in number and relate primarily to the imperative of contributing to the ability of others in the organization to accomplish their goals. Strong intervention meta-norms are present, driven by a clearly articulated mission and by strong sense of collective endeavor. Trust-based organizing tends to be team-oriented, and the intervention of bystanders will usually take place within the context of team processes.

Fourth, *puritanical regimes*. Puritanical regimes are characterized by high norm density and strong intervention meta-norms. The typical puritanical regimes emerge in organizations with a highly institutionalized culture, especially when the external cultural milieu is strongly group-oriented.

Trust-based organizing in puritanical regimes is therefore organization-wide. Shadow norms are tightly defined and organizational bystanders regularly exercise sanctions against norm violators.

Conclusion

Ronald Dore (1999) justly castigates the tendency of current research on trust to examine the uses and benefits of trust from a purely economic perspective. Trust, he argues, is not only an economic good; it is also a social good that increases our sense of well-being. The decline of trust should be seen therefore not only as negative in terms of economic performance; it is also negative socially and emotionally. The example that Dore uses to illustrate his point is interesting in light of the present discussion. He recounts the first time he began to realize that long-held norms no longer apply. The time was the late 1960s and the place was London or, more precisely, the area adjacent to the London School of Economics. As Dore (1999: 9) puts it: 'I still remember my sense that London was no longer such a nice place to live in when I had a bicycle stolen for the second time and decided that henceforth I would have to invest in a lock and chain.'

Looking back at the episode from the vantage point of current notions of trust, we may be surprised that Dore's trust in the morals of his fellow Londoners survived the first occasion his bicycle was stolen. A different reading of the story suggests that Dore did not invest in a lock and chain after losing his first bicycle because he was willing to give his fellow Londoners the benefit of doubt. On a pure costs-benefit analysis this may not be rational: a lock and chain is, after all, cheaper than a new bicycle. But from a social and psychological point of view there is logic here, and the logic is embedded in the notion of shadow norms that is developed in this chapter.

Dore's criticism of the cost-benefit view of trust goes to the heart of the interplay between 'hard' and 'soft' governance. Seeing trust from a purely economic perspective invariably pushes governance towards more rules and more elaborate control mechanisms, in short towards more hard governance. By contrast, seeing trust from a social and psychological perspective reinforces informal processes that govern interaction; in other words, it facilitates the emergence of soft governance. The interplay and balance between the two ultimately depends on context and events: banks are more likely than software firms to rely on hard governance. Incidents of malfeasance on a grand scale are more likely to tilt organizational emphasis towards hard governance, whereas long periods of responsible stewardship are more conducive to the development of soft governance.

Dore's criticism of the 'efficiency' view of trust applies to the origins and subsequent development of shadow norms as well. The rise of shadow norms can be explained purely on evolutionary grounds: shadow norms persist and tend to spread because relationships in which they protect trust are more likely to survive than relationships in which violations of norms trigger immediate exit. Shadow norms, however, are more than another way of calculating the odds of defection. They are a version of the ancient practice of giving others the benefit of doubt. As such they are grounded in the moral imperative that seeks to combine the normative power of values with the practical recognition that trust must withstand the vagaries of changing circumstances and the misunderstandings that often accompany human communication.

References

Atkinson, V. (2002). 'Why I Recommend a Considered Approach to Plagiarism', *Times Higher Educational Supplement*, 26 July: 7.

Axelrod, R. (1986). 'An Evolutionary Approach to Norms', *American Political Science Review*, 80: 1095–111.

Azariadis, C. (1989). 'Implicit Contracts', in J. Eatwell, M. Milgate, and P. Newman (eds.), *Allocation, Information, and Markets*. New York: W.W. Norton.

Barney, J. and Hansen, M. (1994). 'Trustworthiness as a Source of Competitive Advantage', *Strategic Management Journal*, 15: 175–91.

Bartlett, C. and Ghoshal, S. (1998). 'Beyond Strategic Planning to Organization Learning: Lifeblood of the Individualized Corporation', *Strategy and Leadership*, 26: 34–9.

Bendor, J. (1990). 'Norms, Third-Party Sanctions, and Cooperation', *Journal of Law, Economics, and Organization*, 6: 33–63.

——, Kramer, R., and Stout, S. (1991). 'When in Doubt . . . Cooperation in a Noisy Prisoner's Dilemma', *Journal of Conflict Resolution*, 35: 691–719.

Coleman, J. (1990). 'Norm-Generating Structures', in K. Cook and M. Levi (eds.), *The Limits of Rationality*. Chicago: University of Chicago of Press.

De Leeuw, A. and Volberda, H. (1996). 'On the Concept of Flexibility: A Dual Control Perspective', *Omega*, 24: 121–39.

Dore, R. (1999). 'Trust and the Workings of Market Capitalism', *Hume Papers on Public Policy*, 7/3: 2–16.

Harrigan, K. and Hambrick, D. (1985). *Strategic Flexibility: A Management Guide for Changing Times*. Lanham, MD: Lexington Books.

Klein, D. (1997). *Reputation: Studies in the Voluntary Elicitation of Good Conduct*. Lansing: University of Michigan Press.

Lampel, J. and Shapira, Z. (2001). 'Judgmental Errors, Interactive Norms and the Difficulty of Detecting Strategic Surprises', *Organization Science*, 12: 599–611.

Mintzberg, H. (1982). 'A note on that dirty word "Efficiency"', *Interface*, 12/5: 101–5.

Ring, P. and Van De Ven, A. (1992). 'Structuring Cooperative relationships between Organizations', *Strategic Management Journal*, 13: 483–93.

Sabel, C. (1993). 'Studied Trust: Building New Forms of Cooperation in Volatile Economy', *Human Relations*, 46: 1133–70.

Sitkin, S. and Roth, N. (1993). 'Explaining the Limited Effectiveness of Legalistic "Remedies" for Trust/distrust', *Organization Science*, 4: 367–92.

Sunstein, C. (1996). 'Social Roles and Social Norms', *Columbia Law Review*, 96: 903–68.

Uslaner, E. (2002). *The Moral Foundations of Trust*. Cambridge: Cambridge University Press.

Volberda, H. (1996). 'Toward the Flexible Form: How to Remain Vital in Hypercompetitive Environments', *Organization Science*, 7: 359–74.

Williamson, O. (1993). 'Opportunism and its Critics', *Managerial and Decision Economics*, 14/2: 97–108.

Young, P. (1996). 'The Economics of Convention', *Journal of Economic Perspectives*, 10: 105–22.

11

The Governance of Innovation:
The Case of Rolls-Royce plc

WILLIAM LAZONICK AND ANDREA PRENCIPE

Introduction

At the beginning of the twenty-first century, Rolls-Royce plc has remained a
power in the turbofan engine industry, notwithstanding its own troubled history and the relative lack of international success, more generally, of British
companies in high-technology manufacturing industries over the past half
century or so. Its RB211 family of engines enables the company to compete
in the high-thrust turbofan market as one of the 'Big Three' along with
US-based General Electric Aircraft Engines and Pratt & Whitney. The technological foundation of Rolls-Royce's competitive advantage is the RB211's
unique 'three-shaft' architecture that the company began developing in the
second half of the 1960s.

The initial attempt to develop the RB211 for the Lockheed L-1011 jumbo
jet, however, drove Rolls-Royce into bankruptcy in February 1971. Yet, as
a nationalized company under both Labour and Conservative governments,
from 1971 to 1987 Rolls-Royce sustained its investments in the RB211. In
1987 Rolls-Royce was privatized, and since that time has been operating as
a publicly listed corporation. In the late 1990s and early 2000s, Rolls-Royce
surpassed Pratt & Whitney as the number-two aircraft engine company.
At the beginning of 2003, General Electric (GE), along with CFM, its
joint venture with the French company, SNECMA, had 56 per cent of the
total aircraft engine market, Rolls-Royce 20 per cent, and Pratt & Whitney
12 per cent.

The case of Rolls-Royce, therefore, offers a unique opportunity for
an analysis of how a high-tech company sustained the innovation process
over a number of decades, notwithstanding dramatic changes in corporate
ownership. Using a theory of innovative enterprise developed by Lazonick
and O'Sullivan 2000 (see also O'Sullivan 2000; Lazonick 2002; Carpenter,
Lazonick, and O'Sullivan 2003), this study documents the importance to
Rolls-Royce's ultimate success of the abilities and incentives of career managers, most of them engineers, who exercised *strategic control* over the
allocation of the company's resources. We also document the sources of

financial commitment that enabled these strategic managers to sustain the uncertain innovation process until it could generate financial returns.

In focusing on the roles of strategic control and financial commitment in sustaining the innovation process, this study suggests an alternative to conventional agency theory for explaining the relation between the governance of resource allocation and economic performance at Rolls-Royce. According to agency theory, the entrenchment of Rolls-Royce's managers should have resulted in a squandering of the company's resources, not superior economic performance. The fact that these managers exercised strategic control, and developed the RB211, under very different ownership structures also raises questions about the importance of ownership to corporate performance and the conditions under which a high-tech company that must make uncertain and expensive investments in technological development can be exposed to the demands of public shareholders. This study, therefore, sheds light on the role of not only career managers but also public shareholders in the innovation process.

The next section describes how Rolls-Royce's attempt to develop the three-shaft engine for Lockheed at the end of the 1960s resulted in bankruptcy. Then we detail how, as a nationalized company from February 1971 to May 1987, Rolls-Royce continued to develop the RB211, first as an add-on to its military efforts and then in the 1980s as a critical capability in preparation for privatization. The use of financial markets in general and the stock market in particular to sustain the development of the RB211 is also detailed. The final section considers the implications of the Rolls-Royce case for understanding the governance of innovation.

The Origins of the RB211 and the Bankruptcy of Rolls-Royce

The British National Context

Already in the mid-1940s Rolls-Royce had proved to be the most successful and competent British aircraft engine firm. Unlike vertically integrated competitors such as de Havilland and Siddeley Armstrong Motors, Rolls-Royce was an independent engine supplier that could seek orders from any of the airframers. Rationalization of the industry occurred between the end of the 1950s and the beginning of the 1960s. A series of combinations reduced the number of airframers to three (Hawker Siddeley Group, British Aircraft Corporation, and Westland Aircraft) and engine manufacturers to two (Rolls-Royce and Bristol Siddeley Engines). Then in 1966, when it appeared that Bristol Siddeley would join with SNECMA to build the Pratt & Whitney JT9D engine for the Airbus, Rolls-Royce acquired Bristol-Siddeley, and thus became the only British aircraft engine company that could contemplate competing on global markets (Pugh 2001: 94–102). Both Bristol Siddeley Engines and the government (which had recommended the merger of the two companies in the Plowden Report) welcomed the takeover.

The Three-Shaft Engine Architecture

The development of Rolls-Royce's civil business rested on two important decisions: to develop a large turbofan aircraft engine, and to break into the United States market. In 1965 a study indicated an expanding future market for engines rated over 30,000 lb. At Rolls-Royce the first program for a larger turbofan engine was based on the two-shaft Conway turbofan engine. The engine, labeled RB178, was rated at 28,500 lb and had a relatively low bypass ratio. The company's view was that the fuel consumption benefits of a high bypass ratio would be more than offset by the fuel consumption costs attributable to the larger size of the fan, the greater weight of the engine, and the higher installed drag that a high bypass ratio would entail (Cownie 1989; Pugh 2001: 105).

This view changed, however, when 'tests in the US demonstrated that the installed drag penalty of the nacelle was less than half that assumed in European studies' (Ruffles 1992: 3). As a result, the bypass ratio of the RB178 was increased to eight, which in turn led Rolls-Royce's engineers to choose 'a three-shaft configuration as the best for both aerodynamic and mechanical reasons' (Ruffles 1992: 4). This design layout, labeled RB178-51, would provide much higher thrust than the previous RB178. A demonstrator program was launched to test the new technological solution, with the first engine test run taking place in July 1966 (Cownie 1989). The tests revealed a number of mechanical defects related to the revolutionary character of the three-shaft architecture. A shortage of finance meant that the demonstrator program was dropped. Meanwhile, Rolls-Royce started a smaller three-shaft engine program, the Trent, which permitted the company to gain some experience on a lower-rated version of a three-shaft engine. The Trent program was, however, cancelled in 1968. As reported by Cownie (1989: 232), 'many believed that some of the problems later experienced in RB211 development could have been solved earlier if running had continued with the RB178 demonstrator'.

When Boeing launched the 747 aircraft in 1968, Rolls-Royce submitted an engine proposal (the RB178-51) to power the wide-body aircraft (Ruffles 1992). Boeing selected the Pratt & Whitney JT9D, however, mainly because of its larger size. After failing to sell the RB178-51 to Boeing, Rolls-Royce became even more convinced that the future of its aircraft engine business depended on the development of large turbofan engines. Forecast studies showed that sales of Rolls-Royce's existing engines would fall from £58.9m in 1969 to £3.5m in 1975, and revenues from the aftermarket from £36.5m to £31.9m (Cownie 1989). Towards the end of the 1960s, Rolls-Royce had in place two large three-shaft engine projects, namely, the RB207 and the RB211. The RB207 was the larger, rated at over 50,000 lb and proposed for the twin-engined European Airbus, US jumbo jets, and the BAC Two-eleven projects. The RB211 was smaller, rated at 30,000 lb, and proposed for three-engined airliners.

Development of the RB211

In June 1967 Rolls-Royce entered into negotiations with Lockheed to manufacture the RB211, rated at 33,260 lb, for its projected L-1011 three-engined wide-body aircraft (Pugh 2001: ch. 4). The Rolls-Royce marketing team (led by David Huddie) focused its campaign on technological superiority and lower prices. Technological superiority was supposed to derive from not only the revolutionary three-shaft architecture but also the all-composite (Hyfil) fan blade. These technological advances would result in an engine that was 'lighter, cheaper to run, simpler in construction (with 40 per cent fewer component parts) and easier to maintain than existing turbo-fan engines' (Gray 1971: 84). Also, given lower wages in Britain and the further devaluation of the British pound against the US dollar, the RB211 engine was offered at £203,000 compared with £250,000 for the GE engine and £280,000 for the Pratt & Whitney engine. Pratt & Whitney pulled out of the race, while GE cut its price to £240,000. After tough and intense negotiations, Rolls-Royce won the contract by cutting its price to just under £200,000 (Reed 1973). Lockheed announced the launch order for the RB211 in March 1968. Lockheed ordered 150 'ship sets' of RB211 engines (totaling 450 engines), with TWA and Eastern Air Lines as launch airline customers. Air Holding of the United Kingdom ordered 50 Lockheed aircraft, which was politically advantageous for Rolls-Royce because it offset the offshore purchase of British engines and therefore helped the US balance of payments (Cownie 1989).

The news of the Lockheed deal was very well received in Britain. Anthony Wedgwood Benn, Minister of Technology in the Labour government, stated that the contract was 'a terrific boost to British technology and its export potential' (quoted in Gray 1971: 86). The City also welcomed the deal, and Rolls-Royce's share prices moved up from £2.225 to £2.35, adding £30 million to Rolls-Royce's market value (Reed 1973). As pointed out by Gray (1971: 86), however, the optimism was based on the mistaken assumption that, through the company's newly developed computer centre, 'Rolls-Royce's success was due to the careful control of costs'. In fact, Rolls-Royce's success in securing the contract was based on price cutting, a strategy that, as Gray (1971: 86), put it, 'did not require a computer'.

The development of the RB211 was unique for Rolls-Royce. As Harker (1976: 176) summed it up: 'This was a mammoth task; the engine itself was much bigger in overall dimension than anything the company had produced before; it was a different shape and the diameter of the fan was eighty-six inches, which necessitated large machinery to cut metal and required new techniques in welding' (see also Cownie 1989: 234). The task became even more complex when the design specifications of the engine were modified to accommodate changes in the design of the aircraft. By the time the engine was ordered, aircraft performance requirements had increased, with the thrust required from the RB211 rising to 40,600 lb. In 1972, the thrust requirement climbed again to 42,000 lb because of the increased weight of both aircraft and engine. This thrust was twice that of the largest engine that Rolls-Royce had previously produced.

The government's initial contribution was 70 per cent of the launching costs of the RB211, totaling around £47m. It was an exceptional contribution since the government had set a limit to launching aid at 'normally not more than 50%' of the launching costs (DTI 1972: Annex A).[1] To make things worse, the initial launching costs had been seriously underestimated. The as yet unproven technologies being introduced in the RB211 resulted in soaring development costs. *In primis*, the Hyfil carbon fiber that made up the fan blades failed the so-called 'bird strike test'. The fiber was reinforced to strengthen the leading edge of the blades, but this solution caused stresses at the root of the blade (Gray 1971). As a result, the all-composite fan blade was abandoned, and the 'old' solid titanium blades with snubbers were reintroduced. This change, however, added 300 lb to the weight of the engine, thus necessitating expensive redesign work. The sheer size of the engine also required the construction of new testing facilities. As a result, the progress of the program was delayed, and it became highly likely that Rolls-Royce would incur the heavy late-delivery penalties that the Lockheed contract mandated.

Rolls-Royce's Bankruptcy

Rolls-Royce's financial situation started deteriorating towards the end of 1969. In May 1970, Rolls-Royce asked the Industrial Reorganisation Corporation for a loan of £10m. Changes in management were made: first Lord Beeching and Ian Morrow joined the board; then Sir David Huddie, one of the architects of the successful RB211 campaign, stepped down and Hugh Conway (from the Bristol division) replaced him. Also, 3,500 men were made redundant and a small factory (employing 100 men) was closed down. In November 1970, in the face of Rolls-Royce's mounting financial difficulties and a revised estimate of the launching costs of the RB211 to £135m, the government increased its launching aid by a further £42m, its total contribution of £89m representing 66 per cent of the revised cost estimate. Also, the Bank of England agreed to lend £8m to Rolls-Royce, while

---

[1] 'Launching aid is an interest-free financial contribution to the launching costs of a civil aircraft or aero-engine project, repayable as a levy on sales and licences to the extent that these are achieved' (DTI 1972: Annex A).

Midland Bank and Lloyds Bank lent £5m each with the stipulation that they each would have a representative on the Rolls-Royce board (DTI 1972: 7–8; Bowden 2002: 50). This £60m financial package was, however, subject to a reassessment of the development program (DTI 1972). A further change was made to Rolls-Royce management. Sir Denning Pearson, Rolls-Royce Chairman and another architect of the RB211 campaign, stepped down and was replaced by Lord Cole, who had just retired from Unilever.

Notwithstanding changes in management, redundancies and augmented financial aid from the British government, Rolls-Royce was not able to overcome the problems with the RB211 development program. Rolls-Royce internal assessments (reported to the Ministry of Aviation Supply) showed that, due to a number of design modifications and subsequent changes in the production process, development and production targets could not be met. These delays meant a postponement of at least six months for engine deliveries. The DTI estimated that 'a further £110 million cash flow would be required, as compared with the £60 million estimated in September 1970' (DTI 1972: 11). The incoming Conservative government that, while in opposition, 'had adopted a policy of "disengagement" from industry with references to the need to end public support for "lame ducks"' (Hayward 1989: 138), had to decide whether to continue to support Rolls-Royce financially or allow it to go bankrupt. They opted for the second alternative and on 4 February 1971 Rolls-Royce went into receivership.

What went wrong? The problems were technical, financial, managerial, and contractual. The use of Hyfil carbon fiber for fan blades turned out to be a failure. Also, the technological viability of the RB211's revolutionary three-shaft architecture had yet to be demonstrated. As mentioned earlier, the RB178 demonstrator program had been cancelled due to financial shortage, leaving the design team dependent on parametric studies of the Spey and smaller turbo-fan engines. Worse still, the premature death of Adrian Lombard deprived Rolls-Royce of one of the finest 'trouble shooting' engineers in the industry (Hayward 1989: 137).

At the time that the RB211 program was launched, Rolls-Royce was involved in the development of the larger RB207 engine for the European Airbus as well as in a number of military programs (Harker 1976). Although the two civil engines shared a common architecture and several design features, 'development of two large engines, and especially the RB211 to Lockheed's stringent contract terms, was straining [Rolls-Royce's] resources' (Hayward 1989: 136). Also, the acquisition of Bristol Siddeley Engines absorbed financial resources; Rolls-Royce's purchase of Bristol cost £63.6m, £26.6m of which was paid in cash to Hawker Siddeley Aircraft (Hayward 1989: 123). The valuation included about £20m in 'goodwill' and shares in British Aircraft Corporation and Westland, which Rolls-Royce later sought unsuccessfully to sell. The Bristol acquisition placed considerable demands upon managerial resources for rationalizing the engine divisions. In fact,

Rolls-Royce would have to provide additional capital to support the Bristol side of the business at a time when its own liquidity was under pressure from its fateful contract with Lockheed. Hayward (1989: 123) stated that '[w]ith hindsight, it is evident that the determination to prevent P&W [Pratt & Whitney] obtaining a European foothold led Rolls into a precipitated and ill-judged act. Although the merger [with Bristol Siddeley] was not the main cause of Rolls' later problems, it would be a significant contributory factor.'

As for the Lockheed contract, the main problem was that Rolls-Royce had agreed to a relatively low fixed price with, as Hayward (1989: 136) put it, 'strict and onerous penalties for delay, giving Rolls very little leeway in the event of serious technical or financial problems'. Similarly, Harker (1976: 186) emphasized that '[s]ix hundred engines were contracted, but the price did not make sufficient allowance for the unexpected inflation that ensued in the economy or the unanticipated development costs that arose'.

Engineer Control: A Two-Edged Sword

'A basic engineering training is a good training for management and for top engineering decisions' (quoted in Gray 1971: 75). This statement attributed to Sir Denning Pearson summarizes Rolls-Royce's management philosophy. Several commentators underlined the fact that Rolls-Royce was an engineering company run by engineers who were devoted to engineering excellence. This value informed every single allocative decision taken within the firm. Engineering excellence was pursued strenuously, sometimes irrespective of time and cost constraints. As mentioned by an industry expert, allegedly, having laid their hands on a Pratt & Whitney engine, Rolls-Royce engineers were appalled by the crudity of the engineering solutions embedded in the engine. They were also appalled, however, by the fact that the competitor's engine worked.

Rolls-Royce was a paternalistic company that was run by and for its long-time employees, especially its engineers. Getting a job in Rolls-Royce was easier if the applicant had a relative already working for the company. Employees tended to stay with the company for their entire working lives. This attachment occurred not only at the top management level but also on the shop floor. As underlined by Gray (1971: 75): 'Before Rolls-Royce merged with Bristol Siddeley in 1966 only one of their eight directors had been with them for less than twenty-five years. Such links with the past were to be found on every level: in 1964 over a third of the workers in the Derby factory had been employed there since before the Second World War.' Also, Rolls-Royce did not adopt job rotation policies, so that engineers tended to stay within the same department for years and sometimes decades, with the likelihood that they would become experts in a specific component and/or subsystem of the aircraft engine.

The Era of Nationalization

Emergence from Bankruptcy

On the same day that the Rolls-Royce Receiver was appointed, Frederick Corfield, the Ministry of Aviation Supply stated: 'To ensure continuity of those activities of Rolls-Royce which are important to our national defence, to our collaborative programmes with other countries and to many air forces and civil airlines all over the world, the Government has decided to acquire such assets of the aero-engine and marine and industrial gas turbine engine divisions of the company as they may be essential for these purposes' (quoted in DTI 1972: 14). A new company, Rolls-Royce (1971) Limited, was therefore formed and took control of the assets of Rolls-Royce acquired by the government.

At that point the development of the RB211 was almost cancelled. But Lord Carrington, the Minister of Defence, commissioned a technical and cost study that involved veteran Rolls-Royce engineers Fred Morley, Stanley Hooker, and Arthur Rubbra and that gave an optimistic assessment of the RB211 (Pugh 2001: 230). The study argued that the RB211's development problems could be overcome with a six-month delay and a cash flow injection of a further £120m (DTI 1972). According to Gunston (1997: 195), the nationalized company took 'the RB211 on board, funded on a cheese-paring daily basis'. The British government entered talks with Lockheed to renegotiate the RB211 contract. After a lengthy negotiation involving the British and the US governments, Rolls-Royce (1971) Limited and Lockheed signed a new contract for the completion of the RB211 program. Under this new agreement, Lockheed agreed to buy RB211 engines at increased prices. Meanwhile, the US Senate had authorized a federal rescue package for Lockheed, and the British government provided the necessary cash to complete the RB211 program.

According to the 1971 Memorandum of Understanding that outlined the relationship between the British government and Rolls-Royce, the government, as the sole shareholder, maintained ultimate control over strategic planning and financial issues related to the launch of new engine development programs (Hayward 1989). In particular, 'any investment decisions over £25 million (US$41 million) had to be referred back to the government for approval' (Verchère 1992: 33). The government was, however, not involved in the company's day-to-day management, although the Rolls-Royce board agreed to keep it informed about its operations (Hayward 1989).

A number of the government appointees to the new board of Rolls-Royce (1971) Limited were clearly supporters of the RB211 program. They included Sir William Cook, a former scientific adviser to the Ministry of Defence, and Sir St John Elstub, Chairman of Imperial Metal Industries, both of whom had already advised the Heath government on the viability of the RB211 (Pugh 2001: 234–5). Yet, as summed up by Hayward (1989: 140), the bankruptcy and bailout entailed a dramatic challenge to engineer control:

[I]t was soon evident that Rolls required a long period of convalescence and a sharp taste of internal reform. Pearson, Huddie and the Rolls board took the full brunt of the post mortem. There had been fatal flaws in Rolls' management structure and the dominance of engineers at the top of the company was singled out for particular criticism. As one Rolls man would later put it, 'the first thing we had to learn was that the company was not just a playground for engineers to amuse themselves'. Rolls-Royce had to be rebuilt and Sir Kenneth Keith's appointment as chairman in September 1972 marked the start of the process. According to Sir Stanley Hooker, Sir Kenneth found a lack of discipline which appalled him and took on a seven year stint which would lay the conditions for Rolls' revival.

Engineer Control and Bureaucratic Interference

With government and board support for the RB211 program, engineers regained complete control over the evolution of the program itself. In the aftermath of the bankruptcy, a number of Rolls-Royce's most illustrious engineers had come out of retirement. Among them was Sir Stanley Hooker, who, among other things, had led the development of the engine for the Concorde while working at Bristol Aero Engines (Pugh 2001: 90–2). Hooker became both Technical Director and a member of the Rolls-Royce board of directors with the charge of getting the RB211 program back on track. Cyril Lovesey and Arthur Rubbra, both well over 70 years old, worked with Hooker as what he called 'a kind of Chief of Staff committee' (Pugh 2001: 235, quoting from Hooker 1984).

When the Labour government took office in 1974, however, the specter of bureaucratic interference reappeared. Rolls-Royce was put under the control of the National Enterprise Board (NEB) whose role was to oversee the company's operations. Indeed, Rolls-Royce was the main holding of NEB, which in turn came to symbolize Labour's foray into industrial policy. Rolls-Royce management disliked this intrusion; Sir Kenneth Keith, its chairman believed that the NEB added a redundant bureaucratic layer between Rolls-Royce and the government (Hayward 1989: 159).[2] Tony Benn, as Minister of Trade and Industry, had his first meeting with the Rolls-Royce Chairman in March 1974. Keith told Benn that, when he had accepted the Rolls-Royce position in 1972 he had told the Prime Minister, Edward Heath, that he would 'take it on so long as I am not buggered about by junior Ministers and civil servants and officials'. Benn responded that 'while I am in charge I will not accept chairmen of nationalised industries indicating to me that they won't be mucked about by junior Ministers and civil servants: Rolls-Royce

---

[2] See also 'Rolls-Royce: Middle-Man or Medler?', *Economist*, 27 December 1975: 42; 'National Enterprise Board: Rolls-Royce of a Problem', *Economist*, 11 February 1978: 112.

is a nationalised company and must be accountable for what it does' (Pugh 2001: 256–7).

During 1979, over a period that included the election of the Thatcher government in May, there was open hostility between Sir Kenneth Keith and the NEB Chairman, Sir Leslie Murphy. In late 1979 Murphy told Sir Keith Joseph, Thatcher's Minister of Industry, that the Rolls-Royce chairman should be sacked in the light of the company's poor financial performance.[3] In the event, Sir Kenneth retired as chairman, while Sir Keith took control of Rolls-Royce away from the NEB (resulting in the resignation of the entire NEB board), and placed the company in the hands of the Department of Industry.[4]

Worsening Financial Performance and the GE Deal

In 1980 Rolls-Royce's 1,000th RB211 went into production. But from 1979 the company's financial situation worsened. With uncovered foreign exchange as the value of the pound appreciated under the first Thatcher government, as well as a prolonged strike, Rolls-Royce recorded losses of £58m in 1979 (Pugh 2001: 299). A severe recession in the civilian aerospace industry in the early 1980s meant persistent losses for Rolls-Royce.[5] In 1983 Rolls-Royce lost £193m and in 1983 and 1984 delivered only 126 new RB211s, even though the 'worst-case' scenario in the company's 1982 plan had been 350 engines (Pugh 2001: 297, 304). Between 1980 and 1984 Rolls-Royce cut its labor force from 62,000 to 41,000, mainly through voluntary severance and with no industrial disputes (Pugh 2001: 300, 321, 325).

From 1971 to 1979, Rolls-Royce reportedly had received £425m in state aid.[6] From 1979 through 1988 successive governments provided Rolls-Royce with £437m in launch aid, of which £118m was repaid from sales levies (Hayward 1989). The new chairman, Sir Frank McFadzean, appointed at the end of 1979, stated, however, that 'as a chairman of this company I have no intentions of going and clearing everything with civil servants; otherwise I would never run the company. You would never run a business on that basis' (quoted in Hayward 1989: 160).

---

[3] 'NEB and Rolls-Royce: Who Needs a Lame-Duck Hospital?', *Economist*, 17 November 1979: 108.

[4] See 'Industrial Policy: Mrs Thatcher's Awkward Inheritance', *Economist*, 5 May 1979: 120; 'Rolls under Whitehall's Wing', *Economist*, 24 November 1979: 83.

[5] According to a 1984 report in the *Wall Street Journal*, Rolls-Royce lost the equivalent of $253m in 1983, and 'Rolls-Royce last posted a profit—currently equivalent to $9 million—in 1978. Its best year since then was 1981, when it posted income before extraordinary items of $18 million, but a net loss of $4 million after an extraordinary charge of $22 million due to restructuring costs. It had a net loss of $176 million in 1982' (Ingrassia 1984).

[6] 'The Real Problem is Money', *Economist*, 17 November 1979: 108.

In 1984, however, in the aftermath of a string of unprofitable years stretching back to 1979, Rolls-Royce entered into two risk and revenue-sharing partner agreements with General Electric whereby GE took a 15 per cent stake in the development of the medium-sized RB535E4 engine to power the Boeing 757, while Rolls took a 15 per cent stake in the development of a GE engine designed to exceed 60,000 lb (Pugh 2001: 311–19). As reported in an article titled 'Rolls faces up to reality' that appeared in the *Financial Times* the day after the agreement was announced:

By swapping a share in one of its new engines for a stake in one of General Electric's, Rolls has finally moved away from the course which it has followed in the civil engine market for the past 20 years—a course which has taken this proud engineering company into bankruptcy, and which more recently has left it with an increasingly weak position in the market for high thrust commercial engines. (Lambert and Makinson 1984)

The article cites Ralph Robins, who was at the time Director – Civil Engines, as saying (in the words of the journalists) 'that to develop the RB-211 series up to the [60,000 lb+] size range would have effectively required the designers to start with a clean sheet of paper. On this basis the project could have cost $1-1/2 bn or more.'

As a journalist was to write from the vantage point of 1990 on the eve of the first test of the Trent engine, the 1984 RRSP deal had been made because the company's new Chairman, Sir William Duncan, 'believed that any attempt by Rolls to go it alone in developing high-thrust engines would threaten a repetition of the 1971 RB211 crisis. His answer was for Rolls to stay in the game by opting for minority partnership with one of it American rivals' (Lorenz 1990). Or, as another journalist, also writing in 1990, remarked, looking back at the Duncan agreement, 'implicit in the deal was the understanding that Rolls would stay out of the big engine end of the market—shutting it out of the highest growth area and limiting it to a subordinate role' (Crooks 1990: 10).

The Reversal of Strategy: The RB211 Thrust Growth Capability

By 1986, however, some two years after agreeing to the high-thrust RRSP with GE, Rolls-Royce was marketing its own high-thrust engine, the RB211-524D4D, in direct competition with not only Pratt and Whitney's PW-4000 but also GE's CF6-80C2, in which Rolls-Royce still had a 15 per cent stake. In August 1986, much to the displeasure of GE, the RB211-524 secured a £600m order from British Airways for its new long-range jumbo jets. GE claimed that its pact with Rolls-Royce precluded its 'partner' from bidding for the BA order. Rolls-Royce disagreed (Donne and Cassell 1986). Subsequently the GE-Rolls high-thrust RRSP fell apart, with the collaboration being terminated in November 1986 (Crooks 1990; Pugh 2001: 314–19).

Why the reversal of strategy? The improvement in the market for turbofan engines from 1985 clearly had much to do with it; in 1986 Rolls-Royce had pretax profits of £120m and outstanding orders worth £3.1bn (Pugh 2001: 323). Rolls-Royce's engineers also found, over the course of 1984 and 1985, that, because of the modularity embedded in the three-shaft architecture, they could upgrade the RB211 for the big-engine market without increasing the fan diameter, with dramatic savings in development costs compared with Robins earlier estimate (Pugh 2001: 314). Whether or not a change in the top management of Rolls-Royce was a factor in the reversal of strategy is difficult to say. In late October 1984, some eight months after the high-thrust RRSP, Duncan, the Rolls-Royce architect of the agreement, announced that, as of 1 December, Ralph Robins would become Managing Director of the company, the number-two position. A week after the announcement, Duncan suddenly died at the age of sixty-one. He was replaced as Chairman by Sir Francis Tombs, who had been appointed to the Rolls-Royce board as a non-executive director in 1982, and hence was involved in the direction of the company when the pact with GE had been made. From the perspective of 1990, Tombs was able to argue that the agreement with GE 'was leading us nowhere. The decision to pull out was a watershed' (quoted in Lorenz 1990). As a result of the reversal of the decision to take a subordinate role to GE in the development of the high-thrust engine, Rolls-Royce increased its market share of the world civil engine market from 5 per cent at the time of its 1987 privatization to 20 per cent in 1990. The basis of the company's success was, as Crooks (1990) put it, 'Rolls' massive advantage in having the RB211 engine'. As Lorenz (1990) summarized these advantages that, by 1990, had resulted in the Trent engine:

... the RB211 engine core, whose development costs put the company into receivership, has become the key to its survival and success. Its revolutionary design, using three shafts rather than Pratt and GE's two, has proved so flexible that in successive upgradings since 1971 the engine power has been doubled without incurring the huge expense of significant design changes.

The three-shaft is shorter than two-shaft engines, more rigid and therefore more durable. It wears less in service, preserving its outstanding fuel economy over its full life. Along the way Rolls developed a new, wide fan blade, the 'wide-chord' fan, which needs fewer blades to produce the same, or more, power, is quieter and more fuel-efficient than conventional fans. Only with the Trent did the original RB211 fan diameter have to be increased, but no other fundamental change has been made. As a result, the Trent development is likely to cost about £400 (with about 25% being funded by Rolls' partners in the project, including BMW and two Japanese companies). By contrast, industry estimates suggest the GE90 project will cost more than £1 billion.

Corporate Control and Financial Markets

Privatization, Restructuring, and Reorganization

From 1979 Thatcher administration had wanted to privatize Rolls-Royce as part of the Tory policy 'to reduce government intervention in industry and to spread "popular capitalism" through wider share ownership' (Hayward 1989: 160). As one minister put it, 'the business of aerospace must pay its way. Defence considerations apart, there is no reason why aerospace should not be subject to the financial disciplines and opportunities of the marketplace'. Or, in the words of Norman Tebbit, the Minister of Industry who succeeded Keith Joseph, 'the aerospace industry is for making profits, it is not a form of occupational therapy' (both quoted in Hayward 1989: 160).

With losses piling up in the early 1980s, Rolls-Royce was not yet ready to throw away the protection of government ownership. But in late 1984 a recovery in the civil aerospace markets began, and in 1985 and 1986 Rolls-Royce posted substantial profits. In May 1987 Rolls-Royce was privatized with the flotation raising £1.36bn for the government for the sale of its shares to the public. In addition, at the request of Sir Francis Tombs, Rolls-Royce newly appointed Chairman, the government authorized an additional share issue that injected £283m. Notwithstanding the privatization, the British government retained in perpetuity a 'golden share' of Rolls-Royce that gave it the power to veto any takeover attempt. In an effort to limit the possibility of such a situation arising, the privatization limited foreign ownership of Rolls-Royce to 15 per cent of its outstanding shares on a first-come-first-served basis (Hayward 1989). This limitation on foreign ownership was challenged by the European Commission, and was subsequently increased to 29.5 per cent in 1989 and then to 49.5 per cent in 1998.[7]

Once privatized, Rolls-Royce searched for productivity gains through significant organizational restructuring that entailed focusing on core businesses, outsourcing, downsizing, and cost-cutting schemes. This restructuring was pursued with the aim of making the customer, especially civil airlines, central to the strategy of the company. Restructuring also involved an increasing involvement of suppliers and universities as partners in development and research programs. Organizational restructuring was pursued also via several internal programs informed by lean manufacturing, total quality control, and business process re-engineering principles. The aims of these programs were to improve the efficiency of business processes throughout the company and to modify the management structure to improve accountability. At the beginning of the 1990s, Rolls-Royce embarked on an internal quality-enhancing program, labeled Project 2000. The program was clearly inspired

---

[7] 'Investor Limit Up at Rolls-Royce', *New York Times*, 20 July 1989: D5; 'BAe, Rolls-Royce Foreign Ownership Limit Raised to 49.5pct from 29.5', *AFX News*, 12 March 1998.

by the Japanese quality movement and aimed at identifying and eliminating the firm's business processes that did not add value (Verchère 1992).

The supplier base was also rationalized through the reduction of the number of first-tier suppliers and the introduction of a supplier ranking system. Also, in 1998 Rolls-Royce reorganized itself into two types of business units: customer-facing business units with responsibility for identifying and meeting customer needs, and operating business units with responsibility for delivering sub-systems on time, to cost, and to specification. It was expected that this flatter structure would enable clear accountability of the business units (Rolls-Royce 1998).

This intense and profound restructuring resulted in job-cutting throughout the 1990s. The average number of Rolls-Royce's employees steadily declined throughout the decade. In ten years there was a net reduction of about 20,000 employees, accounting for about a third of the work force in 1990. Nevertheless, Rolls-Royce has recognized the importance of a committed and trained labor force. For example, the 1996 Annual Report contended that '[ultimately] our competitive edge lies not in hardware but in the quality of our people' (Rolls-Royce 1996: 17). The 2000 *Annual Report* put it more concretely:

Rolls-Royce is fortunate to have extremely talented and dedicated employees. In the UK, the average length of service is approaching 20 years. This is important in an industry where development and production programmes may have lives of more than 50 years and in which the customer relationship with an individual product may be 25 years or more. (Rolls-Royce 2000: 16)

Over the 1990s the absolute amount of spending on R&D increased constantly, with net R&D as a share of sales in the 6–7 per cent range. Much of this spending (as we shall see in the next section) was aimed at the further development of the RB211. In recent years, the emphasis has been on the generation of technologies that can be exploited across the company's different businesses. Technologies originally developed for aerospace applications are being exploited for energy applications and more recently in the marine business (in particular, computational fluid dynamics tools are being applied to marine propulsion design). New technologies are being researched to reduce the adverse environmental impacts (in terms of noise and emissions) of products. New technologies are also being used to support the more recent move towards the provision of customer support and service.

Corporate Strategy and the Stock Market

As a nationalized company, Rolls-Royce prepared a corporate strategic plan for government approval every year, and relied on corporate revenues, short-term and long-term borrowing, and government support in the form of defense contracts and 'launch aid' (in effect interest-free loans from the government) to maintain its organization and fund expansion. With the privatization of the company in May 1987, Rolls-Royce still had access to these sources of funds, although launch aid would be forthcoming only if other sources were unavailable. The main difference was that, as a publicly traded company, the management of Rolls-Royce was now accountable to the corporation's public shareholders, the vast majority of whom had a purely financial interest in the company.

According to Verchère (1992), after privatization senior managers felt more under public scrutiny by the investment community and private shareholders. As a Rolls-Royce senior manager stated: 'We're becoming much more of a financial and accountability culture than before' (quoted in Verchère 1992: 34). From the beginning of the 1990s Rolls-Royce engaged in 'a three-tier planning discipline comprising a ten-year review of market trends backed by five-year financial and strategic plans' (Verchère 1992: 34). The third tier was a two-year operating plan and budget that was, in turn, informed by quarterly and four-week financial budgets that, according to Verchère (1992: 34), have had 'the net effect of tightening financial controls at all levels, including the shop floor'.

Yet throughout the 1990s Rolls-Royce underperformed the FTSE 100 British stock-market index, with the gap in stock prices increasing perceptibly in the late 1990s (see Fig. 11.1). But how did Rolls-Royce's exposure to the stock market actually affect strategic decision-making and the allocation of resources at the company? Lazonick and O'Sullivan (2002) provide a framework for analyzing the four functions that the stock market can perform in the industrial corporation. First, it can structure the relation between

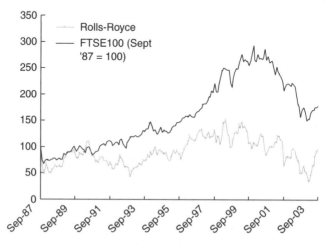

FIGURE 11.1   *Stock price indices, Rolls-Royce plc and FTSE100, September 1987–September 2003 (adjusted close on the first trading day of each month).*

owners and managers in exercising strategic *control* over corporate allocation decisions. Second, it can provide the corporation with *cash* that can be used to restructure the corporate balance sheet, fund operations (including R&D), invest in plant and equipment, or acquire existing physical and intangible assets. Third, it can provide the corporation with its own *combination* currency that can be used instead of or in addition to cash in mergers and acquisitions. Fourth, it can provide the corporation with its own *compensation* currency that it can use, instead of or in addition to cash, to reward employees and other stakeholders.[8] As we shall see in the following account of the relation between Rolls-Royce's corporate strategy and financial markets, the stock market has played all four roles at Rolls-Royce during the past sixteen years.

Ownership and Control

The privatization of the company in 1987 transferred ownership of Rolls-Royce's shares from the British government to institutional investors and households. Table 11.1 shows the size distribution of holdings of ordinary shares on 31 December 1988 and 31 December 2002. It is worth noting that on 31 December 1968, on the eve of the difficulties that had plunged Rolls-Royce into bankruptcy, Rolls-Royce had 59,712 shareholders of which 50,742 were individuals (who held 46 per cent of the number of shares outstanding), while 218 were insurance companies, 948 banks, and 134 pension funds (Bowden 2002: 41–2). Twenty years later, as a reprivatized company, Rolls-Royce had a vastly increased number of small shareholders, but a smaller number of large institutional shareholders held a much larger proportion of the shares outstanding.

TABLE 11.1   *Size distribution of ordinary shareholdings at end-1988, 1991, and 2002*

Size of holding*	31 December 1988			31 December 1991			31 December 2002		
	Number of holders	% of total holdings	% of total shares	Number of holders	% of total holdings	% of total shares	Number of holders	% of total holdings	% of total shares
1–150	612,545	72.32	11.43	345,974	58.21	5.26	119,263	37.06	0.94
151–500				200,769	33.78	4.63	155,370	48.27	2.48
151–1,000	210,226	24.82	8.28						
501–10,000				45,521	7.66	8.66	45,157	14.03	5.07
1,001–10,000	22,491	2.66	6.88						
10,001–100,000	1,099	0.13	5.00	1,348	0.23	4.71	1,457	0.45	2.49
100,001–1,000,000	474	0.06	20.34	574	0.10	21.34	463	0.14	9.25
1,000,001 and over	115	0.01	48.07	149	0.02	55.96	166	0.05	79.77
TOTAL	846,950	100.00	100.00	594,335	100.00	100.00	321,876	100.00	100.00

* The 1988–90 annual reports provide data on shareholding for those with 151–1,000 shares and 1,001–10,000 while the 1991–2002 annual reports provide data on shareholding for those with 151–500 shares and 501–10,000 shares.
Source: Rolls-Royce (1988: 34; 2001: 72).

[8] For an application of this framework, see Carpenter, Lazonick, and O'Sullivan (2003).

As can be seen from Table 11.1, from 1988 to 2002 the number of small shareholders declined, while the concentration of shareholdings among the largest shareholders—all institutional investors—increased dramatically. Whereas in 1988 the 115 holders of more than 1m shares had 48 per cent of Rolls-Royce's shares, in 2002 the 166 largest shareholders had 80 per cent of the shares. As of 6 March 2002, the largest shareholder was, with holdings of 12.08 per cent of the outstanding ordinary shares, Franklin Resources, Inc., a major US-based institutional investor that manages the Franklin-Templeton investment funds. The second largest shareholder was BMW AG with holdings of 9.89 per cent. The German automobile company had acquired these shares as a result of Rolls-Royce's purchase of BMW's stake in a joint aircraft engine venture.

Notwithstanding the growing concentration of shareholding at Rolls-Royce, throughout the period 1987–2003 Rolls-Royce's management was dominated by insiders who, protected from takeover by the British government's 'golden share', remained firmly in control of corporate allocation decisions. The key executive over this period was Sir Ralph Robins. Upon graduating from Imperial College in 1955, Robins, aged twenty-three, had joined the company as an apprentice engineer. He became Managing Director in 1984, Chief Executive in 1991, and Chairman in 1992. A 1999 profile of Robins in *The Financial Times* noted that 'Sir Ralph . . . has been in charge throughout the glory years'. The article went on to say that, while the City remained unimpressed with Rolls-Royce's stock market performance, 'no one in the City has a bad word to say about the slim, pinstriped, impeccably courteous Sir Ralph'. The profile went on to quote one unnamed City analyst who remarked: 'He's everybody's favourite uncle. But his priority is to maintain Rolls as an independent British company. Shareholder value is secondary to him' (Skapinker 1999). Or, more recently, as stated in a newspaper report that followed Robins's announcement of his retirement: 'Sir Ralph Robins, chairman of Rolls-Royce, is no great fan of the City and it of him by the look of the 7 per cent surge in the Rolls-Royce share price that greeted news of his retirement'.[9]

Like Robins, most of the other top executives at Rolls-Royce in the fifteen years after privatization had built their careers with the company. In October 2001 the person whom Michael Howse replaced as Director–Engineering and Technology was Philip Ruffles, an engineer who had joined the company in 1961 at the age of twenty-three. In addition, Ruffles' predecessor as Director–Engineering and Technology was Stewart Miller, an engineer who had joined Rolls-Royce in 1954 at the age of twenty-one and had been appointed to the Board in 1984 before retiring after forty-one years of service

---

[9] 'Outlook: Prickly Sir Ralph Deserves his Place in History', *Independent*, 8 March 2000.

in 1996. Counting Robins and Ruffles, of the nine executive directors who were with the company in 2001, six had joined the company in 1969 or before at an average age of 22.5 years and had on average thirty-seven years of service with the company. Five of these six were engineers. Of the other three, John Rose and Paul Heiden, who joined Rolls-Royce in their thirties, both had finance backgrounds, while James Guyette joined the company subsequent to the Allison acquisition. These executives, who effectively control Rolls-Royce's resource allocation decisions, are long-term career managers, and most of them have spent their entire careers with Rolls-Royce.

Stock as a Source of Cash

Table 11.2 shows the most important items in Rolls-Royce's sources and uses of funds since it was privatized. In addition, we have shown the company's annual net expenditures on R&D, which are deducted as an expense on the profit-and-loss statement, thus reducing the 'funds from operations' figure but which represent in reality an ongoing 'capital' expenditure that the company must be able to fund if it is to stay in business. Based on the data in Table 11.2, Fig. 11.2 illustrates that for most of the 1990s the company's funds from operations plus depreciation charges were just covering capital expenditures (including acquisition costs) plus dividends. Since the late 1990s, however, these sources of funds have been significantly greater than these uses, without sacrificing either R&D expenditures or dividend distributions.

Figure 11.3 shows Rolls-Royce's main financing activities and external fund raising under privatization. As discussed below, the two public share issues (categorized as PSI in Table 11.2) that Rolls-Royce did in 1993 and 1995 were directly related to technological investments—in the first case to fund R&D without taking on more debt, and in the second case to fund the acquisition of Allison Engine. By the late 1990s, when Rolls-Royce did the major acquisition of Vickers, it turned to the bond market rather than the stock market for financing.

Rolls-Royce made substantial profits from 1987 through 1990. As a result, as can be seen in Table 11.2, from 1987 through 1990 the company's funds from operations totaled £732m, almost double its total capital expenditures of £372m. In addition, internal funds also covered the company's expenditures on net R&D, which totaled £734m during the years 1987–90.

After the boom years of the late 1980s, a slowdown hit both the military and the civil segments of the aerospace industry. After suffering an operating loss of £172m in 1992, Rolls-Royce found itself facing the high costs of both sustaining the development of the high-thrust wide-body Trent and rationalizing its existing activities. The first Trent 700 engines for the Airbus 330 were to be delivered in the winter of 1994, and the higher-thrust

TABLE 11.2 *Rolls-Royce plc, sources and uses of funds, 1987–2002 (selected items, £m)*

Year	2002	2001	2000	1999	1998	1997	1996	1995	1994	1993	1992	1991	1990	1989	1988	1987
Sources																
FFO	611	418	479	392	395	311	182	193	41	37	124	100	254	278	217	191
DEP	236	198	238	110	113	92	103	116	109	105	104	64	69	55	43	41
LTB	151	69	510	734	177	2	69	4	0	208	181	335	161	162	155	9
ΔLTD	103	67	-223	530	162	-5	59	-150	-76	48	3	174	-1	-38	146	-70
ΔSTD	-155	39	-146	91	-19	65	0	17	6	-29	214	57	48	-62	-2	-163
SS0	1	16	10	4	14	4	18	15	4	8	0	4	1	0	0	0
PSI	0	0	0	0	0	0	0	332	0	317	0	0	0	0	0	274
DFA	41	168	46	187	213	89	52	153	40	38	12	15	19	8	4	2
Uses																
CPX	314	211	292	381	387	222	142	94	105	130	126	119	112	113	65	82
AOA	28	1	45	653	0	9	3	217	0	0	0	0	0	0	0	0
RLTD	48	2	733	204	15	7	10	154	76	160	178	161	162	200	9	79
CDS	109	84	74	88	65	78	69	57	51	44	64	45	69	55	45	14
Net R&D*	**297**	**358**	**371**	**337**	**310**	**268**	**217**	**206**	**218**	**253**	**229**	**216**	**237**	**161**	**149**	**187**

* As an operations expense, the cost of net R&D is covered by revenues that are deducted in arriving at the 'funds from operations' figure and is not an item in the cash flow (that is, 'sources and uses of funds') accounts. Given its importance to the company, however, the net R&D figures are included so that they can be compared with the cash flow items that are in the sources and uses accounts.

FFO = Funds from operations; DEP = Depreciation; LTB = Long-term borrowing; ΔLTD = Change in long-term debt (= LTB−RLTD); ΔSTD = Change in short-term debt; SS0 = Sale of ordinary shares to employees exercising options; PSI = issue of ordinary shares to the public (net of expenses); DFA = Disposal fixed assets; AOA = Acquisition of assets; RLTD = Reduction of long-term debt; CDS = Cash dividends.

Source: Rolls-Royce (1988–2002).

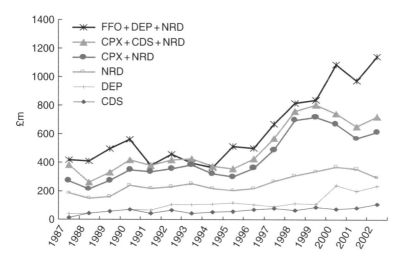

FFO = funds from operations; NRD = net R&D; DEP = depreciation

CPX = capital expenditures; CDS = cash dividends;

LTB = long-term borrowing; PSI = public share issues

FIGURE 11.2   *Rolls-Royce: sources and uses of funds 1987–2002.*

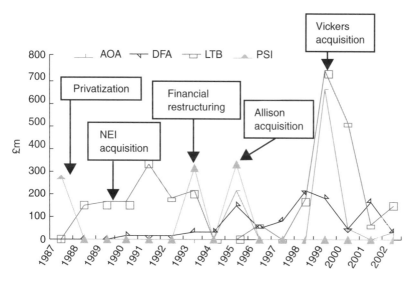

AOA = acquisition of assets; DFA = disposal of assets

LTB = long-term borrowing; PSI = public share issues

FIGURE 11.3   *Rolls-Royce: external funding 1987–2002.*

Trent 800 that was being developed for the Boeing 777 would be tested in September 1993.[10] The rationalization program, which was announced in March 1993, entailed the closing of six of twelve of the company's main manufacturing sites and layoffs of 2,900 people, a workforce reduction of 6 per cent (Tieman 1993).

The company had taken on considerable debt in the lean years of the early 1990s (see Table 11.2). But the company still needed to raise funds from the markets. According to the report in *Extel Examiner*, '[Sir Ralph] Robins [the Chairman of Rolls-Royce] said that it was expected that the rationalisation programme alone will result in a cash outflow of £130 million over this year and next. Against this background Robins said the board had decided to increase the equity base thereby restoring it to a level which, in its opinion, is more appropriate to the sales and activity of the Group.'[11] Instead of taking on more debt, in September 1993 Rolls-Royce announced a rights issue which would raise £307m net of expenses. One new share would be offered to the company's existing shareholders for each four shares that they currently held. A Rolls-Royce press release explained why the company was going to shareholders for more equity capital:

In July this year the financial resources of the Group were strengthened by a successful $300 million bond issue. However the Board of Rolls-Royce does not wish to place undue reliance on bank and other forms of debt financing. The Board believes it appropriate to finance the Group's long term activities predominantly through equity capital rather than debt. This approach was adopted in the Group's capital structure at the time of privatisation in 1987 when the Group came to the stock market with no net debt. The requirement for a rights issue should be seen in the context of turnover which has risen from £1973 million in 1988, when shareholders' funds were £949 million, to £3562 million in 1992 on a similar equity base.[12]

Rolls-Royce had seen its market share of civil aircraft engines rise from 22 per cent in 1992 to 28 per cent in the first half of 1993—placing it just ahead of Pratt & Whitney, and even with GE—but market conditions, intense competition, and the imperative to sustain R&D raised concerns among shareholders about when they would see a resurgence of Rolls-Royce's share price to its post-privatization levels (Tieman 1993).[13] *The Times*'s editorial on the rights-issue announcement observed that 'Rolls-Royce asks a great deal from its shareholders'. In *The Times*'s full report on the condition of Rolls-Royce, reporter Ross Tieman (1993) observed that 'the last time Rolls-Royce needed more cash to develop a new aero-engine,

[10] 'Rolls-Royce plc Interim Results 1993', PR *Newswire European*, 2 September 1993.

[11] 'Royce-Royce 1—Right Issue Offsets Rationalisation Costs', *Extel Examiner*, 2 September 1993.

[12] 'Official Correction: Rolls-Royce—Rights Issue', *Extel Examiner*, 2 September 1993.

[13] 'Extel Financial Exclusive: Rolls-Royce to Fund "R&D at Highest level Ever"— Chairman', *Extel Examiner*, 2 September 1993.

it went bust. This time it is asking shareholders to contribute.' But Tieman (1993) continued:

The need for money is fundamentally different to that which existed 22 years ago, when Edward Heath's government was obliged to bail the company out of its cost over-runs on the development of the RB211 airliner engine. Today, the problem is one of success. But ironically, the RB211 is still at the root of Rolls's financial embarrassment.

Ideally, the prices that Rolls-Royce could secure from the airlines in the new engine market would reflect the improvements in reliability that would save on future servicing and replacement costs. But the generally depressed market conditions since 1989 had led airlines to ground older planes with 'spares-hungry' engines while creating intense competition among the Big Three for new orders, including engines for the Boeing 777, in a multi-sourcing world (Tieman 1993). It was under such economic conditions that, in 1993, Rolls-Royce went to its shareholders for cash.

On the announcement of the rights issue, the price of Rolls-Royce shares fell by almost 7 per cent to 152.5 p. The rights issue was offered at 130 p, a 20.5 per cent discount from the market price on the announcement date. Those British shareholders who did not want to take up the rights issue had a window of opportunity to sell the rights to those who did. At the same time, foreign holdings had reached the maximum of 29.5 per cent, thus restricting foreign sales (Rudd 1993).[14] In the event, the deep discount on the rights issue meant that 87.2 per cent of the 211.6m new ordinary shares offered were taken up by existing shareholders, with the broker underwriting the rest of the issue and offloading the shares at 145 p, mainly to two large institutional investors (Kibazo, Price, and Qureshi 1993). In the process, the proportion of shares that was foreign-owned dropped to 25 per cent (Pain 1993).

In January 1995 Rolls-Royce paid US$525m, equivalent to £328m, to acquire Allison Engine Company, a US military engine supplier that had been founded in 1915 and that from 1929 to 1993 had been a subsidiary of General Motors. Rolls-Royce had made a previous bid for Allison in 1993, but GM had sold the company to a management buyout team for $370m.[15] When Rolls-Royce had announced its plan to buy Allison Engine on 21 November 1994, the news was, according to *Investors Chronicle*, 'welcomed by the City', with Rolls-Royce's share price moving up 2 p to 185 p.[16]

[14] Some foreign investors had already been forced to sell their holdings to comply with the limit. Meanwhile Rolls-Royce lodged a request with the government to raise the limit to 49.5 per cent.

[15] 'Rolls-Royce Buys Allison Engine', *European Information Service*, 5 January 1995; 'Clayton, Dubilier & Rice Completes Sale of Allison Engine Company to Rolls-Royce', *PR Newswire*, 24 March 1995.

[16] 'Popular Shares: R-R Ahead of Allison OK', *Investors Chronicle*, 10 February 1995: 54.

Financial analysts apparently believed the Allison acquisition would be done in Rolls-Royce shares, whose price had risen substantially over the past year and which were listed on the New York Stock Exchange in the form of American Depository Receipts.[17] Allison's current owners were not, however, interested in accepting Rolls-Royce's shares in payment. To finance the acquisition, therefore, in March 1995 Rolls-Royce did a £331m rights issue (net of expenses)—after having raised £307m from shareholders in a rights issue just eighteen months earlier—this time offering one ordinary share at 154p for every 5.4 ordinary shares held on 16 March 1995.

The March 1995 rights issue differed significantly from that of September 1993. Instead of offering new shares directly to existing shareholders, Rolls-Royce, through its sole underwriter N. M. Rothschild & Sons, offered the 227.3 shares to City institutional investors at 154p, which was a discount of just over 5 per cent on the opening price of 164p—and hence less than one-fourth of the discount that the 1993 rights issue had imposed on the company's shares (Rodgers 1995).

Stock as an Acquisition Currency

In late October 1988 Rolls-Royce secretly purchased a 4.7 per cent stake in Northern Engineering Industries (NEI), a power station equipment and heavy engineering group based in Newcastle (Garnet 1988). Rolls-Royce then entered into talks with NEI concerning a friendly bid for the company that would total £360m and be paid mainly in cash, to be covered by Rolls-Royce's cash balances and the proceeds from the Eurobond issue.

Subsequent merger talks between the two companies appeared to have come to an end in late December (Gibben 1988: 19). When the merger was agreed in April 1989, however, no cash was involved. Between the aborted discussions in December and the merger agreement in April, Rolls-Royce's share price rose from 128p to 185p, an increase of 45 per cent, that, compared with the FTSE100, enabled it to outperform the rising stock market by 29 per cent.[18] Instead of cash, seven new Rolls-Royce shares were exchanged for every ten NEI shares, thus valuing NEI at £306 million.[19] In using its shares for the merger, Rolls-Royce was able to maintain control over its cash flow.

The NEI purchase price represented a 23 per cent premium over the price of NEI shares on the date before the disclosure of Rolls-Royce's 4.7 per cent holding in NEI. The new shares issued by Rolls-Royce entailed

---

[17] ADRs track a foreign-based company's share-price movements on its home stock market, but obviate the need for US holders of these securities to assume the exchange-rate risk of holding the actual shares.

[18] 'View from City Road: NEI an "Add-on" for Rolls-Royce', *Independent*, 11 April 1989: 25.

[19] 'Rolls-Royce and NEI to Merge', *PR Newswire European*, 10 April 1989. See also Garnett (1989).

a 16.7 per cent increase in its issued ordinary share capital, thus placing a substantial burden on the NEI acquisition to generate sufficient earnings to maintain existing earnings per share. In 1988 NEI had reported pre-tax profits of £38.5m, equivalent to 22.9 per cent of Rolls-Royce's level of pre-tax profits in that year (Garnett 1989). Thus, the NEI acquisition promised to pay its own way. More importantly, the NEI acquisition started the company on a diversification strategy that, as already described, became focused in the second half of the 1990s around the application of gas turbine technology to energy and marine uses as well as aerospace.

Alongside Rolls-Royce, Vickers was the other major British engineering company to survive the pressures of competition and consolidation over the course of the twentieth century. Indeed the relation between Rolls-Royce and Vickers went back to 1919, when the first non-stop transatlantic flight was made in a Vickers Vimy aircraft powered by Rolls-Royce Eagle engines (Lister 1999). In September 1999, Rolls-Royce announced its proposal to acquire Vickers for £576m in cash—a premium of 53 per cent over Vickers' market capitalization at the time—in order to gain access to its capabilities in marine power systems.[20] As Sir Ralph Robins told reporters: 'Our strategy is to get to No. 1 or 2 in the various markets in which we operate. We are there in aerospace, this will put us there in marine' (Cowell 1999). Vickers shareholders were also given the option of receiving, in lieu of cash, loan notes issued by Rolls-Royce, redeemable at the holder's option in whole or in part at six-monthly intervals directly from Rolls-Royce, but not listed or traded on a stock exchange.[21] With revenues strong in 2000, the company was able to reduce substantially the debt taken on to acquire Vickers.

In 1999 Rolls-Royce made three other acquisitions. To build capabilities in the energy sector, it acquired the rotating compression business of Cooper Cameron, named Cooper Rolls, for £132m in cash. It acquired National Airmotive, a service and repair facility in Oakland California, for £47m in cash. Finally on 31 December 1999 Rolls-Royce purchased the 50.5 per cent shareholding that BMW AG held in BMW Rolls-Royce GmbH for 33.3m shares and the waiver of a £180m loan that BMW owed to Rolls-Royce, for a total acquisition value of £289m. The business was renamed Rolls-Royce Deutschland GmbH (Rolls-Royce Annual Report 1999). It was as a result of this deal that BMW acquired a 10 per cent stake in Rolls-Royce and was, as we have seen, its second largest shareholder as of March 2002.

---

[20] 'Rolls-Royce plc: Proposed Recommended Offer for Vickers plc From Company for £576m', *Global News Wire*, 20 September 1999.
[21] 'Vickers plc—Recommended cash offer—Part 1', *Regulatory News Service*, 20 September 1999.

Stock as a Compensation Currency

After its privatization, Rolls-Royce had two stock-based compensation schemes: (*a*) an Employee Sharesave Plan that, for example in 1995, was available to about 40 per cent of the company's UK employees and 30 per cent of all employees; and (*b*) an Executive Stock Option Plan that covered 46 senior executives in 1987 and 124 in 1999, but was extended to 363 senior executives in 2000 (Rolls-Royce 1988–2001). Under the executive plan, the vesting period was three years with expiration after ten years, and certain company performance criteria had to be met before stock options could be exercised. As stated in the 2000 *Annual Report*:

Depending on performance, executives are eligible to receive options on an annual basis. Options are granted at the mid-market price on the day before the day of issue and normally have to be held for a minimum of three years before they are capable of exercise. They expire after ten years. In line with the [remuneration] committee's view that an increasing proportion of remuneration should be performance related, the exercise of options is subject to a performance condition that the Group's growth in earnings per share (EPS) must exceed the UK retail price index by three percent per annum, over a three-year period. (Rolls-Royce 2000)

The annual reports provide information on the stock option awards to executive directors, including the number of awards in a particular year, exercise prices, and the number of options exercised. From this information it is possible to derive fairly accurate estimates of the extent to which executive directors were able to augment their salaried income (which included bonuses) through the exercise of stock options. For example, Sir Ralph Robins was able to increase his income over the period 1987–2002 by 7.48 per cent through the exercise of stock options, while John Rose increased his income as an executive director (1991–2002) by 3.48 per cent. In fact, most options awarded in the early years expired without being exercised. Nevertheless, at the end of 2002 Robins had over 1m options outstanding and Rose over 2.3m.

Over the period 1987–2002, executive directors received increasingly generous pay even without gains from the exercise of stock options, as Table 11.3 shows. In 1987 the pay of the highest paid Rolls-Royce executive was 9.0 times that of the average pay of all Rolls-Royce employees, while the average pay of all executive directors was 6.1 times that of all employees. By 2002 these figures had risen to 28.9 and 18.2. In addition, in 2001, and in certain cases for 2000, executive directors began receiving quantities of stock option awards that were far in excess of what they had received previously. For example, perhaps as a retirement bonus, Robins received 1,025,618 option awards in 2001, up from 172,674 in 2000 and a previous high of 694,618 in 1995. Rose received 1,680,702 option awards in 2001, up from 408,276 in 2000 and a previous high of 355,392 in 1995 (Rolls-Royce 2000, 2001). In 2002 Rose received 638,298 more options.

TABLE 11.3   *The relative pay of Rolls-Royce executives and Rolls-Royce employees, 1987–2002*

Year	Pay of highest-paid executive to average pay of all employees	Average pay of executive directors to average pay of all employees
1987	9.0	6.1
1988	11.2	6.9
1989	12.5	6.6
1990	14.8	9.5
1991	14.3	7.7
1992	14.4	9.7
1993	14.5	10.6
1994	16.6	11.0
1995	13.3	9.3
1996	14.4	10.7
1997	19.2	12.7
1998	18.5	13.0
1999	18.9	14.9
2000	20.1	13.2
2001	25.0	16.5
2002	28.9	18.2

Source: Rolls-Royce (1987–2002).

Is Rolls-Royce a Success Story?

This case study shows that, despite dramatic changes in the forms of enterprise ownership from the 1960s through the 1990s, Rolls-Royce was able to remain one of the Big Three in the turbofan industry. As a result of continuous investments in the three-shaft RB211 program from the mid-1960s through the 1990s, the company was able to emerge as the industry's technological leader in wide-body engines, notwithstanding the fact that it was Rolls-Royce's initial investments in this program that helped to drive the company into bankruptcy at the beginning of the 1970s. We have argued that the continuity of this development effort can be understood only in terms of the influence of the company's engineers, as strategic decision-makers, over the allocation of the company's resources.

As salaried employees, their own careers depended on the success of the company in developing jet engines. In pursuing this developmental strategy, they made use of government financial support, especially during the period of nationalization, but not at the cost of surrendering their positions of strategic control. Subsequent to the company's 1987 privatization, Rolls-Royce's executives have made astute use of financial markets to fund acquisitions and further technological development while avoiding both loss of strategic control and the threat of bankruptcy. Indeed, it would appear that the career advancement of the current CEO, John Rose, who joined Rolls-Royce in 1984 at the age of thirty-two with a background in finance, was bound up with the successful financial engineering of the 1990s, and in particular the two rights issues of 1993 and 1995. Fundamentally, however, the success of the company over the last decade and a half derives from the sustained development of the RB211, a process that was begun in the second half of the 1960s and continued through the end of the century.

While Rolls-Royce is an exceptional case in the British context, from a comparative-historical perspective on the role of salaried managers in exercising strategic control over corporate resource allocation in high fixed-cost, knowledge-intensive industries, Rolls-Royce's history is by no means unique (see Chandler, Amatori, and Hikino 1997). It is career managers, not public shareholders or government bureaucrats, who have the understanding of the technologies, markets, and competitors in a complex-product industry required to make strategic allocation decisions that stand any chance of generating successful outcomes. At the outset, investments in innovation in such industries are inherently uncertain. The role of strategic managers is not only to make investments in the face of uncertainty but also to immerse themselves in an ongoing learning process about developing technologies, accessing markets, and confronting competitors that can transform uncertainty into economic success.

As outsiders to the industrial corporation, public shareholders are ill-positioned to be involved in these strategic decision-making processes and, indeed, if they were obliged to be so involved they would probably rather sell their shares. In this regard, Rolls-Royce's shareholders, both before the bankruptcy and after privatization, were no exception. The question for them has always been when, not whether, to buy and sell 'ownership' stakes in the company, and in this activity different shareholders of the same company often take very different actions. Bowden (2002: 44), for example, shows that from 1968 to 1969, as Rolls-Royce's seemingly strong financial condition eroded, four major institutional shareholders (including the largest, Prudential Insurance, with holdings in 1968 that were greater than those of the next seven largest shareholders combined) sold their entire holdings while ten others increased the size of their holdings, in many cases substantially. Bowden (2002: 49–51) also recounts how, as Rolls-Royce's financial difficulties deepened in 1970, it was the banks, not the shareholders, who became involved in the affairs of the company.

Since privatization, as we have seen, shareholding in Rolls-Royce has become increasingly concentrated in the hands of large institutional investors. What have they gained? From 1988 through 2002, the average real dividend yield on Rolls-Royce's shares was minus 1.3 per cent, ranging from minus 6.6 per cent in 1990 to plus 2.0 per cent in 2001. In 2001–2 dividends per share were 64 per cent higher than they were in 1992–5. But, with the company's dismal stock-price performance since 1997, the real annual total yield (dividend yield plus price yield adjusted for inflation) on Rolls-Royce's stock has averaged minus 13.2 per cent for 1997–2002 compared with an average of 6.8 per cent for 1988–96. For 1988–2002, the average annual real total yield on Rolls-Royce's shares was minus 3.2 per cent. Whatever else it has been doing since privatization, the company clearly has not been creating value for shareholders. Particularly for the most recent period, therefore, a proponent of agency theory might argue that in fact Rolls-Royce's competitive success—it raised its market share of the civil engine market from 8 per cent in 1987 to about 30 per cent in 2002—represents a case of entrenched management squandering resources that could have been used more productively elsewhere in the economy.

The problem with such a view is that, whatever its stock-market performance, Rolls-Royce is a company that, because of sustained investment in its productive resources, has a technological capability that took decades to develop and that no other company in the world can replicate. The company has been persistently profitable with underlying real earnings per share being somewhat higher in 1997–2002 (when stock-price performance was poor) than in 1988–96. The company provides productive employment to over 39,000 people, of whom the 24,000 in Britain would have by no means been certain of finding another employer in the UK that could have provided them with equivalent career opportunities. The average real annual earnings of these employees were over 50 per cent higher in 2000–2 than they were in 1990–2. While beyond the scope of this chapter, the development of Rolls-Royce's capability clearly has had 'spillover' effects that, especially through their effects on resources available in the British university system, have been beneficial to the training of engineers outside the Rolls-Royce as well as to the technological capabilities of other engineering companies. It may well be that, in the future, Rolls-Royce's top management may become more concerned with their own emoluments (as the British say) than with generating returns on the company's human and physical resources—and in this respect the tripling of average executive director pay in relation to average employee pay from 1987 to 2002 may be a cause for concern. But there is little doubt that over the past several decades the entrenched control of Rolls-Royce's managers over the strategic allocation of the company's resources has resulted in the creation of valuable and unique productive capabilities that certainly the British economy would not otherwise have possessed.

References

Bowden, S. (2002). 'Ownership Responsibilities and corporate Governance: The Crisis at Rolls-Royce, 1968–71', *Business History*, 44/3: 31–62.

Carpenter, M., Lazonick, W., and O'Sullivan, M. (2003). 'The Stock Market and Innovative Capability in the New Economy: The Optical Networking Industry', *Industrial and Corporate Change*, 12: 963–1034.

Chandler, A., Amatori, F., and Hikino, T. (eds.) (1997). *Big Business and the Wealth of Nations*. Cambridge: Cambridge University Press.

Cowell, A. (1999). 'Rolls-Royce to buy Vickers for $933 million', *New York Times*, 21 September.

Cownie, J. (1989). 'Success Through Perseverance: the Rolls-Royce RB211 Engine', *The Putnam Aeronautical Review*, 4: 230–8.

Crooks, E. (1990). 'Aero-Engines: Rolls revs up for new aero-engine battle', *Investors Chronicle*, 24 August.

Donne, M. and Cassell, M. (1986). 'Rolls-Royce Wins Engine Order for 16 BA Jumbo Jets', *Financial Times*, 16 April: 1.

DTI (Department of Trade and Industry) (1972). 'Rolls-Royce Ltd and the RB211 Aero-Engine', statement presented to Parliament by the Secretary of Sate for Trade and Industry by Command of Her Majesty, January.

Garnet, N. (1988). 'Rolls-Royce Takes 4.7 percent of Northern Engineering', *Financial Times*, 1 November: 33.

—— (1989). 'Rolls-Royce to But NEI in Deal Worth £300 Million', *Financial Times*, 11 April 1989: 1.

Gibben, R. (1988). 'Rolls and NEI End Talks', *Daily Telegraph*, 22 December.

Gray, R. (1971). *Rolls on the Rocks: The Story of Rolls-Royce*. Salisbury: Compton Press.

Gunston, B. (1997). *The Development of Jet and Turbine Aero Engines* (2nd edn.). Sparkford: Patrick Stephens Limited.

Harker, R. (1976). *Rolls-Royce: From the Wings 1925–1971 Military Aviation*. Oxford: Oxford Illustrated.

Hayward, K. (1989). *The British Aircraft Industry*. Manchester: Manchester University Press.

Hooker, Sir Stanley (1984). *Not Much of an Engineer*. Marlborough: The Crowood Press.

Ingrassia, L. (1984). 'Rolls-Royce Ltd. Expects to narrow its loss this year', *Wall Street Journal*, 27 August.

Kibazo, J., Price, C., and Qureshi, S. (1993). 'London Stock Exchange: Rolls-Royce Rises', *Financial Times*, 30 September: 50.

Lambert, R. and Makinson, J. (1984). 'Rolls Faces Up To Reality', *Financial Times*, 4 February: 16.

Lazonick, W. (2002). 'The Theory of Innovative Enterprise', in M. Warner (ed.), *International Encyclopedia of Business and Management*. London: Thomson Learning.

—— and O'Sullivan, M. (2000). *Perspectives on Corporate Governance, Innovation, and Economic Performance*. Report to the European Commission (DGXII) under the TSER Programme, www.insead.edu/cgep

———— (2002). *Corporate Governance, Innovation, and Economic Performance in the EU: Project Policy Report*. Report to the European Commission (DGXII) under the TSER Programme, www.insead.edu/cgep

Lister, D. (1999). 'Vickers Consigned to History As Rolls Rides to the Rescue', *The Times*, 21 September.

Lorenz, A. (1990). 'Rolls Turns on Maximum Power', *Sunday Times*, 15 July.

O'Sullivan, M. (2000). 'The Innovative Enterprise and Corporate Governance', *Cambridge Journal of Economics*, 24: 393–416.

Pain, D. (1993). 'Market Report: Rolls Aero Shares Fly High as Horizon Brightens', *Independent*, 13 November: 22.

Pugh, P. (2001). *The Magic of a Name: The Rolls-Royce Story, Part Two: The Power Behind the Jets, 1945–1987*. Cambridge, UK: Icon Books.

Reed, A. (1973). *Britain's Aircraft Industry: What went right? What went wrong?*. London: J. M. Dent & Sons.

Rodgers, P. (1995). 'Rolls Placing Raises £330m', *Independent*, 25 March: 17.

Rolls-Royce (1988-2002). *Annual Reports*. London: Rolls-Royce.

Rudd, R. (1993). 'Rolls-Royce Issues £307m Cash Call', *Financial Times*, 3 September: 17.

Ruffles, P. (1992). 'The RB211: The First 25 Years', 31st Short Brothers Commemoratives Lecture. London, Royal Academy of Engineering, February.

Skapinker, M. (1999). 'Flag-carrier's restorer: Profile of Sir Ralph Robins, Rolls-Royce', *Financial Times*, 13 September: 19.

Tieman, R. (1993). 'Rolls-Royce Asks Investors for Mid-Flight Refuelling', *The Times*, 3 September.

Verchère, I. (1992). 'Rolls-Royce Runs Leaner and Meaner', *Interavia Aerospace Review*, January: 33–7.

PART III

Explaining Difference and Change in Corporate Governance Systems: Beyond the Convergence/Divergence Dilemma

12

Explaining Western Securities Markets

MARK J. ROE

Introduction

How important is corporate law—and its capacity to protect minority stockholders from insider machinations—in building securities markets and separating ownership from corporate control? Quite important, according to most recent analyses, and maybe central. Without strong corporate law protections, securities markets, it is said, will not arise. And if corporate law is good enough in technologically advanced nations, ownership will be diffused away from concentrated ownership into dispersed stock markets.

This new perspective contributes to understanding the fragility of capital markets in transition and Third-World economies, chiefly where even basic contract and property rights are weak. But it has been used—and I argue here it has been overused—to explain primarily the persistence of dominant stockholders and fragile securities markets in many of the world's richest nations in Europe and Asia. I say 'overused' because there is too much that is critical to ownership separation that corporate law *does not even seek to reach* in the world's richest, most advanced nations.

Two conceptual problems afflict the idea that corporate law is primary. Each is sufficient to render the corporate law argument, while still relevant, secondary, not primary.

First, current academic thinking lumps together costly opportunism due to a controller's self-dealing and costly decision-making that inflicts losses on the owners. The former—self-dealing—corporate law seeks to control directly. The latter—bad decision-making that damages shareholders—it does not. Other institutions control the latter, and their strength varies from firm to firm and from nation to nation. Yet owners tend to stay as block-holders—and ownership does not become diffuse, and securities markets remain weak—if stockholders expect that managerial agency costs to shareholders would be very high if ownership were fully separated.

Second, the focus on legal families is probably over-sold. Civil law systems are said to over-regulate, while common law systems, operating through

I make arguments similar to some of those I make here in Roe (2002; 2003*b*). Thanks for comments on the draft of this chapter go to Margaret Blair and Anna Grandori.

wise judges, do not. The theoretical difficulty with this perspective is that American regulatory agencies (such as the Securities and Exchange Commission) arose because common law institutions were thought to insufficiently regulate securities markets.

To recast our angle of vision from a national overview of the system to a micro-perspective, if ownership did not separate from control in a nation (or a firm), we cannot know whether separation was aborted because block-holder rampages are uncontrolled or because *managerial agency costs* would be far too high if ownership were separated. *Either* could have prevented separation. Or one alone could have, with the other not standing in the way. And the first is closely and directly affected by corporate law; the second is not.

Managerial agency costs come in two 'flavors', only one of which corporate law tightly controls. One flavor—machinations that transfer value to the controllers and managers, or 'stealing'—corporate law seeks to control. But the other—'shirking', or pursuing goals other than shareholder value—corporate law largely leaves alone. If underlying economic, social, or political conditions make managerial agency costs very high, and if those costs are best contained by a controlling shareholder, *then concentrated ownership persists whatever the state of corporate law in checking block-holder misdeeds.*

I speculate on what underlying economic, political, and social conditions could make managerial agency costs persistently high. I also speculate on how a shrinking of these agency costs, plausibly now going on in continental Europe, could raise the demand to build legal institutions that facilitate separation. First, for ownership to be separated in the modern economy, distant shareholders seem to need, or at least do better if they have, some pro-stockholder institutions, such as a few of transparent securities markets, aligning compensation systems, intermittent takeovers or other means to control managers, and shareholder primacy norms. (Enron and WorldCom failures show us how fragile these can be even in a nation, like the United States, that favors such institutions.) But some polities, unlike America's, have been hostile to pro-shareholder institutions and don't support them.

Second, some polities further open up the gap between managers and shareholders by encouraging managers to expand, to go slow in down-sizing, to give employees more rights against firms that can be best mitigated for shareholders via concentrated ownership, and so on. When those pressures are strong, dominant stockholders stay in place to resist them. Some nations have pursued a vision of what makes for a just society in ways different from how they have been pursued in the United States. And, hence, it's no surprise that their corporate systems differ.

Third, in corporatist polities, owners and stakeholders have protected themselves by being concentrated enough to be national political players, because that's where the economic pie is divided up (Faccio 2002; Roe 2000).

Some of these pressures are in flux today, but their historical reality is quite concrete. The relationships fit some types of industrial production, especially where soft commitments and close working relationships between owners and workers are critical.

* * *

High-quality, protective corporate law is a good institution for a society to have. It lowers the costs of building strong, large business enterprises. It can prevent or minimize diversions engineered by dominant stockholders, and some institution that minimizes these is a necessary condition for separation to stay stable. It, or a substitute such as reputational intermediaries (DeLong 1991; Miwa and Ramseyer 2000) or stock exchange rules (Mahoney 1997; Roe 2000; Coffee 2001), lowers the cost of ownership separation and seems to precede, or shortly follow after, ownership separation. But, among the world's wealthier nations, corporate law does not primarily determine whether it is worthwhile to build those enterprises and their supporting institutions. It is only a tool, not the foundation. With labor and political institutions in mind, we can better explain why some nations have deep separation and strong stock markets while others, about equally wealthy, do not.

The Argument: Corporate Law as Propelling Diffuse Ownership

Today's dominant academic and policy explanation of why continental Europe lacks deep and rich securities markets is the purportedly weak role of corporate and securities law in protecting minority stockholders, a weakness that is said to contrast with America's strong protections of minority stockholders. A major European-wide research network, leading financial economists, and increasingly legal commentators have stated so (La Porta *et al.* 1998: 1136–7; Bebchuk 1999; Coffee 1999; Becht and Röell 1999).

Leading economists showed that deep securities markets correlate with an index of basic shareholder legal protections. And 'protection of shareholders ... by the legal system *is central* to understanding the patterns of corporate finance in different countries. Investor protection [is] *crucial* because, in many countries, expropriation of minority shareholders ... by the controlling shareholders is extensive' (La Porta *et al.* 2000: 4, emphasis added). According to Modigliani and Perotti (1998: 5), nations with deficient legal regimes cannot get good stock markets and, hence, 'the provision of funding shifts from dispersed risk capital [via the stock market] ... to debt, and from [stock and bond] markets to institutions, i.e., towards intermediated credit'. And legal origin (civil law vs. common law) is said to load the dice in the results.

While the academics are developing a theory and gathering data, international agencies such as the IMF and the World Bank have admirably promoted corporate law reform, especially that which would protect minority stockholders (Iskander *et al.* 1999). The OECD and the World Bank have had major initiatives to improve corporate governance, both in the developing and the developed world (OECD 1999; Nestor 2000; Witherell 2000).

These efforts by the international agencies are valuable at some level. They could well contribute to reaching their goals of more stable enterprises and better economic performance, especially in transition nations. But corporate law, and the reach of government policy-makers through corporate law reform, has limits. And those limits are much closer than the policy-makers and academic theory now discern. Here I demarcate those limits in the world's richest nations beyond which corporate law ceases to be primary. If the limits are close, and the cost of constructing corporate law high, then other development strategies may be seen as even more valuable.[1]

Protecting Minority Stockholders

The basic law-driven story is straightforward. Imagine a nation whose law badly protects minority stockholders against a block-holder extracting value from small minority stockholders. A potential buyer fears that the majority stockholder would later shift value to itself, away from the buyer. So fearing, the prospective minority stockholder does not pay pro rata value for the stock. If the discount is deep enough and cannot be accurately priced (or if the transfer diminishes firm value), then the majority stockholder decides not to sell, concentrated ownership persists, and stock markets do not develop.

To approach the problem from the owner's perspective, posit large private benefits of control. The most obvious benefits that law can affect are those that the controller can derive from diverting value from the firm to himself. The owner might own 51 per cent of the firm's stock but retain 75 per cent of the firm's value if the owner can over-pay himself in salary, pad the company's payroll with no-show relatives, use the firm's funds to pay private expenses, or divert value by having the 51 per cent-controlled firm

---

[1] I do not address here *how* valuable those corporate law initiatives are. That is, if the advantages of securities markets can be cheaply achieved through other means, then those substitutes might make securities markets development of secondary importance to general economic development. It is plausible that well-developed securities markets *reflect* economic development and only secondarily help induce it. The development agencies are pursuing securities market development as, one assumes, a means to general economic development, in the belief that it is a strong cause, not a minor reflection. But if it is a reflection, then the agencies' efforts might go better into building the underlying foundations. (And the effort here in this chapter becomes one of explaining why we see, or don't see, strong securities markets, not in planning how to get them.)

overpay for goods and services obtained from a company totally owned by the controller. Strong fiduciary duties, strong doctrines attacking unfair interested-party transactions, effective disclosure laws that unveil these transactions, and a capable judiciary or other enforcement institution can reduce these kinds of private benefits of control.[2] The owner considers whether to sell to diffuse stockholders. With no controller to divert value, the stock price could reflect the firm's underlying value. But the rational buyers believe, so the theory runs, that the diffuse ownership structure would be unstable, that an outside raider would buy up 51 per cent of the firm and divert value, and that the remaining minority stockholders would be hurt. Hence, they would not pay full pro rata value to the owner wishing to sell; and the owner wishing to sell would find that the sales price to be less than the value of the block if retained (or if sold intact) (La Porta *et al.* 1997, 1998; Bebchuk 1999; Modigliani and Perotti 1997, 1998).

Hence, the block persists. The controller refuses to leave control 'up for grabs' because, if it dips below 51 per cent control, an outsider could grab control and reap the private benefits.

The Attractions of a Technical Corporate Law Theory

The quality-of-corporate-law argument is appealing. Technical institutions are to blame, for example, for Russia's and the transition nations' economic problems. The fixes, if technical, are within our grasp. Humans can shape the results. Progress is possible, one could believe, if we just can get the technical institutions right. And, one might further believe, if we make these technical fixes, economic development will follow. And, as a descriptive matter, if we don't see ownership separation in Germany, France, and Scandinavia, it must be because a technical fix is missing, one we can provide as easily as downloading a computer program across the Atlantic Ocean. But if it turns out that deeper features of society—industrial organization and competition, politics, conditions of social regularity, or norms that support shareholder value—are more fundamental to inducing securities markets, we would feel ill at ease because these institutions are much harder for policy-makers to control.[3] These institutions might change over time (and seem to have been changing in Europe), but they are not in the hands of a technocrat drafting corporate law reform.

---

[2] Private benefits also arise from pride in running and controlling one's own, or one's family's, enterprise. On this, corporate law has little direct impact.

[3] To be clear, I am not speaking simply of corporate law but also of securities law, and of the quality of regulators and judges, of the efficiency, accuracy, and honesty of the regulators and the judiciary, of the capacity of the stock exchanges to stymie the most egregious diversions, and so on. Cf. Black (2000).

As self-contained academic theory, there is little to quarrel with in the quality-of-corporate-law argument. It is sparse and appealing. Good corporate law lowers the costs of operating a large firm; it is good for a nation to have it because it seems to cost so little. But we need *more* to understand why ownership is not separate from control *even where core corporate law is good enough*. Where managerial agency costs due to potential dissipation are substantial, concentrated ownership persists *even if conventional corporate law quality is high*.

Given the facts that we shall develop in the third section—there are too many wealthy, high quality corporate law countries *without* much separation—the quality-of-corporate-law theory needs to be further refined or replaced. This we do next in the second section of the chapter.

Corporate Law's Limits

How Managerial Agency Costs Impede Separation

Managers would run some firms badly if ownership were separated from control. Effective corporate laws constrain managers' *overreaching* but do much less to directly make them operate their firms well. A related-party transaction can be attacked or prevented where corporate law is good; judges examine these transactions and remedy them. But judges leave unprofitable transactions untouched, with managers—when untainted by self-dealing—able to invoke corporate law's business judgment rule to deflect direct legal scrutiny.

Consider a society (or a firm) in which managerial agency costs from dissipating shareholder value would be high if ownership were separated but low if it were not, because a controlling shareholder can contain those costs. When high but containable by concentration, concentrated shareholding ought to persist *even if corporate law fully protects minority stockholders from insiders' overreaching*. Block-holders would weigh their costs in maintaining control (in lost liquidity and diversification) against what they would lose if managerial agency costs were high. Control would persist even if corporate law were good.[4]

This is a basic but important point, and it is needed to explain the data that we look at in the next section.

Improving Corporate Law Without Increasing Separation

The basic but often missed argument in the prior section—that variance in managerial agency costs can drive ownership structure, and that managerial agency costs can vary greatly *even if conventional corporate law is quite good*—can

---

[4] This section and its brief model draw on Roe (2002).

be stated formally in a simple model. High managerial agency costs can preclude separation *even if there is high-quality conventional corporate law.*
Let:

A_M = the managerial agency costs to shareholders from managers' dissipating shareholder value, to the extent avoidable via concentrated ownership.

C_{CS} = the costs to the concentrated shareholder in holding a block and monitoring (that is, the costs in lost liquidity, lost diversification, expended energy, and, perhaps, error).

When A_M is high, ownership concentration persists whether or not law successfully controls the private benefits that a controlling shareholder can siphon off from the firm. Further, let

V = value of the firm when ownership is concentrated.

B_{CS} = the private benefits of control, containable by corporate law.

Consider the firm worth V when ownership is concentrated. Posit first that managerial agency costs are trivial even if the firm is fully public. As such, the private benefits of control, a characteristic legally malleable and reducible with protective corporate law, can determine whether ownership separates from control. Consider the controller who owns 50 per cent of the firm's stock. As such she obtains one-half of V plus her net benefits of control. (In this simple first model, the value of the firm remains unchanged whether it has a controlling stockholder or is fully public.) She retains control when the following inequality is true:

$$V/2 + B_{CS} - C_{CS} > V/2. \tag{1}$$

The left side is the value to the controlling stockholder of the control block: half the firm's cash flow plus the private benefits diverted from minority stockholders minus the costs of maintaining the block (in lost diversification and liquidity). The right side is the value she obtains from selling the block to the public. Equation (1) states that, as long as the private benefits of control exceed the costs of control, then concentrated ownership persists. Because corporate law can dramatically shrink the private benefits, B_{CS}, corporate law matters quite a bit in equation (1). This is the current theory[5] that we next amend.

We amend by introducing A_M, managerial agency costs from dissipating shareholder value in ways that a controlling shareholder would avoid. If those managerial agency costs are non-trivial, then the controller's proceeds from selling into the stock market would be $(V - A_M)/2$. Concentration

---

[5] See Bebchuk (1999), who models the problem; see also Coffee (2001); La Porta, Lopez-de-Silanes, and Shleifer (1999); La Porta *et al.* (1997; 1998).

persists if and only if

$$V/2 + B_{CS} - C_{CS} > (V - A_M)/2. \tag{2}$$

To rearrange: concentration persists if the net benefits of control $(B_{CS} - C_{CS})$ are more than the controller's costs of diffusion $(A_M/2)$:

$$B_{CS} - C_{CS} > -A_M/2. \tag{3}$$

Or, further re-arranging, concentration persists if:

$$B_{CS} + A_M/2 > C_{CS}. \tag{4}$$

Quality-of-corporate-law theory predicts that diffusion fails to occur when $B_{CS} > C_{CS}$, with corporate law the means of containing B_{CS}. That is correct but incomplete. Where A_M is high, diffusion does not occur *even if B_{CS} is zero and corporate law perfect, because A_M could take over and drive the separation decision.* B_{CS}, the controlling shareholder's private benefits, are relatively unimportant if A_M is very high. Only when $A_M \to 0$ do legally malleable private benefits determine diffusion.[6]

These simple relations adapt to much complexity here. For instance, if the controller can no longer manage well then the sign on agency costs, A_M, changes. Similarly, the relationships can absorb uncertainty. That is, most business decisions are made under uncertainty. The billion-dollar factory that turns out to have been a bad investment is not, if the decision to build was made by agents, necessarily an agency cost. Mistakes are not necessarily agency costs. Rather, if the agent was more likely than a sole owner to overestimate the probabilities of success (because the agent benefited even from moderately unprofitable expansion), then this 'extra' portion of mis-estimate (the *increased* probability of taking on the project, the increased investment in the project once started, and so on) becomes the agency cost that (astute) close ownership would reduce. According to Levinthal (1988: 182), 'It is not the industriousness of top management that is the issue, but the qualitative nature of the decisions they make.'

Corporate Law's Limited Capacity to Reduce Agency Costs

One might reply that core corporate law when improved reduces *both* the controlling stockholder's private benefits (B_{CS}, by reducing the controller's capacity to siphon off value) *and* managerial agency costs (A_M, by reducing

---

[6] The best-developed model of the corporate law problem begins by assuming a population of firms that is more valuable when diffusely owned than when privately-owned (see Bebchuk 1999). As such, its author does not have to address managerial agency costs, since these are assumed away as central for the population under discussion. But it is here where the critical calculus can occur whether firms go public. (Not all other analyses of the relationship between corporate law and ownership diffusion confine their inquiry so adroitly.)

the managers' capacity to siphon off benefits for themselves). And it does so, one might mistakenly then argue, about equally.

1. The Business Judgment Rule. This criticism, however, fails to reflect what American corporate law really does. Managerial agency costs are the sum of managers' overreaching (unjustifiably high salaries, self-dealing transactions, and so on) *and* their mismanagement (that is, the part of their mismanagement that a stronger owner would avoid). Economic analyses typically lump these two together and call them 'agency costs'. But agency costs come from stealing *and* from shirking. It is correct to lump them together in economic analyses *as a cost to shareholders* because both costs are visited upon shareholders. For example, Fama (1980) notes that agency costs come from 'shirking, perquisites or incompetence'. But it is incorrect to think that *law* (especially American corporate law) minimizes each cost to shareholders equally well.

The standard that corporate law applies to managerial decisions is, realistically, no liability at all for mistakes, absent fraud, or conflict of interest (Dooley and Veasey 1989: 521; Bishop 1968; 1095). *But this is where the big costs to shareholders of having managerial agents lie, exactly where law falls silent.*

Conventional corporate law—the law of corporate fiduciary duties, which common law is said to be particular adept at—does little or nothing to directly reduce shirking, mistakes, and bad business decisions that squander shareholder value. The business judgment rule is, absent fraud or conflict of interest, nearly insurmountable in America. It insulates directors and managers from the judge, removing them from legal scrutiny. Most American analysts think that one wouldn't want the judge second-guessing managers on a regular basis.

2. Controlling Shareholders. One might refine this analysis by accounting for controlling shareholder error. But the costs of these errors are usually thought to be smaller than legally uncontrollable managerial error. True, similar legal doctrines (the business judgment rule) shield the controlling shareholder from lawsuits for a non-conflicted mistake. But, because the controlling stockholder owns a big block of the company's stock, it internalizes much of the cost of any mistake (unlike the unconstrained managers). A controller has some incentive to turn the firm over to professional managers if he realizes they would make the firm more profitable. (And, as I mentioned, in those settings where the controller would overall be worse than unconstrained managers, we then should get diffusion. A_M's sign flips.)

Even if Law Critically Affects Both

Still, one might reject the proposition that law is secondary in inducing good management for shareholders. Law affects those other institutions that indirectly control managerial agency costs (competition, compensation, takeovers, transparency, and so on), and one might believe *these* laws to be central to whether public firms can arise and whether ownership can be separated from control.

But, even so, the structure of my argument—of *corporate* law's limits—persists. The institutions and law that affect managerial agency costs of running the firm differ from the institutions and laws that affect insider machinations. The two sets are *not* identical. If one society does better with one set than with the other, then the degree of diffusion should be deeply affected. Corporate law might minimize insider transactions in both nations, but the other laws in one might fail to reduce managerial agency costs from running the firm, or even increase them.

That is, assume arguendo that corporate law, broadly defined, can, if 'unleashed', affect both private benefits and managerial agency costs. But, if other institutions *also* affect managerial agency costs, then corporate law could be perfect but these *other* institutions would determine the degree of ownership separation through their effect on managerial agency costs from running the firm. These other institutions might vary across nations and systematically determine, or affect, the degree of ownership separation across nations.

The Difficulty of Seeing Legal Origins as Causal

Moreover, a theory based primarily on legal origins is weakened by the means of regulation in the United States. America uses a regulatory agency, the Security and Exchange Commission (SEC), as the primary regulator of stock markets. This agency, though, is not a common law mechanism. As such, it is unclear where the *legal* advantage, if it has any, arose for the United States as compared with continental European civil law nations. Perhaps civil law nations have to regulate less than they usually might, so as to be effective in securities market. But common law has to regulate more. (And the impression one has is that civil law nations actually regulate securities markets *less* than their emblematic level.) Civil law nations may simply have decided for reasons exogenous to the legal system—more about that in the next subsection—*not* to regulate securities markets, because for some reason—say, political—making good security markets was not a national priority.

The Tight Limits to the Purely Legal Theory

Thus, the basic theory I propose here is that, first, if one observes persistent block-holding, one cannot a priori know whether the blocks persist because minority stockholders fear the controller or because they fear the *managers*, who might dissipate shareholder value if the controlling stockholder disappears. Even if better corporate law usually increases diffusion in rich nations with adequate but not outstanding corporate law (a proposition open to theoretical challenge, see Roe 2003*a*: 181[7]), concentration might be due to high managerial agency costs in running the firm and have little to do with core corporate law's constraints on insider machinations.

If distant shareholders fear unrestrained managers, the controller cannot sell stock at a high enough price and thus she keeps control to monitor managers or to run the firm.

Second, stock markets are regulated, not left to the unadorned common law. This is so even in common law nations. Indeed, common law nations may regulate stock markets more than civil law nations do. As such, a theory based on legal origins—that civil law regulates, while common law judges—is not prima facie convincing. Even today, when corporate structures go awry—think of Enron—and fiduciary duties fail, the systemic reaction, even in a common law nation like the US, is to regulate—think of Sarbanes-Oxley of 2002—*not* to rely primarily on judge-made common law fiduciary duties.

Data: Political Variables as the Strongest Predictor of Ownership Separation

If a society's institutions do not promote shareholder value, or if a society adds institutions that raise managerial agency costs (because it wants managers loyal to a wider spectrum of interests than elsewhere), then ownership separation ought to be narrower than elsewhere.

Politics Can Increase Managerial Agency Costs

In nations where labor institutions—whether via social democracy or corporatist power-sharing or other cooperative arrangements—are strong, one would expect managerial agency costs to shareholders to often be higher in firms that had ownership and control divided than in nations where such labor institutions were weaker.

Two channels would be in play, one through the firm and the other through institution-building: First, through the firm, the polity would tend to promote non-profit-maximizing expansion (and make it even harder to contract when firms' capabilities are misaligned with markets). And there would be more bargaining over the surplus, with some of that bargaining at the national political level and some inside the firm. Concentrated owners could often bargain better in such polities. Second, nations in which labor or the left held significant political power could be unwilling to build the institutions that facilitate distant shareholding, such as building good securities regulation, promoting profit-building institutions, facilitating shareholder

---

[7] The idea is that when corporate law is 'passable'—neither excellent nor atrocious—then improving it could make distant shareholders *more* comfortable with a controller, and therefore *more* willing to buy minority stock. See also Roe (2000; 2002).

control over (or influence on) managers, and enhancing shareholder primacy norms that induce managers to align themselves with stockholders, even those stockholders that cannot control the managers day-to-day.

If this is right, and one or both of these channels is strong, then one could hypothesize a basic model with testable implications. Greater labor protection should predict weaker ownership separation. Consider the results in Table 12.1 and Fig. 12.1 from OECD data indexing the level of job protection in the OECD.

With a small sample like, this multiple controls are hard, and the small 'n' makes the econometric behavior here tricky. But consider the results in Table 12.2 when we control for two measures of corporate law, one the well-known La Porta *et al.* (1998) index and a less well-known measure of the control premium in the world's richer nations from Dyck and Zingales (2002). Each legal measure standing alone predicts separation. But look at what happens when we combine the legal measures with the political one.

The bottom-line: employment protection *strongly dominates the two measures of corporate law.*[8] Roughly, these results suggest that controlling insider

TABLE 12.1 *Employment protection and ownership separation*

Country	Employment protection	Widely-held at 20% for medium-sized corporations (med 20)
Australia	4	0.30
Austria	16	0.00
Belgium	17	0.20
Canada	3	0.60
Denmark	5	0.30
Finland	10	0.20
France	14	0.00
Germany	15	0.10
Italy	21	0.00
Japan	8	0.30
Netherlands	9	0.10
Norway	11	0.20
Sweden	13	0.10
Switzerland	6	0.50
United Kingdom	7	0.60
United States	1	0.90

Note: Employment protection measures how strongly a nation's law protects employees from being fired. (It is an inverse, relative measurement: a value of 1 means the employees are relatively unprotected; 17 means that they are well protected.) It aggregates specific employment rules in each nation in the OECD (OECD 1994). Widely-held at 20% measures the dispersion of stock in public companies. It is a nation-by-nation index, compiled by La Porta, Lopez-de-Silanes, and Shleifer (1999), of the portion of companies that are widely-held in a slice of mid-sized firms in each nation. A company was classified as not being wide-held if it has a stockholder owning 20% or more of the firm's stock.

[8] Indeed, it is robust even to "throwing" both legal indicators at it, as a commentator suggested.

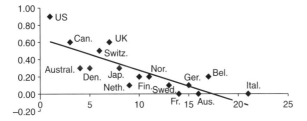

Technical data: Separation (med 20) v. employment protection

Regression	S = −0.04EmpPro + 0.65
Adj R-Sq	0.64
t-stat	−5.24***

FIGURE 12.1 *Employment protection as predicting mid-sized firms' separation.*
*** Significant at the 0.0005 level.
Source: The x-axis is an index of employment protection compiled by the OECD (1994); the y-axis is an index of ownership concentration in mid-sized public companies, compiled by La Porta, Lopez-de-Silanes, and Shleifer (1999). The data for both items are arrayed in Table 12.1.

TABLE 12.2 *Employment protection vs. corporate law in predicting separation*

	Dependent variable: ownership separation in mid-cap companies				
Corp. law: La Porta	0.14 (3.69***)			−0.03 (−0.57)	
Corp. law: control premium		−1.07 (−1.94*)			0.43 (0.87)
Employment protection			**−0.04** **(−5.24***)**	**−0.03** **(−2.62**)**	**−0.05** **(−4.39***)**
R^2	0.53	0.18	0.64	0.71	0.72

Note: This table shows how well two determinants of ownership separation predict the dispersion results in Table 12.1. The dependent variable is the degree of ownership dispersion in the mid-cap companies in each nation, as listed in Table 12.1. The independent variables are employment protection and the quality of corporate law.

   The third data column shows the labor index of employment protection (from Table 12.1) nicely predicting ownership dispersion. The labor predictor is robust to two measures of corporate law quality, one from La Porta, Lopez-de-Silanes, and Shleifer (1999: 492) and the other from Dyck and Zingales (2002). The first index of corporate law quality, from La Porta, indexes corporate law features that are thought to protect outside shareholders from insider over-reaching; the second measures the premium paid for a control block above the trading value of minority stock. (A high premium suggests small shareholders are poorly protected; a low premium, well-protected.) The two indices of corporate law quality predict ownership separation in these rich nations, but they are not robust to adding the employment protection index. The latter strongly dominates corporate law in predicting the degree of ownership separation in the OECD, as is indicated in the third, bold-faced, row.

overreaching—the type of costs of public firms that law can reach—gets us at most (only) half-way to making public firms viable. If the political environment impedes manager-shareholder alliances, the second type of agency costs to shareholders would rise, and ownership could not easily be separated from control, *even if controller machinations are contained*. In fact, in most of these 'models' law doesn't significantly increase the predictive power of left-right politics alone.[9]

Do Block-holders Increase or Decrease Value?

A pure law-driven theory would predict that increasing block-holding would decrease the value of minority shares. A pure managerial agency cost theory would predict the opposite. An integrative theory would look for both.

But bigger block-holders in many countries *increase* the value of minority stockholders' shares (Roe 2003*b*). This is not a relationship consistent with the legal theory. But it is one consistent with a managerial agency cost theory, that block-holders restrain managerial agency costs. And it is a result that fits with the political theory I have advanced, because for these countries in particular political and employment pressures are strong, and it is plausible that dominant stockholders are able to create more value for shareholders than do managers acting alone.[10] Overall, there are mixed results, some studies finding block-holders demeaning minority shareholder value, some showing them enhancing it, others showing offsetting effects. These overall results suggest that the legal theory again is insufficient in explaining the strength of ownership separation. Both effects—diversionary and agency cost—seem to be in play.

---

[9] See Roe (2003*a*). Surely the correlation here does not prove the theory. And, even if the basic theory—a relationship between labor and ownership concentration—is right, other channels linking the two are possible. Visible ownership concentration might have provoked labor protection. Or the two may work hand in hand: high human capital industries might dominate in some nations, and they may fit well with concentrated owners (who can make soft deals better than can distant stockholders). The commonality between the footnoted relationships and the textually-noted ones is that institutional protection of minority stockholders plays a secondary role in determining whether ownership is separated or stays close.

[10] Reality is more complex. First, distant shareholders might suffer through two channels. They might suffer the controllers' machinations, but the agency cost minimization may be so great that it exceeds the controllers' diversions of private benefits. Second, endogeneity might lead the low private benefits companies to have dominant stockholders, while the high private benefits companies build barriers to keep controllers out or they never go public. Nevertheless, the dominant observable effect is hard to reconcile with weak law primarily determining separation as opposed to being a secondary factor.

And the Not-So-Rich Nations?

One might observe that many poorer nations have decrepit corporate law institutions. This is true, and possibly weak corporate law is holding them back, but the coincidence of bad law and a bad economy does not tell us enough. To learn that, say, Afghanistan has poor corporate law does not tell us whether its weak economy and low degree of ownership separation are primarily due to its weak corporate law or to its *other* weak institutions. If the other institutions, particularly the other property rights institutions, are decrepit, *these* may be the critical debilities preventing Afghanistan from developing wealth and complex private institutions that get it ready for public firms and ownership diffusion. Only then, when it gets that far, will we be able to tell whether weak corporate law holds it back. The omitted variable might be weak property rights institutions generally, with weak corporate law institutions just a visible and perhaps minor surface manifestation of the deeper weakness.

In any case, we are here focusing on the world's richer nations, not its poorer nations. Even if corporate law is the institution holding back the transition and developing nations—an unlikely hypothesis—the data indicate that it is not holding back every one of the richer nations from getting stronger securities markets and sharper ownership separation. Something else is.

Other data are consistent. There are too many studies showing that increasing block-holders in many countries *increase* the value of minority stockholders.

Conclusion: Politics and Corporate Law as Explanations for Securities Markets

We should be skeptical about a pure, or even a primarily, law-based theory or legal-origins theory for predicting ownership separation and stock market strength in the wealthy West. True, strong corporate law that protects distant stockholders is good to have. It is useful in building efficacious business enterprises and has utility in explaining some key aspects of corporate differences around the world, especially in transition and developing nations. For deep securities markets and strong ownership separation, nations probably need it or a substitute.

But the quality-of-corporate-law argument has limits, and these limits are probably much closer than is commonly thought. High-quality corporate law is insufficient to induce ownership to separate from control in the world's richest, most economically advanced nations. Technologically advanced nations in the wealthy West can have the potential for fine corporate law in theory, and several have it in practice, but ownership would *not* become separated from control wherever managerial agency costs are high. And managerial agency costs, unlike insider self-dealing, are *not* closely connected with corporate law. Indeed, American corporate law's business judgment rule has corporate law *avoid* dealing with managerial agency costs.

By examining a restricted sample of the world's richest nations, we can move towards two conclusions, one strong and the other weak. The strong one focuses on the richer nations in the wealthy West: studies that examine corporate law worldwide tend to over-predict the importance of corporate law in the world's richest nations. It seems almost intuitive that these nations—where contract can usually be nicely enforced—shouldn't have much technical trouble developing satisfactory corporate law or good substitutes. Some, by measurement, already have. If ownership still hasn't separated widely, then other institutional explanations are probably in play. The weak conclusion focuses on the world's transition and developing nations. We cannot conclude that improving corporate law is irrelevant there (because we have examined here only the restricted set of the world's richest nations). But we can offer the weak conclusion that the development agencies may do everything right in getting the corporate law institutions of these nations ready for ownership separation, and it is at least possible that no one comes to the party.

The quality of conventional corporate law does not fully explain why and when ownership concentration persists in the wealthy West, because core *corporate law does not even try to directly prevent managerial agency costs from dissipating a firm's value*. The American business judgment rule keeps courts and law out of basic business decisions and that is where managers can lose, or make, the really big money for shareholders. Non-legal institutions control these costs. In nations where those *other* institutions, such as product competition or incentive compensation, fail or do less well, managerial dissipation would be higher and ownership cannot as easily become separate from control as it can where dissipation is lower. Corporate-law quality can be high, private benefits of control low, but if managerial agency costs from dissipation are high, separation will not proceed. Even if we believed law to be critical to building these *other* institutions, the analysis would persist because *different* laws support the agency cost controlling institutions (antitrust and product market competition; tax law and incentive compensation; and so on).

Moreover, the regulatory character of the means by which securities law is made seems to run counter to the strengths of the common law system—it operates through rules and regulations, not common law, judge-made fiduciary duties. The SEC's regulatory character thus casts some doubt on the primacy of legal origins, that is, the idea that legal origins heavily affect the ability to protect minority stockholders.

Variation in other institutions could explain why managerial agency costs are not low enough. If other institutions induce managers, if untethered, to stray from shareholder profit-making, then shareholders would be less likely to untether the managers. When those other institutions are strongly in play, then corporate law—even corporate law writ large—no longer primarily determines the degree of separation.

A nation need not control insider machinations and motivate managers equally well; and, to the extent it does one better than the other, concentration and diffusion are deeply affected. The diffusion decision is based on the *sum* of private benefits of control and managerial agency costs. Even if traditional corporate law drives private benefits to zero, concentration should persist if managerial agency costs are high.

Data are consistent. Several nations have, by measurement, good corporate law, but not much diffusion and hardly any separation. These nations also have a potential for high managerial agency costs if ownership and control were separated: relatively weaker product market competition and relatively stronger political pressures on managers to disadvantage shareholders. Political variables predict separation well, and they dominate corporate law quality in predicting separation in the wealthy West.

The quality of a nation's corporate law cannot be the only explanation of why diffuse Berle-Means firms grow and dominate. Perhaps, for some countries at some times, it is not even the principal one.

References

Bebchuk, L. (1999). *A Rent-Protection Theory of Corporate Ownership and Control* (Law and Economics Working Paper). Cambridge, MA: Harvard University (Discussion Paper No. 260).

Becht, M. and Röell, A. (1999). 'Blockholdings in Europe: An International Comparison', *European Economic Review*, 43: 1049–56.

Bishop, J. Jr. (1968). 'Sitting Ducks and Decoy Ducks: New Trends in the Indemnification of Corporate Directors and Officers', *Yale Law Journal*, 77: 1078–103.

Black, B. (2000). 'The Core Institutions That Support Strong Securities Markets', *Business Lawyer*, 55: 1565–607.

Coffee, J. (1999). 'The Future as History: The Prospects for Global Convergence in Corporate Governance and Its Implications', *Northwestern University Law Review*, 93: 641–707.

—— (2001). 'The Rise of Dispersed Ownership: Theories of Law and the State in the Separation of Ownership and Control', *Yale Law Journal*, 111: 1–82.

DeLong, B. (1991). 'Did J.P. Morgan's Men Add Value?', in P. Temin (ed.), *Inside the Business Enterprise: Historical Perspectives on the Use of Information*. Chicago: University of Chicago Press.

Dooley, M. and Veasey, E. (1989). 'The Role of the Board in Derivative Litigation: Delaware Law and the Current ALI Proposals Compared', *Business Lawyer*, 44: 503.

Dyck, A. and Zingales, L. (2002). 'Why are Private Benefits of Control so Large in Certain Countries and What Effect does this Have on their Financial Development?'. Working paper, Chicago: University of Chicago, January (forthcoming, *Journal of Finance*).

Faccio, M. (2002). 'Politically-connected Firms: Can they Squeeze the State?' Social Science Research Network working paper.

Fama, E. (1980). 'Agency Problems and the Theory of the Firm', *Journal of Political Economy*, 88: 288–307.

Iskander, M., Meyerman, G., Gray, D., and Hagan, S. (1999). 'Corporate Restructuring and Governance in East Asia', *Finance and Development*, 36: 42–5.

La Porta, R., Lopez-de-Silanes, F., and Shleifer, A. (1999). 'Corporate Ownership Around the World', *Journal of Finance*, 54: 471–517.

La Porta, R., Lopez-de-Silanes, F., Shleifer, A., and Vishny, R. (1997). 'Legal Determinants of External Finance', *Journal of Finance*, 52: 1131–55.

——————————(1998). 'Law and Finance', *Journal of Political Economy*, 106: 1113–50.

—————————— (2000). 'Investor Protection and Corporate Governance', *Journal of Financial Economics*, 58: 3–27.

Levinthal, D. (1988). 'A Survey of Agency Models of Organizations', *Journal of Economic Behavior and Organization*, 9: 153, 182.

Mahoney, P. (1997). 'The Exchange as Regulator', *Virginia Law Review*, 83: 1453–500.

Miwa, Y. and Ramseyer, M. (2000). 'Corporate Governance in Transitional Economies: Lessons from the Pre-War Japanese Cotton Textile Industry', *Journal of Legal Studies*, 29: 171–203.

Modigliani, F. and Perotti, E. (1997). 'Protection of Minority Interest and the Development of Security Markets', *Managerial and Decision Economics*, 18: 519–28.

—— (1998). 'Security Versus Bank Finance: The Importance of a Proper Enforcement of Legal Rules'. Unpublished manuscript. Cambridge, MA: MIT Sloan School of Management.

Nestor, S. (2000). *Corporate Governance Trends in the OECD Area: Where Do We Go From Here?* (Working paper). Paris: OECD.

OECD (Organization for Economic Cooperation and Development) (1994). *The OECD Jobs Study: Evidence and Explanations—Part II—The Adjustment Potential of the Labour Market*. Paris: OECD.

—— (1999). *Principles of Corporate Governance*. Paris: OECD.

Roe, M. (2000). 'Political Preconditions to Separating Ownership from Corporate Control', *Stanford Law Review*, 53: 539–606.

—— (2002). 'Corporate Law's Limits', *Journal of Legal Studies*, 31: 233–71.

—— (2003a). *Political Determinants of Corporate Governance*. Oxford: Oxford University Press.

—— (2003b). 'Institutional Foundations of Ownership Separation in the West.' Working paper.

Witherell, W. (2000). 'Corporate Governance: A Basic Foundation for the Global Economy', *The OECD Observer*, Summer: 24–6.

13

Convergence of Corporate Governance during the Stock Market Bubble: Towards Anglo-American or European Standards?

STEEN THOMSEN

Introduction

It is now widely recognized that there are large differences in corporate governance between the US and the UK on the one hand and continental Europe on the other (for example, Baums, Buxbaum, and Hopt 1994; Roe 1994*b*; Prowse 1995; Vives 2000; Gugler 2001; Barza and Becht 2001). In recent years some scholars have argued that European governance systems are converging to US–UK standards (Coffee 1999, 2002; Hansmann and Kraakman 2001, 2002; Denis and McConnell 2002). Others have argued that convergence is unlikely because of both path dependencies and the relative efficiency of the European model (Bebchuck 1999; Bebchuck and Roe 1999; Roe 1994*b*). But so far little systematic evidence has been produced on the issue, and the potential drivers of convergence have not been subject to empirical analysis.

This chapter provides some empirical evidence by analyzing the evolution of ownership concentration among 2,238 large US and European companies in 1989–98. I show that, contrary to general belief and to the few previous empirical studies (Guillen 2000; Khanna, Kogan, and Palepu 2002), the data appears to support a *mutual convergence hypothesis*. Not only has ownership concentration in Europe decreased and thus converged to US standards, in the US and UK it has increased and thus de facto converged to European standards (Thomsen 2001, 2003). Moreover, I try to provide a deeper analysis of the observed empirical trends: what does theory have to say about convergence in ownership structure, what has in fact happened, and to what extent can theory explain the observed changes? Unlike previous studies by Guillen (2000) and Khanna, Kogan, and Palepu (2002), this chapter can make use of time series data at the firm level. A major advantage of this approach is its ability to test for changes over time rather than to infer them

I am grateful to B.V. Phani and Michael Emil Ollinger for research assistance and to Ruth Aguilera for helpful comments.

from cross-sections. Moreover, firm level data open the opportunity of going beyond the convergence question in the absolute ('yes' or 'no') to a more fine-grained examination and explanation of which firms do and which do not exhibit convergence over time. An additional advantage is the ability to control for the effects of variables like firm size and industry, which may spuriously influence the findings.

A few caveats are in order, however. First, while there are advantages to focusing on in-depth analysis of one quantifiable variable, ownership concentration is only one dimension of corporate governance, and convergence in this dimension need not be accompanied by convergence in other dimensions like board structure, incentive systems, stakeholder relations, and so on. Aguilera and Jackson (2003: 461) have recently argued that the dichotomy between path dependence and convergence may need to be replaced by a more complex appreciation of '*simultaneous processes of continuity and change across national boundaries*'. Clearly, an overall understanding of context and other dimensions of governance are important in interpreting any given empirical phenomenon. In the interpretation and discussion of the empirical results, I therefore turn to context as well as the broader question of overall convergence in governance.

Second, it is now evident that the 1990s were a special period, most likely an outlier, because of the spectacular increase in stock prices that took place across the world and particularly in the US and UK. Figure 13.1 shows the Dow-Jones index over a 100-year period to underline this point.

As can be seen from Fig. 13.1, the stock market boom 1980–2000 was spectacular compared with other periods in US history. Stock prices rose by a factor 10 from index 1,000 to index 10,000 over this period. This compares with an index that remained flat at around 10,000 over the preceding two-decade period 1960–80. The last similar bull market 1940–60 came after a world war and a world depression in the 1930s. The 1980–2000 bull market took place in a period of falling inflation, which implies a change in relative prices that exerted a powerful pull on companies worldwide to cater to the needs of stock market investors and thus induced a particular corporate governance regime. Moreover, although stock markets rose across the world, the stock index rose faster in the US and UK than in continental Europe (Holmstrom and Kaplan 2003), and, in a period of deregulation, globalization, and integration of financial markets, the largest stock markets in the world clearly exerted a particularly powerful influence on corporate governance practices. The diffusion of stock option compensation, investor activism, best practice codes, shareholder value—even the concept of corporate governance—bear witness to this trend.

However, since the turn of the millennium the boom has been replaced by a collapse with a 50 per cent decline in the global stock market index from March 2000 to March 2003 (currently somewhat less). We would therefore not expect corporate governance trends from the 1990s to continue into the

FIGURE 13.1   *Dow-Jones industrial average 1898–2002 (logarithmic scale).*

present decade. In more than one sense, therefore, the 1990s now belong to economic history.

The Convergence/Divergence Debate

While there are many dimensions of corporate governance, this chapter will focus on ownership structure and particularly ownership concentration. The classic distinction here is between the *market-based* models of the US–UK, in which ownership concentration among large companies is low, and the alternative ('bank-based' or 'control-based') models of continental Europe, in which ownership concentration is high. Ownership structures in *market-based systems* are held to be characterized by large and liquid stock markets and significant share ownership by institutional investors and other portfolio investors. In contrast, the *control-based systems* of continental Europe are held to be characterized by smaller and less liquid share markets and a larger share of stock held by (founding) families, corporate investors (cross-holdings), and governments (Barza and Becht 2000).

These differences have been attributed to different levels of minority investor protection (La Porta, Lopez-de-Silanes, and Shleifer 1999; La Porta *et al.* 2000) and to regulatory limitations on the role of large investors in the economy (Roe 1991, 1994*a*). In addition economic theory would suggest variations because of international differences in country size, firm size, and industry structure (Hansmann 1996; Pedersen and Thomsen 1999). According to Johnson and Shleifer (2001), the economic, 'Coasean', perspective predicts convergence of governance structures when the economic environment converges, while both the legal and political views would require political intervention to harmonize rules and regulation. However, legal systems and political regulation tend to be highly stable over time, and there appears to have been little formal convergence in company law between continental Europe and the US for the past decades (Coffee 1999). Moreover, 'Coaseian convergence' is to some extent a straw man, since Coase (1960) in fact maintained that transaction costs are significant in most real-world situations and influence the allocation of resources. Thus, when transaction costs are high corporate governance structures and corporate policies will not respond automatically (or efficiently) to changes in the economic environment.

Bebchuck (1999) and Bebchuck and Roe (1999) specifically explain why ownership concentration will not automatically adjust to efficient levels, that is, why a controlling shareholder structure with high ownership concentration will not automatically evolve into low ownership concentration even if this would maximize the financial value of the firm. One important reason is the existence of private benefits to controlling shareholders, which are not shared with minority investors. When firms have already adopted a mixed ownership structure with some minority investors, prospective gains by selling more shares to the public must be shared by these investors, and this reduces the incentive to give up private control benefits (Bebchuck and Roe 1999). Bebchuck (1999) therefore predicts that control-based governance systems will emerge when the private benefits of control are large. Similarly, inefficiently low rates of ownership concentration may persist in market-based systems. Here managerial control benefits may give rise to persistence of market-based governance structures (dispersed ownership). Because of vested interests in maintaining the status quo, incumbent managers may resist the formation of controlling blocks (Bebchuck and Roe 1999) and fight hostile takeovers. Gains from formation of large blocks of control will again be shared with the market, reducing the incentive to form such blocks in market-based systems (Shleifer and Vishny 1997).

Other factors at the system level are also believed to create barriers to change of ownership structure (Bebchuck and Roe 1999). Ceilings and other limitations on ownership by financial institutions, as in the US, limit their ownership shares of individual firms (Roe 1991). The existence of complementary institutions in a given system—for example, a large and well-functioning stock market as in the US–UK or an active bank sector as in Germany—may influence the ownership and capital structures of firms based in that system (Roe 1994a). Legal systems may provide varying degrees of protection of minority investors (La Porta et al. 1998). Finally, the incumbent organizations/institutions will lobby for continuation of their own existence (North 1990).

So, according to the legal and political perspectives, there are strong reasons to assume that different corporate governance systems will persist. In other words, there should be no convergence over time. The no-convergence hypothesis has been supported by the few previous attempts at statistical testing.

Khanna, Kogan, and Palepu (2002) used a recent-year (2000) cross-sectional dataset on governance practices gathered from private rating organizations, and tested to what extent these de facto governance measures and the de jure measures constructed by La Porta et al. (1998) are influenced by measures of economic integration. They found no evidence of formal or functional convergence to US standards, but some evidence of formal convergence between country pairs. However, they are unable to test for time series convergence on a cross-sectional dataset.

Guillen (2000) compares indicators of convergence at the country level. He notes that the share of Anglo-American countries in world foreign direct investment is decreasing, that the ownership shares of institutional investors vary increasingly across countries, that corporate debt-equity ratios show no systematic tendency to convergence to US standards, and that hostile takeovers remain a primarily Anglo-American phenomenon.

Contrary to the no-convergence hypothesis, Hansmann and Kraakman (2001) have proposed a strong-form convergence hypothesis according to which the Anglo-American market model has in fact become the global corporate governance standard for companies and countries across the world. Moreover, Gilson (2001) and Coffee (1999) observing that formal governance structures like company law change only slowly but that other indicators point to convergence, have proposed the idea of functional convergence, that is, that the formal structure remains unchanged while there is de facto convergence in company behavior.

Hansmann and Kraakman (2001) point to three mechanisms of governance convergence: logic (persuasive arguments for the superiority of one model), example (of competitive success of one model), and demonstrated competitive advantages. They also mention harmonization and changes in corporate law as a weak force making for convergence. Convergence in regulation may come about if politicians imitate the laws and policies of other countries because they are persuaded by logical arguments and/or a desire to improve international competitiveness, economic growth, or employment. Such could, for example, be the case with the proposed EU takeover directive (EU Commission 2001, 2002), which aims to stimulate the market for hostile takeovers in Europe. Alternatively, governance structures may converge if corporate decision makers respond in the same way to similar challenges (for example, the growing importance of institutional investors).

However, even though the formal governance structure is unchanged, there may be convergence in behavior. Gilson (2001) makes an important distinction between formal and functional convergence: companies within a particular institutional framework may change their behavior in order to succeed or survive in international competition even though the formal structure is unchanged. Coffee (1999) argues that a number of forces pull and push towards convergence: the growth of European stock markets, disclosure harmonization, the appearance of institutional investors, harmonization of international accounting standards, migration to foreign markets, and the need for global scale. He emphasizes foreign listings in the US as a migration from European to US governance. But at the same time, he argues, the forces of inertia are very strong: rent seeking by incumbent interest groups, reluctance of controlling shareholders to give up their control premiums by selling out, historical path dependencies, and complementarities between various elements of each system, which make it difficult to change one element without also changing a number of others. In other words, strong forces for convergence meet strong forces for resistance and inertia. The outcome of this dilemma, Coffee argues, is that formal governance structures change very little, but that a functional convergence in corporate governance takes place as European companies adopt American change standards and behavior.

So far, however, there has been little direct empirical evidence to support their ideas and there has also been some uncertainty concerning the precise mechanism by which convergence would take place. In this chapter, I propose from an economic perspective that *internationalization*, particularly the emergence and massive growth of a global stock market, created a corporate governance regime that stimulated convergence during the 1990s. More specifically, I argue that globalization promoted convergence in corporate ownership structures through three different mechanisms: (i) growth and internationalization of world equity markets, (ii) product market internationalization, and (iii) diffusion of ideas.

Internationalization of Equity Markets

A channel for convergence is the massive growth and internationalization of equity markets in which profit-seeking investors can strike mutually advantageous deals with companies in other governance systems and thus transact around formal barriers. In global capital markets this may be the direct result of an attempt to attract capital from the same investors. It is worth noting that the US stock prices (Dow Jones) first increased by 300 per cent during the 1980s and then again increased by 300 per cent during the 1990s

(Thomsen 2001). The high-tech index NASDAQ increased even more. Other countries followed suit, although the US–UK markets appear to have outperformed continental Europe (Thomsen 2001, 2003). This marks a change of relative factor prices, which was large enough to influence the world economy and particularly to set the agenda for corporate governance during the 1990s. Moreover, financial markets became international during the same period. Van den Berghe (2002) documents significant internationalization of European equity markets, which implies global competition to attract shareholder funds. Among listed companies, international share ownership has increased considerably as a share of total ownership in most European countries over the period 1990 to 1998. In rough figures international ownership increased from 12 per cent to 15 per cent in Germany, from 14 per cent to 35 per cent in France, from 8 per cent to 12 per cent in Italy, from 16 per cent to 36 per cent in Spain, and from 12 per cent to 24 per cent in the UK. It also increased significantly up to more than 30 per cent in the Nordic countries (Thomsen 2001), but only marginally in the US, from 7 per cent to 7 per cent plus. Likewise Coffee (2002) documents an increasing tendency for foreign firms to list on the New York Stock Exchange. This too is likely to have had a direct impact on corporate governance. In continental Europe, for example, ownership concentration is likely to have decreased as companies issued new equity to international investors and large inside owners (families, company groups, governments) decided to reduce their control of firms because this improved their standing from an investor viewpoint or simply because they became convinced that was the modern way to go. In principle, the reverse might have happened in the US–UK, although the argument here is less convincing. Some level of ownership concentration—a visible 'owner'—may be seen as an advantage by foreign investors investing in the US–UK. And to some extent European companies may export European business structures by taking unusually large ownership positions in British or American firms.

Internationalization of Product Markets

Internationalization of product markets is another channel for convergence. With more intense competition in product markets, the pressure to reduce capital costs and to improve managerial control will increase (Coffee 1999). Hansmann and Kraakman (2001) highlight demonstrated competitive advantage as a driver of convergence. The mechanism here could be that governance structures, which effectively discipline managers, lower agency costs and thus increase competitiveness and profitability. US companies that face head-on competition with international rivals with concentrated ownership could therefore be more likely to succeed (and less likely to fail) if they have ownership structures that are more concentrated than other US companies.

Internationalization by Ideas

In addition to hard economic pressure, more subtle forces, such as diffusion of ideas, may also be at work (Thomsen 2000). Hansmann and Kraakman (2001) cite logic (persuasive arguments for the superiority of one model) and examples (of competitive success) as causes of convergence. They also mention harmonization and changes in corporate law as a weak force towards convergence. Generally, the internationalization-by-ideas hypothesis is difficult to test, but could predict general imitation of national models that are perceived as successful because of high growth rates. This would then imply faster convergence to US–UK standards because of the excellent relative performance of the American economy during the past decade (Holmstrom and Kaplan 2003). The evidence presented by Alvaro Cuervo-Cazurra and Ruth Aguilera (Chapter 14, this volume) on the spread of codes of best governance practice can be regarded as a case in point. Cuervo-Cazurra and Aguilera demonstrate how best-practice corporate governance codes originated in the US–UK and later spread to the rest of the world. This trend could be regarded as a (weak) indicator of convergence in what Aguilera and Jackson (2003) term 'managerial ideologies'. They also demonstrate, however, that the speed of diffusion is sensitive to economic variables like stock market size, openness to international trade, and investment.

These three forces work in the same direction when influential shareholders or company managers adopt international governance structures that are perceived to work better, for example when European managers adopt US–UK governance principles because comparable companies in the US–UK have higher market value, lower capital costs, or other perceived advantages. In global capital markets this may be the direct result of an attempt to attract capital from the same investors, or it may be a more indirect imitation of 'new' corporate governance.

Data and Measurement

This chapter tests the convergence hypothesis in the case of ownership concentration. The data are drawn from a comprehensive electronic database on large listed firms across the world (Worldscope-Disclosure various years) and consists of two datasets combined:

- all EU and US companies that had net sales and net assets exceeding US$2bn in 1998 (France, Germany, Italy, as well as the UK); and
- the total number of companies in twelve smaller European countries (Austria, Belgium, Denmark, Finland, Greece, Ireland, Luxembourg, Netherlands, Norway, Portugal, Spain, Sweden) for which information is available in the Worldscope database.

The smaller countries are included both to avoid the large-country bias and to increase the number of different legal systems in the analysis. The combined

TABLE 13.1 *List of variables*

Code	Description	Definition
C	Ownership concentration	The fraction of 'closely held shares' (chs). Closely held shares are shares held by block-holders including officers, directors (and their families), trusts, pension/benefit plans, and shares held by another corporation or individuals that hold more than 5% .
Frslsp	Internationalization (I)	Foreign sales/Total sales (%)
Mbv	Firm value (Market-to-book)	(Market price-year end * Common shares outstanding/common equity at year-end).
Size	Firm size	Log (Total assets)
Firm	Firm effect	Firm number (categorical variable)

Source: Worldscope (1999).

dataset contains 2,242 companies over ten years, a total of 15,475 firm-year observations (somewhat less than $10 \times 2242 = 22,420$ because of missing information for some companies). The variables are described in Table 13.1.

Ownership concentration is measured by the fraction of closely held shares (Worldscope-Disclosure 1997) including shares held by owners who hold more than 5 per cent; shares held by officers, directors and their families, shares held in trust, shares held by another corporation (except in a fiduciary duty by banks), or shares held by pension or benefit plans. Previous research has found a high correlation between closely held shares and another concentration measure, the share of the largest owner (Thomsen and Pedersen 2000). Since this measure is bounded between zero and 100, I checked whether a logit transformation made any difference for sign and significance of the coefficients but, since it did not, I kept the original measures, which make the coefficients easier to interpret.

Convergence. Theoretically, convergence is a process by which two governance structures come to resemble one another over time. Given that ownership concentration in continental Europe (C_{EU}) is higher than ownership concentration in the US/UK (C_{US}), convergence formally requires that $d(C_{EU} - C_{US})/dt < 0$ which means either $d(C_{EU})/dt < 0$ (convergence to Anglo-American standards) or $d(C_{US})/dt > 0$ (convergence to European standards) or both (mutual convergence). The speed of convergence—dC/dt—can be estimated by a simple regression of ownership concentration over time (year) using firm-level data. In essence this means that the time trend(s) of ownership concentration is the object of analysis.

Stock market pull/pressure is measured by the market-to-book value of equity (mbv), a standard valuation measure. In theory, a high valuation signals profitable investment opportunities (the classical rationale for Tobin's q) and thus a need for external finance. In this case, mbv is intended to capture the influence that the stock market surge exerted on convergence in ownership concentration. Large block-holders have had a stronger incentive to sell out if the price of their stock was high and so convergence could be more pronounced for high-value companies.

Product market internationalization is measured as international sales divided by total sales. This measure was adopted as a baseline because it is a standard measure in the literature (for example, Gomes and Ramaswamy 1999) and because it was generally available for European as well as US companies. However, it includes both exports and revenue generated by foreign investment. The rationale for including this variable is that greater exposure to international competition could mean greater pressure to adapt efficient ownership structures (that is, to converge to an efficient norm).

In addition, I use the following self-explanatory variables: *Country* (country of incorporation), *System* ('US–UK', if firms are incorporated is either US or UK, 'EUROPE' otherwise), *Time* (year of observation), *Firm size* (log total assets).

Results

The average fraction of closely held shares 1989–98 in two governance regions (the US/UK and continental Europe) is depicted in Fig. 13.2.

Figure 13.2 reveals large difference in ownership concentration between the US–UK and Europe. The fraction of closely held shares at around 50 per cent in Europe is between four and fives times higher than is the US–UK, where only 10 per cent of the stock is closely held on average. There also

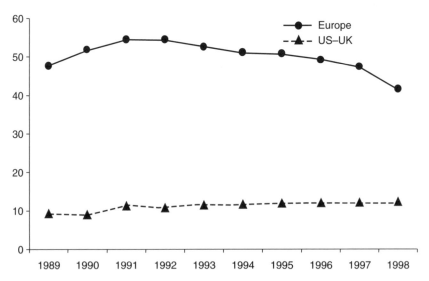

FIGURE 13.2   *Closely held shares (per cent), Europe and US–UK, 1989–98.*
Source: Author's datasets.

TABLE 13.2   *Time trend in ownership concentration—by system*

Estimate	Europe (15 countries)	US/UK (2 countries)
Time Trend	−0.0036***	0.0043***
(t-Value)	(−3.4030)	(4.9487)
N *(Firms)*	1618	620

Notes: 1. The time trend (b) is estimated by the regression $c = a + bt$, where c is ownership concentration, t is time and a and b are estimated coefficients.
2. *** indicates significance at the 1% level.

appear to be indications of convergence. Ownership concentration declines in continental Europe from around 50 per cent at the beginning of the 1990s to a little more than 40 per cent at the end of the decade. In the US–UK there are signs of a slow upward trend. Ownership concentration increases from a little less than 10 per cent to a little more. The two systems appear to be slowly converging in this respect, but the speed of convergence seems to be higher in continental Europe.

However, graphs can be deceptive, particularly at a highly aggregated level, and closer analysis is clearly needed for drawing definite conclusions. For example, effects of a changing population of firms, country effects, firm size and, industry as well as the impact of possible convergence drivers need to be sorted out.

Estimates of the time trend of ownership concentration by system are provided in Table 13.2.

Ownership concentration is found to decrease by 0.4 percentage points a year or around 4 per cent over the decade in Europe and to *increase* at the same rate in the US–UK. These rates are relatively slow. If these rates of change continued, it would take the two systems between thirty and forty years to converge perfectly.

The regressions fail to support the visual impression from Fig. 13.2 that convergence was slower in the US–UK than in Europe. One reason is that simple averages are sensitive to sample variations. For example, Fig. 13.2 indicates that ownership concentration in Europe increased slightly from 1989 to 1991, but this turns out to be mainly a result of increasing the sample size. From 1991 the sample size is relatively stable.

Table 13.3 repeats the same analysis by country. To control for sample variations it also corrects for fixed effects (that is, firm differences in ownership concentration) in the last column.

If we start from the bottom, ownership concentration tends to increase significantly both in the US and in the UK and at roughly the same speed. A majority of the European countries experienced declines, but the trend is significant only in France, Italy, the Netherlands, and Sweden—countries in

TABLE 13.3   *Time trend in ownership concentration, by country*

Country	Time trend	T-value	N (firms)	N (firm years)	Trend adjusted for firm effects	T-value (adjusted trend)
Austria	−0.012	−1.596	53	204	−0.014	−2.08
Belgium	−0.001	−0.412	128	894	0.004	3.23
Denmark	−0.004	−1.133	150	811	−0.004	−2.47
Finland	0.004	1.097	100	816	−0.000	−0.20
France	−0.013	−3.094	87	682	−0.010	−4.29
Germany	0.001	0.211	113	730	0.003	1.91
Greece	0.009	0.807	77	183	−0.018	−1.88
Ireland	−0.002	−0.534	61	564	0.001	0.26
Italy	−0.010	−3.712	167	890	−0.005	−3.29
Luxembourg	−0.001	−0.067	8	40	0.008	1.79
Netherlands	−0.014	−3.606	167	974	−0.003	−1.58
Norway	−0.002	−0.737	117	851	−0.002	−1.18
Portugal	0.022	4.071	72	388	0.016	4.51
Spain	0.000	−0.129	137	906	0.006	2.68
Sweden	−0.013	−4.863	184	1,349	−0.016	−9.76
United Kingdom	0.005	3.020	117	978	0.002	2.15
United States	0.004	4.315	504	4,215	0.000	0.07

Note: The time trend (b) is estimated by the regression $c = a + bt$, where c is ownership concentration, t is time, and a and b are estimated coefficients.

which stock markets boomed and international share ownership grew significantly over the period. Italy has experienced a clear reduction in government ownership because of privatization and an increase in individual share ownership, which usually consists of smaller stakes (FESE 2002). France too has seen some privatization, but somewhat surprisingly an increase rather than a decrease in government ownership (FESE 2002).

The trend towards less concentrated ownership is clearly not uniform. One European country, Portugal, actually seems to have experienced a significant *increase* in ownership concentration, but this may be partly due to measurement error. FESE (2002) notes that ownership information is missing for a large segment (19 per cent) of the Portuguese stock market and that this percentage has been increasing over time. In other cases there seem to be countervailing forces in line with the complexity hypothesis proposed by Aguilera and Jackson (2003). In Germany private non-financial companies ('Germany inc.') were reducing their share of total share ownership up to 1998, while private financial companies increased their share (FESE 2002), which points to deconcentration because financial investors typically spread their portfolios across many companies (although banks have historically taken large stakes in Germany companies, they appear not to have increased their stakes during the 1990s). However, unlike in many other countries, international ownership did not increase significantly in Germany during the 1990s, and government ownership actually *increased* over the period, presumably as a consequence of reunification. In Norway, a decline in individual investor ownership and an increase in institutional investment could have increased ownership concentration. Moreover, the share of government ownership increased but this reflects relative price changes (that is, an increase in the relative value of the state-controlled Norwegian oil company Statoil, in which the Norwegian government holds a controlling share). However, at the same time foreign ownership increased and corporate shareholders declined as a share of the total market (FESE 2002), so that forces making for ownership concentration were counterbalanced by forces making for deconcentration.

When one controls for firm effects, the increasing trend remains significant in the UK but is insignificant in the US. Apparently, the increase in the US was attributable to entry by new firms with high ownership concentration (for example, many high-tech start-ups) and exit by old-economy firms with dispersed ownership due to mergers and acquisitions. In continental Europe, there is still a negative trend for the majority of the countries after one controls for firm effects, but quite a few (five) experienced increases in ownership concentration among the incumbent firms. This seems to reinforce the general impression that, while there appears to have been an aggregate tendency towards less concentrated ownership, the trend was influenced by country-specific factors like privatization and the attractiveness of the national stock market to foreign investors which was again influenced by both policy and country-specific economic conditions.

Additional information on the nature of the convergence process can be obtained by breaking down the time trends by the identity of the largest owner (Table 13.4). Unfortunately, the data only contains information about owner identity at the end of the observation period (1998), and this needs to be taken into consideration when interpreting the results.

TABLE 13.4   *Time trend in ownership concentration 1988–1998, by largest owner 1998*

Largest owner	EUROPE		US–UK	
	Time trend	T value	Time effect	T value
Bank	−0.001	−0.246	0.007	1.084
Company	−0.002*	−1.856	0.012***	3.133
Family	−0.010***	−2.948	0.003	0.794
Government	−0.012***	−2.151	−0.011	−1.619
Financial Institution	−0.008***	−2.919	0.006***	4.397
Portfolio investor (<5%)	−0.018***	−2.804	−0.001	−1.316

***, **, and * = significant at 1%, 5%, and 10%, respectively.

In Europe, ownership concentration seems to have declined for all ownership categories. But the trend is not significant for bank-owned companies and it is quite slow for company shareholders (companies owned by other companies, a characteristic feature of business groups). Apparently owners with access to finance from sources other than the stock market have been better able to resist convergence. This points to the stock market as an important driver of ownership convergence in Europe.

In the US–UK, the increase in ownership concentration appears to be attributable to a tendency for financial investors and corporate owners to increase their stakes in individual companies. This is in line with previous research, which indicates that the market-based stock markets responded positively to a higher ownership share by financial institutions (for example, Thomsen and Pedersen 2000, and references). One reason may be that greater ownership concentration is perceived to lead to better monitoring. It is also possible that foreign non-financial companies took larger ownership stakes in Anglo-American companies during the period, although this is not verifiable in the data. In contrast, ownership concentration fell for companies with end-of-period government and portfolio investor ownership. This probably reflects reductions in government ownership and either a reduction of individual portfolio shareholdings over the period or the result of other kinds of block-holders selling out.

Table 13.5 examines some possible convergence drivers. One way of doing this would have been to use the estimated ownership concentration time trend by firm as the dependent variable in a new regression analysis, but this loses a great deal of information (and many degrees of freedom) since ownership trends need not be constant over the period. Instead I chose to analyze how the estimated time trends co-vary with stock market pressure (mbv) and product market internationalization using interaction effects (t * INT and t * mbv). To the extent that the t * int or t * mbv interaction effects are significant and positive they, indicate that the speed of convergence is higher

TABLE 13.5   *Determinants of ownership concentration*

Dependent variable: C	US/UK	EUROPE
Time	0.001 n.s.	−0.000
Internationalization	−0.0051***	0.001
Internationalization * Time	0.0001***	−0.000
Market-to-book value	0.0000	0.062*
Market-to-book value * Time	−0.0000	−0.001*
Firm size (assets)	−0.0000	−0.000
F-test firm effects (significance level)	0.0001	0.0001
F-test model (significance level)	0.001	0.001
R-square (including firm effects)	78%	83%

***, ** and * = significant at 1%, 5%, and 10%, respectively.

for more international firms or firms with a higher stock-market valuation. This approach retains the original dataset and makes it feasible to control for firm effects (that is, to include a dummy for each firm in the regression), which can capture levels effects of nation, industry, and other variables that are time-insensitive (or at least do not vary within the period of observation), including stable differences between, for example, research-intensive and non-research-intensive firms.

The table regresses ownership concentration on time (year), internationalization (measured by *frslsp*, the ratio of foreign to total sales), stock-market valuation (measured by the market-to-book value of equity), firm size (total assets), and some interaction effects between them. In this connection, the most interesting aspect is the interaction effect with time, which estimates how the speed of convergence is influenced by internationalization and firm value respectively. The models control for firm effects on the level of ownership, which should capture a number of cross-sectional effects, including for example firm differences that remain stable over the period as well as industry and nation effects. R-square is therefore quite high (around 80 per cent). In this connection firm size is also included as a control variable to control for the rather robust finding in the literature that larger firms have more dispersed ownership (see, for example, Demsetz and Lehn 1985). The firm size * time interaction effects turned out to be insignificant and were dropped.

In the US–UK it turns out that there is a negative main effect of internationalization but a positive interaction effect with time. The main effect indicates that more international firms *ceteris paribus* had less concentrated ownership, which is possibly attributable to a need to issue more equity to outsiders to finance extra investments related to internationalization. But the positive interaction effect implies that more international firms tended to experience larger increases in ownership concentration (faster convergence) over time, indicating perhaps that convergence pressures were stronger for more international firms. The effect of firm size was negative, as predicted, but firm value did not appear to have any systematic effect. In other words high-value firms did not experience greater ownership concentration, which is understandable because higher value implies that it is more expensive to acquire and hold a large ownership stake.

In Europe, the internationalization effects were insignificant. One reason for this may be that average internationalization is generally much higher in Europe, so that marginal variations may be relatively unimportant. But there were signs of a (weakly significant) positive main effect of firm value. And the firm value * time interaction effect was negative (although also only weakly significant). Apparently firms whose value increased over the period experienced greater dispersion of ownership, possibly because incumbent owners decided to reduce their holdings (or alternatively those that did were rewarded by the market). Contrary to expectation the size effect was insignificant, presumably because it was captured by the fixed effects.

TABLE 13.6   *Correlation of convergence by industry in US–UK and Europe*

N = 18 industries	Pearson correlation between observed convergence in the US–UK and EUROPE (level of significance)
Significant convergence (0/1 dummy)	−0.050
	(0.840)
Speed of convergence (time trend)	−0.025
	(0.920)

In summary, the convergence process in the US–UK appears to be driven partly by product market internationalization, while convergence in Europe may be more related to stock market trends.

To further probe into the nature of the convergence process in the two systems, Table 13.6 compares convergence indicators in eighteen industries in which there were an acceptable number of firms (eight to ten) in each industry and system category. The approach here is to examine whether a general tendency for an industry in one system to converge is associated with a tendency for companies in the same industry to converge in the other system.

The table first examines whether significant convergence at the industry level (significantly positive time effects in the US–UK, significantly negative time effect in continental Europe) is correlated across systems. Convergence at the industry level is coded as a dummy variable in each system, and the correlation between the two dummy variables is examined by a correlation analysis. If there is convergence in one industry in one system, does this increase the probability that there will be convergence in the same industry in the other system? This turns out not to be the case. There is no significant correlation between industry convergences in the two systems. An alternative test below regresses the speed of convergence by industry in one system on the speed of convergence in the other system and these turn out not to be correlated either (a significant negative correlation could have been a sign of a gravitational pull towards a global mean). In other words, the convergence process appears to be driven by different system effects rather than by common industry forces pulling or pushing firms in certain industries to convergence to an industry norm somewhere in between the two system extremes.

Discussion

This chapter has found support for the proposition that there was slow mutual convergence in ownership concentration in the 1990s. Among 2,238 companies over the period 1989–98 ownership concentration increased in the US–UK and decreased in Europe. The drivers of convergence were different, however. The convergence appears to be driven in part by internationalization in the US–UK and by stock market trend pressure in Europe, but not by specific industry effects.

The theoretical implications of these findings are important since this is some of the first quantitative evidence of corporate governance convergence. Moreover, the possibility that even the US or UK might converge to an international standard introduces a new dimension in the corporate governance discussion. Finally, the chapter has suggested and found support for some credible drivers of convergence, namely stock market pull/push and product market internationalization.

Is mutual convergence an isolated phenomenon or is it part of a more systematic tendency? Aguilera and Jackson (2003) point to the complexity and possible contradictions of convergence-divergence trends. However, several trends point to mutual convergence (Thomsen 2001, 2003).

First, there are quite a lot of indications that European corporate governance became more American and stock-market driven during the 1990s. Examples include the growing power of institutional investors (Coffee 1999; van den Berghe 2002), an increasing number of hostile takeovers (*The Economist* 2000), the spread of stock option-based managerial compensation (Murphy 1999) and increases in leverage through share buy-backs and higher dividends (Warner 1998).

Second, US–UK governance has also effectively become more European in other dimensions than ownership structure. With regard to board structure, management and control in the US–UK have increasingly been separated by the appointment of non-executive directors (Monks and Minnow 2001), subcommittees composed of non-executives (Cadbury code, NYSE code) and separation of the roles of CEO and board chair (for example, the Cadbury and Higgs codes in the UK). With regard to the banking system US financial deregulation has relaxed the separation of investment and commercial banking and allowed banks to assume a more prominent role in the American economy (Financial Services Modernization Act 1999; *The Economist* 1999). That too is a step in a European direction.

Finally, the stakeholder perspective—sometime regarded as a cornerstone of European governance—has attracted increasing attention in US management research and practice during the 1990s (Clarkson 1995; Donaldson and Preston 1995; Agle, Mitchell, and Sonnenfeld 1999; Jawahar and McLaughlin 2001). As Gerald Davies has pointed out, it is symbolic that the President of the Coca-Cola Company, which used to claim that it existed to generate wealth for its shareholders now states: 'Fundamentally, the Coca-Cola Company is built on a deep and abiding relationship of trust between it and all its constituents: bottlers . . . customers . . . consumers . . . shareowners . . . employees . . . suppliers . . . and the very communities of which successful companies are an integral part. That trust must be nurtured and maintained on a daily basis.' Compare this with the earlier mission statement: 'At The Coca-Cola Company, our publicly stated mission is to create value over time for the owners of our business. In fact, in our society, that is the mission of any business: to create value for its owners' (quote from the CEO 1981–97, Goizueta 1996).

However, convergence in some dimensions of corporate governance does not automatically imply convergence in other dimensions. As part of cross-checking on the conclusions of this chapter, I examined trends in capital structure (debt/equity ratios) using the same dataset as in this chapter and found that European companies have decreased their leverage during the 1990s. Given the traditional view that European governance is bank debt-based this might by some be taken as an indication that European corporate governance is changing in a more US–UK market-oriented direction. But I found no systematic tendency for US–UK companies to increase their leverage. In this dimension one might therefore speak of unilateral convergence to US–UK standards.

Aguilera and Jackson (2003) specifically point to the role of labor markets, but even here there are several trends, which point to convergence to US–UK standards. For example, unionization—the share of the workforce organized in labor unions—is traditionally much lower in the US–UK than in continental Europe. But during the 1990s unionization rates declined throughout continental Europe—and even in the US–UK (for example, Checchi and Lucifora 2002). In this way even labor markets have become more market-based.

Conflicting evidence raises the fundamental issue of what aspects of the corporate governance system are more fundamental and how deep the perceived convergence trends actually are. Economists would probably point to ownership structure and government (de)regulation as the most important factors, but sociologists, political scientists, and organizational theorists would not necessarily agree to this.

Finally, even if one remains within a single theory frame (for example, the law and economics convergence debate), there is the issue of the importance and significance of the observed trends. Has US corporate governance fundamentally changed because of a slight increase in ownership concentration? And might we not in the next decade experience, for example, a decline in ownership concentrations? On this issue changes in Europe seem to be larger and more significant than the changes in the US–UK. But for the reasons presented in the introduction it is clearly misguided to extrapolate trends from the booming 1990s into the present decade.

References

Agle, B., Mitchell, R., and Sonnenfeld, J. (1999). 'Who Matters to CEOs? An Investigation of Stakeholder Attributes And Salience, Corporate Performance, And CEO Values', *Academy of Management Journal*, 42: 507–25.

Aguilera, R. and Jackson, G. (2003). 'The Cross-National Diversity of Corporate Governance: Dimensions and Determinants', *Academy of Management Review*, 28: 447–65.

Barza, F. and Becht, M (eds.) (2001). *The Control of Corporate Europe*. Oxford: Oxford University Press.

Baums, T., Buxbaum, T., and Hopt, K. (eds.) (1994). *Institutional Investors and Corporate Governance*. Berlin: De Gruyter.

Bebchuck, L. (1999). *A Rent Protection Theory of Corporate Ownership and Control* (NBER Working Paper 7203). Cambridge, MA: NBER.

—— and Roe, M. (1999). 'A Theory of Path Dependence in Corporate Ownership and Governance', *Stanford Law Review*, 52: 127–70.

Berghe, Lutgart van den (2002). *Corporate Governance in a Globalising World: Convergence or Divergence? A European Perspective*. Dordrecht: Kluwer.

Checchi, D. and Lucifora, C. (2002). 'Unions and Labour Market Institutions in Europe', *Economic Policy*, 17: 361–408.

Clarkson, M. (1995). 'A Stakeholder Framework for Analysing and Evaluating Corporate Social Performance', *Academy of Management Review*, 20: 92–117.

Coase, R. (1960). 'The Problem of Social Cost', *The Journal of Law and Economics*, 3: 1–44.

Coffee, J. (1999). 'The Future as History: The Prospects for Global Convergence in Corporate Governance and its implications', *Northwestern University Law Review*, 93: 641–707.

—— (2002). 'Convergence and Its Critics: What are the Preconditions to the Separation of Ownership and Control', in J. McCahery *et al.* (eds.), *Corporate Governance Regimes: Convergence and Diversity*. Oxford: Oxford University Press.

Demsetz, H. and Lehn, K. (1985). 'The Structure of Corporate Ownership: Causes and Consequences', *Journal of Political Economy*, 93: 1155–77.

Denis, D. and McConnell, J. (2002). *International Corporate Governance: A Survey*. Working Paper No. 2001/2002-007. West Lafayette, IN: Krannert Graduate School of Management, Purdue University.

Donaldson, T. and Preston, L. E. (1995). 'The Stakeholder Theory of the Corporation: Concepts, Evidence, and Implications', *Academy of Management Review*, 20/1: 65–91.

The Economist (1999). 'Finance and Economics: The Wall Falls', 30 October: 79–81.

—— (2000). 'Europe's New Capitalism: Bidding for the Future', 12 February: 71–4.

EU Commission (Commission of the European Communities) (2001). *Company Taxation in the Internal Market* (Bolkestein Report). Com (2001) 582 Final. Brussels, 23 October.

—— (2002). *Proposal for a Directive of the European Parliament and of the Council on Takeover Bids*. Com (2002) 534 Final 2002/0240 (Cod). Brussels, 2 October.

FESE (Federation of European Securities Exchanges) (2002). *Share Ownership Structure in Europe*. www.fese.be/statistics/share_ownership/index.htm.

Gilson, R. (2001) 'Globalising Corporate Governance: Convergence of Form or Function', *American Journal of Comparative Law*, 49: 329–57.

Goizueta, R. (1996). *Why Share-owner Value?* (CEO Series no. 13). St Louis: Center for the Study of American Business, Washington University in St Louis.

Gomes, L. and Ramaswamy, K (1999). 'An Empirical Examination of the Form of the Relationship Between Multinationality and Performance', *Journal of International Business Studies*, 30: 173–88.

Gugler, K. (2001). *Corporate Governance and Economic Performance*. Oxford: Oxford University Press.

Guillen, M. (2000). 'Corporate Governance and Globalization: Is There Convergence Across Countries?', *International Comparative Management*, 13: 175–204.

Hansmann, H. (1996). *The Ownership of Enterprise*. Cambridge, MA: Belknap Press.

——— and Kraakman, R. (2001). 'The End of History for Corporate Law', *Georgetown Law Journal*, 89: 439–68.

——— ——— (2002). 'Towards A Single Model for Corporate Law', in J. McCahery *et al.* (eds.), *Corporate Governance Regimes: Convergence and Diversity*. Oxford: Oxford University Press.

Holmstrom, B. and Kaplan, S. (2003). *The State of U.S. Corporate Governance: What's Right and What's Wrong?* (Working Paper No. 9613). Cambridge, MA: NBER.

Jawahar, I. M. and McLaughlin, Gary L. (2001). 'Toward a Descriptive Stakeholder Theory: An Organizational Life Cycle Approach', *The Academy of Management Review*, 26/3: 397–414.

Johnson, S. and Shleifer, A. (2001). 'Coase and Competence in Development' (unpublished working paper). Cambridge, MA: Harvard University.

Khanna, T., Kogan, J., and Palepu, K. (2002). 'Globalization and Corporate Governance Convergence? A Cross-Country Analysis' (working paper). Cambridge, MA: Harvard Business School.

La Porta, R., Lopez-de-Silanes, F., and Shleifer, A. (1999). 'Corporate Ownership Around the World', *Journal of Finance*, 54: 471–519.

La Porta, R., Lopez-de-Silanes, F., Shleifer, A., and Vishny, R. (1998). 'Law and Finance', *Journal of Political Economy*, 106: 1113–55.

——— ——— ——— ——— (2000). 'Investor Protection and Corporate Valuation', *Journal of Financial Economics*, 58: 3–27.

Most, B. (2002). 'Socially Responsible Investing: An Imperfect World for Planners and Clients', *Journal of Financial Planning*, 15/2: 48–55.

Monks, R. and Minnow, N. (2001). *Corporate Governance*. Oxford: Blackwell.

Murphy, K. (1999). 'Executive Compensation', in O. Ashenfelter, and D. Card (eds.), *Handbook of Labour Economics*, Vol. 3. Amsterdam: North-Holland.

North, Douglas C. (1990). *Institutions, Institutional Change and Economic Performance*. Cambridge: Cambridge University Press.

Pedersen, T. and Thomsen, S. (1999). 'Economic and Systemic Explanations of Ownership Concentration Among Europe's Largest Companies', *International Journal of the Economics of Business*, 6: 367–81.

Prowse, S. (1995). 'Corporate Governance in an International Perspective: A Survey of Corporate Control Mechanisms Among Large Firms in the U.S., U.K., Japan and Germany', *Financial Markets, Institutions and Instruments*, 4: 1–61.

Roe, M. (1991). 'A Political Theory of Corporate Finance', *Columbia Law Review*, 1: 10–67.

——— (1994*a*). *Strong Managers, Weak Owners—The Political Roots of American Corporate Finance*. Princeton: Princeton University Press.

——— (1994*b*). 'Some Differences in Corporate Governance in Germany, Japan and America', in T. Baums, T Boxhaul, and K. Hop (eds.), *Institutional Investors and Corporate Governance*. Berlin: de Gruyter.

Shleifer, A. and Vishny, R. (1997). 'A Survey of Corporate Governance', *Journal of Finance*, 52: 737–83.

Thomsen, S. (2000). 'Internationalisation by Ideas', in T. Almor and N. Hashai (eds.), *FDI, International Trade and the Economics of Peacemaking: A Tribute to Seev Hirsch*. Tel Aviv: Academic Studies Division, College of Management.

—— (2001). 'Convergence Goes Both Ways: An Alternative Perspective on the Convergence of Corporate Governance Systems', in M. Neville and K. Sørensen (eds.), *The Internationalisation of Companies and Company Laws*. Copenhagen: DJØF.

—— (2003). 'Convergence of Corporate Governance Systems to European and Anglo-American Standards', *European Business Organization Law Review*, 4: 31–50.

—— and Pedersen, T. (2000). 'Ownership Structure and Economic Performance in the Largest European Companies', *Strategic Management Journal*, 21: 689–705.

Vives, X. (ed.) (2000). *Corporate Governance: Theoretical and Empirical Perspectives*. Cambridge: Cambridge University Press.

Warner, J. (1998). 'Buyback Fever Hits Europe; Continental Companies are Snapping Up their Shares', *Business Week*. 11 May: 46.

Worldscope (1999). *Data Definitions Guide*. Bethesda, MD: Disclosure Inc.

Worldscope-Disclosure (various years). *Compact D CD-ROM*. Bethesda, MD: Disclosure Inc.

14

The Worldwide Diffusion of Codes of Good Governance

ALVARO CUERVO-CAZURRA AND RUTH V. AGUILERA

Introduction

Good corporate governance is beneficial for the country. Countries with good governance systems become better locations not only for domestic firms to operate but also for foreign companies to invest. Good governance facilitates interactions among parties and the development of the country (World Bank 1997, 2002). It also helps the development of external capital markets necessary for firm investment (La Porta, Lopez-de-Silanes, and Shleifer 1999; La Porta *et al.* 1997, 1998, 2000) and facilitates economic growth (Levine 1999).

Good governance can be promoted by developing corporate governance practices. These are, in theory, established to ensure that the firm is run in a profit-maximizing manner and that the rights of shareholders and, sometimes, stakeholders are protected. The initial discussion on corporate governance practices focused on the protection of shareholder rights from misbehavior by managers (Fama and Jensen 1983*a*,*b*; Jensen and Meckling 1976). However, recent debates reveal the existence of different types of shareholders with private objectives that differ from the maximization of the value of the overall firm. These studies highlight the need to protect the rights of minority shareholders from the misbehavior of not only managers but also large shareholders (Barclay, Holderness, and Pontiff 1993; Cuervo-Cazurra 1997, 1999; Shleifer and Vishny 1997). Another strand of the literature has focused on the need to develop corporate governance practices that protect the rights of not only shareholders but also of other stakeholders in the firm (Aguilera and Jackson 2003; Alkhafaji 1989; Freeman 1984).

In this chapter, we study corporate governance practices that are bundled in codes of good governance. Codes of good governance are a set of 'best practice' recommendations regarding the behavior and structure of the board

©Alvaro Cuervo-Cazurra and Ruth V. Aguilera, 2003

Anna Grandori and Steen Thomsen's comments helped to improve previous versions of this chapter. Financial support from the University of Minnesota International Programs, the University of Illinois CIBER and Fewcett Grant, and Bocconi University are gratefully acknowledged. This chapter was completed while the first author was a Visiting Professor at the Department of Applied Economics and Management, Cornell University. All errors remain ours.

of directors. Although the board of directors can serve several functions (Cuervo-Cazurra 1996), we focus on its role as a control mechanism. Moving beyond the convergence-divergence debate, we study the diffusion of codes by asking: (*a*) why codes develop; (*b*) how fast the first code emerges; and (*c*) who the actors involved in their development are.

This chapter contributes to the literature in four ways. First, drawing on the seminal work on legal systems and corporate control by La Porta and colleagues (La Porta, Lopez-de-Silanes, and Shleifer 1999; La Porta *et al.* 1997, 1998, 2000), we provide an understanding of how corporate governance practices can strengthen the legal system in the protection of the rights of shareholders (Aguilera and Cuervo-Cazurra 2004; Morgan and Engwall 1999). Second, we suggest theoretical explanations of the reasons and dynamics of the development of codes of good governance worldwide. This theoretical exercise extends previous research on codes analyzing the determinants and consequences of the development of a code of good governance in a single country (for example, Cadbury 2000; Pellens, Hillebrandt, and Ulmer 2001; Stiles and Taylor 1993) or describing codes of good governance in several countries (for example, Gregory 1998, 1999; Gregory and Simmelkjaer 2002; Van den Berghe and de Ridder 1999). Third, we go beyond the debate on convergence-divergence on corporate governance practices by examining how a converging trend, namely, the emergence of codes in different countries, has led to divergence in the speed of diffusion. Finally, we contribute to the literature by stressing the difficulties in transferring practices across countries, which lead to different speeds of diffusion. We highlight the importance of the exposure to foreign knowledge, in addition to willingness and understanding (for example, Grant 1996; Szulanski 1996), in the explanation of the transfer of knowledge across countries.

The rest of the chapter is organized as follows. In the second section, we describe codes of good governance, their potential contribution in improving national corporate governance systems, and their historical evolution. In the third section, we review the factors triggering the adoption of codes of good governance worldwide. We borrow from institutional theory to build our arguments. In the fourth section, drawing on the knowledge-based view of strategic management, we propose a theoretical model to explain the speed in the worldwide diffusion of codes, and conduct an empirical test of our model. In the fifth section we describe the differences in the issuers of codes of good governance across and within countries. We conclude the chapter with a summary of our main findings and their implications for theory and research in corporate governance.

Improving Corporate Governance: Codes of Good Governance

All countries need to improve their prevailing corporate governance. Good governance is not part of a country's endowment but has to be fostered.

Countries with poor corporate governance can improve it in two main ways: changing the overall corporate governance system and introducing innovations in the existing corporate governance system.

The national governance system can potentially be reinvented to heighten shareholders' protection, as has been the case in transition economies that lacked measures for protecting private property rights (Coffee 1999). These countries are exceptional cases. They usually embarked on the creation of a corporate governance system and a new legal framework as part of the overall transformation of the economic and political system—from public ownership of productive resources and allocation of their use through command, towards private ownership and allocation through price mechanism (Blanchard 1997; Svejnar 2002).

The transformation of the corporate governance system does not have to be this radical, however. Countries can improve their existing legal framework to deal with new governance challenges (World Bank 1997). However, in general this is not an easy proposition. Introducing changes into an existing legal system is a difficult and lengthy process, not least because of the political consensus required. More importantly, the legal system is deeply embedded in the institutional legacies of a given country (Roe 1994) and it is part of a system of institutions that change very slowly (North 1990).

Alternatively, sets of corporate governance practices can be introduced to address the deficiencies in the corporate legal system incorporating the idiosyncrasies of the country's corporate governance system (Shleifer and Vishny 1997), ownership patterns (Barca and Betch 2001; Bebchuck and Roe 1999; Bergloff 1990), or stakeholder rights (Aguilera and Jackson 2003). This customization of practices responds to the limitations in the use of practices developed in one legal system into another (Cuervo 2002; Cuervo-Cazurra 1998).

Codes of Good Governance

One important practice developed to improve national corporate governance is codes of good governance. They present a comprehensive set of norms on the role and composition of the board of directors, relationships with shareholders and top management, auditing and information disclosure, and the selection, remuneration, and dismissal of directors and top managers. Although the specific code recommendations vary across countries, the two principles every code rests on are 'the need for adequate disclosure and the need for appropriate checks and balances in the governance structure' (Cadbury 2000: 9). Ultimately, codes attempt to improve the overall corporate governance of firms, especially when other mechanisms such as takeover markets and legal environments fail to ensure adequate protection of shareholders' rights. Although most of these codes are not statutory, firms nevertheless tend to adopt them. There are two reasons explaining such adoption. First, in several countries, listing rules require quoted firms to adopt the recommendations of the codes or justify the reasons of non-compliance with the country code of good governance in their annual reports. This 'comply or explain' mandatory disclosure requirement adopted by most stock exchanges encourages firm compliance. Surveys in countries where codes have been issued show that publicly traded companies tend to respond to code recommendations (Gregory and Simmelkjaer 2002). For example, Pellens, Hillebrandt, and Ulmer (2001) surveyed German companies in the DAX100 and found that 95.6 per cent of the firms agreed with the German code of good governance and 48.5 per cent had already implemented some of the code guidelines. Second, codes of good governance serve as a signal of the quality of the firm and may give automatic legitimization to adopting firms because of the additional information made available to shareholders. The adoption of codes provides shareholders with information on the corporate governance practices that are (or are not) being implemented in the firm. This information gives them the opportunity to either voice their disagreement with how the company is being governed or—if they do not agree with it—to sever the relationship (Hirschman 1970). As such, firms that adopt the recommendations will be perceived as showing more concern for shareholders than those that do not do so.

The adoption of the recommendations of the codes has induced changes in firms. The adoption of the codes forces firms to change their corporate governance practices to comply with, if not the spirit, at least the letter of the code, and improve upon previous protection of shareholders, especially minority ones. Existent research reveals that codes of good governance influence firm behavior in several ways. First, Canyon and Mallin (1997) and Weir and Laing (2000) show that, despite the voluntary nature of the Cadbury Report, British-quoted firms to a large extent comply with the code's recommendations, such as the appointment of board subcommittees or the presence of outside directors in the board, and other recommendations that were not explicit in the code such as dual leadership, the functional separation of CEO and Chairman of the board. Second, it has been demonstrated that adopting some of the practices recommended by the codes is directly related to higher firm performance. For instance, Weir and Laing (2000) tested a sample of 200 British firms in 1992 and 1995 and showed that market returns were higher when firms followed the Cadbury Report and established a remuneration committee. Similarly, Dahya, McConnell, and Travlos (2002) demonstrate that the adoption of the Cadbury Report in 1992 increased CEO turnover in the UK—reflecting the need for the separation of Chairman and CEO—and heightened the sensitivity of CEO turnover to poor performance. Finally, highly publicized financial scandals have contributed to the adoption of codes of good governance. This is corroborated by statements such as: 'On December 1992, when Sir Adrian Cadbury and his committee published their final report on "The Financial Aspects of

Corporate Governance," they started a train of events that changed the face of British boards and led to a *worldwide* movement for the reform of corporate governance' (Stiles and Taylor 2001: v, emphasis added). Stiles and Taylor continue: 'Following the Cadbury Code, most large quoted companies changed their board structures ... reducing their size boards, separating the roles of the chairman and the chief executive, appointing a new group of "independent" non-executive directors, and establishing board committees' (2001: vi).

Historical Development of the Codes of Good Governance

The first code of good governance came into being in the United States in the late 1970s in the midst of great corporate ferment with business, legal, academic, and political constituencies squaring off on what should be the role of the board of directors. In the context of charges and countercharges surrounding the takeover movement, the Business Roundtable issued a report in January 1978 titled *The Role and Composition of the Board of Directors of the Large Publicly Owned Corporation*, which was, according to Monks and Minow (1992), a response to the trend of corporate criminal behavior and an attempt to pass legislation curbing hostile takeovers. The Business Roundtable report, chaired by J. Paul Austin, CEO of Coca-Cola at the time, turned out to be a claim for the legitimacy of private power and the enforcement of accountability. The report shifted the role of directors from being merely 'ornaments on a corporate Christmas tree' (Mace 1971) to proclaiming the director's main duties as: (i) overseeing management and board selection and succession; (ii) reviewing the company's financial performance and allocating its funds; (iii) overseeing corporate social responsibility; and (iv) ensuring compliance with the law (Charkham 1995). It was drafted as the first guidelines to improve governance capacity in US corporations.

In the United States, the Securities Exchange Commission, the New York Stock Exchange, and the Roundtable, among others, continued to issue codes from the late 1970s. However, it was not until a decade later that another country created a code of good governance. In 1989, the Hong Kong Stock Exchange issued its first Code of Best Practice, Listing Rules, and in 1991 the Irish Association of Investment Managers drafted the Statement of Best Practice on the Role and Responsibility of Directors of Publicly Listed Companies. Despite the slow start, the development of codes grew rapidly in the early 1990s, especially following the Cadbury Commission's report (1992) in the United Kingdom. The Cadbury Report became the flagship guideline in corporate governance codes that deliberately challenged the effectiveness of voluntary regulation and corporate democracy (Stiles and Taylor 1993).

Figure 14.1 shows the evolution of codes of good governance in capitalist countries by country and number of codes developed. The emergence of codes of good governance across countries did not follow a gradual path.

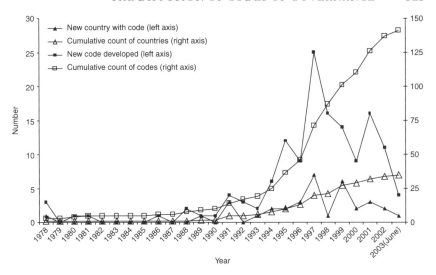

FigURE **14.1**   *Dynamics of codes of good governance worldwide: Number of countries and
number of codes, 1978–2003.*
Source: Authors' calculation using data from CAGN (1999), ECGI (2003), ECGN
(2000), Gregory (1998, 1999), Gregory and Simmelkjaer (2002), Van den Berghe
and de Ridder (1999), and World Bank (2000).

As noted, there is a gap between the first code issued in the United States in
1978 and the second code published in Hong Kong in 1989. After 1989, new
codes appeared steadily throughout the early 1990s and, particularly since the
publication of the Cadbury Report in 1992, there has been an exponential
rise in the adoption of codes and overall shareholder activism. This path
in the emergence of codes in the 1990s is correlated with the increasing
discussion of shareholder value that emerged across corporate governance
systems around the world and increasing activism in global stock markets.

An additional impetus in the development of the codes of good governance came from the work of supra-national bodies, particularly the
Organization for Economic Cooperation and Development (OECD) among
developed countries, and the World Bank among developing countries. The
OECD issued the influential 'OECD Principles of Corporate Governance',
which the OECD member countries adopted as non-binding principles to
improve their corporate governance regulation. The World Bank promoted
the development of good governance in general and good corporate governance in particular as part of the recommendations for the transformation
of economic systems in developing countries, especially in the 1990s. It also
acted as a catalyst in the development of corporate governance and codes
of good governance in transition economies. These countries, however, are
not part of our analyses. Other supra-national bodies that have issued codes

are the European Union and pan-European associations and bodies, and the Commonwealth. By the middle of 2003, thirty-five developed and developing countries had issued at least one code of good governance. In this list we do not include codes issued by supranational bodies. Countries that developed codes of good governance earlier continue to develop subsequent codes. This resulted in a total of 141 codes of good governance develop by the middle of 2003. As some areas were addressed by a code, new requirements appeared, inducing the development of other codes to address them. As such, even countries that had already developed codes of good governance continued improving their corporate governance system by issuing new ones to address existing limitations in the protection of shareholders.

Development of Codes of Good Governance: Effectiveness and Legitimization

Guidelines and codes of corporate governance are important as they provide a voluntary means for the adoption of essential practices of good governance. Identifying the factors that influence the development and diffusion of governance practices in different countries permits a better understanding of their impact despite the lack of formal legal rules (Strang and Soule 1998). Diffusion studies explain the adoption of new practices within a social system by referring to two main theoretical sources: efficiency (or rational) accounts and social legitimization (Strang and Macy 2001; Tolbert and Zucker 1983). Rational accounts point to the efficiency or effectiveness gains that may follow innovation or the adoption of a practice. Alternatively, social legitimization suggests that practices are adopted because of their growing taken-for-granted improving qualities, which make adoption socially expected.

The efficiency and legitimization theoretical perspectives are often posed as mutually exclusive categories where, early in the process of diffusion, practices are adopted because of their unequivocal effects on efficiency or effectiveness, while later adoption is seen as a social legitimization process regardless of net benefit. Nevertheless, as pointed out by Strang and Macy, this dichotomy is theoretically costly because 'ideas about rationality and effectiveness come to be cast in opposition to ideas about imitation' (2001: 148). Hence, we argue that these two theoretical rationales, usually presented as incompatible, can be reconciled and thereby account for the spread of practices across countries with different economic organization. We do so by proposing two different mechanisms shaping effectiveness and legitimization. In particular, we propose that, while endogenous forces influence effectiveness factors in a given country, exogenous pressures lead to legitimization by triggering the adoption of taken-for-granted practices.

In Aguilera and Cuervo-Cazurra (2004) we theorize and empirically test the factors that led to the development of codes of good governance between 1988 and 1999 in a sample of forty-nine countries, which includes twenty-four countries that had developed codes. We theorize that codes of good governance are triggered by (i) endogenous forces increasing their corporate governance effectiveness and by (ii) exogenous forces legitimizing the corporate governance system.

Endogenous Forces to Increase Effectiveness in the Corporate Governance System

Codes of good governance are capable of solving deficiencies in the corporate governance system, particularly workings of the board of directors as the direct corporate governance mechanism that oversees the management of the firm on behalf of shareholders. Hence, following this logic, we expect that countries with less effective corporate governance systems are more likely to develop new governance practices such as codes of good governance. We look at two measurements of effectiveness in the protection of shareholders rights: type of legal tradition and ability of minority shareholders to shape firm governance.

Deficiencies in the corporate governance system are linked to the legal tradition of a country (La Porta, Lopez-de-Silanes, and Shleifer 1999; La Porta *et al.* 1997, 1998, 2000). As indicated by La Porta *et al.* (1998), countries with common-law legal systems grant better legal protection to investors than countries with a civil-law legal system. Among the latter, the French-based legal system is the least effective in protecting shareholder rights (La Porta *et al.* 1998). Hence, in principle, we argue that codes are adopted to make up for the lack of minority shareholder protection in the legal system and are more likely to be adopted in countries with civil-law traditions.

Empirical tests undertaken in Aguilera and Cuervo-Cazurra (2004) find that this logic is not supported. They show that codes of good governance are less likely to be developed in countries with a civil-law legal tradition and more likely to be developed in countries with a common-law legal tradition. Two explanations account for this counterintuitive result. First, in order to deal effectively with the changing global competitive environment, corporate governance practices need to be continuously updated and aligned with global standards. Consequently, countries with strong shareholder protection rights embedded in their legal system, such as the common-law legal tradition, are more likely to continue fostering effective governance practices via codes of good governance. As such, codes are developed to fill in gaps in the legal system in the overall protection of shareholders. Second, the intrinsic characteristics of the common-law legal system facilitate the enforceability of the codes of good governance. Although in the common-law legal system practices that are 'good' business practice tend to be enforceable by the courts, in civil-law legal systems such practices are not enforceable unless they become codified into law (Cuervo 2002). Thus, in countries with a common-law legal system, the development of codes of good governance can provide additional mechanisms to protect shareholder rights, whereas this is not automatically the case in countries with a civil-law legal tradition.

However, countries and families of legal systems vary in the ability of minority shareholders to challenge the workings of the board of directors and managers in corporate decision-making. Particularly relevant to the adoption of codes is the existence of laws that already regulate the relationships between shareholders and boards of directors. La Porta *et al.* (1998) constructed an anti-director index to measure a country's degree of minority shareholders rights protection, which evaluates the mechanisms available to shareholders to protect themselves against expropriation by the board of directors. In countries with strong anti-director rights, minority shareholders have more mechanisms available to influence corporate decision-making and protect their rights, whereas, in countries with weak anti-director rights, shareholders are less protected and directors are less accountable. Therefore, we expect that the adoption of codes of good governance serves as a mechanism to compensate for weak anti-director shareholder rights in the legal system. This is accomplished by encouraging the development of instruments that increase the country's corporate governance effectiveness such as promoting firm transparency and board accountability towards shareholders. Empirical findings in Aguilera and Cuervo-Cazurra (2004) confirm that the adoption of codes of good governance tend to be issued in countries with weak anti-director shareholder rights, providing support for the effectiveness account. All in all, codes complement a country's legal system in the overall protection of shareholders in the country.

Exogenous Forces to Legitimize the Corporate Governance System

The development of codes of good governance is influenced not only by the endogenous need to increase effectiveness and hence compensate for potential deficiencies in the corporate governance system, but also by exogenous pressures to introduce practices that are socially legitimate or widely perceived as appropriate (Tolbert and Zucker 1983). In Aguilera and Cuervo-Cazurra (2004) we show that three exogenous factors influence the likelihood of code development at the country level: globalization pressures exemplified by economic openness, government liberalization, and the significant presence of foreign institutional investors.

First, a country's economic integration in the world economy in terms of international trade facilitates the transfer of knowledge across countries and the diffusion of codes of good governance. Moreover, integration of a national economy into world trade reduces the possibility of shielding governance inefficiencies behind barriers of trade. This economic openness is positively related to the adoption of codes, although the relationship is not statistically significant. Second, the withdrawal of government presence in the economy and the subsequent need to redesign the governance structure of newly privatized firms explains the adoption of codes. Thus, the transfer of property rights from the government to private hands opens a window of opportunity to promote sound governance principles in firms that used to have strong ties to the government. We find that processes of government liberalization in a given country are positively related to the adoption of codes. Finally, institutional investors need the assurance that their investments are going to be protected since they may not hold enough capital or information to influence decision-making. In effect, institutional investors are willing to pay a premium for good governance (McKinsey 2000). That is, they search for firms that have good governance practices and are eager to promote the adoption of codes of good governance. We demonstrate that the presence of foreign institutional investors is positively related to the adoption of the number of codes.

In conclusion, codes are developed in response to a combination of endogenous and exogenous pressures to solve deficiencies in a country's corporate governance system. Internal pressures aim to increase effectiveness in the system, and exogenous pressures seek to acquire legitimization. These two theoretical logics—effectiveness and legitimization—usually presented as being incompatible, can be reconciled and thereby account for the spread of practices across countries with different governance systems.

Speed of Worldwide Diffusion of Codes of Good Governance as Transfer of Knowledge

We extended the analysis of factors triggering the worldwide adoption of codes of good governance with a study of the speed in the diffusion of codes among those countries that have developed them. The details of this appear in Cuervo-Cazurra and Aguilera (2003). The specific research question we tackle is: what are the determinants of the speed in the development of the first code in a given country? We conceptualize 'speed of code development' as how early the first code of good governance was developed in a given country. This is another dimension to consider when analyzing the diffusion of practices. As we have discussed above, the diffusion of practices is usually presented as a discussion of the efficacy versus legitimization of adopting a practice.

However, diffusion arguments assume that it is easy to transfer the knowledge embedded in a practice across organizational or in this case, country boundaries. Instead, the knowledge-based view shows that the transfer of practices tends to be complex, both within the firm (Grant 1996; Kogut and Zander 1992; Szulanski 1992; Von Hippel 1994; Zander and Kogut 1995) and across countries (Kogut 1991; Kogut and Zander 1993). Therefore, to fully capture the complexity understanding of the diffusion of practices across countries, we need to examine not only the factors that influence the diffusion of practices, but also the factors that influence the speed in the transfer of practices across countries.

The development of the first code is a critical initial step towards the development of additional codes. The first code will generally cover some of the deficiencies in the national corporate governance system, but there are always new issues that appear as corporations and their governance changes over time. Subsequent codes can address areas that were not properly dealt with in previous codes, or areas that have appeared as new demands for additional governance. As such, codes of good governance are not a one-time solution to corporate governance problems, but part of an evolving pattern of corporate behavior, or more adequately misbehavior, and the solutions to it. However, the most difficult code to develop is the first one, as it requires being aware of the existence, acknowledging its need, and its analysis and adaptation. Once the first code is developed, subsequent codes will emerge more easily. Therefore, we study the speed of development of the first code of good governance in a given country.

The Speed in Diffusion as a Problem of Transferring Knowledge across Countries

We analyze the determinants of the speed in the diffusion of practices across countries as a problem of transferring codified knowledge across countries (Kogut and Zander 1993). This approach has a long tradition in technology research (for example, Roberts 1983) and is increasingly being used in management research (Grandori and Kogut 2002). Whereas some view the transfer of practices across countries as not particularly problematic, the literature has acknowledged that knowledge transfer is in fact difficult (Grant 1996; Kogut and Zander 1992; Teece 1980), and particularly problematic across countries (Kogut 1991; Kogut and Zander 1993; Teece 1977).

Most of these studies analyze the transfer of knowledge among parties already involved in a transaction, whether units within the same company (Szulanski 1996; Hansen 2002; Winter and Szulanski 2001) or partners in an investment project (Almeida, Song, and Grant 2002; Teece 1980). These studies indicate two key factors that facilitate the transfer of knowledge: understanding and willingness. Understanding refers to the necessity to be able to de-codify each other's knowledge (Arrow 1974; Cohen and Levinthal 1990; Grant 1996; Szulanski 1996). Willingness refers to the need for the two parties involved in the transaction (the source and the recipient of knowledge) to be sufficiently motivated to establish interactions and share their knowledge (Kerr 1975; Milgrom and Roberts 1992; Szulanski 1996).

The receiving party must also be exposed to the existence of this knowledge in the first place. This is not a problem when the transfer of knowledge is between parties that are formally related—either because it is part of the best practices of the firm and may help other units (see, for example, Szulanski 1996) or because it is part of formal relationships to transfer knowledge from one firm to another (for example, Teece 1980). However, this exposure may not be the case in the transfer of knowledge across countries among entities that are not formally related. Therefore, we will discuss exposure to foreign knowledge as a third determinant of the transfer of codified knowledge across countries.

Hence, we now specify the hypotheses in our particular setting, codes of good governance worldwide. We argue that the speed in developing the first code of good governance in a country depends on three factors: understanding of foreign knowledge, willingness to use foreign knowledge, and exposure to foreign knowledge.

The understanding of codes of good governance in other countries speeds the development of a code because governance practices codified in one country can be understood and applied to another (Arrow 1974; Cohen and Levinthal 1990; Grant 1996). In the case of codes of good governance, these practices are already codified and simplified as 'best governance practices' when they are assembled in the code. This reduces the additional problems of transferring knowledge in terms of tacitness and complexity of the knowledge (Kogut and Zander 1992; Nonaka 1994). The challenge becomes one of teachability across countries (Kogut and Zander 1992, 1993).

The ability to learn about the codified knowledge embedded in codes depends on the similarity of the institutions across countries (Johanson and Wiedersheim-Paul 1975). One of the key institutions influencing code content is the legal system (La Porta *et al.* 1998). The two legal families as described by La Porta *et al.* (common law and civil law) have different understanding of corporate behavior and accountability. The first code was issued within a common-law system, the United States. Hence, institutional similarity leads to a speed advantage in the adoption of codes in countries that have a common-law legal tradition. Practices developed in one country transfer more easily to other countries that have similar institutions, as managers are able to understand the information transferred more easily. Therefore, we expect that countries with a common-law legal system are likely to adopt codes more quickly than countries with civil-law legal systems.

The willingness of using foreign knowledge is correlated with the expected returns (Milgrom and Roberts 1992; Szulanski 1996), which influence the speed of development. Following this logic, we predict that the speed in the development of new practices such as codes of good governance will also depend on their expected returns. Specifically, in the case of the codes of good governance, benefits stem from filling gaps in the existing legal system regarding the protection of minority shareholders. Hence, we expect that countries with legal systems that do not provide appropriate protection for minority shareholders will be more likely to take the lead in developing codes. Codes of good governance help address deficiencies in the legal system, and are an easier and cheaper way to do so, since altering the legal system is a complex process (Coffee 1999) because it involves changes in a large system (Whitley 1999).

The willingness to develop codes will also be dependent on the relative importance of capital markets in the economy. Corporate governance problems are more likely to appear in public companies in which managers or large shareholders are better equipped to expropriate other shareholders. In private companies, the concentration of shares is higher and the overseeing of managers is stronger (La Porta *et al.* 1998). We expect that the speed in adopting codes of good governance increases if there is a large benefit in terms of shareholder protection. Higher benefits compensate for the costs of developing codes of good governance. The benefits in developing codes of good governance can be separated into the impact on the number of companies and the size of the capital markets. Countries with a large number of companies listed benefit more from the fast development of capital markets, as there are more companies that can improve their corporate governance. Moreover, countries whose capital markets are an important source of external firm financing, those that have a large economic size, also benefit from the improvement in corporate governance. In sum, we expect a direct relationship between the country's development of capital markets and the speed in the development of the code.

Speed in the transferability of practices is influenced by the exposure of potential code developers to foreign governance practices and in particular codes. This factor is not part of other discussions of knowledge transfer since these already have identified the knowledge to be transferred, hence concentrating on analyzing dimensions of willingness and understanding that facilitate the transfer. However, in the transfer of practices across countries among entities that are not related to each other, exposure to foreign knowledge becomes relevant. In this case, there are no mechanisms that facilitate the exposure to knowledge, such as boards of directors (Davis and Thompson 1994) or competitive interactions (Guler, Guillen, and MacPherson 2002). Hence, exposure to foreign knowledge comes indirectly, from other exchanges among countries, such as trade and investment flows. Countries more open towards international trade and investment are more likely to be exposed not only to diverse goods, services, and capital but also to new knowledge. Transferability of knowledge across countries can be part of the transfer of product and services, or through trade. Hence, we expect that countries more open to trade tend to develop codes more quickly. Alternatively, the transferability of knowledge across countries can accompany the transfer of capital for investment. This is more relevant when investments are done in the capital markets. Foreign direct investment in private firms suffers less from corporate governance problems since the foreign investor can always establish the appropriate controls. Portfolio investments are more vulnerable to corporate governance problems because they do not have control over the firm, as their investments are below 10 per cent of the stock of the firm. Hence, we expect that countries with a large foreign equity investment are more likely to develop codes of good governance quickly.

Research Design

To test these arguments, we built a comprehensive database of codes of good governance developed worldwide from 1978, the year the first code of good governance was developed, until June of 2003, the time of writing. Our main sources of information are the European Corporate Governance Network (2000), and the European Corporate Governance Institute (2003), and the World Bank (2000). In order to complete and cross check information, we consulted Commonwealth Association for Corporate Governance (1999), Gregory (1998, 1999), and Gregory and Simmelkjaer (2002), and Van den Berghe and de Ridder (1999). Our database includes only codes of good governance. We exclude laws or legal regulations, revisions, and new editions of original codes, corporate disclosure codes, reports on the compliance with the codes issued, codes on the behavior of top management, consulting firm reports, and individual company codes. We analyze capitalist countries. We have excluded 'transition' and socialist economies because the changes that accompany their transformation from communism to capitalism require a different approach to corporate governance. By the middle of 2003, thirty-five countries had issued 141 codes of good governance. Table 14.1 summarizes the number of codes issued in each country, the year when the first code was developed, and the types of issuers of codes.

Table 14.2 summarizes the variables, explains their measurement in detail, and provides data sources. We defined speed of development, our dependent variable, as how early the first code of good governance is developed in each country. We operationalize it as a count variable that measures the years that have passed since a given country developed its first code of good governance until 2003. We use this measure to be able to interpret the coefficients of the independent variables directly. The sooner the first code of good governance was developed in the country, the more years have passed from then until 2003. We measure understanding of foreign knowledge in terms of the similarities in the legal system, using a dummy variable that indicates whether the legal system is a common-law legal system (English origin), which is the legal system of the first country that issued a code, the United States. We operationalize willingness to use foreign knowledge in terms of deficiencies in the protection of shareholders and in terms of the size of capital markets. We measure deficiencies in the protection of minority shareholders by using the indicator of the anti-director rights in the legal system (La Porta *et al.* 1998). We measure the importance of capital markets in terms of number of domestic public companies

TABLE 14.1 *Issuers of codes of good governance worldwide, 1978–2003*

Country	First code developed						Cumulative number of codes						
	Stock exchange	Government	Directors' assocs.	Managers' assocs.	Profess. assocs.	Investors	Total	Stock exchange	Government	Directors' assocs.	Managers' assocs.	Profess. assocs.	Investors
English-law legal system (15 countries)													
Australia	1	0	0	0	0	0	4	2	0	1	0	0	1
Canada	0	0	0	0	0	1	7	4	1	0	0	1	1
Cyprus	1	0	0	0	0	0	1	1	0	0	0	0	0
Hong Kong	1	0	0	0	0	0	7	3	0	0	0	4	0
India	0	0	0	1	0	0	2	1	0	0	1	0	0
Ireland	0	0	0	0	0	1	2	0	0	0	0	0	2
Kenya	1	0	0	0	0	0	1	1	0	0	0	0	0
Malaysia	0	1	0	0	0	0	3	2	1	0	0	0	0
Pakistan	0	0	0	0	0	0	1	1	0	0	0	0	0
Singapore	1	0	0	0	0	0	2	1	1	0	0	0	0
South Africa	0	0	1	0	0	0	2	0	0	2	0	0	0
Sri Lanka	0	0	0	1	0	0	1	0	0	0	1	1	0
Thailand	1	0	0	0	0	0	1	1	0	0	0	0	0
UK	0	0	1	0	0	0	26	5	4	2	0	4	11
USA	0	0	0	1	0	0	30	4	2	5	6	4	9
All	7	1	2	3	0	2	90	26	9	10	7	14	24
French-law legal system (12 countries)													
Belgium	0	0	1	0	0	0	5	1	0	2	1	1	0
Brazil	0	0	1	0	0	0	2	1	0	1	0	0	0
France	0	0	1	1	0	0	7	2	0	0	4	0	1
Greece	1	0	0	0	0	0	2	1	0	0	1	0	0
Indonesia	0	1	0	0	0	0	1	0	1	0	0	0	0
Italy	0	1	0	0	0	0	2	1	1	0	0	0	0
Malta	1	0	0	0	0	0	1	1	0	0	0	0	0
Mexico	1	0	0	0	0	0	1	1	0	0	0	0	0
Netherlands	1	0	0	0	0	0	3	1	0	0	0	0	2
Peru	0	0	0	0	0	1	2	1	0	0	0	0	1

Table (rotated landscape). Column headers are not present on this page; the first six numeric columns report counts of countries and the remaining columns report firm counts (total followed by six categories).

	(1)	(2)	(3)	(4)	(5)	(6)	Total	(1)	(2)	(3)	(4)	(5)	(6)
Portugal	1	0	0	0	0	0	1	1	0	0	0	0	0
Spain	1	0	0	0	0	0	3	2	0	0	1	0	0
All	4	2	1	1	0	0	30	11	3	2	9	1	4
Scandinavian-law legal system (3 countries)													
Denmark	0	0	0	1	0	0	2	0	1	0	0	0	1
Finland	1	0	1	1	0	0	2	0	1	0	1	0	0
Sweden	0	0	0	0	0	0	3	0	1	0	0	0	2
All	1	0	1	2	0	0	7	0	3	0	1	0	3
German-law legal system (5 countries)													
Austria	1	0	0	1	0	0	1	1	0	0	0	0	0
Germany	0	0	1	0	0	1	7	0	3	0	3	0	2
Japan	0	1	0	0	0	0	3	0	0	1	2	0	1
Korea	1	0	0	0	0	0	1	1	0	0	0	0	0
Switzerland	0	0	0	1	0	1	2	1	0	1	0	0	0
All	2	1	1	2	0	2	14	3	3	2	5	0	3
Common-law legal system, total (15 countries)	7	1	2	3	0	2	90	26	9	10	7	14	24
Civil-law legal system, total (20 countries)	7	3	3	5	0	2	51	14	9	4	13	1	10
All countries, total (35 countries)	14	4	5	8	0	4	141	40	18	14	20	15	34
Common-law legal system, % (15 countries)	46.7	6.7	13.3	20.0	0.0	13.3	100.0	28.9	10.0	11.1	7.8	15.6	26.7
Civil-law legal system, % (20 countries)	35.0	15.0	15.0	25.0	0.0	10.0	100.0	27.5	17.6	7.8	25.5	2.0	19.6
All countries, % (35 countries)	40.0	11.4	14.3	22.9	0.0	11.4	100.0	28.4	12.8	9.9	14.2	10.6	24.1

Source: Authors' calculation using data from CAGN (1999), ECGI (2003), ECGN (2000), Gregory (1998, 1999), Gregory and Simmelkjaer (2002), Van den Berghe and de Ridder (1999), and World Bank (2000).

TABLE 14.2 *Variables and measures*

Variable	Measure	Sources
Speed of development of first code	Years between the first code of good governance was developed in the country and 2003.	Database of codes of good governance by country based on data from CAGN (1999), ECGI (2003), ECGN (2000), Gregory (1998, 1999), Gregory and Simmelkjaer (2002), Van den Berghe and de Ridder (1999), and World Bank (2000)
Common-law legal system	Dummy: 1 if the legal system is common-law based (English), 0 otherwise.	Data from La Porta *et al.* (1998) based on data from Reynolds and Flores (1989).
Anti-director measures in the legal system	An index aggregating shareholder rights labeled as 'anti-director rights'. The index is formed by adding one when: (i) the country allows shareholders to mail their proxy votes to the firm; (ii) the shareholders are not required to deposit their shares prior to a general shareholder meeting; (iii) cumulative voting or proportional representation of minorities in the board of directors is allowed; (iv) oppressed minorities mechanism is in place; (v) the minimum percentage of share capital that entitles a shareholder to call an extraordinary shareholders meeting is less than or equal to 10%; (vi) shareholders have pre-emptive rights that can be waived only by a shareholder vote. The index ranges from 0 to 6.	Data from La Porta *et al.* (1998)
Number of public domestic firms	Number of domestic companies in the stock market, in hundreds.	Data from World Bank (2003) WDI database
Size of capital markets	Market capitalization at the end of the year as a percentage of GDP.	Data from World Bank (2003) WDI database
Trade openness	Imports and exports as a percentage of GDP.	Data from World Bank (2003) WDI database
Investment openness	Inward foreign portfolio investment flow in equity as a percentage of gross domestic capital formation.	Data from World Bank (2003) WDI database
Level of development	GDP in PPP terms per capita in thousand of US$.	Data from World Bank (2003) WDI database

and in terms of market capitalization as a percentage of gross domestic product (GDP). Finally, we operationalize the exposure to foreign knowledge in two ways, through trade, measuring the importance of trade as a percentage of GDP, and through investment, measuring the importance of inward foreign portfolio investment as a percentage of gross capital formation.

We control for the level of development of the country by measuring the level of GDP per capita in power purchasing parity terms. Countries with wealthier populations are more inclined to develop codes of good governance more quickly because people are more likely to save and invest, either directly as part of individuals' savings strategy by directing their saving into investment funds in the stock market, or indirectly within the pension system by directing premiums into pension funds in the stock market. Using the alternative control of GDP for country size yields similar results.

The results of the analysis are subject to some limitations. We have restricted the set of countries that we analyze to thirty-three, and excluded Cyprus and Malta from the list in Table 14.1. We do this because we are using the measure on deficiencies in the legal system from La Porta *et al.*'s (1998) dataset, which includes only thirty-three of the thirty-five capitalist countries with codes of good governance. To ensure consistency among the independent variables, we analyze them in the same year, 2001, except for the legal system and its deficiencies, which we obtained from La Porta *et al.* (1998) dataset. We acknowledge that the variables are likely to change over time, but in this chapter we are interested only in getting a good sense of the influences on the speed of development rather than the specific impact of each variable on the speed. Hence, we will not discuss the size of the coefficients but rather their sign and statistical significance. The limited number of countries precludes an in-depth analysis of all potential influences.

We use a Poisson regression to analyze the determinants of the speed of the development of the codes of good governance because our dependent variable is constructed as a count variable: number of years passed from the adoption of the first code in the country until 2003. A positive (negative) coefficient of the independent variable indicates a higher (lower) likelihood of a rapid development of the first code of good governance in the country. We also analyze the determinants of the speed of the development of the codes of good governance using alternative duration models (Weibull, lognormal, log-logistic) to check for the robustness of the results of the Poisson model. The results, not reported, are in line with the ones of the Poisson model. We use the following specification:

Speed of development of the code $= \beta_0 + \beta_1 * $ *common-law legal system* $+ \beta_2 * $ *Anti-director measures in the legal system* $+ \beta_3 * $ *Number of public domestic companies* $+ \beta_4 * $ *Market capitalization* $+ \beta_5 * $ *Inward foreign equity investment* $+ \beta_6 * $ *Openness of country to trade flows* $+ \beta_7 * $ *Control for development of country* $+ \varepsilon$

Speed of Diffusion: Results and Discussion

Table 14.3 provides the means, standard deviations, and correlation matrix of the variables used in our analyses. The correlation matrix appears to indicate some correlations between the independent and the dependent variable. There is a high correlation between the legal system and the anti-director measures. We conducted further analyses to check for potential problems this correlation may have on the reported results. The analyses, not presented here, indicate that the presented results are valid.

Table 14.4 shows the results of the analysis of the determinants of the speed of development of the codes. The coefficients tend to be in line with our expectations. They provide support for the arguments that the first code is more likely to develop faster in countries where there is more understanding of, willingness of, and exposure to foreign knowledge. The coefficients of the common-law system, of the size of capital markets in number of firms and in economic importance, and of the openness of the country to foreign investment are positive and statistically significant, as expected. The coefficient of the anti-director measures is positive but not significantly different from zero. The coefficient of the openness to trade is negative and statistically significant, contrary to expectations.

We check the robustness of our findings by examining the effects that the United States has. The United States was the earliest country to develop codes and has by far the largest capital markets and economic development. Its sheer size may be pulling the results of our analysis (Model 1 in Table 14.4). Model 2 presents the analysis of the model excluding the United States from the computations. Our results hold when we exclude the United States case, although the number of public companies ceases to be statistically significant.

In sum, the speed of development of the first code of good governance depends on the understanding of foreign knowledge, the willingness to use foreign knowledge, and exposure to foreign knowledge: that is, understanding of foreign knowledge coming from similar institutional environments, particularly the legal system, willingness to use foreign knowledge provided by the expected benefit in terms of the protection of minority shareholders of public companies, and exposure to foreign knowledge through equity flows.

There is an unexpected finding from our predicted variables of influence on speed of development. Openness to foreign trade appears to have a negative influence on the speed of the development of codes of good governance. An explanation for this unexpected result is that countries with greater trade openness are not necessarily going to be exposed to innovative corporate governance practices because the exchange tends to be around goods. Firms are exposed to foreign knowledge on the quality of product or productive processes only. However, in the investment of capital,

TABLE 14.3 *Summary statistics and correlation matrix*

	Mean	Std. dev.	(1)	(2)	(3)	(4)	(5)	(6)	(7)
1. Speed of first code	6.757	4.623	1						
2. Common-law legal system	0.424	0.501	0.422*	1					
3. Anti-director measures	2.424	1.250	0.504**	0.700***	1				
4. Number of domestic public firms	10.231	15.422	0.574***	0.369*	0.413*	1			
5. Economic size of capital markets	78.322	67.244	0.451**	0.199	0.323+	0.111	1		
6. Trade openness	90.500	70.401	0.050	0.290	0.068	−0.272	0.473**	1	
7. Investment openness	23.493	31.842	0.289	0.025	−0.119	−0.192	0.132	0.469**	1
8. Control for level of development	18.323	10.169	0.492**	−0.185	0.050	0.136	0.516**	0.206	0.410*

***, **, *, and + indicate statistical significance at 0.1%, 1%, 5%, and 10% respectively.

Source: Cuervo-Cazurra and Aguilera (2003).

Table 14.4   *Analysis of the speed of development of codes of good governance worldwide*

		Dependent variable: Speed of development of first code	
		Model 1. All countries	Model 2. All countries except US
Understanding of foreign knowledge	Common-law legal system	**0.400*** (0.200)	**0.451*** (0.204)
Willingness to use foreign knowledge	Anti-director measures	0.029 (0.105)	0.004 (0.105)
	No. domestic public firms	**0.009*** (0.003)	0.005 (0.003)
	Economic size capital markets	**0.002*** (0.001)	**0.003*** (0.001)
Exposure to foreign knowledge	Investment openness	**0.007**** (0.001)	**0.007**** (0.001)
	Trade openness	**−0.002*** (0.001)	**−0.002*** (0.001)
	Control for level of development	0.015$^+$ (0.008)	0.013$^+$ (0.008)
	Intercept	1.010*** (0.191)	1.118*** (0.203)
	Loglikelihood	−70.459	−67.477
	Wald Chi2 (7)	204.63***	153.26***
	N	33	32

Note: White's heteroskedasticity-consistent standard errors are given in parentheses.
***, **, *, and $^+$ indicate statistical significance at 0.1%, 1%, 5%, and 10% respectively.
Source: Cuervo-Cazurra and Aguilera (2003).

there is exposure to corporate governance practices as there is an important link between capital and good governance.

Overall, the speed of the development of the first code is explained by the transfer of knowledge across countries, transfer that is difficult because of the limitations on the use of practices developed in one legal system in another (Cuervo-Cazurra 1998; Cuervo 2002). Codes developed in each country tend to deal with similar aspects of corporate governance, particularly the need for checks and balances in the firm and the benefits from transparency and disclosure. However, their particular recommendations differ across countries in order to deal with differences in terms of corporate governance systems (Shleifer and Vishny 1997), ownership patterns (Berglof 1990; Bebchuck and Roe 1999; Barca and Betch 2001), or stakeholder rights (Aguilera and Jackson 2003). The codes of good governance should not be taken as an indication of the convergence of corporate governance systems in different countries towards the Anglo-Saxon or any other model in particular. All countries need to improve their prevailing corporate governance system, enjoying different speeds in the development of the first code as a result of their particular characteristics.

The Issuers of Codes of Good Governance

Finally, we complement the analysis of the worldwide diffusion of codes of good governance with a description of the issuers of the codes. By accounting for the type of issuer, we will have a better appreciation for why codes are subsequently developed and how strongly they are enforced. We classify the types of issuer of codes of good governance into six categories: (i) stock exchange, when the issuer is the stock exchange or the overseer of the stock exchange (securities and exchange commission); (ii) government, when the issuer is the central or federal government or one of its ministries; (iii) directors' association, when the issuer is an association of directors; (iv) managers' association, when the issuer is an association of managers; (v) professional association, when the issuer is an association of accounting or law professionals; and (vi) investor's association, when the issuer is an institutional investor or an association of investors. Codes developed by the stock exchange in collaboration with other organizations are classified as being issued by the stock exchange.

Although codes of good governance are sets of governance practices that aim to improve corporate governance in the firm, the main objectives and the specific recommendations vary with the issuers. The power to enforce the practices in the firm also varies with the issuers, with different coercive, normative, and isomorphic pressures helping diffuse the codes across firms (Di Maggio and Powell 1983).

We divide issuers into four groups according to their perceived objectives in developing the codes. First, the stock exchange and the government are interested in promoting the development of practices that facilitate growth of capital markets in particular or of the economy in general. Unlike other issuers, these two actors have the power to impose codes of good governance on firms. They can enforce their recommendations when they transform codes into requirements for the listing of public firms or into laws for the creation of companies.

Second, investor associations are interested in the adoption of practices that facilitate their evaluation of the companies in which they invest. They can force firms to adopt the recommendations on the codes through their fiduciary power as representatives of shareholders, either themselves or individuals who provide the investment firms with money to manage. In addition to having the power to voice their disagreement with the way in which the company is run, they have the ability to exit the relationship with the firm if they dislike the current corporate governance. This second option, however, is not always available to passive investing firms that diversify their portfolio according to pre-established indexes.

Third, professional associations are interested in practices that aid their work and establish standards across companies, especially in areas of transparency and reporting. They have the normative power of imposing the codes on the firm through the requirements of the professionals who work for the firm.

Fourth, directors' associations and managers' associations are interested in facilitating their work in the firm. Although on some occasions managers and directors clash, directors who are not direct representative of shareholders tend to be managers in other firms. This double nature of the directors, in many cases, aligns the objective of both groups towards developing codes that improve the governance of the company by establishing norms that reduce internal conflicts between the board and management. The double nature also helps in the transmission of corporate governance practices across companies related through common directors (Davis and Thompson 1994). Codes developed by directors' and managers' associations are normative in character. Alternatively, directors' and managers' associations may develop codes of good governance as a way to reassure shareholders of the ability of managers and directors to police themselves, tying their own hands (Jensen and Meckling 1976). Their adoption across companies may be done, in addition to the normative pressures, as part of an isomorphic movement in which firms copy the practices of the better firms.

We analyze the relationship between the evolution of codes and the types of issuers in two ways: by the type of issuer of the first code in the country, and by the type of issuer of all codes in the country. Figure 14.2 shows the development of codes of good governance by type of first issuer in

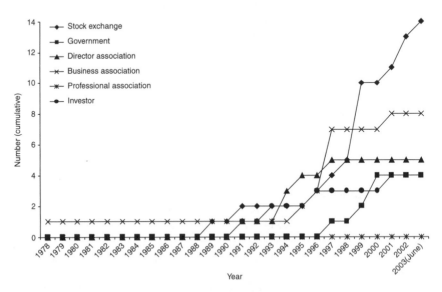

FIGURE 14.2   *Dynamics of codes of good governance worldwide: Type of issuer of first code, 1978–2003.*
Source: As for Fig. 14.1.

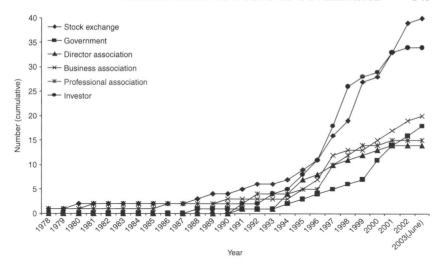

FIGURE **14.3**   *Dynamics of codes of good governance worldwide: cumulative type of issuer of code, 1978–2003.*
Source: As for Fig. 14.1.

the country. The analysis of Fig. 14.2 reveals that the type of first issuer has shifted over time as codes are developed in different countries. Managers' associations and stock exchanges conceived the initial codes, and they were succeeded by investors and professional and directors' associations that played a very active role particularly after 1992. Only in the late 1990s have governments issued codes of good governance; governments are more likely to issue enforceable laws than voluntary codes. Moreover, the issuer of the first code of good governance in each country reveals the active role of coercive issuers, particularly the stock market. The first codes in the country were issued by the stock market in fourteen countries, by managers' associations in eight countries, by directors' associations in five countries, and by investors' associations and government in four countries. Professional associations did not issue any first code. Therefore, the popular claim that institutional investors were the primary instigators of good governance (Useem 1996) is not supported by our data, though these investors may have pressured the stock exchange commissions to issue a code of good governance. Instead, the active role played by managers' and directors' associations indicates their collective desire to bring more effectiveness to their existing corporate governance systems.

However, the analysis of the types of issuers of all codes—not only the first code of each country, as discussed before—reveals the active role of investors and investors' associations. Figure 14.3 illustrates the cumulative development of all issued codes of good governance. The main difference from the conclusions of the previous arguments is the very active role of investors in developing codes of good governance. Although investors have generally not taken the lead in developing the first code, they have nevertheless showed great interest in the improvement of corporate governance systems through the use of the codes. Of the 141 codes developed by mid-2003, the stock exchanges had developed 40 codes while investors' associations had produced 34 codes. The other types of issuers had generated considerably fewer codes. Managers' associations issued 20 codes, a remarkable number given that the codes establish, in many cases, controls over managers' own behavior. Governments developed 18 codes, which do not include laws that were also created to accompany the changes in corporate governance in the country. Professionals' associations generated 15 codes. Finally, directors' associations issued 14 codes, despite being the body that was subject to regulation with the development of the codes.

The importance of one or another type of issuer may depend on the legal system in which the code is developed. In the common-law system, 'good' business practices tend to reach the level of enforceability in courts, whereas in civil-law legal systems such practices do not have the enforceability in courts unless they become codified into law or are among the requirements for public firms (Cuervo 2002). This differential in enforceability may be reflected in the nature of the issuers. We explore this by looking at the information presented at the last three rows in Table 14.1. We study two aspects: the type of issuer of the first code in each country, and the type of issuer of all the codes. First, when we compare the nature of the first code issuers, we see that stock exchanges are by far the most common type of issuer in both groups of countries, although more often in countries with a common-law legal system, where they issued almost one in every two first codes. In countries with a civil-law legal system, managers' associations, directors' associations, and, especially, the government take a more active role in developing the first code, while in countries with a common-law legal system investors are more active. Second, when we compare the nature of the issuer of all the codes, we observe also differences across legal systems. The stock exchange takes a similar active role regardless of the legal system in the country, issuing almost three out of every ten codes. In countries with a common-law legal system, investors', directors', and professionals' associations take a more active role, however, while in countries with a civil-law legal systems, the government and, particularly, managers' associations take the lead in developing codes of good governance.

The type of issuer differs not only across groups of countries by legal system but also within each country. Twenty-four countries have more than one code of good governance. Only in two countries is the type of issuer the same. In the rest, the type of issuer varies within the country.

In sum, whereas the forces that influence the development of codes of good governance affect several countries, the specific nature of the codes of good governance, in particular the type of issuer, varies across and within countries. Despite the apparent similarities in the development of codes across different countries, however, this does not indicate a convergence across corporate governance systems. All countries need to improve their prevailing corporate governance system. The codes help each country improve its current corporate governance system rather than converge towards another system. The continual development of codes among those countries that have already developed them and the differences in speed of development and types of issuers illustrate this argument.

Conclusion

In this chapter, we have analyzed different issues surrounding the diffusion of corporate governance practices around the world. In particular, we explore the worldwide diffusion of one corporate governance practice, namely, codes of good governance. These are voluntary guidelines with different levels of enforcement depending on the country where they are issued. Generally speaking, codes are developed in order to improve the country's corporate governance system to promote investment and growth. Even though there is a convergence in the issuance of codes in the 1990s, partly motivated by the spread of the focus on shareholder value and the internationalization of capital markets, our analysis goes beyond the convergence-divergence debate and looks at the specific mechanism triggering the development of codes, the speed of their development, and differences in types of code issuers. The study of these three dimensions demonstrates that, despite common environmental factors affecting all countries, each country is embedded in its individual path-dependent trajectory that will influence the reasons to enact codes, how fast, and by whom. In addition, from a preliminary content analysis of the different codes, we could also appreciate that the emphasis in their content is significantly different depending on the particular issues that they aim to address, ranging from family firms to shareholder relations. Finally, it is also noticeable that good corporate governance is a dynamic process requiring constant updates and improvements over time.

We argue that codes of good governance help to solve deficiencies in a country's corporate governance system (Aguilera and Cuervo-Cazurra 2004), although there is no indication that they are designed in light of a particular 'ideal type'. Moreover, we discuss the difficulties in the diffusion of practices across countries and demonstrate empirically that the speed in the adoption of the first code depends on the understanding of foreign knowledge, on the willingness to use foreign knowledge, and on the exposure to foreign knowledge, a factor not commonly discussed in knowledge transfer studies (Cuervo-Cazurra and Aguilera 2003).

This chapter is an important first step in the examination of the forces influencing the diffusion of new corporate practices around the world and a test, as well as an extension, of the work of La Porta and colleagues (La Porta, Lopez-de-Silanes, and Shleifer 1999; La Porta *et al.* 1997, 1998, 2000) on corporate governance and control across countries. We explore these issues drawing on institutional theory and the knowledge-based view. These theoretical approaches allow us to explain diffusion patterns in terms of more than simple convergence-divergence arguments. In effect, we believe that the explosion of codes in the 1990s is a consequence of both divergence and convergence and the relevant questions are about the factors determining these organizational innovations at the country level. Finally, we provide a comprehensive analysis of the codes of good governance that complements previous studies on the determinants of development of the codes of good governance worldwide (Aguilera and Cuervo-Cazurra 2004). As such, this chapter opens new ground for research on the codes of good governance in particular and corporate governance practices in general.

References

Aguilera, R. and Cuervo-Cazurra, A. (2004). 'Codes of Good Governance Worldwide: What is the Trigger?', *Organization Studies*, 25: 417–46.

——and Jackson, G. (2003). 'The Cross-National Diversity of Corporate Governance: Dimensions and Determinants', *Academy of Management Review*, 28: 447–65.

Alkhafaji, A. F. (1989). *A Stakeholder Approach to Corporate Governance: Managing in a Dynamic Environment*. New York: Quorum Books.

Almeida, P., Song, J., and Grant, R. (2002). 'Are Firms Superior to Alliances and Markets? An Empirical Test of Cross-Border Knowledge Building', *Organization Science*, 13: 147–61.

Arrow, K. (1974). *The Limits of Organization*. New York: Norton.

Barca, F. and Becht, M. (eds.) (2001). *The Control of Corporate Governance*. Oxford: Oxford University Press.

Barclay, M., Holderness, C., and Pontiff, J. (1993). 'Private Benefits from Block Ownership and Discounts on Closed-End Funds', *Journal of Financial Economics*, 33: 263–91.

Bebchuck, L. and Roe, M. (1999). 'A Theory of Path Dependence in Corporate Ownership and Governance', *Stanford Law Review*, 52: 127–70.

Berglof, E. (1990). 'Capital Structure as a Mechanism of Control: A Comparison of Financial Systems', in M. Aoki, B. Guftafsson, and O. Williamson (eds.), *The Firm as a Nexus of Treaties*. London: Sage.

Blanchard, O. (1997). *The Economics of Post-Communist Transition*. New York: Oxford University Press.

Cadbury, A. (2000). 'The Corporate Governance Agenda', *Corporate Governance*, 8: 7–15.

Cadbury Commission (1992). *Code of Best Practice: Report of the Committee on the Financial Aspects of Corporate Governance*. London: Gee and Co.

CAGN (Commonwealth Association for Corporate Governance) (1999). 'CAGN Guidelines. Principles for Corporate Governance in the Commonwealth: Towards Global Competitiveness and Economic Accountability' (mimeo). Marlborough, New Zealand: CAGN.

Canyon, M. and Mallin, C. (1997). 'A Review of Compliance with Cadbury', *Journal of General Management*, 2: 24–37.

Charkham, J. (1995). *Keeping Good Company: A Study of Corporate Governance in Five Countries*. New York: Oxford University Press.

—— and Simpson, A. (1999). *Fair Shares: The Future of Shareholder Power and Responsibility*. New York: Oxford University Press.

Coffee, J. (1999). 'Privatization and Corporate Governance: The Lessons From Securities Market Failure', *Journal of Corporation Law*, 25: 1–39.

Cohen, M. and Levinthal, D. (1990). 'Absorptive Capacity: A New Perspective on Learning and Innovation', *Administrative Science Quarterly*, 35: 128–52.

Cuervo, A. (2002). 'Corporate Governance Mechanisms: A Plea for Less Code of Good Governance and More Market Control', *Corporate Governance*, 10: 97–107.

Cuervo-Cazurra, A. (1996). 'Tres Visiones Teóricas de las Funciones del Consejo de Administración' [Three Theoretical Perspectives on the Functions of the Board of Directors], *Situacion*, 2/3: 119–34.

—— (1997). 'Estructura de Propiedad y Comportamiento de la Empresa: Objetivos Alternativos de los Accionistas en Espana' [Ownership Structure and the Behavior of the Firm: Alternative Objectives of Shareholders in Spain] (Ph.D. dissertation). Salamanca: University of Salamanca.

—— (1998). 'La Reforma del Consejo de Administración en España: Límites a la Aplicación de los Modelos Anglosajones' [The Reform of the Board of Directors in Spain: Limitations to the Application of Anglo-Saxon Models]. *Información Comercial Española*, 769/March: 9–21.

—— (1999). 'Grandes Accionistas y Beneficios Privados: El Caso de Bancos Como Accionistas de Empresas no Financieras' [Large Shareholders and Private Benefits: The Case of Banks as Shareholders of Non-Financial Firms]. *Investigaciones Europeas de Dirección y Economía de la Empresa*, 5: 21–44.

—— and Aguilera, R. (2003). 'The Speed of Cross-National Transfer of Best Practices'. Mimeo. Minneapolis: University of Minnesota.

Dahya, J., McConnell, J., and Travlos, N. (2002). 'The Cadbury Committee, Corporate Performance, and Top Management Turnover', *Journal of Finance*, 57: 461–83.

Davis, G. and Thompson, T. (1994). 'A Social Movement Perspective on Corporate Control', *Administrative Science Quarterly*, 39: 141–73.

DiMaggio, P. and Powell, W. (1983). 'The Iron Cage Revisited: Institutional Isomorphism and Collective Rationality in Organizational Fields', *American Sociological Review*, 48: 147–60.

ECGI (European Corporate Governance Institute) (2003). *Index of Codes*. www.ecgi.org/codes/all_codes.htm (3 June).

ECGN (European Corporate Governance Network) (2000). *Corporate Governance Codes, Principles and Recommendations*. www.ecgn.ulb.ac.be/ecgn/codes.htm (1 March).

Fama, E. and Jensen, M. (1983a). 'Agency Problems and Residual Claims', *Journal of Law and Economics*, 26: 327–59.

Fama, E. and Jensen, M. (1983b). 'Separation of Ownership and Control', *Journal of Law and Economics*, 26: 301–25.

Freeman, R. (1984). *Strategic Management: A Stakeholder Approach*. Boston: Pitman.

Grandori, A. and Kogut, B. (2002). 'Dialogue on Organization and Knowledge', *Organization Science*, 13: 224–31.

Grant, R. (1996). 'Toward a Knowledge-Based Theory of the Firm', *Strategic Management Journal*, 17/Winter special issue: 109–22.

Gregory, H. (1998). 'International Comparison of Board "Best Practices" — Investor Viewpoints'. Mimeo. New York: Weil, Gotshal & Manges LLP.

——(1999). 'Comparison of Board "Best Practices" in Developing and Emerging Markets'. Mimeo. New York: Weil, Gotshal & Manges LLP.

——and Simmelkjaer II, R. (2002). *Comparative Study of Corporate Governance Codes Relevant to the European Union and its Member States*. Final Report by Weil, Gotshal & Manges LLP. New York: Weil, Gotshal & Manges LLP.

Guler, I., Guillen, M., and MacPherson, J. (2002). 'Global Competition, Institutions, and the Diffusion of Organizational Practices: The International Spread of ISO Quality Certificates', *Administrative Science Quarterly*, 47: 207–32.

Hansen, M. (2002). 'Knowledge Networks: Explaining Effective Knowledge Sharing in Multiunit Companies', *Organization Science*, 13: 232–48.

Hirchman, A. (1970). *Exit, Voice and Loyalty*. Cambridge, MA: Harvard University Press.

Jensen, M. and Meckling, W. (1976). 'Theory of the Firm: Managerial Behavior, Agency Costs and Ownership Structure', *Journal of Financial Economics*, 3: 305–60.

Johanson, J. and Wiedersheim-Paul, F. (1975). 'The Internationalization of the Firm: Four Swedish Case Studies', *Journal of Management Studies*, 12: 305–22.

Kerr, S. (1975). 'On the Folly of Rewarding A, while Hoping for B', *Academy of Management Journal*, 18: 769–83.

Kogut, B. and Zander, U. (1992). 'Knowledge of the Firm, Combinative Capabilities, and the Replication of Technology', *Organization Science*, 3: 383–98.

—— ——(1993). 'Knowledge of the Firm and the Evolutionary Theory of the Multinational Corporation', *Journal of International Business Studies*, 24: 625–45.

Kogut, B. (1991). 'Country Capabilities and the Permeability of Borders', *Strategic Management Journal*, 12/Special Issue on Global Strategy: 33–47.

La Porta, R., Lopez-de-Silanes, F., and Shleifer, A. (1999). 'Corporate Ownership Around the World'. *Journal of Finance*, 54: 471–517.

—— —— ——and Vishny, R. (1997). 'Legal Determinants of External Finance', *Journal of Finance*, 52: 1131–50.

—— —— —— ——(1998). 'Law and Finance', *Journal of Political Economy*, 106: 1113–55.

—— —— —— ——(2000). 'Agency Problems and Dividend Policies around the World', *Journal of Finance*, 55: 1–33.

Levine, R. (1999). 'Law, Finance, and Economic Growth', *Journal of Financial Intermediation*, 8/1–2: 8–35.

Mace, M. (1971). *Directors: Myth and Reality*. Boston: Harvard Business School Press.

McKinsey (2000). *Investor Opinion Survey*. McKinsey & Company. June. www.mckinsey.com/features/investor_opinion/index.html

Milgrom, P. and Roberts, J. (1992). *Economics, Organization and Management*. Englewood Cliffs, NJ: Prentice Hall.

Monks, R. and Minow, N. (1992). *Power and Accountability: Restoring Balance of Power Between Corporations, Owners and Societies*. New York: Harper Business.

—— —— (1995). *Corporate Governance*. Cambridge, MA: Blackwell Business.

Morgan, G. and Engwall, L. (1999). 'Regulatory Regimes', in G. Morgan and L. Engwall (eds.), *Regulation and Organizations: International Perspectives*. New York: Routledge.

Nonaka, I. (1994). 'A Dynamic Theory of Knowledge Creation', *Organization Science*, 5: 14–37.

North, D. (1990). *Institutions, Institutional Change, and Economic Performance*. New York: Cambridge University Press.

Pellens, B., Hillebrandt, F., and Ulmer, B. (2001). 'Implementation of Corporate Governance-Codes in German Practice–An Empirical Analysis of the DAX 100 Companies', *Betriebs-Berater*, 56: 1243–50.

Reynolds, T. and Flores, A. (1989). *Foreign Law: Current Sources of Codes and Basic Legislation in Jurisdictions in the World*. Littleton, CO: Rothman.

Roe, M. (1994). *Weak Owners, Strong Managers: The Political Roots of American Capitalism*. Princeton, NJ: Princeton University Press.

Shleifer, A. and Vishny, R. (1997). 'A Survey of Corporate Governance', *Journal of Finance*, 52: 737–83.

Stiles, P. and Taylor, B. (1993). 'Benchmarking Corporate Governance: The Impact of the Cadbury Code', *Long Range Planning*, 26: 61–71.

—— —— (2001). *Boards at Work: How Directors View their Roles and Responsibilities*. Oxford: Oxford University Press.

Strang, D. and Macy, M. (2001). 'In Search of Excellence: Fads, Success Stories, and Adaptive Emulation', *American Journal of Sociology*, 107: 147–82.

—— and Soule, S. (1998). 'Diffusion in Organizations And Social Movements: From Hybrid Corn To Poison Pills', *Annual Review of Sociology*, 24: 265–90.

Svejnar, J. (2002). 'Transition Economies: Performance and Challenges', *Journal of Economic Perspectives*, 16: 3–28.

Szulanski, G. (1996). 'Exploring Internal Stickiness: Impediments to the Transfer of Best Practice within the Firm', *Strategic Management Journal*, 17: 27–43.

Teece, D. (1977). *The Multinational Corporation and the Resource Transfer Cost of Technology Transfer*. Cambridge: Ballinger.

—— (1980). 'The Diffusion of an Administrative Innovation', *Management Science*, 26: 464–70.

Tolbert, P. and Zucker, L. (1983). 'Institutional Sources of Change in Formal Structure of Organizations: The Diffusion of Civil Service Reform, 1880–1935', *Administrative Science Quarterly*, 28: 22–39.

Useem, M. (1996). *Investor Capitalism: How Money Managers Are Changing the Face of Corporate America*. New York: Basic Books.

Van den Berghe, L. and de Ridder, L. (1999). *International Standardisation of Good Corporate Governance: Best Practices for the Board of Directors*. Boston: Kluwer.

Von Hippel, E. (1994). ' "Sticky Information" and the Locus of Problem Solving: Implications for Innovation', *Management Science*, 40: 429–39.

Weir, C. and Laing, D. (2000). 'The Performance-Governance Relationship: The Effects of Cadbury Compliance on UK Quoted Companies', *Journal of Management and Governance*, 4: 265–81.

Whitley, R. (1999). *Divergent Capitalisms: The Social Structuring and Change of Business Systems*. Oxford: Oxford University Press.

Winter, S. and Szulanski, G. (2001). 'Replication as Strategy', *Organization Science*, 12: 730–43.

World Bank (1997). *World Development Report 1997*. Washington, DC: World Bank.

—— (2000). *Corporate Governance: Best Practices*. www.worldbank.org/html/fpd/privatesector/cg/codes.htm (3 March).

—— (2002). *World Development Report 2002*. Washington, DC: World Bank.

—— (2003). *World Development Indicators*. Washington, DC: World Bank.

15

From Colleague to Employee: Determinants of Changing Career Governance Structures in Elite Law Firms

RYON LANCASTER AND BRIAN UZZI

Introduction

In contrast to research on the governance of corporations, research on the governance of professional service firms is spare (Malos and Campion 1995; Greenwood, Hinings, and Brown 1990; Sherer and Lee 2002). This lack of research is interesting because professional firms are at the center of commerce in law, accounting, and consulting. Their governance structures are distinctive in that the fundamental governance principle of separation of ownership and management found in other business firms does not exist or is blurred in professional firms that use the partnership model of governance (Hinings, Brown, and Greenwood 1991; Howard 1991; Gilson and Mnookin 1989; Maister 1982; Sander and Williams 1992). The traditional partnership governance structure of professional service firms appears to be transforming as many firms in accounting, banking, and now law are adopting corporate-based models of governance.

This chapter examines the changing governance structures in elite law firms during the late 1980s through the mid-1990s. We focus on the career structures that reflect the partnership governance system and how it is changing into a structure that is more 'corporate' in nature. This change centers on the introduction of new types of non-partner track job arrangements into the traditional partnership model that had been used by large law firms for over a hundred years. Under the traditional partnership governance system, all attorneys in the firm are either partners, who are owners and managers, or associates, who are 'on track' to partnership. The socialization, training, and monitoring of associates is accomplished under constant supervision of partners and who motivate associates to work excessive hours for relatively low pay with the deferred prospect of making partner at the firm. Associates who failed to make partner were expected to permanently leave the firm for employment elsewhere. In the mid-1980s, the introduction of new, non-partner track positions such as 'senior attorneys' and 'staff attorneys' into the traditional partnership structure altered the partnership governance structure. Like typical positions in corporation, these positions are salaried,

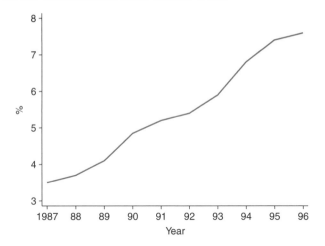

FIGURE 15.1   *Percentage of attorneys in non-partner track positions, 1987–1996.*
Source: NALP (1988–97).

offer no promise of partnership or even of indefinite employment, and diffuse governance over work processes to a wider and more specialized set of employees while concentrating ownership in a smaller set of partners (Sherer and Lee 2002). The increasing incidence of these new positions is seen in Fig. 15.1, which shows the spread of these new governance positions, indicating that there has been both a large percentage increase in the frequency of these positions and a steady growth trend of about 0.5 per cent a year since 1987.

In our analysis we review and test two arguments that have been offered to explain this change using panel data on the 100 largest US law firms from 1987 to 1995. First, we examine theories of the role of race and gender in law firms, which argue that law firms modified their governance structures in order to retain women and minorities disadvantaged by the traditional partnership structure of the large law firm (Hagan and Kay 1995). Second, we examine the tournament model offered by Galanter and Palay (1991) that argues that law firms modified their governance structures as a result of excessive growth and turnover, forcing firms to adopt innovative structures that expanded upon the partnership governance system. We begin with a review of the historical significance of the partnership governance model in the large law firm and how labor market and competitive changes reduced the model's traditional benefits.

Governance Structures in the Modern Large Law Firm

The large law firm is a product of the twentieth century (Nelson 1988). In the nineteenth century, the American legal profession was composed almost entirely of solo-practitioners. Aspiring lawyers either attended graduate school in law or apprenticed with existing lawyers to earn the right to practice. With the coming of large corporations at the end of the nineteenth century, corporate legal practice became consolidated into larger firms where partners could specialize and leverage each other's human and social capital for corporate clients with diverse legal needs.

During the beginning of the twentieth century, law firms began to provide specialized representation in different practice areas (such as banking, labor, real estate, and probate) and in the latter half of the twentieth century began to expand in size (Nelson 1992). In 1968, the largest law firm in the United States had 169 lawyers (Galanter and Palay 1990); thirty years later the largest law firm in the US, Baker & McKenzie, had 2,343 attorneys nation-wide (*National Law Journal* 1999). A summary of the current composition of largest 250 US law firms from 1989 to 1997, grouped into size quintiles, is presented in Table 15.1. It shows that the largest 50 law firms in the US averaged over 500 attorneys, with roughly 187 partners and 317 associates. For all of the 250 largest firms, the average size was 273 attorneys, with 110 partners and 150 associates. The starting salaries of associates tend to be moderate relative to jobs in banking and finance or consulting, which require equivalently long hours. Most firms are headquartered in large cities but are dispersed regionally with an average of nearly seven branch offices, and predominately work for large corporate clients that possess their own large legal departments—which suggests that their markets are competitive and their clients have substantial in-house alternatives to buying legal services externally.

TABLE 15.1 *Descriptive statistics of the largest 250 US law firms, 1990–1997*

Size quintile	Firm characteristics						
	Offices	# of attorneys	# of partners	# of associates	Costs-starting salary	% with main office in major city	# in-house at clients
1	10.73	527.55	186.59	317.46	$74,171	76.8	53.3
2	6.95	297.86	119.53	161.75	$69,661	64.8	43.9
3	5.86	221.79	98.29	111.93	$65,187	56.0	49.3
4	4.69	176.72	79.20	91.02	$63,363	57.9	43.5
5	4.58	143.73	65.88	71.07	$61,722	36.8	34.4
Mean	6.56	273.00	109.68	150.31	$66,830	58.3	45.7

Note: Data are from *The National Law Journal* and the *Of Counsel 500*. The number of cases ranges from 1,052 to 2,000 due to missing data for some of the variables. Major cities include New York, Boston, Philadelphia, Chicago, Houston, Dallas, San Francisco, and Los Angeles.

To govern the skill development and administration of new talent that was dispersed widely around the firm, had specialized expertise, and was given considerable autonomy over the pacing and execution of the law, the 'Cravath system' was developed, named after the lead partner of the first firm to utilize it, Cravath, Swaine, & Moore (Swaine 1948). Under the Cravath system, law firms became organized as two-tiered legal partnerships with partners at the top and associates below them. Partners participated in all significant managerial decisions and governed their own behavior under the rule of 'jointly and severable' liability, which meant that all partners were liable for the gains and losses of all other partners—a system that tended to keep unreasonable risk-taking behavior as well as shirking to a minimum (Carr and Mathewson 1990; Gilson 1990). In return, partners were residual claimants upon the firm's income obtained after all of the firm's fixed costs had been paid (Carr and Mathewson 1990; Daniels 1992). The sharing of profits could be lockstep, with all partners at the same level of seniority receiving an equal share, or through a more complicated formula that included seniority, marginal productivity, development, and promotions (Gilson and Mnookin 1985; Daniels 1992).

While partners were free to govern their own behavior, a key governance activity of partners was the management of new recruits. Associates were recently minted lawyers who worked for a fixed salary in the firm, learning how to practice law from experienced partners (Nelson 1988). A unique aspect of the governance structure of the Cravath system was the 'up-or-out' decision for retaining new associates. Associates would be hired directly from law schools and apprentice at the firm for a fixed number of years (typically between five and nine) with the prospect of making partner. Associates that were not retained as a partner in the firm were permanently let go. The purpose of the 'up-or-out' system was to motivate associates to increase their responsibility and legal expertise through the possibility of promotion. Associates who did not make partner were asked to leave the firm, since, as Swaine (1948) put it:

A man who is not growing professionally [i.e., did not make partner] creates a barrier to the progress of the younger men within the organization and himself, tends to sink into a mental rut—to lose ambition; and loss of ambition induces carelessness. It is much better for the man, for the office and for the clients that he leaves while he still has self-confidence and determination to advance. The frustrated man will not be happy, and the unhappy man will not do a good job. (Cited in Sherer and Lee 2002: 105)

Thus, the possibility of becoming partner motivated associates to avoid shirking, invest in their human capital, and act in the interests of the firm. However, if the associate was passed over for partner, the motivations were absent and the associate was a potential liability to the firm.

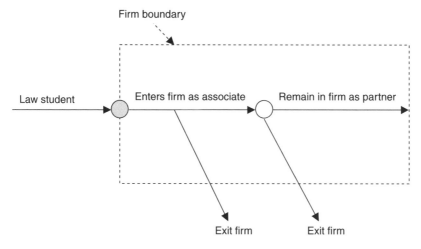

FIGURE 15.2   *Model of traditional career paths.*

Figure 15.2 diagrams the traditional governance model of law firms. Upon completion of law school, lawyers face a choice whether to join a private firm or to work in some other form of practice. Upon entering, they are an associate for a set number of years before the partnership decision. During this time, they are able to leave the firm for another firm, government or corporate work, or to leave the profession all together. At the partnership decision, they are either elected to partner or permanently leave the firm.

This governance system promoted a number of key benefits for law firms. It encouraged entrepreneurship on the part of partners and, to a lesser extent, associates by motivating partners to grow a portfolio of practice areas with numerous clients and in numerous areas of law. Furthermore, it supported the development of long-term relationship that promoted collaboration and teamwork among highly skilled specialists (Lazega 2001). Finally, the Cravath system socialized young lawyers into corporate practice and helped screen for the best performing associates for partner (Heinz and Laumann 1982).

In the mid-1980s, several factors outside the firm began to decrease the governance benefits of the traditional Cravath system. Principal among these changes were new desires in the work preferences of newly minted attorneys and an increasingly more competitive market for law firm services in which corporate clients stressed efficiency (Galanter and Palay 1991; Daniels 1992; Nelson 1988). On the side of labor, increasing numbers of lawyers wanted careers and families, which led young lawyers to see the benefits of partnership as now opposed to family interests (Hagan and Kay 1995). Consequently, new lawyers expressed less willingness to work excessive hours, what became known as the 'tyranny of the billable hour', for the slim possibility of partnership. This was especially true for women and minorities who did not see proportionate increases in their rates of making partner even though they were equally represented in new graduating classes at top law schools. Associates in corporate practice often bill up to 2,000 hours a year, forcing talented women who want to have children to choose between corporate practice and their families (Seron 1996; Hagan and Kay 1995).

The pressure on law firms to meet the new demands of top law schools graduates was exacerbated by credible employment alternatives to private law firm practice that arose during the same period. In particular, elite corporations and banks created large in-house legal departments that opened up new employment opportunities with similar status and benefits but without the excessively long hours expected in large law firms. The establishment of in-house legal departments not only created and legitimized alternative career opportunities for top graduates but meant that law firms' key clients were gaining expertise in the practice of law and in the evaluation of legal services by their outside law firms. This meant that an increasingly important aspect of law firm success was efficiency. Compared with corporations' tall hierarchies and separation of ownership and control, and the trend among investment banks and accountancies to adopt the corporate system, the traditional partnership structure of the law firm looked out of date. It also looked inefficient. How could a firm with 500 employees be efficiently managed with the same structure as the 'mom-and-pop' corner law firm? Consequently, law firms began to recognize that a movement away from the traditional partnership model could increase external legitimacy (Heinz and Markham-Bugbee 1986) and offer the firm a way to create positions for infrequently needed specialists, retain near-partner quality associates in whom the firm had already invested, and increase the division of labor in the firm (Nelson 1988; Sherer and Lee 2002).

Law firms adapted to these pressures by instituting significant changes in their governance structures. A significant change was the creation of new career paths that deviated from the Cravath system, in particular the staff attorney and senior attorney. The senior attorney position was used to retain or recruit talented associates but took them off the partner track. The senior attorney forgoes the possibility of partnership in return for salaried employment, a decreased workload, and the opportunity for greater specialization. In contrast, staff attorneys are hired fresh out of law school on one- to three-year adjunct contracts and are expected to leave at the end of their contracts. These tracks proved attractive to lawyers and firms alike, with firms retaining talented lawyers without diluting their partnership while allowing associates to stay if they were unable or unwilling to do the work necessary for becoming partner at a large firm.

These governance changes also offered new economic benefits to law firms. Because they allowed the firm to offer more flexible and less demanding work commitments, as well as an alternative to the straight 'up or out' decision, they enhanced firms' ability to compete with corporate in-house

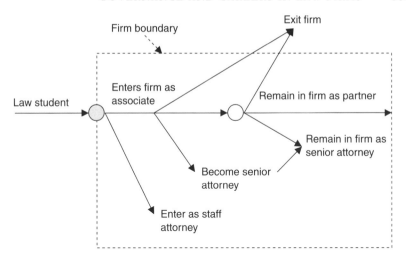

FIGURE 15.3   *Model of corporatist career paths.*

positions, leading to more gainful recruitment and retention of valued talent. Additional career paths also permitted the law firm to manage specialists and make reversible investments in new practice areas. Finally, these positions permitted existing partners to concentrate ownership within a smaller set of partners by increasing the size (and returns) of the firm without increasing the number of partners at the same rate as the firm grew larger.

Figure 15.3 presents a corporate governance model in law firms. The beginning of the path is the same, with the choice to enter a firm in private practice or not. Associates then face a set number of years before the partnership decision. The potential for exit is still available, but some firms allow associates to switch to alternative career tracks before the partnership decision by becoming senior attorneys. Some of these positions still leave the lawyer open for partner, while others are permanent non-partner positions, allowing the lawyer to remain in the firm without having to become a partner.

Accounting for the Spread of New Governance Arrangements

The historical review of the governance systems of law firms suggests that both demographic and economic forces explain the emergence and spread of non-partnership governance arrangements in firms. Demographic change arguments suggest that the Cravath system was designed to optimize governance arrangements in elite law firms where associates were willing to trade-off most other pursuits in the hope of making partner and that this system was supported by cultural norms in which stay-at-home spouses could specialize in domestic and child-rearing functions while associates concentrated all their energies on work (Hagan and Kay 1995). With the large influx of women into the profession, the separation of work and family life functions was difficult for women to support because they often performed both roles, creating perceptions that the standard governance model relatively disadvantaged women's chances of making partner.

Consistent with these arguments, Hagan and Kay's (1995) study of Canadian lawyers found that women had a much lower chance of making partner than did men and that the difference in partner rates was largely attributable to differences in who takes parental leave—partner-track women take parental leave whereas men do not. The tensions between the work requirements of corporate practice and of childcare responsibilities appear to put women in a disadvantaged position in the firm.

Consistent with the view that women do not proportionately advance to partner at the same rate as men, Table 15.2 presents the proportion of women and minority associates in large law firms. It indicates that, while women comprise almost half of all associates, they continue to be underrepresented among partners. For example, in 1996 women accounted for 41 per cent of all associates but only 13 per cent of all partners in large law firms.

Table 15.2 also indicates that the success of minorities under the Cravath system appears to be similar to women. While minorities entered the profession in large number later than did women, their proportional representation at the partner level is still unbalanced. Of the roughly 10–13 per cent of minority associates that enter large law firms, only 3 per cent reach partner. There are several factors that account for this disparity. Minorities tend to

TABLE 15.2   *Percentage of women and minority partners and associates at large US law firms, 1986–1996*

Year	Women		Minorities	
	Associate	Partner	Associate	Partner
1986	34	7	5	1
1987	38	8	7	2
1988	41	10	6	2
1989	38	9	6	2
1990	41	10	7	2
1991	42	11	8	2
1992	41	12	8	2
1993	39	12	9	3
1994	40	12	10	3
1995	40	13	12	3
1996	41	13	13	4

Note: Data drawn from 73 large US law firms. The data are described in the data and methods section.

receive lower levels of training at the associate level and are not given the opportunities to build up a base of clients (Wilkins 2000). In addition, there are disincentives for minorities to build up the skills needed for long term success in legal practice, instead focusing on sending signals to partners that they are partner material, which leaves them less opportunities to invest in their own human capital and client networks (Wilkins and Gulati 1996). Finally, there are still indications that there are racial preferences for promoting white associates to partnership ranks (Lempert, Chambers, and Adams 2000; Wilkins and Gulati 1996).

The under-representation of women and minorities poses a number of problems for the firm. First, if human capital is randomly distributed across gender and racial lines, then losing women or minorities to other employment opportunities will diminish the overall level of talent in the firm. Second, clients are now expecting their legal counsel to be more diverse, and less diverse firms are less likely to gain new contracts. Corporate legal departments have been more favorable to hiring and promoting women and minority lawyers, leading to a more diverse client (Wilkins 2000; Hagan and Kay 1995). Many of the large US corporations and banks now require a disclosure of the demographic composition of firms who bid on projects, and use this in the hiring decision to favor firms with more women and minorities (Skolnick 1991; Silas 1984). State and local governments also require their outside counsel to be diverse, disadvantaging firms that have low numbers of women and minorities (Blodgett 1992; Knapp and Grover 1994). Finally, there are indications that more diverse firms perform better, through the ability to attract and retain clients as well as drawing on a greater pool of human capital (Pearce, Hickey, and Burke 1998; Uzzi and Lancaster 2003).

These statistics reinforce the perception that the Cravath system failed to promote equal opportunity for all competing groups and involved high personal costs that were beginning to be viewed as anachronistic with the work needs of some of the best young lawyers, creating a double bind for law firms with large proportions of women or minority associates. On the one hand, they project the perception that women are not equally represented in the firm, which limits their ability to recruit the best women associates. On the other hand, to balance gender and minority representation they would have to promote a proportionately larger number of women associates to partner relative to men, a change that would be difficult in the near term if one presumes that the proportion of men, women, and minority associates qualified for partnership at elite firm is about equal (Eaves, Png, and Ramseyer 1989; Hagan and Kay 1995; Chambers 1989; Seron 1996). This suggests that setting up new career governance arrangements would allow firms to retain women and minority lawyers with the promise of alternative and possibly more flexible work arrangements when there exist pessimistic perceptions of advancement in traditional partnership track positions.

Hypothesis 1: *The greater the proportion of female associates, the more likely a firm is to adopt non-partnership governance arrangements.*

Hypothesis 2: *The greater the proportion of minority associates, the more likely a firm is to adopt non-partnership governance arrangements.*

By the same arguments, if the lack of equal representation at the partner level increases the likelihood that a firm adopts new governance arrangements, then equal representation should decrease the probability of adoption because it promotes the optimistic perceptions that the current model is working, enabling these firms to attract the best women and minority talent without the need to invest in costly new systems of governance. Furthermore, firms with greater numbers of women and minority partners shift internal resources around, which help in the training and promotion to partner of more women and minority associates (Chambliss and Uggen 2000). This implies firms with better representation of women and minority partners could avoid pressures to change their governance arrangements to satisfy the needs of new graduates.

Hypothesis 3: *The greater the proportion of female partners, the less likely a firm is to adopt non-partnership governance arrangements.*

Hypothesis 4: *The greater the proportion of minority partners, the less likely a firm is to adopt non-partnership governance arrangements.*

In an influential article and book, Galanter and Palay (1990, 1991) proposed that changes in the governance structure of law firms can be explained by the economic factors underpinning the recent and rapid growth of law. Using ideas from transaction cost economics and from agency theory, they argued that the tournaments to make partner under the Cravath system explains the distribution of career tracks in the firm. In a tournament, associates are not given their full wages but instead are given an opportunity for a deferred bonus in the form of partnership. This aligns the associates' interests with that of the partners, removing the risk of opportunistic behavior (shirking, theft of capital, early exit) on the part of associates.

In order for this tournament to work effectively, associates must be able to estimate their chances of making partner, which creates an incentive for firms to fix the percentage of associates making partner each year. A governance problem arises, however, when the number of associates partnered each year is greater than the number of partners that retire, because, to make each new partner in the firm profitable, the firm must hire from two to five new associates—a condition known as leverage. Using this logic, Galanter and Palay reasoned that a firm using the traditional Cravath system must maintain exponential growth to optimally motivate associates and maintain profit levels. However, such rapid growth through partnership is constrained by competition for scarce top talent and a lucrative client base.

This places special pressures on fast-growth firms that need to establish other methods of growth. One strategy for growth is through the establishment of governance arrangements that increase the length of time to partnership as well as leverage over non-partner track attorneys. A greater time to partnership allows firms to better match promotions with retirements and the rate of client development, while non-partner track attorney permit partners to gain leverage without the need to increase the size of the pool of associates who expect partner. This suggests that:

Hypothesis 5: *The faster the rate of firm growth, the greater the likelihood of adoption of non-partnership governance arrangements.*

Non-partner track positions can also provide firms with an option for retaining good talent that didn't make partner but that received firm-specific training and socialization at the firm during the tournament. Similarly, these new positions could offer winning talent that had been denied partner the option of a salaried, non-billable hourly position, albeit one that was of lower status. The *American Lawyer* registered the testimonial of Richard Spizzirri, a Davis Polk partner, who gave this rationale for the corporatist structure.

To lose someone [an associate denied partner] who's that good is crazy ... maybe some of them would prefer to stay on a somewhat different basis if we had a program ... 'Up-or-out maybe' just doesn't make sense anymore ... You've invested a lot of effort in training good lawyers, good people, nice people. All of a sudden, when they reach their highest level of proficiency, they're forced by the system to look elsewhere for employment ... Other professional service organizations such as accounting firms and the investment banks, which ten years ago were organized like law firms, have created a more fragmented hierarchy ... If it is such a good thing for them, are we missing something? (Pollock 1982, cited in Sherer and Lee 2002).

These arguments suggest that firms that bore the costs of training associates but that could not retain all qualified persons as partners would be motivated to recapture some of their socialization and firm-specific investment costs through new job categories. If firms with the highest levels of turnover are experiencing the greatest economic retention costs, then firms with high turnover should be more likely to adopt these new governance structures. This suggests:

Hypothesis 6: *The greater the law firm's exit rates, the greater the likelihood that it adopt non-partnership governance arrangements.*

The creation of new governance arrangements is not costless to the tournament model, however. In addition to significant new investments in administrative structures and job routines, they also represent a break in the traditional culture of the large law firm. The creation of these new positions can run at odds with the norms and values of the wide profession (Daniels 1992). By virtue of passing the bar, all lawyers, no matter their area of specialty or place of schooling, are deemed to have earned the same proficiency to practice law. Consequently, the corporate model introduced a new stratification system that conflicted with graduates' professional training, socialization, and mindset that law is a 'calling' (Daniels 1992).

Thus, for firms in which the organizational culture is part of professional values of equality and highest level of quality, conflict is likely to accompany attempts at changing the governance structure of the firm by adding new types of lawyers, *except* in firms that have had a culture of employing salaried support staff to do legal work. In these cases, the creation of new career paths for attorneys can more easily fit into the traditional partnership culture as an extension of the use of support staff, decreasing the conflict associated with adding these positions. In addition, the presence of a greater amount of support staff indicates the existence of governance rules and routines for managing these support staff that can be extended to managing non-partner track attorneys. Hence:

Hypothesis 7: *The higher the ratio of support staff, the more likely is the firm to adopt non-partnership governance arrangements.*

Data and Measures

To test these hypotheses, data were collected for the years 1986 through 1996 from *Martindale-Hubbell Law Directory*, *The American Lawyer 100*, *National Law Journal*, *Directory of Legal Employers*, and *Of Counsel*. The sample consists of all law firms that were included in nine years of *The American Lawyer 100* to create a balanced panel. *The American Lawyer 100* is an annual survey of 250 large US law firms that asks questions about the law firm's size, practice areas, office branches, and fiscal standing. The 100 most profitable firms (in terms of their overall profits per partner) in the US are then reported in the *American Lawyer*, along with their responses to the survey. This survey design creates an unbalanced panel, since each year asks the same items, but of different firms. To create a balanced design, we included only the seventy-seven firms that appeared in the survey in all eleven years of our study. In addition to firms that did not appear in all eleven years of our study, one firm was dropped because of missing data and one firm was dropped because of a local merger that made comparison across years impossible. This left us with a panel of seventy-five firms. Other firms were involved in mergers but with small firms or firms in another city, which did not affect our focus on the main office of each firm. We then used this sample to collect additional data from the other sources (described below). Table 15.3 presents summary statistics and correlations of the variables used in our model.

TABLE 15.3 *Summary statistics and correlations*

	Mean	S.D.	Min	Max	1.	2.	3.	4.	5.	6.	7.	8.	9.	10.	11.	12.	13.	14.	15.
1. New senior Attorney	0.06	0.23	0	1	—														
2. New staff Attorney	0.05	0.21	0	1	0.14	—													
3. Growth rate	0.05	0.10	−0.67	0.52	0.06	0.06	—												
4. # attorneys (log)	5.42	0.36	3.95	6.53	0.03	−0.01	−0.13	—											
5. (# attorneys (log))²	29.46	3.88	15.61	42.61	0.03	0.00	−0.13	1.00	—										
6. % Female partners	0.11	0.04	0.01	0.38	−0.08	−0.03	−0.06	−0.19	−0.18	—									
7. % Minority partners	0.02	0.03	0	0.51	−0.09	0.00	−0.05	−0.21	−0.20	0.23	—								
8. % Female associates	0.40	0.11	0.17	1.46	−0.02	0.01	−0.03	−0.18	−0.18	0.43	0.12	—							
9. % Minority associates	0.08	0.07	0	1	−0.07	0.04	−0.04	−0.17	−0.16	0.29	0.38	0.41	—						
10. Non-legal staff/# attorneys	1.75	0.38	0.61	3.88	0.07	0.00	0.09	0.22	0.22	−0.17	−0.11	−0.09	−0.05	—					
11. Exit rate of associates	0.11	0.08	0	0.58	0.04	−0.02	−0.05	−0.18	−0.18	0.08	0.01	0.14	0.18	0.15	—				
12. Gross revenues (log)	4.85	0.51	3.65	6.57	−0.06	−0.01	−0.13	0.54	0.55	−0.02	0.10	−0.14	0.18	0.21	−0.13	—			
13. Costs of goods sold	73.14	9.59	45	91	0.04	−0.08	−0.14	0.40	0.40	−0.02	−0.02	−0.01	0.22	0.13	0.08	0.43	—		
14. # clients	6.61	6.98	1	54	−0.06	−0.04	−0.13	0.41	0.43	0.02	0.02	−0.13	0.06	0.25	−0.09	0.62	0.21	—	
15. # in-house counsel at clients	43.74	33.32	1	206.83	−0.03	−0.04	−0.05	0.18	0.19	0.06	0.08	0.00	0.14	0.01	0.03	0.19	0.17	0.16	—
16. East coast firm	0.51	0.50	0	1	0.04	−0.08	−0.06	0.30	0.30	−0.16	−0.09	−0.07	−0.03	0.16	0.08	0.03	0.56	0.01	−0.04
17. 1989	0.09	0.29	0	1	−0.01	0.13	0.15	−0.02	−0.02	−0.14	−0.10	−0.06	−0.13	0.08	−0.02	−0.08	−0.05	−0.17	−0.10
18. 1990	0.09	0.29	0	1	0.01	0.04	0.10	0.03	0.03	−0.06	−0.08	0.01	−0.08	0.13	0.02	−0.01	−0.06	0.06	0.03
19. 1991	0.09	0.29	0	1	−0.03	−0.04	−0.08	0.04	0.04	0.02	−0.04	0.04	−0.04	0.07	0.04	0.02	−0.04	0.10	0.03
20. 1992	0.09	0.29	0	1	−0.05	−0.02	−0.21	0.03	0.03	0.05	−0.02	0.03	−0.01	−0.03	0.05	0.04	−0.04	0.08	0.05
21. 1993	0.09	0.29	0	1	−0.03	0.02	−0.22	0.03	0.03	0.05	0.03	−0.04	0.01	−0.06	−0.02	0.06	0.05	0.10	−0.27
22. 1994	0.09	0.29	0	1	−0.05	−0.06	−0.11	−0.01	−0.01	−0.01	0.06	0.00	0.08	−0.06	0.01	0.09	0.07	0.06	0.09
23. 1995	0.09	0.29	0	1	−0.05	−0.02	−0.10	0.00	0.00	0.11	0.10	0.00	0.17	−0.12	−0.11	0.13	0.15	0.01	0.19
24. 1996	0.09	0.29	0	1	−0.07	−0.02	0.05	0.02	0.03	0.16	0.19	0.03	0.23	−0.20	−0.11	0.18	0.16	0.06	0.16

Dependent Variables

Our dependent variables are the adoption of the *senior attorney position* and the adoption of the *staff attorney position* in the firm. We created this variable from the *Directory of Legal Employers* when a firm indicated the presence of a senior attorney position and/or a staff attorney position when they were not present in the previous year's *Directory*. This allows us to measure the year in which the position was created, but not the actual date. This was coded 1 for adoption, 0 for at risk of adoption. The *Directory of Legal Employers* is an annual survey of law offices around the country. It provides a narrative description of the firm, data on the firm's hiring and promotion practices, employment demography, practice areas, location of branch offices, opportunities for part-time work, and starting salary for new associates.

Independent Variables

All independent variables were lagged by one year. The *growth rate* of the firm was calculated by taking the difference between the size at t and t − 1 and dividing by the size at t − 1. We calculated the *exit rate of associates* as the number of associates in the previous time period plus the number of new hires, minus the number of current associates, divided by the number of associates in the previous time period:

$$\text{exit rate} = \left(\frac{\#associates_{t-1} - \#associates_t + \#hires_t}{\#associates_{t-1}} \right)$$

The *proportion of female partners* and *associates* as well as the *proportion of minority partners* and *associates* was measured as the number of attorneys in that subclass divided by the total in that class. For example, the proportion of female partners was measured as the number of female partners divided by total number of partners. Minorities represented all non-white associates. We measured the *ratio of non-legal staff to attorneys* as the number of functional staff (paralegals, support staff, and other professionals) employed by the firm divided by the total number of attorneys in all categories at the firm (including associates, partners, staff attorneys, and senior attorneys).

Control Variables

Gross revenues measured the gross revenues of the firm. This variable was logged to normalize its distribution. To control for differences in the firms' *costs of goods sold*, we used the common measure of the yearly starting salary of the firm's associates; partners receive a share of the residual profits rather than a salary, and therefore are not part of the cost of goods sold (Hagan *et al.* 1991; Gilson and Mnookin 1985). *Size* of the firm measured as the log of the total number of attorneys, including partners, associates, staff attorneys, and senior attorneys employed at the firm at time t.

To control for the market position of the law firm, we include several controls for the law firm's clients. We drew on research that has shown that the greater the *number of in-house counsels* employed by the client, the more informed the client is about, and the more carefully it can screen, the quality and internal structure of the law firm (Suchman 1998; Nelson 1988: 59). We calculated the average number of in-house counsels in a law firm's network of clients by summing the number of in-house counsel of each client and dividing it by the number of clients. To control for client's bargaining power and size, we used the *total number of* Fortune 250 corporation and bank *clients* of each law firm in the sample.

Finally, we included a dummy variable indicating whether or not the firm was headquartered on the *east coast*. Additionally, we included dummy variables for each *year*, with 1987 being the reference category. In separate analyses, we included controls for law firm practice area, but as these were not significant and did not affect the results of our other variables, they were not included in the analyses presented here.

Model

We tested our arguments using a pooled cross-section random effects logit model. This allows us to examine time-varying firm characteristics that affect the adoption of senior attorney and staff attorney positions. Firms that did not adopt by 1996 were right-censored. Once a firm had adopted a specific new position, it was taken out of the risk set for that model and did not provide further cases. Unfortunately, our data do not allow us to examine the very first cases of implementation of these positions. Nevertheless, the number of firms that adopted either position before our observation window of 1987 is small. For senior attorneys, four firms in our sample had adopted them by 1987, and two firms for staff attorneys. These firms were excluded from our analyses.

Results

Table 15.4 lists the regression results of our analysis of the adoption of the senior and staff attorney positions. The first column presents our results for senior attorneys. Most of our year indicator variables are positive and significant, indicating an increasing likelihood of adopting the senior attorney position over time, which is consistent with Fig. 15.1. East cost firms, which are generally the larger and most prestigious of the large US law firms, were significantly less likely to adopt new governance positions, while firms with higher salary costs were more likely to adopt the position. Organizational revenues and the number of clients failed to attain significance.

TABLE 15.4   *Random effects logit of predictors of adopting new governance position*

Firm demographics	Adopt senior attorney	Adopt staff attorney
% Female associates	0.157***	−0.030
	(0.046)	(0.036)
% Minority associates	0.133	0.228*
	(0.112)	(0.105)
% Female partners	−0.510**	−0.245*
	(0.184)	(0.115)
% Minority partners	−2.148***	0.872**
	(0.574)	(0.305)
Tournament model		
Growth rate	4.315	5.117†
	(4.386)	(2.950)
Exit rate of associates	−10.979†	−17.460**
	(6.178)	(6.635)
Ratio of non-legal staff to attorneys	2.181**	2.230†
	(0.964)	(1.338)
Controls		
# of attorneys (log)	0.339	3.073*
	(1.540)	(1.427)
Gross revenues (log)	2.468	0.335
	(1.792)	(1.220)
Costs of goods sold	0.081***	0.017*
	(0.019)	(0.009)
# of clients	−0.092	−0.042
	(0.095)	(0.110)
# In-house counsel at clients	0.032*	0.011
	(0.014)	(0.015)
East coast firm	−2.147†	−10.991***
	(1.277)	(2.612)
1989	1.433	10.410***
	(1.675)	(2.763)
1990	4.897***	11.610***
	(1.474)	(3.131)
1991	7.173***	9.327***
	(2.100)	(2.895)
1992	9.393***	12.956***
	(2.529)	(3.531)
1993	12.385***	15.851***
	(2.913)	(3.990)
1994	12.166***	10.488*
	(3.103)	(4.860)
1995	12.290***	16.738***
	(3.063)	(4.378)
1996	−23.795	17.475***
	(13.624)	(4.643)
Constant	−34.017**	−38.009**
	(10.854)	(11.538)
N	401	496
# of firms	73	71

Note: Data drawn from 73 large US law firms. The data are described in the data and methods section.
† $p < .10$, * $p < .05$, ** $p < .01$, *** $p < .001$.

The second column presents our results for the adoption of the staff attorney position in the firm. Again, we find that the effects for our year dummies are positive and significant, indicating an increasing likelihood of adoption over time. Consistent with the findings of senior attorney position, east coast firms were less likely to adopt the staff attorney position, while firms with higher salary costs were more likely to do so. There were no significant effects for the number of clients, the size of their in-house legal staff, or the total revenues of the firm.

Consistent with our demographic arguments, we found a generally uniform relationship between the adoption of new forms of governance and the race and gender distribution of the firm—although these effects varied with the type of new position that was adopted. As predicted in hypothesis 1, we found that, the greater the percentage of female associates in the firm, the greater the likelihood of adopting senior attorney positions. The effect for minority associates was also positive but failed to attain significance. Also consistent with hypotheses 3 and 4, we found that firms with a higher proportion of either female or minority partners were less likely to adopt senior attorneys.

The results for staff attorney were less consistent. Consistent with hypothesis 2, firms with a higher percentage of minority associates were significantly more likely to adopt the staff attorney position, but there was no significant effect for female associates as predicted by hypothesis 1. For partners, the percentage of female partners decreased the likelihood of adoption, supporting hypothesis 3, but the effects for minority partners was positive and significant, the opposite of what hypothesis 4 predicted. In both models, we were concerned that our demographic variables were collinear with one another, creating these different results. In order to ensure that our results were represented in the underlying data and were not simply a statistical artifact, we ran both models with each demographic variable entered on its own. In these results, each variable had the same direction and level of significance as in the complete models reported here, indicating that the collinearity among these variables did not drive our results.

While we lack systematic data and theory to resolve this conflicting result, one explanation follows from past work and aggregate data on the distribution of women and minorities in large, elite law firms. During this period, women represented around 40 per cent of all associates, a percentage consistent with the proportion of women graduating from law schools (Abel 1989; Hagan and Kay 1995). Thus, the creation of the staff attorney position would not advantage female hires because they already have a strong presence in these firms. However, minorities are still distinctly under-represented at these firms. It is possible that the creation of the staff attorney position allows for greater opportunities for newly minted minority lawyers by providing them with membership, even if temporary, at an elite law firm, and that minority partners support these positions to advantage other minority lawyers.

The results suggest mixed support for the economic determinants of adoption. Consistent with hypothesis 5, we found that higher growth rates are positively associated with the adoption of staff attorneys. However, growth rate had no effect on the adoption of senior attorneys. These results suggest that the problems of growth are associated with shifts to a more corporate governance structure but that the two indicators of governance, staff attorneys and senior attorneys, may address the governance problem differently. One explanation is that fast growth also requires rapid hiring, which would make the hiring of staff attorneys easier than senior attorneys. Staff attorneys are hired straight out of law school on annual contracts, and have no expectation of becoming partners in the firm, whereas senior attorneys because of their seniority in the profession take longer to identify and recruit from competing firms.

Hypothesis 6 predicted that higher exit rates would lead to higher adoption rates. We find the opposite effect in both models. This indicates that firms that have a harder time retaining associates are less likely to adopt the senior attorney track. One explanation may be that our turnover measure of these firms is picking up on voluntary job changes rather than involuntary up-or-out job changes, a condition that is possible during this time period when lateral moves among associates increased along with the booming economy (Heinz, Nelson, and Laumann 2001). As some scholars have noted, during the 1990s law firms 'came to be regarded as talent depositories that could be raided' in order to satisfy the demand for skilled personnel at American companies, in particular Internet-based companies (Heinz, Nelson, and Laumann 2001: 353). If the exit rate represents voluntary job changes then, the need to create alternative tracks that help the firm recoup socialization and training investments in associates that they could not promote is no longer the primary concern. Rather, the opposite is true: how to retain top talent that they would like to promote? If this were indeed the case, then the establishment of non-partner track positions would be inversely related to exit rates because firms would have no need to expand the tournament through these new governance positions.

Consistent with hypothesis 7, we found that increases in the ratios of non-legal staff to attorneys was significantly and positively related to adoption of both senior attorney and staff attorney positions. This suggests that firms with experience in managing non-partner positions in their firm have acquired experience and cultural norms that particularly support the adoption of new forms of governance that extend the partnership model to include non-partnership track job positions.

Conclusion

In this chapter, we analyzed some of the key changes in the governance structure of large law firms. Law firms, like many other professional service firms, have been changing their governance structure to look more like their corporate clients. However, this has been an understudied topic in governance research. In particular, we examine how law firms created new positions outside of the traditional Cravath system of governance. These new positions concentrated ownership, created more flexible and less demanding work commitments, and allowed for the retention of talented attorneys who did not want to try to make partner in these firms. These changes also gave firms a greater ability to retain specialists as well as giving them more flexibility to respond to competitive shifts in the marketplace. Overall, these changes in career structures in large law firms amount to a wholesale change from the traditional governance structure of professional service firms to a governance structure that more closely approximates a corporate governance structure.

The competitive situation facing large law firms exposed them to external pressures for greater accountability and efficiency. In addition, law firms faced internal pressures for better opportunities for advancement and better work conditions as greater job opportunities for talented lawyers in corporate legal departments made the working conditions in large law firms less attractive for associates. In this chapter, we examined two sets of factors that have been advanced in the literature as to why law firms have changed their governance structure.

We examined the effects of demography on governance change, where new governance structures are better at retaining female and minority associates. Women and minorities are typically disadvantaged under the Cravath system and, while they were entering large law firms as associates, firms were having a difficult time promoting and retaining them. At the same time, their clients were asking for a more diverse workforce, pressuring law firms to innovate in order to retain their women and minority lawyers. Thus, we hypothesized that firms who had more women and minority associates would be more likely to change their governance structure, while firms that had found ways in which to promote them under the Cravath system would be less likely to adopt new governance arrangements.

We also examined the effects of the internal labor market and organizational structure of the firm. The Cravath system of governance creates an exponential growth function for the firm, where the firm has to hire between two and five new associates for each newly promoted partner. This diluted the ownership of the firm as more and more attorneys became partner, and made the firm more difficult to coordinate and manage. Firms that were having difficulty in retaining their associates had to find new ways of retaining talented lawyers who found better working conditions in corporate legal departments, causing firms to invest heavily in their training only to see them leave for other career opportunities. In addition, these new governance arrangements challenged the traditional culture of law firms and of legal practice, creating conflict within firms. However, this conflict could be mitigated if the firm had already made extensive use of non-attorney professional services, particularly in the form of specialized professionals (economists, accountants, and so on) and of paralegals. Therefore, we hypothesized that firms that were growing at high rates, had high levels of associate exits, and had a higher proportion of support staff would be more likely to adopt new governance structures.

Overall, we found strong support for our hypotheses. Firms with greater proportions of female and minority associates were more likely to adopt new governance structures, supporting our hypotheses that these new governance structures provide a way of retaining those associates who are disadvantaged under the Cravath governance system. We also found that, the higher the proportion of female partners, the less likely a firm was to adopt new governance structures. This substantiates our argument that firms that have found ways to retain and promote to partner female associates have less need to modify their governance structure. However, the effects for minority partners differed by type of governance. For senior attorneys, or permanent associates, the results were the same as for women partners, indicating a firm that has already solved the problem of retaining minority associates. However, for staff attorneys, the effects were positive. This indicates that minority partners use their position to increase opportunities for minority lawyers, even if they have no hope of staying in the firm.

We also found strong support for our hypotheses about the structure of the labor market of the firm. We found that firms with higher growth rates were more likely to adopt staff attorneys, but that this had no effect for the adoption of senior attorneys. Because high growth rates imply an immediate need for talent, and because staff attorneys are in effect temporary employees, it is easier for the firm to hire them for short-term needs. The results also supported our hypothesis that firms with higher proportions of support staff are more likely to adopt new governance structures, since these firms will experience less cultural conflict and have existing routines for managing staff. Finally, the effects of the exit rate of associates were strong and significant, but in the opposite direction of our hypothesis. While we lack the data to explore this finding, it is possible that firms with high exit rates have less of a problem retaining associates that they would like to keep but not to promote to partner, and have a greater problem retaining associates that the firm would like to promote.

An important result of this research is that the effects of our hypothesized relations often differed by the type of governance structure. This is not entirely unexpected, since the type of governance structure used is tied to different job structures. These job structures provide different types of benefits for the firm. Thus, the type of governance adopted will depend on the situation of the firm and what the specific set of problems facing the firm is. This also indicates that different governance changes solve different governance problems, and that certain factors will affect the likelihood of adopting different types of governance structures in varying ways.

Our results speak more generally to governance research. In a number of articles and books, Williamson (1975; 1981) has argued that the governance structure of professional service firms should be structured around the nature of transactions between lawyers providing the professional services. We make a similar argument in this chapter, in that the governance structure of law firms is primarily determined by the nature of labor contracts between attorneys. However, we differ from Williamson in that the type of labor contracts used is determined not simply by transactions between lawyers but also has to do with factors external to the transaction. In particular, we find that the demographic composition of the workforce and the competitive situation facing law firms affects whether or not law firms will adopt new governance structures. Furthermore, we find that these factors have different effects depending on the type of governance structure used, indicating that these factors external to the transaction help shape the governance structure of law firms. This suggests that the environment surrounding transactions has a significant effect on governance structures independent of the nature of the transaction.

The pressures law firms are facing are not unique to law firms, nor are the governance changes. Law firms had provided one of the more important models for the governance of professional service firms during the twentieth century; and now, as they change their governance structures, they are again serving as a model. Changes in law firms are similar to changes that are affecting accounting, banking, and consulting. While changing governance structures provides better fit in many ways to changing environmental conditions, these changes are not without costs to the profession. Concentration of ownership, the ability of firms to increase their size and market share, the consolidation of elite practice, and hierarchical firm structures are all outcomes of these changes. Yet these changes challenge the very nature of professional work by making it harder to maintain professional autonomy or acquire high-level human capital (Abbott 1988; Abel 1989). What this means for professional work is unclear but, as professions come to look more like the corporations they provide services to, it becomes harder for them to maintain their distinctiveness.

Finally, it is unclear what the performance implications of these changes are. According to Williamson, the shift towards hierarchical contracts that these new governance arrangements contain should reduce the risk of opportunism, thereby increasing the overall performance of the firm. However, these governance changes challenge the culture of law and of professional autonomy in significant ways, increasing the risk of greater conflict within the firm (Daniels 1992; Abel 1989). Thus, it is possible that these new governance structures increase performance but, if a firm moves too far away from the traditional governance structures, its performance might suffer due to the increased conflict within the firm. In a related project, preliminary results suggest that this is indeed the case, where the optimal performance level for a firm is with a hybrid governance structure (Uzzi and Lancaster 2003). In this structure, the firm maintains a traditional Cravath governance system, with some elements of these new governance structures. This provides a balance between the gains in efficiency and flexibility from the new systems while maintaining the traditional culture of legal practice and prevents conflict from disrupting the operations of the firm.

References

Abbott, A. (1988). *The System of Professions: An Essay on the Division of Expert Labor.* Chicago: University of Chicago Press.

Abel, R. (1989). *American Lawyers.* Oxford: Oxford University Press.

Blodgett, N. (1992). 'Room for Minorities: Firms Advised that a Diverse Workforce is Good for Business', *American Bar Association Journal*, 78: 35–6.

Carr, J. and Mathewson, F. (1990). 'The Economics of Law Firms: A Study in the Legal Organization of the Firm', *Journal of Law and Economics*, 33: 307–30.

Chambers, D. (1989). 'Accommodation and Satisfaction: Women and Men Lawyers and the Balance of Work and Family', *Law and Social Inquiry*, 14: 251–88.

Chambliss, E. and Uggen, C. (2000). 'Men and Women of the Elite Law Firm: Reevaluating Kanter's Legacy', *Law and Social Inquiry*, 25: 41–68.

Daniels, R. (1992). 'The Law Firm as an Efficient Community', *McGill Law Journal*, 37: 801–34.

Eaves, D., Png, I., and Ramseyer, J. (1989). 'Gender, Ethnicity, and Grades: Empirical Evidence of Discrimination in Law-Firm Interviews', *Law and Inequality*, 7: 189–214.

Galanter, M. and Palay, T. (1990). 'Why the Big get Bigger: The Promotion-to-Partner Tournament and the Growth of Large Law Firms', *Virginia Law Review*, 76: 747–811.

——— (1991). *Tournament of Lawyers: The Transformation of the Big Law Firm.* Chicago: University of Chicago Press.

Gilson, R. (1990). 'The Devolution of the Legal Profession: A Demand Side Perspective', *Journal of Political Economics*, 99: 420–5.

—— and Mnookin, R. (1985). 'Sharing among the Human Capitalists: An Economic Inquiry into the Corporate Law Firm and How Partners Split Profits', *Stanford Law Review*, 41: 313–92.

——— (1989). 'Coming of Age in a Corporate Law Firm: The Economics of Associate Career Patterns', *Stanford Law Review*, 41: 567–95.

Greenwood, R., Hinings, C., and Brown, J. (1990). '"P²-Form" Strategic Management: Corporate Practices in Professional Partnerships', *Academy of Management Journal*, 33: 725–55.

Hagan, J. and Kay, F. (1995). *Gender in Practice: A Study of Lawyers' Lives.* New York: Oxford University Press.

——Zatz, M., Arnold, B., and Kay, F. (1991). 'Cultural Capital, Gender, and the Structural Transformation of Legal Practice', *Law & Society Review*, 25: 239–62.

Heinz, B. and Markham-Bugbee, N. (1986). *Two-Tier Partnerships and Other Alternatives: Five Approaches*. Chicago: American Bar Association.

Heinz, J. and Laumann, E. (1982). *Chicago Lawyers: The Social Structure of the Bar*. Chicago: University of Chicago Press.

—— Nelson, R., and Laumann, E. (2001). 'The Scale of Justice: Observations on the Transformation of Urban Law Practice', *Annual Review of Sociology*, 27: 337–62.

Hinings, C., Brown, J., and Greenwood, R. (1991). 'Change in an Autonomous Professional Organization', *Journal of Management Studies*, 28: 375–93.

Howard, J. (1991). 'Leadership, Management and Change in the Professional Service Firm', *Business Quarterly*, 55: 111–18.

Knapp, V. and Grover, B. (1994). 'The Corporate Law Firm: Can It Achieve Diversity?', *National Black Law Journal*, 13: 298–307.

Lazega, E. (2001). *The Collegial Phenomenon: The Social Mechanisms of Cooperation among Peers in a Corporate Law Partnership*. Oxford: Oxford University Press.

Lempert, R., Chambers, D., and Adams, T. (2000). 'Michigan's Minority Graduates in Practice: The River Runs Through Law School', *Law and Social Inquiry*, 13: 678–701.

Maister, D. (1982). *Managing the Professional Service Firm*. New York: Free Press.

Malos, S. and Campion, M. (1995). 'An Options-Based Model of Career Mobility in Professional Service Firms', *Academy of Management Review*, 20: 611–44.

NALP (National Association for Law Placement) (1988–97). *National Directory of Legal Employers*. Chicago: Harcourt.

National Law Journal (1999). 'The NLJ 250', 13 December.

Nelson, R. (1988). *Partners with Power: Social Transformation of the Large Law Firm*. Berkeley: University of California Press.

—— (1992). 'Of Tournaments and Transformations: Explaining the Growth of Large Law Firms', *Wisconsin Law Review*, 1992: 733–50.

Pearce, J., Hickey, J., and Burke, D. (1998). 'African Americans in Large Law Firms: The Possible Costs of Exclusion', *Howard Law Journal*, 42: 59–71.

Pollock, E. (1982). 'Applying the "Principal" Principle', *American Lawyer*, 4: 8.

Sander, R. and Williams, E. (1992). 'A Little Theorizing about the Big Law Firm: Galanter, Palay, and the Economics of Growth', *Law and Social Inquiry*, 17: 391–414.

Seron, C. (1996). *The Business of Practicing Law: The Work Lives of Solo and Small-Firm Attorneys*. Philadelphia: Temple University Press.

Sherer, P. and Lee, K. (2002). 'Institutional Change in Large Law Firms: A Resource Dependency and Institutional Perspective', *Academy of Management Journal*, 45: 102–19.

Silas, F. (1984). 'Business Reasons to Hire Minority Lawyers', *American Bar Association Journal*, 70: 52–4.

Skolnick, J. (1991). 'Doing the Right Thing is Good for Business', *The Compleat Lawyer*, 8: 20.

Suchman, M. (1998). 'Working without a Net: The Sociology of Legal Ethics in Corporate Litigation', *Fordham Law Review*, 67: 837–74.

Swaine, R. (1948). *The Cravath Firm and Its Predecessors*. New York (privately printed).

Uzzi, B. and Lancaster, R. (2003). 'Organizational Evolution and Prosperity: Networks, Culture, and the Economic Adaptation of Large Law Firms' (Working Paper). Evanston, IL: Department of Sociology, Northwestern University.

Wilkins, D. (2000). 'Rollin' on the River: Race, Elite Schools, and the Equality Paradox', *Law and Social Inquiry*, 25: 527–55.

—— and Gulati, G. (1996). 'Why are there so Few Black Lawyers in Corporate Law Firms? An Institutional Analysis', *California Law Review*, 84: 493–614.

Williamson, O. (1975). *Markets and Hierarchies: Analysis and Antitrust Implications*. New York: Free Press.

—— (1981). 'Economics of Organization: The Transaction Costs Approach', *American Journal of Sociology*, 87: 548–77.

Index

Numbers in bold type indicate a figure or table.